VOLCKER

When Washington Shut Down Wall Street:
The Great Financial Crisis of 1914 and the Origins of
America's Monetary Supremacy

Financial Options: From Theory to Practice (coauthor)

Principles of Money, Banking, and Financial Markets (coauthor)

Financial Innovation (editor)

Money (coauthor)

Portfolio Behavior of Financial Institutions

VOLCKER

The Triumph of Persistence

WILLIAM L. SILBER

BLOOMSBURY PRESS
New York • London • New Delhi • Sydney

Published by Bloomsbury Press, New York

All papers used by Bloomsbury Press are natural, recyclable products made from wood grown in well-managed forests. The manufacturing processes conform to the environmental regulations of the country of origin.

Library of Congress Cataloging-in-Publication Data

Silber, William L.
Volcker : the triumph of persistence / William L. Silber.—1st u.s. ed.
p. cm.
Includes bibliographical references and index.
ISBN 978-1-60819-070-6 (alk. paper)
1. Volcker, Paul A. 2. Economists—United States—Biography. 3. Board of Governors of the Federal Reserve System (U.S.)—officials and employees—Biography.
4. United States—Economic policy—1971–1981. 5. United States—Economic policy—1981–1993. 6. Monetary policy—United States—History—20th century.   I. Title.
HB119.V6S55 2012
332.1'1092—dc23
[B]
2012003042

First U.S. Edition 2012

1 3 5 7 9 10 8 6 4 2

Typeset by Westchester Book Group
Printed in the U.S.A. by Quad/Graphics, Fairfield, Pennsylvania

In Memory of Pauline R. and Joseph F. Silber

Contents

Introduction

More Than a Central Banker

Five American presidents, three Democrats and two Republicans, spanning nearly half a century, have called on Paul A. Volcker to serve the government and the people of the United States. John F. Kennedy made him deputy undersecretary of the treasury for monetary affairs in 1963; Richard Nixon named him undersecretary of the treasury for monetary affairs in 1969; Jimmy Carter appointed him chairman of the Federal Reserve Board, America's central bank, in 1979; Ronald Reagan reappointed him chairman in 1983; and in 2008, President-elect Barack Obama named him chairman of the President's Economic Recovery Advisory Board.

Carlo Ciampi, the former president of Italy, sent Volcker a three-word letter upon hearing of President Obama's assignment. The message sits in a chrome frame on Paul's desk: "We trust you."

Volcker earned his unparalleled credibility over the course of his professional career by approaching public service as a sacred trust. His contributions spread beyond the narrow confines of finance, including investigating the oil-for-food scandal at the United Nations and chairing the commission to settle claims against Swiss banks by victims of the Holocaust. But his tenure as chairman of the Federal Reserve Board between 1979 and 1987 built his legacy. During that time, Volcker did nothing less than restore the reputation of an American financial

1

system on the verge of collapse. In the last great economic crisis, the epic battle against the Great Inflation of the 1970s, Paul Volcker was the hero. Jack Kimm, a resident of Anchorage, Alaska, penned the following message to him when Volcker left office in 1987. "Losing you at the Fed seems and feels like losing George Patton in the middle of war."[1]

This book began as the story of a determined central banker who confounded the critics while defeating an entrenched inflation in America, but turned out to be much more. I will show that Paul A. Volcker not only restored price stability in the United States, but also led a battle for fiscal responsibility in America. Volcker never held elective office, but his refusal to accommodate the Reagan-era budget deficits by creating money—what economists call monetizing the deficit—forced up real interest rates during the mid-1980s until Congress delivered a plan to balance the budget.

Volcker relied on public opinion, integrity, and persistence to overcome the political pressure to finance government spending the easy way, by printing money rather than by taxation. Congress created the Federal Reserve System, America's central bank, and can abolish it with a simple majority vote. Volcker deflected repeated threats, including a bill of impeachment, and stuck to his principles. His tenure at the Federal Reserve began the process of reining in the deficit. Volcker promoted the goal of fiscal integrity that Ronald Reagan had promised to the American people, turning Reagan into Reagan.

Foreigners rewarded the United States for its monetary and fiscal discipline by investing in U.S. securities and by treating the dollar as a safe haven currency. The United States enjoys lower interest rates and a higher standard of living because countries from China to South Korea send clothing and children's toys to America in exchange for U.S. dollars. Current Federal Reserve chairman Ben Bernanke credits Volcker's policies with setting "the stage for decades of economic growth and stability."[2]

Volcker's linkage of responsible monetary policy with fiscal virtue carries a message for today, as the United States emerges from the greatest financial crisis since the Great Depression. Unprecedented low interest rates and easy money policies to lower unemployment provoke fears of rekindling inflation when the economy recovers, and the enormous structural budget deficit confronting America fans those fears. The Federal Reserve promises to reverse field to contain inflationary pressures, but that commitment is suspect, with the memory of recession still fresh, unless Congress and the president agree to a balanced budget at full employment. Reckless fiscal policy threatens the dollar's status as a reliable international store of value and the exorbitant privilege that confers on American consumers.

The need to integrate monetary and fiscal policies gained intellectual currency in 2011, when Thomas Sargent was awarded the Nobel Prize in Economics. The New York University economist considers that "Good monetary policy is impossible without good fiscal policy."[3] Sargent advanced the concept of rational expectations in economic behavior and offered historical evidence from the hyperinflations of the 1920s that credible monetary policy needs grounding in fiscal responsibility. Volcker learned the power of expectations while an apprentice on the trading desk at the Federal Reserve Bank of New York. I will show that his subsequent policies revealed an appreciation of rational expectations before that principle gained acceptance.

This book is divided into four parts. Part 1 sets the stage, describing Volcker's formative years at home, in school, and his early work experience at the Federal Reserve Bank of New York. Part 2 chronicles his role surrounding President Nixon's suspension of the dollar's convertibility into gold on August, 15, 1971, America's final break with the gold standard, which Volcker considers "the most significant single event" in his career.[4] Part 3 traces Volcker's actions as chairman of the Federal Reserve Board from 1979 through 1987 to defeat an escalating inflation that President Jimmy Carter cited as promoting a "crisis of confidence" in America.[5] Part 4 describes his role in formulating what President Obama labeled the Volcker Rule in 2010, designed to protect the American taxpayer from having to repeat a bailout of a crippled financial system. A brief prologue weaves the common theme underlying the three crises—1971, 1979, and 2010—that tested Paul Volcker.

This biography of Volcker's professional life tells the story of how principle, determination, and pragmatism blend into effective leadership. Volcker understood the need to compromise, and some of his concessions, such as the bailout of Continental Illinois, the seventh-largest U.S. bank in 1984, set a costly precedent in public policy. But he knew where to draw the line, when to build credibility and when to spend it. And that good judgment turned Paul Volcker into an American financial icon.

Paul cooperated in this project by arranging for the release of thousands of documents from the U.S. Treasury and the Federal Reserve System that are the foundation of this biography. He added a personal touch by sitting (not always happily) for one hundred hours of interviews. He also shared his school records and reports that had been carefully guarded by his mother, Alma Volcker. However, this is not an authorized biography: Paul did not think it appropriate to exercise editorial control over the final product. He refused to read it until after it went to press. Nevertheless, Volcker's presence towered over this project despite his efforts to impose distance. He is alive and well at the writing of this final draft, and that surely had an impact on my thinking.

I have tried to remain objective by drawing on a lifetime studying the intricacies of money and finance, but my choosing to unravel the Volcker mystique did not occur by accident. In 1966, at age twenty-three, I taught my first class to twelve graduate students at what is now called the Stern School of Business at New York University. Most of the students in this seminar in money and banking were older than I, including Alan Greenspan, who had just returned to school to begin his work toward a doctorate. (He got an A.) I later served for almost ten years with Ben Bernanke on the Economic Advisory Panel of the Federal Reserve Bank of New York. Greenspan and Bernanke followed Volcker as Federal Reserve chairmen and acknowledge standing on the shoulders of a titan, and that perspective is close to where I was when this project started. Upon further review, I agree with that assessment, but as I have outlined in this introduction, for much broader reasons than I originally thought.

A letter from Paul Volcker dated March 17, 2008, launched this venture. His note to me, written a day after the Federal Reserve System, America's central bank, arranged a bailout of the investment banking firm Bear Stearns, read, "Thanks so much for that message—all the more on a day that I'm feeling rather depressed about current problems taking the 'Fed' to or beyond the limits!"

My message to Paul Volcker, sent a week earlier, had nothing to do with Bear Stearns, the Federal Reserve, or the crisis that refused to die. It had to do with a conversation I had relayed to Paul about my student Rebecca Solow. Rebecca had told me, "I have been keeping my grandfather up-to-date about your lectures. He was most pleased with what I have learned, especially when you told us that Paul Volcker was the greatest Federal Reserve chairman in American history." That observation may not be controversial today, but it was far from the consensus a generation ago.

Rebecca's grandfather is Robert Solow, winner of the 1987 Nobel Prize in Economics. Bob is witty and personable, in addition to being very smart. He is also a die-hard Keynesian who, like so many public intellectuals, lamented Paul Volcker's anti-inflation policy of the early 1980s, and the accompanying unemployment, as it unfolded. He described the Federal Reserve as "stuck in the embarrassing position of having their finger in the dike and believing they are the country's last hope."[6] If *he* wants his granddaughter to appreciate the Volcker legacy, which requires historical perspective, then so, too, should everyone else.

Prologue

The Three Crises of Paul Volcker

On Thursday, January 21, 2010, Paul Volcker and Vice President Joseph Biden flanked Barack Obama behind the lectern in the White House's Diplomatic Reception Room, site of Franklin Delano Roosevelt's fireside chats during the Great Depression. After a yearlong battle among the administration's economic advisers, the president was about to unveil the financial regulatory plan Volcker had advocated. Volcker's main adversaries, Treasury Secretary Timothy Geithner and White House National Economic Adviser Lawrence Summers, stood like soldiers at parade rest awaiting the president's orders. Volcker radiated his usual cheer, as though he were attending a funeral rather than celebrating a victory.

Volcker had been appointed chairman of the President's Economic Recovery Advisory Board in November 2008, a newly created oversight panel reporting to Obama. Volcker was eighty-one, and his bald head fringed with white hair highlighted the generation gap with Geithner, Summers, and other members of the president's economic brain trust. "They are younger than my kids," he observed later to anyone who would listen.[1] Volcker's appointment had raised expectations in some quarters. *Newsweek* magazine commented, "Ah, finally an adult."[2] But with little staff and no policy responsibilities, he disappeared from view soon after the election. When a reporter implied that Volcker had lost influence, Paul responded, "I did not have [any] to start with."[3]

Few would say that going forward.

The president offered a brief history in his opening remarks.

> Over the past two years more than seven million Americans have lost their jobs in the deepest recession our country has known in generations . . . But even as we dig our way out of this deep hole it's important that we not lose sight of what led us into this mess in the first place. This economic crisis began as a financial crisis when banks and financial institutions took huge, reckless risks in pursuit of quick profits and massive bonuses. And to avoid this calamity, the American people . . . were forced to rescue financial firms facing [crises] largely of their own making.[4]

Obama's populist analysis rings true. Excessive risk taking, enabled by easy access to borrowed funds by brokerage firms such as Bear Stearns and Lehman Brothers, and by insurance giant AIG, turned a decline in home prices into a financial earthquake. President Obama wanted to redesign the regulatory system to avoid future bailouts.

"Limits on the risks major financial firms can take are central to the reforms that I have proposed . . . We simply cannot accept a system in which hedge funds or private equity firms inside banks can place huge risky bets that are subsidized by taxpayers . . . It's for these reasons that I'm proposing a simple and common sense reform, which we're calling the Volcker Rule, after this tall guy behind me."[5]

Obama hooked his thumb like a hitchhiker in Volcker's direction, just in case the assembled press had failed to notice the financial giant standing behind him. The president cracked a smile, and Vice President Biden laughed. Volcker nodded his large head, apparently enjoying the recognition he deserved. Few knew how upset he was.

Volcker had been fighting a losing battle for a year, pushing his vision of regulatory reform, including a comprehensive plan to restrain banks from reckless risk taking. Geithner and Summers had beaten down his proposals, labeling them a throwback to the 1950s, when commercial banks were different from the rest of finance. Now that all financial institutions did the same thing, it made no sense to single out banks for a separate set of restrictions.

Volcker felt marginalized. "They considered me an old man . . . which I may be, but banks are still the center of the American financial system. As long as we protect them with government-sponsored deposit insurance and provide loans from the central bank as needed, they should be treated differently. So I took my *Back to the Future* regulatory framework directly to Congress."[6]

Volcker's testimony before the House Banking and Financial Services Committee on September 24, 2009, caught the attention of Vice President Joseph Biden, who said, "His position makes sense to me and it'll make sense to the American people."[7] Biden urged Obama to reconsider, rescuing Volcker from the Dumpster.[8]

Volcker had met with the president in the Oval Office immediately before the news conference on January 21, 2010, but the Volcker Rule designation caught him by surprise. The christening had been a last-minute suggestion to Obama by David Axelrod, the president's chief political strategist. Most people would have paid for the naming rights to a presidential initiative, but not Paul Volcker. His first thought was "Now, why did he do that?"[9]

Volcker could find fault with the *Mona Lisa*. He made those who viewed the glass as half-empty seem like wild-eyed optimists. Paul thought the label with his name attached sounded boastful, like a Madison Avenue advertisement. His mother was a Lutheran and his father an Episcopalian, but they both taught that Presbyterian modesty was a cardinal virtue. He also worried that the Volcker Rule label would narrow his life into two words of limited scope. He doubted that Alois Alzheimer, a noted psychiatrist, would be pleased with his memorial.

Volcker had always fought like a zealot to get his way, but withdrew when the limelight reflected too brightly off his brow. This time he relented. He lent his name to Obama's initiative because this would be his last chance to set the American monetary system on the right course. Volcker had emerged from the shadows twice before, launching new financial arrangements in August 1971 and in October 1979, when crises threatened to undermine American leadership in world finance. January 2010 would be his third and final installment.

Before the monetary meltdown of the new millennium, Volcker had confronted two financial disasters that had simmered over many years. The promise by the U.S. Treasury to convert dollar holdings of foreign central banks into gold had served as the foundation of the Bretton Woods System of fixed exchange rates since the end of World War II. But a decade of eroding U.S. balance of payments during the 1960s threatened America's promise and undermined the greenback's credibility as international money. The escalating crisis convinced Volcker, as undersecretary of the treasury for monetary affairs in 1971, to recommend cutting the dollar's link to gold. The suspension was announced by President Nixon on August 15, 1971, and Volcker then negotiated the transition to the system of floating exchange rates that we have today.

The absence of gold as its anchor tested American finance. A decade of monetary mismanagement under the leadership of Arthur Burns, appointed by Nixon as chairman of the Federal Reserve System, America's central bank, nearly destroyed U.S. financial credibility. The escalating inflation during the 1970s led President Jimmy Carter to appoint Volcker as Federal Reserve chairman in 1979.

Volcker initiated a new program of monetary control on October 6, 1979, allowing real interest rates to fluctuate widely to reduce inflationary expectations, but his main contribution occurred later. His policy of preemptive restraint during the economic upturn after 1983 increased real interest rates and pushed Congress and the president to adopt a plan to balance the budget. The combination of sound money and fiscal integrity sustained the goal of price stability through Volcker's departure in 1987 and served as a prototype going forward. His leadership of the Federal Reserve from 1979 through 1987 revived confidence in the central bank—almost as though he had restored the gold standard—and ushered in a generation of economic stability.

Volcker's approach to crisis control cannot be reduced to a precise metric. It is an art form, a blend of principle and compromise, like the justice administered by a frontier sheriff. Volcker never acted hastily, always trying to preserve the status quo. And like a reluctant peace officer pressed into making a stand, he was not above using controversial tactics to restore order.

In 1971 he accepted capital controls, an undesirable interference with free trade, while basing exchange rates on the dollar rather than gold.

In 1982, when skyrocketing interest rates threatened to bankrupt Mexico and impair the capital positions of America's largest banks, Volcker papered over the problem with questionable loans. In 1984, when Continental Illinois, the seventh-largest bank in the United States, nearly failed, he helped rescue the embattled giant from bankruptcy, and in the process sanctioned the problematic principle of Too Big to Fail in American finance. Both bailouts permitted the battle against inflation to proceed.

Volcker chose to defend an ambitious goal, sustaining both the domestic and the international integrity of the U.S. currency. Some view the two faces of the dollar as separate objectives, but he insists, "They are the same. Preserving purchasing power at home promotes confidence in the dollar abroad."[10] His success as an inflation fighter revived trust in the Federal Reserve System and maintained the greenback as the world's reserve currency. Americans have been able to consume more than they have produced domestically thanks to the dollar's role as international money. The United States exports financial services to the rest of the world, in exchange for cars, televisions, and manhole covers.

Volcker's victory over inflation had unintended consequences. The generation of economic growth and low inflation that followed between 1987 and 2007 fostered a myth that the business cycle had disappeared and encouraged excessive risk taking by consumers and investors, who borrowed more than they could reasonably expect to repay. The crisis simmered as regulators relaxed safeguards no longer needed under the so-called Great Moderation.

Paul Volcker expected trouble.

In a speech at Stanford University in February 2005 he said, "Baby boomers are spending like there is no tomorrow . . . and we are buying a lot of houses at rising prices."[11] He warned that "The capital markets which have been so benign in providing flexibility . . . can become a point of great vulnerability." And then predicted "Big adjustments will inevitably come . . . And as things stand it is more likely than not that it will be financial crises rather than policy foresight that will force the change."

Volcker knew whereof he spoke. His prediction that crisis would force change came from experience. In 1971 he proposed allowing a

"foreign exchange crisis to develop without action or strong intervention by the U.S.," and to use "suspension of gold convertibility" as negotiating leverage for currency revaluation.[12] In 1979 he used the growing
popular disgust with the inequities of inflation to galvanize support.
"People were prepared to sacrifice to win the battle. I could not have
pushed the anti-inflation program without favorable public opinion."[13]
In 1984 he agreed with Senator John Heinz at hearings in the Senate
that "an inevitable consequence" of the Federal Reserve's tight monetary policy and high interest rates might be a crisis that forced Congress and the president to reduce the federal deficit.[14] Congress passed
the Gramm-Rudman-Hollings Act the following year, a first step toward budgetary reform that cheered financial markets, despite its flaws.

Almost no one paid attention to Volcker's warning in 2005. He was
old, old-fashioned, and a worrier by nature. He had been eclipsed by
time and circumstance. Less than 10 percent of young adults knew
who had preceded the then-chairman of the Federal Reserve, Alan
Greenspan, when Volcker gave his 2005 speech.[15]

The monetary meltdown that began in 2007 changed everything.
The upheaval threatened to destroy American financial credibility.
Bear Stearns and Lehman Brothers, two of the country's preeminent
investment banks, evaporated over separate weekends in March and
September 2008. The collapse of those giants threatened to undermine
the financial trust that the United States exports to the rest of the world.

Volcker returned in 2010 to repair the system he had rescued twice
before, and as with those earlier efforts, his plan combined principle
and compromise to achieve a noble goal. But unlike 1979, when he was
the sheriff, and unlike 1971, when his position at Treasury carried ad-
ministrative power, Volcker relied primarily on patience and persistence to implement his plan. The Volcker Rule became law on July 21,
2010, a testament to the moral authority he had earned in fifty years of
public service.[16]

PART I

Background

CHAPTER 1

The Early Years

Paul A. Volcker learned integrity at home. He was born on September 5, 1927, in Cape May, New Jersey, to Alma and Paul A. Volcker Sr. In 1930 his family moved to the northern part of the Garden State when Paul Sr. became the town manager of Teaneck, a small suburban community five miles west of New York City. Volcker Sr., a civil engineering graduate of Rensselaer Polytechnic Institute in upstate New York, rescued the town from the Great Depression and managed its affairs for twenty years, creating a zoning system, a paid fire department, and civil service for township employees.[1] "The population doubled while my dad was manager," Volcker recalls. "I've always been proud of his success."[2]

A quote from George Washington hanging on the wall in his father's office burrowed into young Paul's brain: "Do not suffer your good nature . . . to say yes when you ought to say no; remember that it is a public not a private cause that is to be injured or benefited by your choice."[3] Paul Volcker Sr. lived by those words, going to extreme measures to avoid even the hint of impropriety, no matter what the consequence, sometimes at young Paul's expense.

Dick Rodda, the Teaneck recreation director, had hired fifteen high school students, including Buddy Volcker, as Paul was called, to work part-time as safety monitors after a snowstorm. When Paul Sr. found out, he called Dick to his office and said, "I want Buddy off the payroll . . . I want you to fire him." When Dick protested, Paul Sr. said, "If you won't fire him I'll find a new recreation superintendent who will." Dick Rodda did as he was told.[4]

Paul watched his father purge the emotion from every decision, deliberating like the pipe smoker he was. "If someone came by on a Monday with a request he had not considered before, he would say, 'Come back on Thursday and I'll have an answer.' He almost turned procrastination into a virtue. He was thoughtful and scrupulous, weighing every option in the process. I learned never to make a decision before its time . . . for better and worse."[5]

As far back as he can remember, Paul craved his family's approval. It began when he was five, in kindergarten, the day he brought home his first evaluation from Miss Constance Palmer. Maybe every boy thinks that his first teacher is beautiful, but he insists she really was. "I remember when she led me by the hand into the circle with the other kids. I liked the attention until she added a note to my report: 'Paul does not take part in group discussion and does not play well with others.'"[6] Those comments worried his parents, especially when his sisters chimed in, "And when Buddy plays with his friends they hardly ever speak." Their concern only deepened Buddy's natural reticence.

Paul's reserve continued as he grew older, creating a serious handicap with the opposite sex. During high school, he was too self-conscious to ask a girl out on a date. But his shyness also had an upside, blossoming into self-reliance. He became a Brooklyn Dodgers fan simply because all his friends rooted for the Yankees or the Giants, who played just a few miles away, across the George Washington Bridge. They considered Brooklyn a foreign country, where people spoke a different language. Paul found that he liked being a contrarian.

A curious blend of insecurity and self-confidence emerged in young Paul. At times the insecurity dominated, especially when it came to report cards. He worried about his father's signature on the card. When he did well, his father would embellish the *V* in his name, as though he was signing the Declaration of Independence; when his grades fell short, a simple *PAV* flowed from his father's pen. "I always wanted the fancy 'Volcker' on the back of the card but did not get it often enough."[7]

Paul Volcker Sr. graded like a headmaster: no nonsense . . . and no hugs or kisses either. The tension rose when Paul applied to college in the spring of 1945. His father suggested his alma mater, Rensselaer. Paul decided to apply to Princeton, just to see if he could make it. The application form itself was intimidating—it felt like parchment when he filled it out—but two weeks later he was accepted. His father tried to persuade him not to go, with a warning: "Prep school students will do better at Princeton than a graduate from Teaneck public high. You'll find out that you're not so smart."[8]

Paul decided to take a chance to prove a point.

Uncle Sam almost accomplished what Paul Sr. failed to do. A formal invitation arrived in April 1945, soon after the Princeton acceptance, requesting that Paul visit his local draft board for a physical exam. The war was winding down in Europe, and Paul had been unhappy when the captain of the Teaneck varsity jumped the gun and volunteered. "We were having a championship season on the basketball court, and that derailed our prospects. When I went for the physical I thought about crouching down so that I would not exceed the maximum acceptable six-foot, six-inch height. I didn't try very hard and was rejected with a physical deferment . . . I've always regretted that decision, wondering whether I let myself and my country down."[9]

Volcker concentrated on economics and basketball at Princeton between 1945 and 1949. Much to his disappointment, he was far better at economics, despite his elongated frame. "I never got along with the coach," Volcker complains, sounding like a benchwarmer covering up for bad footwork or bad hands, "so I didn't play much."[10] Perhaps that is why he found refuge with Princeton's two famous German-born economists, Friedrich Lutz and Oskar Morgenstern, who had come to America after Hitler's rise to power. Lutz taught Volcker about money and banking, his lifelong preoccupation; Morgenstern taught him to worry, his lifelong compulsion.

Morgenstern is best known for his book *Theory of Games and Economic Behavior*, published in 1944 with John von Neumann, one of the most famous mathematicians of the twentieth century.[11] Volcker never studied much game theory, a formal approach to strategic decision making, beyond what Morgenstern had discussed in class, but the professor left his mark by turning Paul into a professional skeptic.

Morgenstern worried about the relevance of economics. He said that "unless [economics] offers a contribution to the mastering of practical life . . . it is but an intellectual plaything . . . similar to chess."[12] Morgenstern probably disliked chess because the Russians dominated it, but he really did want economics to be more than just a game and warned that "insufficiency of data is in great part responsible for the fact that economic policy is so often lacking in rationality."[13] Back then, his colleagues spent most of their time thinking rather than doing.

Oskar Morgenstern would soon write *On the Accuracy of Economic Observations*, published in 1950, warning against the mistreatment of economic data. He did not mince words: "It [is] grotesque to see the *New York Times*, for example, often reporting on its front page that 'consumer prices' have 'risen' or 'fallen' by 1/10 of 1 percent without any qualifying word about the significance of this change in a mere index of doubtful validity."[14]

Volcker recalls Morgenstern's shocking example of data on international gold movements, which often made front-page headlines throughout the world. "Oskar showed numerous years in which Britain's reported gold imports from the United States differed substantially from America's reported gold exports to the U.K. This logical inconsistency made a mockery of further analysis."[15]

Volcker spent most of his days at Princeton reading and playing basketball, not necessarily in that order. "I devoured Friedrich Hayek's *Road to Serfdom*.[16] His defense of free enterprise made me wary of government intervention—and proud to be an American, even though Hayek warned against our creeping socialism. As for coursework, I listened to what the professors had to say and found that I could get As by repeating their views, almost verbatim, on the exams."[17]

Princeton dealt with students who were too smart for their own good by requiring a thesis for graduation—a lengthy tome on some weighty subject that could not be written while shooting baskets. Paul responded to the looming deadline by ignoring the problem. With less than a semester left, he had done nothing.

According to Volcker, Professor Frank Graham, assigned as his thesis adviser, saved him. "I decided to write on Federal Reserve policy after World War II. It turned out more complicated than I had anticipated. Professor Graham gave me great advice: to write first and edit later. I would submit a handwritten chapter on yellow legal-size paper on a Friday afternoon, and he would return it the following Monday with detailed comments and corrections. I was too embarrassed not to push ahead."[18]

Graham, an expert in international trade, flattered Volcker with his attention. Paul had always been too shy and insecure to meet with professors. "I thought they did not have time for me."[19] Graham pushed his young protégé, hoping he would pursue graduate study in economics, and Paul ultimately submitted his thesis with a week to spare, graduating summa cum laude in the process. Volcker would follow this "procrastinate and flourish strategy" throughout his professional career. "I found that it worked, so I never changed." And then he adds, "Besides, it gave me time to think and to get it right."[20]

Volcker continued his studies in economics while attending the Graduate School of Public Administration at Harvard in 1950 and 1951, listening to lectures by, among others, Alvin Hansen, the foremost expositor of the new Keynesian theory of activist government intervention. "Hansen was a great teacher," Volcker recalls, "but I had cut my teeth in economics as an undergraduate at Princeton. I was very skeptical."[21]

Volcker received his master's degree from Harvard in 1951 and then left for the London School of Economics, armed with a Rotary Club fellowship to write his doctoral dissertation. Paul spent most of his time traveling through Europe. "I found a girlfriend who kept me busy. And when time got short, there was no Professor Graham to save my hide. I still feel bad about not completing my degree. I had also disappointed my father, who had saved the clipping from the local newspaper when I received the fellowship. He was an active member of the Rotary Club. I screwed up a good opportunity."[22]

Paul redeemed himself by pursuing a career in public service, like his father. Paul Sr. helped by getting his son an interview at the Federal Reserve Bank of New York. The New York Fed is the most important of the twelve regional Federal Reserve Banks that serve as branches of America's central bank, headed by the Federal Reserve Board in Washington, D.C. The New York Bank, a fortress-like building in Lower

Manhattan, serves as the observation post of the Federal Reserve System, located two blocks from the New York Stock Exchange and within walking distance of the numerous government bond dealers that buy and sell securities with the Federal Reserve every day.

Robert Roosa, vice president of the Research Department at the Federal Reserve Bank of New York, molded Volcker's thinking after he was hired as an economist in 1952. Roosa drafted Volcker to help produce *Federal Reserve Operations in the Money and Government Securities Markets*, a little red booklet (107 pages long) that instructed a generation of policy makers about central bank strategy.[23] Illinois senator Paul Douglas, chairman of the congressional Joint Economic Committee, described Roosa as "probably the foremost authority on the technical operation of the money market in Government securities."[24] He had become an expert after transferring in 1954 from the New York Bank's Research Department to the open market desk, where traders bought and sold securities for the Federal Reserve System.

Roosa's move to the practical side of the Federal Reserve was unprecedented. Economists were considered too cerebral for the instinct-driven trading business, and in the mid-1950s they were segregated in research, barely a notch above the accountants. Roosa broke further ground by putting the twenty-seven-year-old Volcker in the trading room—as an observer, of course. The experience married theory and practice in Volcker's brain and altered the trajectory of his career. If Oskar Morgenstern had convinced Paul that data were essential, but fraught with error, then Robert Roosa gave him the opportunity to examine data under a microscope—data from the heart of Wall Street.

Volcker encountered a new world when he entered the trading room at the New York Fed. Unlike modern trading facilities, decorated with computer terminals and multicolored electronic displays, the 1955 model carried the stark imprint of a black-and-white movie production. A U-shaped desk, equipped with telephone consoles for each trader, filled the entire space, while a large chalkboard hanging on the wall at the open end of the U recorded the relevant statistics, much like a primitive scoreboard at a baseball game. Prices of government bonds, which were frozen in print in the Research Department, now danced in Volcker's head during phone conversations with Wall Street's bond dealers. Shorthand words for buying and selling could make the conversations sound like gibberish. It took a practiced ear to decipher the meaning of "9 bid, offered at 10, 100 by 100," but Paul caught on quickly and reveled in the details, feeling as though he had been initiated into a secret fraternity.[25]

On Wednesdays, when commercial banks had to meet their required reserves prescribed by the Federal Reserve, Volcker would work past midnight on his weekly report for the Federal Reserve's Open Market Committee. The committee, referred to as the FOMC, is the central bank's decision-making body. It consists of the seven members of the Federal Reserve Board, appointed by the president of the United States, plus five of the twelve regional Reserve Bank presidents, who serve on the FOMC on a rotating basis.

The FOMC was run by the then chairman of the Federal Reserve Board, William McChesney Martin, who had been appointed by President Harry Truman in 1951 and would serve until 1970. Martin was a former banker, just like everyone else on the board in the mid-1950s. Perhaps the economy was a lot simpler in those days, but the absence of economists bore the chairman's imprint.[26] Martin thought economists' forecasts rivaled the accuracy of fortune teller predictions, probably an insult to the fortune tellers: "If the decision were mine alone, I would dispense with [that] kind of analysis."[27] He also felt that economists lacked the practical experience needed of central bankers.

With Martin at the helm, it is not surprising that economist Paul Volcker failed to make the distribution list of those permitted to read the weekly report that he wrote. His wife, Barbara, taunted him: "You can write it but can't read it. What's wrong with these people?"[28]

Barbara, a pretty woman with short dark hair that she denigrated as mousey, had majored in irreverence at Pembroke College, part of Brown University. She had been married to Paul for less than two years at the time and did not appreciate his midnight scribbling. Paul knew that she was right about the Fed, as she was about most things. The rigid bureaucracy would wear him down. But he also knew that his memoranda to the FOMC mattered, even though he was a mere economist, because they came from his observer status on the open market desk. He had the credibility of an embedded reporter on the front lines. He even went to an FOMC meeting as Roosa's scribe and recalls thinking, "It would be nice to sit around the table as a member of the board."[29]

Volcker's memos bristled with facts and figures: how many securities were bought or sold, at what prices, who was buying and who was selling, and perhaps most important, what the dealers expected interest rates to do in the near term. Dealers profit by anticipating whether interest rates will decrease or increase, whether bond prices rise or fall. They make money buying before prices jump and selling before they drop. Volcker paid attention to the details, especially the link between expectations and behavior, and recognized the importance of fitting the pieces together, much as he had in his boyhood hobby of building model airplanes. Every plane, made from balsa wood and paper, with a rubber band to crank the propeller, was perfectly balanced, ready to fly.

The Fed's trading room was a bridge between economic research and the real world, and Volcker had crossed the span and liked what he saw. He remained a reporter rather than a player on the trading desk until 1957, when he took another step toward real-world practice and joined the Chase Manhattan Bank. Chase Manhattan took its name from Salmon P. Chase, Abraham Lincoln's treasury secretary during the Civil War, and from the Bank of Manhattan, founded by Aaron Burr, the vice president of the United States who killed the first treasury secretary, Alexander Hamilton, in America's most famous duel.

Unlike at the Fed, where memos crept through the bureaucracy at the speed of a turtle, ideas at Chase Manhattan could accelerate like an express train. Volcker worked in the economics department but gained access to upper management as the secretary of a weekly meeting among senior officers of the bank. His summaries for the group raised his profile in the executive suite, exposure that ultimately brought a call from George Champion, president of the bank.

Champion, who had joined Chase in 1933, asked Volcker to come by to discuss his most recent memo. Champion must have liked what he heard, because he said, "Sit down a minute. I'm worried about our [international] trade position. It seems to me we are getting less competitive, and it could affect the dollar. What do you think?"[30]

Volcker had not thought much about foreign trade since listening to Harvard specialist in international economics Gottfried Haberler describe the intricacies of foreign exchange and the balance of payments.

Volcker began to dust off his class notes, eager to apply what he had learned.

But he never got the chance. Robert Roosa had other plans for him.

After narrowly defeating Richard Nixon in the 1960 presidential race, John F. Kennedy identified Cuba and the balance of payments as the two most difficult problems confronting America.[31] Cuba made sense. Back then, some fanatics resisted writing with red ink to avoid a hint of Communist sympathy. But aside from a few financiers and professors, almost no one cared about the balance of payments. Robert Roosa, by then a senior vice president at the Federal Reserve Bank of New York, was one of the few. He also knew enough to help.

Paul Samuelson, the Nobel laureate MIT economist who educated millions of Americans with his basic textbook and dazzled his colleagues with wit and mathematics, advised Kennedy on his major economics appointments. He recommended Roosa to the president-elect for the key position as undersecretary of the treasury for monetary affairs.[32] Roosa's job was to fix the balance-of-payments problem.

What was Kennedy worried about? Less than two weeks before the 1960 election, the *New York Times* ran a front-page headline that got everyone's attention like a thunderclap: "Kennedy Pledges He Will Maintain Value of Dollar."[33] Until then, most Americans did not realize that the dollar was in any kind of danger, but Kennedy's promise touched a nerve. No one wanted a decline in the value of the dollar. A few days later the Republicans added a similar assurance.[34] Suddenly everyone worried.

Kennedy's promise meant that the United States would continue to redeem U.S. dollars in gold at the rate of thirty-five dollars per ounce. The pledge applied to foreign central banks that held dollars they received from exporters shipping goods across the Atlantic—the French, who sent wine; the Italians, who sent cheese; and most of all, the Germans, who sent Volkswagens. Americans had not been entitled to redeem their own dollars in gold since 1933, when Franklin Delano Roosevelt made it illegal for U.S. citizens to hold gold, other than as jewelry.

America's promise to redeem dollars at the rate of thirty-five dollars per ounce of gold was the cornerstone of the world's payments system. The U.S. commitment, along with the system of fixed exchange rates among the world's currencies, under the supervision of the International Monetary Fund, had emerged from a three-week meeting, in July 1944, in Bretton Woods, New Hampshire. The Bretton Woods Agreement served as the Magna Carta of international finance for a quarter of a century, until August 1971.

In Volcker's view, the Bretton Woods Agreement was conceived in a "burst of intellectual energy" that has never "been seen before or since."[35] A month after D-day, the Allied landing in Normandy, France, on June 6, 1944, President Franklin D. Roosevelt invited delegates of the Allied countries to the conference that would design the postwar monetary and financial environment. Roosevelt was aware that much bloodshed remained, but he insisted that "even while the war for liberation is at its peak . . . representatives of free men should [plan] . . . for an enduring program of future economic cooperation."[36] Roosevelt believed that "economic diseases are highly communicable," and international trade was an antidote to world conflict, a vaccination against another world war. He said, "Commerce is the lifeblood of a free society."[37]

U.S. treasury secretary Henry Morgenthau headed the American delegation to the conference. On July 1, 1944, he arrived in Bretton Woods, a sleepy village in the White Mountains, noted until then as a refuge for hay fever sufferers rather than as a gathering place for world financiers. He had left a sweltering Washington, D.C., and his first thought upon breathing the crisp mountain air was that he should have packed woolen socks.[38] He was joined at the Mount Washington Hotel conference center by more than seven hundred representatives from forty-four countries, including sixteen ministers of finance and central bankers.[39]

The American group included the then-chairman of the Federal Reserve Board, Marriner Eccles, and highlighted powerful politicians: Dean Acheson, an assistant secretary of state, and Robert F. Wagner, chairman of the Senate Banking Committee. The famed British economist John Maynard Keynes—author of the most influential economic treatise of the twentieth century, *The General Theory of Employment, Interest and Money*, which created the "Keynesian

School" of economics—led the delegation from the United Kingdom, and he was joined by other members of British academic aristocracy: Dennis Robertson, professor of political economy at Cambridge, and Lionel Robbins, professor at the London School of Economics.

Most of the countries represented at Bretton Woods followed the American and British recipes: politicians for power with a sprinkling of academics for flavor. Absent from the conference were representatives of the Axis powers (Germany, Japan, and Italy) and neutral countries, most notably, Switzerland, home of powerful international banks and foreign currency speculators. Argentina was excluded because its "continuing support of the Axis" rendered it unfit to "to sit down with the United Nations in important war and postwar conferences."[40] The conference in New Hampshire was an Allied operation, just like the invasion of Normandy.

The Bretton Woods Agreement was the brainchild of John Maynard Keynes and Harry Dexter White, a U.S. Treasury economist serving as the only technical expert in the American delegation.[41] The objective was to restore the golden age of international trade that had flourished for a generation prior to the outbreak of World War I. Most countries adhered to the gold standard before 1914, protecting citizens against inflation by promising to redeem paper currency in gold. The gold content of each currency also fixed the rate of exchange among different currencies: Americans could always get one British pound for $4.86 and could always exchange one dollar for five French francs. As a result, a company such as John Deere, headquartered in Moline, Illinois, knew how much it would earn in dollars whether it shipped tractors to Liverpool, Marseilles, or Kansas City. The absence of fluctuating exchange rates made international trade no more complicated than a visit to the flea market on the other side of town.

The problem with resurrecting the gold standard after World War II was that America had almost all the gold—$20 billion worth buried in Fort Knox.[42] No country could credibly promise to redeem its currency in gold except for the United States. The Bretton Woods Agreement anchored the international payments system on America's hoard, tethered by the U.S. pledge to exchange dollars for gold at the rate of $35 per ounce, with every other country agreeing to fix its currency relative to the dollar. Fixing exchange rates to the dollar required a commitment by central bankers to buy and sell currencies at the agreed-upon rate. Success meant the Bretton Woods System would mimic the stability of the gold standard.

Fixed exchange rates under the Bretton Woods Agreement would also avoid the trade wars of the Great Depression, when countries fought among themselves to devalue their currencies to promote exports. The "butter battle" between New Zealand and Denmark demonstrates the futility of competitive devaluations.[43] New Zealand started the fight by devaluing its currency in 1930 to lower the effective price of its butter exports to England, hoping to sell more to cost-conscious Londoners. Denmark retaliated with its own devaluation to neutralize New Zealand's advantage. The process continued until 1933 and left each country's total butter exports exactly where they had started. Competitive devaluations made British consumers happy because they paid less for their butter, but no one else benefited, except perhaps the foreign exchange speculators in Switzerland.

The Bretton Woods System of fixed exchange rates would pit governments, and their central bankers, against speculators in a war that lasted a generation. Central banks tried to tame the forces of supply and demand to keep exchange rates fixed, while speculators did their best to make money by anticipating central bank failure to prevent devaluation. Speculators would sell weak currencies hoping to buy them back after they declined in value. In one of the early skirmishes, British officials blamed "the gnomes of Zurich" for mounting "speculative attacks against sterling."[44] Gnomes are imaginary, but speculators are not.

By 1960, speculators scared everyone, including candidates for the most powerful position on earth, the American presidency. JFK affirmed America's pledge to redeem U.S. dollars in gold in October of that year, in response to speculator attacks on America's credibility.

Speculators look like normal people, except they smoke big fat Cuban cigars. They try to buy something (anything) in anticipation of selling at a profit after the price goes up. Or they sell first and try to buy later at a lower price. Some speculators focus on stocks, others on bonds, and still others on Super Bowl tickets. (Ticket scalpers are speculators by another name.)

In October 1960, gold speculators tested America's promise to keep the price of the precious metal at thirty-five dollars per ounce. Transactions among dealers in gold bullion had taken place since March 22, 1954, in the London headquarters of the 150-year-old private banking firm N. M. Rothschild and Sons.[45] The free-market price, sometimes referred to as the London gold fixing, was established every day in an auction conducted by the dealers gathered in the boardroom under the gaze of eighteenth-century Rothschild portraits hanging on the wood-paneled walls.[46] The price was "fixed" to balance demand for bullion with supply, with orders transmitted to the dealers from investors, gold mines, and central banks throughout the world.

The U.S. Treasury had maintained the price in the London fixing within a few cents of thirty-five dollars by selling gold if excess demand prevailed at that price and by buying if there was excess supply. On October 20, 1960, two weeks before the presidential election, speculators suspected that America might abandon its commitment to sell gold in the free market. They flooded the London dealers with buy orders and, much to everyone's surprise (except the speculators), the price jumped to levels that had never been seen before.[47]

Paul Volcker sat in his office at Chase Manhattan Bank on that explosive day in October. During the previous two days, he had watched the price poke above $35.08, the exact level at which the U.S. Treasury promised to deliver gold.[48] Paul recognized the danger to American credibility. Prices had always bounced off the ceiling as private groups—mining companies and foreign banks—sold gold, confident that the U.S. Treasury would hold the line. These private sellers, in fact, kept a lid on the price without the Treasury having to sell gold.

A colleague stuck his head into Volcker's office, looking as though he had glimpsed the hereafter, and said, "The gold price is forty dollars." Paul stared at his ashen-faced friend. "That can't be, you mean thirty-five dollars and forty cents."[49] Volcker thought that even $35.40 would be a terrible blow to American prestige, proof that the United States had failed to meet its obligations. And then they checked the news ticker. Speculative purchases on October 20, 1960, had, in fact, driven the price of gold to $40.00 per ounce, an unprecedented number at the time.

Roosa had tutored Volcker, and everyone passing through the New

York Fed, that America's pledge to gold ranked alongside the pursuit of happiness for all citizens, and he had advised the Kennedy campaign to issue the promise not to devalue.[50] Newspaper reports identified the source of the speculative buying. "Most of the demand came from the Continent and particularly from Zurich . . . Swiss bankers have advised their foreign customers to buy gold for deposit there."[51] These reports were denied as total fabrications by the mythical dwarf-like creatures, the gnomes, evidently living in Zurich, guarding their new treasure. But gnomes and speculators cannot be trusted.

The jump in the price of gold from thirty-five dollars to forty dollars meant that the dollar had depreciated against gold—technically called devaluation. It would now take an extra five dollars to purchase an ounce of the precious metal. Editors at the *New York Times* admonished the public with a message worthy of Jeremiah's Book of Lamentations. "We would all do well to think seriously about the warning we have been given by the London gold market."[52]

Robert Triffin, an expert in international trade from Yale, advocated a criminal indictment of America. "A devaluation of the dollar . . . would be . . . a wanton crime against the people of this country, and against the friendly nations who have long accepted our financial leadership and placed their trust in the United States dollar."[53]

And Richard Nixon, battling JFK for the presidency, piled on in a gang tackle. "The United States cannot afford a debasement of our currency."[54] To all parties involved, what was at stake was nothing less than the stability of the relatively new global financial system.

Volcker believed that America had a moral obligation to uphold its commitment to Bretton Woods and to maintain "the sanctity of the $35 gold price."[55] But he also thought the consequences of devaluation extended beyond ethics. The rumor was that Joseph P. Kennedy, JFK's father, had told his son, "A nation was only as strong as the value of its currency."[56] Perhaps that is why JFK half humorously listed military power behind a strong currency as a determinant of international prestige: "Britain has nuclear weapons, but the pound is weak, so everyone pushes [Britain] around."[57]

Volcker also recalled a comment from Chase's president, George Champion, about a Southeast Asian country he had visited: "It has a strong currency . . . so it's a country we can trust."[58] These sweeping generalizations, linking a country's currency and its stature, nestled comfortably in Volcker's brain beside the lessons he had learned from economic history: before 1914, Britain ruled the world with the pound sterling.

Volcker applauded Kennedy's pledge to maintain the price of gold at thirty-five dollars per ounce. But he knew that simply saying so would not stop the speculators. Oskar Morgenstern had taught him that economists probably knew nothing, or maybe even less than nothing, with one big exception: supply and demand, not words, determine price. Speculator buying (demand) had driven up the price of gold, and would continue to drive up the price further, as long as speculators doubted America's commitment to supply unlimited amounts of gold to the free market at thirty-five dollars an ounce. Volcker knew exactly what fed the doubts that had led to the buying frenzy on October 20, 1960: America's weak balance of payments.

Speculators examine the balance of payments the way bookies review the racing form. The balance of payments is a record of a country's imports and exports. It also determines the supply and demand for a currency in the foreign exchange market. When Americans import Japanese TV sets or German radios, they offer dollars in exchange for foreign currency to pay for their purchases. When the Germans and the Japanese buy American airplanes or invest on the New York Stock Exchange, they offer their currency in exchange for dollars to pay for their purchases. A deficit in America's balance of payments means U.S. demand for Sony TVs and Blaupunkt radios exceeds Japanese and German demand for Boeing aircraft and General Electric stock, with a corresponding buildup of dollars abroad.

A balance-of-payments deficit predicted trouble.

America was the proud owner of $19.5 billion in gold in December 1959, just about the same amount it had fourteen years earlier, at the end of 1945.[59] Less than nine months later, however, in September 1960, a month before the speculative outburst, the U.S. gold stock had declined by almost a billion dollars, to $18.7 billion.[60] The *Wall Street Journal* put the drop for the week ending September 21, 1960, into perspective with the headline "Largest Regular Weekly Decline Since 1931."[61] The *Journal* explained the root cause as "the continuing deficit in this country's balance of payments with the rest of the world."[62]

Foreigners had more dollars than they needed, so the central banks of Europe and Asia sent their surplus greenbacks to the U.S. Treasury with a polite but firm request to exchange their dollars for gold, as was their right under the Bretton Woods System.

Prospects for a Kennedy victory over Richard Nixon fanned speculator worries about America's balance of payments. According to the press, European central bankers attributed the flurry of gold speculation to expectations that "Senator Kennedy will win the U.S. election . . . [and] that a Kennedy election will mean renewed U.S. inflation."[63] Inflation means higher prices, making U.S. products less competitive abroad and leading to fewer exports, worsening America's balance of payments. Speculators were not merely speculating when it came to Kennedy's economic policy; his advisers supported greater inflation to achieve another goal: full employment.

Paul Samuelson was John F. Kennedy's tutor in Keynesian economics, and he had just coauthored an article with his MIT colleague Robert Solow (a future Nobel Prize winner, just like Samuelson), explaining that a country could reduce unemployment if it tolerated an increase in inflation.[64] The trade-off between inflation and unemployment was the guiding principle of mainstream economics for nearly a generation. This doctrine would later come under attack from Milton Friedman, founder of the "monetarist school," and would be blamed for accelerating inflation almost beyond control. But in 1960, Samuelson's opinion defined the mainstream, certainly for the young presidential candidate.

After the election, when Samuelson touted Roosa with high praise for the job as undersecretary of the treasury for monetary affairs, Kennedy, who at that time was still looking to fill the position of secretary, finally said, "If this fellow is so good, why don't we give him the top job?"[65] Samuelson answered, "You can't do that. He is too young." Samuelson's response entertained Kennedy, who noted that Roosa was only a year younger than he, but Kennedy took the advice.[66]

The outlook for inflation had emboldened the gold speculators, forcing JFK to pledge fealty to the value of the dollar. He appointed Roosa to the crucial position at the Treasury to help calm the markets. Roosa's anti-inflationary credentials, honed at the Federal Reserve Bank of New York, matched his commitment to America's obligations under Bretton Woods.

Ironically, Roosa would battle Samuelson's allies at the President's Council of Economic Advisers (CEA) who wanted to promote full employment with a dollop of inflation. Volcker, at the time working for Roosa as an economist, recalls, "At the Treasury we had two main enemies: a State department that did not want the balance of payments to influence foreign policy and a CEA that did not want it to interfere with domestic policy. We had very little room to maneuver."[67]

The Council of Economic Advisers, located in the Executive Office Building next door to the White House, consists of three members appointed by the president, plus a staff of about twenty economists on leave from academic posts. Future Nobel Prize winners decorated the CEA during those years, including James Tobin of Yale, Kenneth Arrow of Stanford, and Robert Solow, Samuelson's colleague from MIT. These economists believed they could engineer full employment just as physicists believed they could put a man on the moon.

Roosa arranged a presidential appointment for Volcker as deputy undersecretary of the treasury for monetary affairs so that he could serve as Treasury's point man in confronting the CEA.[68] Volcker felt like a rookie in a home-run-hitting contest against the 1927 Yankees, and relied on Morgenstern skepticism as his Louisville Slugger.

Volcker recalls: "It all sounded too easy. Push this button twice and out pops full employment. Equations do not work as well on people as they do on rockets. I remember sitting in class at Harvard listening to [the fiscal policy expert] Arthur Smithies say, 'A little inflation is good for the economy.' And all I can remember after that was a word flashing in my brain like a yellow caution sign: 'Bullshit.' I'm not sure exactly where that came from . . . but it's a thought that never left me."[69]

CHAPTER 2

Apprenticeship

Paul Volcker's long and torturous battle with inflation began when he was a teenager, preparing for his departure to Princeton in 1945. His mother offered twenty-five dollars a month for living expenses, just like his sisters, but he protested, "Mother, when they went to school, twenty-five dollars was really worth something. Prices have gone up a lot since then. And besides, I'm a boy and have higher expenses."[1]

Alma Volcker looked at her son. "Really?" She had gone to Vassar and graduated as valedictorian of her class with a degree in chemistry, at a time when most women had thought about neither college nor chemistry. "Well, it was good enough for them, so it'll be good enough for you."

Paul turned to his siblings for support, but it would not be easy. They had always worried about everyone spoiling him, as the youngest in the family and the only son to carry on the Volcker name. Ruth and Louise, more than ten years older than Paul, had gone to college during the Depression. And Virginia, three years older, was nearly finished. Much to his delight, however, they all agreed, so he confronted his mother again.

"My sisters say that I should get more because of inflation."

But Alma Volcker would not budge. "I don't care about that. You'll still get twenty-five dollars."

At first Paul thought his mother wanted to teach him lesson in frugality, a family trait he himself still practices today with the dedication of a monk. He had seen his father wear suits long after they had frayed at the cuffs and knew that his sisters sewed their own clothes. Perhaps his mother was worried about the spendthrift ways of the prep school boys he would befriend at Princeton. Years later, he learned the truth. His father had tried to enlist in the army but was too old. In a burst of patriotic thrift, he refused a salary increase throughout the war, despite the inflation. "That didn't change the facts, but it explained it all, and made a lasting impression."[2]

Keynesians often dismiss the inequities of inflation as a nuisance, an irritant that can be ignored for the common good. A little inflation is certainly an acceptable price for running the economy at full throttle. But Volcker's favorite author as an undergraduate, Friedrich Hayek, fueled his suspicion that it was not quite so simple. The Austrian émigré's ode to free enterprise warned against the alleged virtues of inflation: "It should be specially noted that monetary policy cannot provide a real cure for [unemployment] except by a general and considerable inflation . . . and that even this would bring about the desired result only . . . in a concealed and underhand fashion."[3]

Hayek meant that inflation worked by subterfuge, tricking people into thinking they are better off as their wages rise, only to disappoint them when they are confronted later with higher prices to match. According to Volcker, "Hayek's words forever linked inflation and deception deep inside my head. And that connection, which undermines trust in government, is the greatest evil of inflation."[4]

Hayek also denied the claim by Keynesians that inflation could permanently stimulate the economy. When worker expectations catch up with reality, as they inevitably must, the illusion of higher real wages is exposed as a fraud, and inflation loses its power to promote more employment. The end result is simply higher inflation and increased resentment, because rising prices do not affect everyone the same way.

Hayek's message made logical sense to Volcker, even though it clashed with the emerging Keynesian consensus. It was reinforced by his Princeton professors. "I don't think I heard the name of John Maynard Keynes until I got to Harvard. At Princeton they taught the famous quantity theory of money as though they heard it directly from David

Hume in 1750," says Volcker.[5] "Friedrich Lutz was about forty at the time, but from the perspective of an eighteen-year-old, he might as well have been two hundred and forty. He taught us that too much money created inflation."[6]

Volcker had applied those lessons during the fall of 1948 in writing "The Problems of Federal Reserve Policy Since World War II," his undergraduate thesis. Prices had surged in the United States immediately after the war, triggered by the pent-up demand for consumer goods, the removal of wartime controls, and an enlarged stock of money. Volcker wrote, "A swollen money supply presented a grave inflationary threat to the economy. There was a need to bring this money supply under control if the disastrous effects of a sharp price rise were to be avoided."[7]

He concluded with an indictment of the Federal Reserve's performance worthy of Milton Friedman, a lifelong critic of the central bank: "Although the inflation problem continually raised its head in a disconcerting manner . . . the counter-measures taken have not [been] . . . a realistic attempt to combat the danger . . . The Federal Reserve System had no definite criteria of policy to follow."[8] Volcker lamented the central bank's failure to ensure price stability, its most important responsibility.

Paul Volcker's anti-inflationary sentiments prepared him perfectly for the U.S. Treasury in January 1962. President Kennedy had enlisted Robert Roosa to offset the pro-inflation bias of his Council of Economic Advisers and to oversee international economic affairs. Roosa drafted Paul Volcker as his personal watchdog. "I could hardly wait to get to Washington," Volcker recalls. "It's hard to re-create the excitement of working for a young vibrant John F. Kennedy. My main concern was that they would solve all the problems before I got there to help."[9]

He had nothing to worry about. The U.S. Treasury served as the guardian of American gold. And the dwindling reserves in Fort Knox threatened American finance.

Gold has served as a store of value ever since King Tut passed into the afterlife with a treasure chest of the metal, in addition to his famous mask. Gold developed into money, something useful for making payments, in part because it is a good store of value. But many things are valuable and are not used as money, such as the New York Yankees, Buckingham Palace, and French antiques. Gold serves as money because in addition to holding its value, it is easily divisible and standardized.

More than 2,500 years ago, King Croesus invented gold coins by dividing the precious metal into a fixed number of grains and then certifying its weight with his stamp of approval.[10] Gold in the form of standardized coins facilitated all types of payments, to the tailor for a brand-new suit, to the local tavern for a neighborhood celebration, and of course to the king's tax collector for waging war and building castles.

Before 1933, U.S. gold coins, such as the famous twenty-dollar double eagle and the less-well-known ten-dollar eagle and five-dollar half eagle, had circulated as American currency alongside the familiar Federal Reserve notes still used today. The U.S. Mint, a bureau within the Treasury Department, created these coins out of gold bullion brought in for minting. The Treasury would also exchange paper dollars into gold at the rate of $20.67 in currency per ounce of gold.[11]

People preferred dollar bills rather than gold for most payments because gold is physically dense, making it cumbersome to carry and costly to ship. A gold bar, worth about $8,000 in 1933, is slightly smaller than an ordinary brick and weighs about as much as two bowling balls.[12] As long as people knew they could convert dollars into gold, as the U.S. Treasury promised, they chose not to bother. They would rather hold dollar bills for convenience, or better yet, put the money into their neighborhood bank, where it would earn interest. Gold coins served primarily as Christmas presents for children of privilege rather than as pocket change for everyday shoppers.

All this changed in March 1933. President Franklin Roosevelt wanted to allow banks to expand credit without the limitations of gold, to help rescue the economy from the ravages of the Great Depression. He pushed Congress to pass a law authorizing a Presidential Executive Order requiring American citizens to turn in all gold coins and receive paper currency in exchange.[13]

Now that people had to give up the precious metal, of course, they did not want to. FDR's treasury secretary, William Woodin, ordered the president's directive printed up like Wanted Dead or Alive posters, exhorting the public "To deliver . . . all gold coin" or face criminal penalties, including a "$10,000 fine or 10 years imprisonment, or both."[14] He then distributed the placards to post offices throughout the country for display along with other criminal notices from the postal inspection service.

U.S. citizens complained about the dictatorial decree and squirreled away their gold in safe-deposit boxes, while litigating (unsuccessfully) that Congress had abrogated their inalienable rights.[15] Mary Meeker, a recently unemployed fifty-one-year-old single woman, sent a latter dated April 30, 1933, to the *New York Times*, summarizing the complaint:

> I was frugal in the use of my earnings, and what I managed to save . . . amounted to about $31,000.00 . . . A few months ago I became very much disturbed over the financial situation in this country and decided to withdraw my money from savings banks, convert it into gold and place it in safe deposit boxes . . . Congress [then] adopted the banking emergency bill requiring all persons to convert into currency . . . all gold coin . . . under penalty of a heavy fine or long imprisonment . . . We were assured that the bills we received in exchange for gold . . . were just as good and just as valuable . . . Will you kindly explain to me where I will stand in the event President Roosevelt does revalue the dollar by reducing the gold content? I worked for many years to accumulate the $31,000.00 in gold that I turned over . . . under duress of the law enacted by Congress at the behest of President Roosevelt . . . The government now holds my gold and all I have to show for it is the Federal Reserve notes given me in exchange for it.[16]

Money is a social contrivance, worth something only because others will accept it in payment for real things. A dollar retains its value if prices remain stable, which is precisely what the gold standard accomplished by allowing people to convert paper dollars into gold. It prevented inflation by controlling the printing press, holding the creation of paper dollars in check, for better or worse. The restraint on prices made Mary Meeker happy, but it also prevented banks from expanding credit to jump-start the economy.

Loosening the link with gold provided some leeway for the central bank to expand credit during a crisis, such as the Great Depression. And as long as the Federal Reserve managed its mandate responsibly, so that price increases did not become a way of life, dollars provided a safe store of value. Of course, that is precisely what worried Mary Meeker—she trusted gold more than the Federal Reserve. And she was right to worry.

The Gold Reserve Act of January 1934 established the secretary of the treasury as the czar of American gold.[17] It specified that "all gold coin . . . shall be formed into bars . . . as the Secretary of the Treasury may direct." It gave the secretary the power to "prescribe the conditions under which gold may be . . . transported, imported, and exported . . . for industrial, professional, and artistic use." And finally, to stabilize the international value of the dollar, it gave the treasury secretary the right to "deal in gold and foreign exchange." As far as gold was concerned, the secretary of the treasury was like a grand pooh-bah, an exalted official in charge of all matters, and worthy of the title Lord High Everything Else.[18]

The 1934 legislation also devalued the dollar, reducing its gold content to 13.714 grains of pure gold, which translated into a price of $35.00 per ounce rather than $20.67, but it did not take the United States off the gold standard.[19] It softened the link between money and the precious metal by preventing Americans from exchanging paper dollars into gold, but the Federal Reserve still had to hold a reserve of 40 percent in gold against its liabilities, such as the familiar Federal Reserve notes Americans use as currency. Without further legislation, this "gold cover" provided an upper limit on credit creation by the central bank. Moreover, foreign central banks retained the right to exchange paper dollars for gold. The United States had to manage its monetary affairs so that the U.S. Treasury could meet America's international obligation to redeem dollars in gold.

President Kennedy put Undersecretary of the Treasury for Monetary Affairs Robert Roosa in charge of defending America's gold reserves, which had declined to nearly $17 billion by the time Kennedy took office in 1961.[20] Roosa's assignment was more difficult than it appeared, because over $11 billion of that hoard was immobilized as gold cover for Federal Reserve liabilities.[21] America's immediate obligations to foreign central banks amounted to double the remaining $6 billion of free gold.[22]

Roosa assigned the job of helping him protect the gold stock to Paul Volcker when he arrived at the Treasury in 1962. At times the task bordered on the mundane. The 1934 prohibition against U.S. citizens investing in gold lasted forty years, until 1974, and Volcker had to prevent gold coins from entering the country without a proper visa.[23] He responded to numerous requests for exemptions from regular people like Mary Meeker of thirty years earlier, efforts that tested his diplomatic skills.

Volcker felt bad about being unable to make exceptions for sentiment, including the letter he had to write to a Mr. Schubert in Oklahoma City:

> I understand and sympathize with your feelings in connection with the fact that the Collector of Customs in Kansas City detained gold coins which you [received as a] bequest from your deceased brother. Unfortunately they cannot be allowed under present regulations governing the importation of gold coins . . . only genuine and lawfully issued gold coins of exceptional numismatic value may be acquired abroad and imported to the United States. The determination as to exceptional value is made with reference to the coin itself and not the individual wishing to import it.[24]

Volcker could not single out Schubert (or his brother) for special treatment, because the gold coin restriction did not play favorites. JFK's brother-in-law Sargent Shriver had been honored in Germany for his work as director of the Peace Corps. When he returned to the United States with a solid-gold medallion presented by the German government, it was promptly seized by the Customs Bureau. Shriver appealed to Treasury Secretary Douglas Dillon (Roosa's boss) for help, and Dillon turned the matter over to Volcker. Shriver made his case to Volcker like the good lawyer he was.[25]

"What if I had won an Olympic gold medal?"

"We make an exception for Olympic medals."

"What about a 1729 King George Gold Guinea?"

"It gets the okay as a collector's coin."

"So what's wrong with my medallion?"

"It doesn't fit either category."

"That's ridiculous."

"You're probably right. Do you want me to ask Secretary Dillon to instruct the Customs Bureau to make an exception?"

"I'll think about it."

According to Volcker, "Shriver was sore as a boil at being denied his gold medallion, an award he had been given for exceptional public service. But Shriver knew it would have looked bad to fight the law, so he waited until after resigning as director of the Peace Corps before successfully reclaiming his medal."

Roosa responded to President Kennedy's challenge to protect America's commitment to redeem dollars in gold with a blizzard of innovations. His first initiative was to organize an international consortium, called the "Gold Pool," to help defend the fixed price.[26] Germany, the United Kingdom, Italy, France, Switzerland, the Netherlands, and Belgium agreed to help the United States fix the thirty-five-dollar price of gold by jointly selling gold in the London market if excess demand pushed up the price and buying gold if excess supply pushed it down. This was good for the entire world, since it maintained international financial stability under the Bretton Woods System, but it was a bonanza for the United States, like living in the Magic Kingdom, since it solidified the dollar as the world's reserve currency.

A reserve currency serves like a checking account, a vehicle for exchanging payments, for central banks and financial institutions. The Bank of Japan, for example, would use dollars to settle obligations with the Bank of France. Business firms with extensive exports and imports would do the same, making dollars the international medium of exchange. Not everyone understood the benefits to America of having a reserve currency, not even JFK, who had pledged allegiance to gold to help sustain the dollar's supremacy as international money.

Kennedy knew that "if everybody wants gold, we're all going to be ruined because there isn't enough gold to go around," and he believed that "gold really should be used for international payments."[27] But JFK also worried about the political repercussions, and invited

Undersecretary of State George Ball to balance the views of his financial brain trust. Ball thought that the Treasury's monetary objectives might compromise national security. "Should [we] become more heavily involved in Southeast Asia . . . there is a fair chance that our European friends would walk away from us . . . [and] it would be a real temptation to exploit our own balance of payments difficulties . . . for political purposes." Ball then added, "We're not persuaded that it is at all vital to the United States that we . . . be the principal reserve currency."[28]

Kennedy interrupted and turned to his Treasury team: "What *is* the advantage to the United States of our being a reserve currency?"[29]

Volcker knew that if JFK had posed that question while working for Roosa at the Federal Reserve Bank of New York he would have been dispatched to the sub-basement, fifty feet below sea level, right next to the gold vault, for indoctrination under the care and guidance of Tomás de Torquemada. Roosa believed with the faith of a zealot that America had an obligation to "provide the principal reserve currency for the monetary system of the world—a duty which involves special responsibilities as well as conveying special opportunities."[30]

In answering the president, however, Roosa skipped the responsibilities and focused on the opportunities, something tangible that JFK could take to the bank. "[A reserve currency] makes it possible for us . . . year in and year out . . . to finance any [balance-of-payments] deficit we may run very readily, because you have the world accustomed to holding dollars. When you run behind for a year you don't have to negotiate a credit, they just hold dollars . . . This is a situation similar to that of any commercial bank. If it controls the rate at which it creates credit, it can go on creating credit and perform a general service as well and make a profit."[31]

Roosa told the president that the dollar's status as a reserve currency allowed America to import more goods and services than it exported, and to enjoy a higher standard of living than otherwise. The advantage did not go unnoticed, and would eventually destroy the Gold Pool.

Roosa asked Volcker to craft a second initiative to defend America's commitment to redeem dollars in gold. He wanted a plan to remove the "gold cover" that immobilized the bulk of America's gold stock. Recall that the Federal Reserve had been required to maintain a reserve of 40 percent in gold against its liabilities, such as the dollar bills Americans use as currency. In 1945, Congress lowered the required "gold cover" to 25 percent, but that still isolated $11 billion of America's $17 billion hoard in solitary confinement in Fort Knox.[32]

Volcker responded with a ten-page memorandum for the president's signature. He proposed creating a commission to examine the question of whether the gold cover should be abolished and suggested Allan Sproul as chairman of the committee.[33] He knew Sproul's view on gold.

Sproul had retired as president of the Federal Reserve Bank of New York in 1956, while Volcker toiled on the Fed's trading desk. He had used his influential position to disparage the role of gold in promoting monetary restraint: "The integrity of our money does not depend on domestic gold convertibility. It depends upon the great productive power of the American economy and the competence with which we manage our fiscal and monetary affairs . . . Discipline is necessary in these matters but it should be the discipline of competent and responsible men; not the automatic discipline of [gold], a harsh and perverse mechanism."[34]

Sproul denounced the inflexibility of gold, a rigidity that had hampered the Federal Reserve's response to the Great Depression. His argument echoed British economist John Maynard Keynes's famous denunciation of gold as a "barbarous relic," and confirmed the Federal Reserve as watchdog over U.S. monetary affairs. He would have recommended abolishing the gold cover. Nevertheless, Roosa dispatched to cold storage Volcker's recommendation for a presidential commission.

Roosa's change of heart came from circumstance rather than substance. He wrote to Volcker that "After extensive consideration . . . all of us felt uneasy over calling attention to the [gold] reserve ratio matter at a time when our balance of payments figures about to be released were . . . showing so large a deficit . . . It also became clear that the appointment of such a commission in conjunction with . . . other measures would likely stir up unrest."[35] Roosa emphasized the delicacy of the topic by concluding with "I do not know how many people were involved with you in the preparation of this memorandum. I think the best procedure for you would be to tell each of them orally that the matter is dropped for the time being. You might also check with Mr. Daane

[Volcker's immediate boss] . . . so that he will know that the matter is being quietly put to one side for the time being."

Roosa's detailed instructions to sequester the topic surprised Volcker, as though he were a child who could not keep a secret. A simple CONFI-DENTIAL stamp would have been sufficient. But Volcker also knew that the link between money and gold evoked deep feelings, like the emotions in a crime of passion. Treasury Secretary Douglas Dillon had told the president of the sharp "division in the banking fraternity, with people who know something about foreign markets, like [the] New York banks, generally in favor of removing [the gold cover] and the people from the Middle West violently opposed because they think it means we're going to have printing press money."[36]

Volcker fully expected these emotions to surface again when the Treasury revisited the gold cover, but he was surprised by who led the charge.

Charles de Gaulle pursued gold the way Henry VIII did wives. On February 4, 1965, he called a news conference to denounce the dollar as the world's reserve currency, pleading for the resurrection of gold as king of international finance. Instead, he sparked a revolution that turned the yellow metal into just another speculative asset.

President de Gaulle gathered seven hundred journalists in the Grand Ballroom in the Elysée Palace, built for French royalty in the eighteenth century and now serving as home to the president of the Fifth Republic, no less regal to most of France than Louis XVI. *Le General* began with an ode to gold that qualifies as great financial poetry (there is almost no competition): "International trade should rest . . . on an undisputable monetary basis bearing the mark of no particular country . . . on no other standard than gold—gold that never changes, that can be shaped into ingots, bars, coins, that has no nationality and that is eternally and universally accepted as the inalterable fiduciary value *par excellence.*"[37]

Charles de Gaulle had an obsession with gold, but his proposal reflected a deep resentment of America's favored status under the Bretton Woods System. He noted that the rationale for American dominance, rooted in the devastation of World War II, had passed. "Western European states have been restored to such an extent that the total of their

gold reserves equals that of the Americans . . . [and therefore the] tran-
scending value attributed to the dollar has lost its initial foundation."[38]
The French president felt that the dollar's role as a reserve currency gave
the United States an "exorbitant privilege" that permitted America to
finance an "invasion" of French industry.[39]

De Gaulle was only partly right. Americans did not want to invade
France—that is what Germans did—but he was right about the "exorbitant privilege," the same privilege that Roosa had explained to President
Kennedy in the Oval Office. The dollar's role as international money allows America to import French champagne without having to export
anything tangible in return—other than greenbacks. Of course, De
Gaulle ignored that the world uses dollars as a universal medium of exchange because the United States is a free and open economy, providing
a safe haven currency that transcends international borders.

The president of France backed his dollar bashing with action. De
Gaulle moved $400 million in French gold, consisting of 25,900 bars
weighing a total of 350 tons, from the basement vault of the Federal Reserve Bank of New York in Lower Manhattan, where most countries of
the world store their precious metal, to the Banque de France in Paris.[40]
The high density of gold creates a logistical nightmare, taxing the most
experienced shipping executive. Bars are packed four to a wooden box,
in a bed of sawdust to avoid damage to the soft metal. Each box is tied
with steel strapping and distributed throughout an aircraft to balance
the weight. De Gaulle thought the transfer made sense. He wanted the
gold in Paris when the world returned to the gold standard. De Gaulle
also withdrew French forces from NATO, the North Atlantic Treaty Organization, to complete his divorce from America's influence.[41]

De Gaulle's performance benefited from perfect timing. Four days
before the French president's tirade, on February 1, 1965, the U. S. Congress took up a bill to loosen the gold cover requirement in an effort to
bolster America's defense of the dollar.[42] According to the *New York
Times*, the Treasury's free gold had declined to about $2 billion, which
amounted to less than 15 percent of America's obligations to foreign
central banks.[43] A *Times* editorial emphasized American vulnerability
by linking the gold cover to "France's reported decision to exchange . . .
dollars for gold."[44]

Congress took the easy way out. It removed the gold cover against

Federal Reserve liabilities to commercial banks but left intact the required backing against Federal Reserve notes, the currency used for day-to-day transactions.[45] The compromise bought time, postponing a confrontation with conservatives who wanted gold to remain the permanent bulwark of American finance. A speculative frenzy would soon provide midwestern zealots the opportunity to do battle.

Volcker left the Treasury in December 1965 and returned to Chase Manhattan Bank as director of forward planning. During the last year in Washington, he began to have impure thoughts: that De Gaulle had a point. Productivity in Western Europe had caught up with American ingenuity, leaving the dollar overvalued. The German currency, in particular, was too cheap, encouraging American citizens to import anything with a price tag in deutsche marks. This meant that America's balance-of-payments deficit would persist and the gold outflow would not disappear by anyone's tinkering with the gold cover. "I could not help thinking that a more fundamental revaluation of currencies was required. Back then, such ideas were considered heresy at the Treasury, worthy of a Siberian exile. And besides, I had a family to support. It was time to leave."[46]

Paul Volcker never did anything just for the money, but the jump in annual salary to $35,000 at Chase, compared with $18,000 at the Treasury, made a difference. He and Barbara had two children, ten-year-old Janice and seven-year-old Jimmy, and they had lived comfortably enough while he worked in Washington. But Jimmy had been born with cerebral palsy, and according to Paul, "Barbara insisted we treat him like an able-bodied person. The additional income at Chase would certainly help."[47]

Jimmy had gone to a Catholic school, Mater Dei, in Bethesda, Maryland, simply because it was the only mainstream school that would accept him—after Barbara begged. Paul did what fathers do. He introduced his son to baseball at age five by tossing him balls to hit in the front yard of their home in Chevy Chase, Maryland, often until nightfall, using a four-legged homemade contraption to help Jimmy stand. After they moved to the New York bedroom community of Montclair, New Jersey, Paul turned Jimmy into a full-fledged baseball fan, unfortunately rooting for the New York Mets, now that the Dodgers had deserted to the West Coast. "The Mets were the laughingstock of the major leagues," Jimmy says, "but I was hooked after my dad took me to more games than I was prepared for. I know he did it on purpose. It was good therapy. He would shuffle along beside me while I maneuvered with canes and on leg braces, except after my operations, when he pushed me in a wheelchair."[48]

According to Paul, Jimmy's progress exceeded expectations.

> I remember how difficult it was getting him to walk . . . so much so that I worried about his entire future, whether he would be able to hold a job or get married. When Jimmy turned four, I did something that pained me more than anything I've ever done. He desperately wanted a Superman outfit, and I said, "I'll get it for you after you walk." Well, he tried and tried, falling down more times than I could count. And when he finally took two steps he looked at me and said, "See, I can do it. Now I want to look like Superman." He brought tears to my eyes as I mumbled, "I knew you could do it." And then I ran out to buy the outfit, cape and all . . . It's hard to believe that in Montclair he walked to elementary school with Janice. Barbara and I were so proud.[49]

Paul swallows hard and then forces a smile. "Jimmy did much better than the Mets and far better than the American dollar . . . which barely survived 1968."[50]

Volcker watched speculators attack the golden underpinnings of international finance in March 1968 from his office at Chase, the same vantage point he had during the October 1960 confrontation. But unlike the earlier flare-up, which fizzled like a shooting star, this one crippled the system.

The U.S. Treasury's gold stock stood at $12 billion at the start of 1968, but only $1 billion of that total was available to meet America's obligation to foreigners.[51] The bulk of America's gold still served as required backing for currency issued by the Federal Reserve, the "gold cover" against the tens and twenties Americans use for day-to-day transactions. Currency in circulation had expanded with growth in the economy, raising the gold requirement.

Foreign central banks held more than $15 billion in official dollar reserves at the beginning of 1968 and could exchange those dollars for gold at the U.S. Treasury at the rate of $35 per ounce under the Bretton Woods System.[52] In addition, more than $25 billion in dollar-denominated deposits appeared on the books of European commercial banks.[53] Every self-respecting Swiss schoolchild knew that these foreign holdings of dollars could overwhelm the Treasury's $1 billion of free gold in the blink of a speculator's eye. In case Americans failed to notice, however, a front-page headline in the *Wall Street Journal* spelled out the details: "Paper-Money ... Tying Up Additional Gold ... Cuts Supply Available to Meet Foreign Claims."[54]

President Johnson asked Congress to eliminate the remaining gold cover for currency in his State of the Union address in January 1968.[55] The United States would then have the entire gold stock at its disposal to defend the promise to redeem dollars in gold. Congressional testimony supporting the president's proposal arrived from every corner of American finance, including the leading monetarist, Milton Friedman, from the University of Chicago; a respected Keynesian, Charles Kindleberger from MIT; and the quintessential millionaire David Rockefeller, from Chase Manhattan Bank.[56] Nevertheless, the House of Representatives remained skeptical, voting to approve the administration's bill by a slim majority, 199–190. The Senate prepared to take up the measure in early March.

Speculators responded to the confusing signals by draining gold in record amounts from the world's central banks during the first two weeks of March 1968. The United States lost nearly 900 tons of gold valued at $1.0 billion, almost equaling the $1.2 billion decline for the entire year of 1967 (which had been a very bad year).[57] Volume in the London gold market often hit 100 tons per day, ten or twenty times larger than normal.[58] One of the bullion dealers said, "It can't go on this way: something has to happen."[59]

Real people joined the frenzy as well. Not in the United States, of course. Americans were still barred from investing in gold. But at the Bank of Nova Scotia in Toronto, on March 4, 1968, a thirty-two-year-old mechanical engineer bought fifty ounces of gold while claiming, "I'm not speculating, I'm protecting. I'll give it a year. If nothing comes of it I'm selling out."[60] A line of unsatisfied speculative buyers stood at the teller's window in the basement of the bank at closing time, some of them clutching envelopes stuffed with American dollars.

Deliberations in the Senate over the gold cover went poorly. The bill to eliminate the requirement caused an outbreak of insomnia among midwestern skeptics of central banking.[61] Gordon Allott, the senior Republican senator from Colorado, complained that "the last vestige of restraint on money and currency . . . is removed by this bill. Money expansion decisions would be left . . . to the sole discretion of the Federal Reserve Board, which is answerable to no one." Allott's suspicion of central banking is as American as Andrew Jackson, but the senator was not nearly as tough as Old Hickory, who destroyed the Second Bank of the United States. He simply wanted Congress to continue as a central police station: "I am not suggesting that Congress carry out day-to-day management of our currency and money supply, but it certainly should not short-circuit the alarm system."

Senator William Proxmire of Wisconsin, who knew more about banking and finance than just about anyone in the Senate, tried to persuade Allott that his opposition to the bill suffered from good intentions and bad execution. "What the Senator overlooks . . . is that the main part of our money supply is not in the form of currency, it is demand deposits . . . [and even] Dr. Milton Friedman . . . the one expert economist quoted by the distinguished Senator from Colorado . . . would be among the first to say that it would be hopeless to attempt to limit the money supply by limiting currency."

Allott acknowledged Proxmire's expertise by saying, "The Senator . . . is entirely correct—currency is just one part of the money supply," and then launched a mixed metaphor straight from the American heartland to illustrate his point: "But . . . the tail is the only part of the dog I can get ahold of. I am going to hang on to it and try to keep it from wagging the dog clear out of the ball park."

On March 14, 1968, the Senate voted 39–37 to repeal the 25 percent gold reserve requirement against currency, severing the final link between gold and the domestic money supply.[62] The razor-thin majority reflected an undercurrent of distrust toward central bankers within the legislative branch of the U.S. government. It is not surprising that the favorable vote failed to mollify speculators throughout the world.

Speculators worried that even the *entire* stock of gold in the U.S. Treasury could not support the thirty-five-dollar price for very long. Americans were simply spending too much overseas, leaving too many dollars in foreign hands. President Johnson had sounded desperate during his State of the Union address, asking Americans to avoid trips abroad to keep dollars in the United States.[63] But begging New Yorkers to visit the Grand Canyon instead of the Riviera could not solve America's balance-of-payments problem; cutting Vietnam War expenditures to curtail inflation might have worked, but that was not part of the president's plan.

On Friday, March 15, 1968, Queen Elizabeth shut down the London gold market in response to an emergency request from President Lyndon Johnson.[64] A Zurich banker had summed up the consequence of the speculative frenzy: "Don't they realize, these people who are buying gold, that they are destroying the whole monetary system of the world?"[65]

Representatives of the Gold Pool met at the Federal Reserve Board in Washington on Saturday, March 16, 1968, to determine their strategy.[66] Central banks had been defending the thirty-five-dollar price by selling gold when there were too many buyers, including jewelry manufacturers and Arab sheikhs, and buying when there were too many sellers, usually gold producers such as Russia and South Africa. The Gold Pool worked within the law of supply and demand—and speculator demand had been outstripping supply.

After two days of deliberation the central bankers released a communiqué announcing the new rules: "The U.S. Government will continue to buy and sell gold at the existing price of $35 an ounce in transactions with monetary authorities . . . [but will] no longer supply gold to the London gold market or any other gold market."[67] The formal statement praised the U.S. legislation eliminating the gold cover but claimed that their new policy was needed to conserve the world's stock of monetary gold.

The central bankers had built their own version of the Berlin Wall, separating the official monetary gold market from the private sector's counterpart. They picked up what chips were still theirs and went off to play on their own, with all transactions in their fraternity taking place at the official price of thirty-five-dollars per ounce. As for the outsiders, speculators and real people, they could do as they wished and decide on whatever price they pleased. There would be a two-tier market for gold: one for central bankers at a fixed thirty-five-dollar price and another for everyone else at a freely determined price.

To most Americans the new rules for the gold market seemed as relevant as the rules about splitting aces at the blackjack tables in Las Vegas (probably less relevant). Some, such as Joseph Rokovich, working at a construction site on West Forty-Third Street in Manhattan, were mostly optimistic: "I figure our leaders know what they're doing—I hope."[68] Others sounded confused, like John Wright, a bank security guard at the New York Bank for Savings in Times Square: "I'm not worried . . . But if this keeps on maybe the dollar won't be worth anything."[69]

John Wright should have been worried about the dollar's value. Not so much because of the two-tier gold market, but because Congress had removed the gold cover from U.S. currency, short-circuiting Senator Allott's alarm system. Federal Reserve chairman William McChesney Martin had helped to convince legislators that failure to eliminate the requirement would impair economic growth: "Federal Reserve notes in circulation [must] increase each year with the growth of the economy." Milton Friedman invoked integrity to support removing the gold cover. "Twice before when gold reserve requirements came close to being a constraint the requirements were loosened. This is the third time . . . The legal requirement for a gold cover is therefore . . . a delusion . . . In the interest of plain honesty [it] . . . should be removed."[70] Chairman Martin concurred, emphasizing that the gold cover "discipline" does not control the money supply, but rather decisions of the Federal Reserve control it.[71]

Congress had good reason to trust Martin's commitment to monetary stability. As an assistant secretary of the treasury in 1951, William McChesney Martin had incurred the displeasure of his boss, Treasury Secretary John Snyder, by taking a principled stand supporting Federal Reserve independence. He had negotiated the famous "accord" that freed the central bank to pursue an anti-inflationary policy.[72] Martin then became chairman of the Federal Reserve Board and implemented a policy of price stability that would last almost a generation. But not every head of America's central bank would follow his example.

Paul Volcker's memo to Roosa back in 1962, proposing a presidential commission to remove the gold cover, had reflected his great faith in William McChesney Martin: "He was very nice to me when I first arrived at the Treasury and I never forgot that. He earned my respect by devoting himself to Federal Reserve independence, and then delivering on his promise to contain inflation. He is one of my heroes."[73] In 1968, after Congress removed the gold cover and the central bankers abandoned the Gold Pool, Volcker thought Martin could still maintain domestic stability, but he worried that the international monetary system "had fallen into jeopardy."[74] He thought that the two-tier gold market was a barometer of tension in the Bretton Woods System.

Speculators who had bought gold at thirty-five dollars per ounce before March 15, 1968, made a tidy profit. The withdrawal of central banker supply from the London gold market acted like the popping of a champagne cork. The free-market price of bullion jumped to thirty-eight dollars when the market reopened two weeks later, an increase of nearly 10 percent.[75] And the twenty-dollar double eagle, which Americans (even Sargent Shriver) could buy from their favorite coin dealer, surged more than 25 percent.[76] The price increase reflected expectations that the United States would eventually devalue the dollar.[77]

Volcker thought that, going forward, foreign central banks might purchase gold from the United States "to hedge against the possibility of an eventual American embargo on gold."[78] If the United States could change the rules in March 1968 and stop selling gold to the private market, it could amend them further by refusing to sell gold to other central banks. The specter of America suspending gold convertibility to other monetary authorities kept foreign central bankers awake at night. They had good reason to worry.

PART II

Confronting Gold, 1969–1974

CHAPTER 3

Battle Plan

It was Monday, January 20, 1969, and Paul Volcker stood at the window of his corner office on the second floor of the Treasury Building, watching the motorcade advance at coronation speed along Pennsylvania Avenue. He had left his position as director of forward planning at Chase Manhattan Bank and had been appointed undersecretary of the treasury for monetary affairs in the new administration. It was the same job Robert Roosa had held under President Kennedy, and Volcker relished the challenge, knowing that America's problems had risen like a flood tide. He had watched Roosa seal cracks in the dikes with financial putty to preserve America's commitments. Now an inflationary upsurge threatened to overwhelm the levees and drown the dollar.

As Nixon's inaugural parade disappeared from view, Volcker thought about Kennedy's message to manage America's balance of payments because we were "the principal banker of the free world." He believed JFK had understated our obligations: "Price stability belongs in the social contract. We give the government the right to print money because we trust our elected officials not to abuse that right, not to debase the currency by inflating. Foreigners hold our dollars because they trust our pledge that those dollars are equivalent to gold. Failure to maintain those promises undermines trust in America. And trust is everything."[1]

Volcker looked at the blank space on the wall behind the desk and wanted to fill the void with his father's DO NOT SUFFER YOUR GOOD NATURE . . . plaque.[2] It had disappeared after Paul Sr. died in 1959. Paul believed his father had accomplished much between 1930 and 1950, rescuing Teaneck from a financial crisis that began in 1929. On January 20, 1969, he wanted to follow in his father's path, to rescue the country from the financial setbacks that threatened to diminish America's stature in the world. He wanted to make his father proud, to show he understood the lesson: Public service is a sacred trust. He would miss his father at the formal swearing-in.

Volcker had nearly dismissed the idea of working for the new administration two months earlier, when Richard Nixon defeated Hubert Humphrey. He recalled how Nixon, as Dwight Eisenhower's vice-presidential running mate in 1952 and 1956, had smeared the Democratic presidential candidate Adlai Stevenson as being soft on communism. Nixon said Stevenson's "shocking lack of understanding" of the Communist fifth column was evidence of "exceedingly bad, perhaps dangerously bad judgment" that made him unfit for the presidency.[3] Volcker had campaigned for Adlai Stevenson, and like most Democrats, he never forgave Nixon for the slander.

Stevenson, whose bald pate and huge brain justified the egghead label, dazzled everyone with oratory. He poked fun at himself by saying, "A politician is a statesman who approaches every question with an open mouth." He also delivered a message: "All progress has resulted from people who took unpopular positions."[4] Volcker liked what Stevenson said and how he said it. He recalled how Stevenson described Nixon as "A man of many masks . . . shifty . . . rash and inexperienced."[5] Richard Nixon was the enemy.

Volcker felt guilty knowing he would be working for Stevenson's executioner, but his passion for public service smothered his guilt. He wanted to make a difference and believed that Nixon's foreign policy experience, earned as Eisenhower's globe-trotting vice president, might help find a more permanent solution to the dollar crisis that had escalated along with the Vietnam War and inflation. He could not resist the opportunity.

Empathy arrived from several prominent Democrats. The former chairman of President Kennedy's Council of Economic Advisers, Walter Heller, wrote, "It is probably no secret to you—though I tried to

keep it from highest authority, so as not to prejudice your chances—
that you were my number one candidate as [undersecretary] in the
Nixon Administration."[6] Sargent Shriver, eventually the Democratic
Party's vice-presidential candidate in 1972, understood Volcker's moti-
vation. "My heartfelt congratulations on your nomination . . . There is
no question your new job is something of a hot seat, but I imagine that
is one of the elements that attracts you to it."[7]

National Security Memorandum Number Seven from Henry Kissinger,
labeled SECRET at the top and SECRET at the bottom, greeted Volcker
on January 21, 1969, a day after the inauguration. "The President has
directed the creation of a permanent Working Group to make recommendations on U.S. International Monetary Policy to the National
Security Council (NSC) and to implement policy decisions."[8] Kissinger's memo designated Volcker as the chairman of the working group
and asked that a study on international monetary policy be delivered
to the NSC by February 15, 1969.

Volcker was not happy. He did not want Kissinger sticking his Harvard nose where it did not belong. The position of undersecretary of
the treasury for monetary affairs reported to the secretary of the treasury and not to the president's national security adviser, which is what
Kissinger was at the time. Volcker's responsibilities covered domestic
finance, including managing the public debt of the United States, and
international economic affairs, covering balance-of-payments analysis
and foreign exchange operations. Volcker believed that the mix of domestic and international responsibilities "made it the best job in the
government for an economist."[9] Charls Walker, the undersecretary of
the treasury, administered the politically sensitive areas: the Internal
Revenue Service, the Secret Service, the Bureau of Customs, and the
Bureau of the Mint. Kissinger should have been poking around in
Walker's business, the sexier side of the Treasury.

But Volcker knew that the balance of payments could provoke national security concerns. He recalled JFK's threat years before to cut
off military aid to Europe unless the Europeans promised not to attack
the dollar as the world's currency. At a presidential news conference,
the first broadcast live to Europe via the Telstar satellite, Kennedy had

said: "The United States will not devalue its dollar. And the fact of the matter is the United States can balance its balance of payments any day it wants if it wishes to withdraw its support of our defense expenditures overseas and our foreign aid."[10] According to the *New York Times*, the Telstar transmission ended abruptly at this point (perhaps not accidentally), allowing the Europeans time to think about whether they wanted America's guns and its dollars, or neither.

At a fundamental level, Volcker believed in the strong currency/strong country connection. "Those of us on the financial side certainly thought that the stability and strength of our currency was important to sustaining the broad role of the United States in the world."[11] He recalled with a smile the words of William McChesney Martin during a confrontation with McGeorge Bundy, the White House national security adviser under Kennedy and Johnson: "The stability of the dollar would be more important to American security . . . than precisely how many troops we had in Germany."[12] Volcker had no interest in letting the new national security adviser extend his tentacles into the Treasury. Not a cuddly type by temperament, he considered Kissinger's embrace somewhat premature; they hardly knew each other at the time.

Henry Kissinger began his tenure as Nixon's national security adviser well before Paul Volcker arrived on the scene, and had used the head start to extend his bureaucratic reach. Volcker could not help admiring Kissinger's turf building, and would follow that blueprint going forward, but he would have enjoyed it more had it not come from his backyard. Volcker knew that Kissinger had the president's ear and could not be shut out entirely. He built a boundary by adding the following sentence to Kissinger's memo, leaving only a narrow opening for national security concerns: "The Secretary of the Treasury will refer those issues of importance for basic defense and foreign policy decisions . . . to the NSC for early consideration."[13] Volcker then walked the revised memo to his boss, Treasury Secretary David Kennedy, for a ratifying signature.

Volcker never heard another word about National Security Memorandum Number Seven, perhaps because Kissinger had more important things to worry about. But Kissinger had confirmed Volcker as chairman of a working group to make recommendations on U.S. international monetary policy. This interagency task force, with representatives from the Department of State, the Council of Economic Advisers, the National Security Council, and the Federal Reserve Board, became known as the "Volcker Group."[14] The Volcker Group monitored international financial policy between 1969 and 1974. Paul should have sent Kissinger a birthday present—every year in perpetuity.

Volcker had expected trouble before becoming manager of Nixon's balance-of-payments team. He had watched the free-market price of gold rise steadily from thirty-eight dollars on April 1, 1968, to forty-two dollars on January 21, 1969, the day he negotiated his détente with Kissinger. Less than three weeks later, Volcker provoked an outcry from the White House that would not end so pleasantly.

On February 12, 1969, Volcker appeared at a news conference in Paris during a meeting with European bankers and finance ministers to discuss reforms of the international monetary system. The price of gold had made an all-time high in the London market, signaling a red alert. A reporter asked Volcker whether allowing greater flexibility in foreign exchange rates would prevent a further breakdown of the system. Volcker knew exactly where that particular line of thinking had originated, and he responded as though he were swatting a pesky horsefly. "It's being discussed in academic circles, and that's where it can stay."[15]

The previous evening, Volcker had been initiated into an exclusive clique of international financiers, known as Working Party 3 (WP3), with a warning about such radical ideas.[16] A confusing drive after dark brought him to a Parisian home in a wooded suburb that resembled a mysterious hideaway. After crackers and cheese, Cecil de Strycker of the Belgian central bank took him aside for a private chat in a dimly lit basement that smelled from wine fermenting in wooden kegs. De Strycker summarized the WP3's complaints by shaking his European finger at Volcker and saying, "If all this talk about flexible exchange rates brings down the system, the blood will be on your American head."

Volcker did not need much encouragement to belittle floating exchange rates, Milton Friedman's pet proposal for monetary reform. He recalled with distaste Friedman's debate with Roosa over the merits of Bretton Woods and fixed exchange rates.[17] The two men had battled to a standoff, like champion sumo wrestlers locked in the middle of the ring, except when Friedman took the argument to a personal level. He said that floating exchange rates would "put an end to the occasional crisis, producing frantic scurrying of high government officials from capital to capital . . . Indeed this is, I believe, one of the major sources of the opposition to floating exchange rates. The people engaged in these activities are important people and they are all persuaded that they are engaged in important activities. It cannot be, they say to themselves, that these important activities arise simply from pegging exchange rates."[18]

Friedman's cynical reference to "scurrying of high government officials" and "important people . . . engaged in important activities" displeased Volcker. They were not-so-veiled indictments of his mentor, Robert Roosa, who had done more than his share of "frantic scurrying" while at the Treasury. And now Volcker occupied the same position.

Volcker believed in the benefits of Bretton Woods for international trade, just as Roosa did: "Under a fixed-rate system, there is an established scale of measurement, easily translatable from one country to another, which enables merchants, investors, and bankers of any one country to do business with others on known terms."[19] Bretton Woods creates for world trade the type of stability enjoyed by a businessman in New York who exports to Hell, Michigan, or Paradise, Pennsylvania: A dollar in Hell or Paradise is the same as a dollar in New York.

The White House, however, launched a frontal attack on Volcker's suggestion to quarantine floating exchange rates in the ivory tower. The *Washington Post* headlined a rebuke from "high officials" in the administration, identified as Nixon's Council of Economic Advisers (CEA): "We would not be doing our job if we were not exploring the question [of floating exchange rates]."[20] The CEA was "at a loss to explain Volcker's comment, except to suggest that it must have been off the cuff and not completely thought through."[21]

Secretary of Labor George Shultz, a Nixon favorite who would head two other cabinet departments, supported the CEA. In a subcommittee meeting of the cabinet, he urged the CEA to testify before the congressional Joint Economic Committee in favor of these "new approaches."[22] Shultz, a labor economist by trade, had been a dean at the University of Chicago, home base of Milton Friedman, and would provide a direct pipeline into the administration for Friedman's views.

Volcker understood the arguments in favor of floating exchange rates as well as anyone, having heard them from just about every academic economist he respected, including Lawrence Ritter, his good friend and confidant.[23] Ritter, a finance professor at New York University, had written two bestselling books, one on baseball and another on banking—Volcker's favorite intellectual interests.[24] Ritter's congressional testimony in favor of floating exchange rates had triggered a dismissive "What's wrong with your friend?" from Roosa.[25]

According to the academics, floating exchange rates would cure U.S. balance-of-payments deficits by allowing the price system to work its magic. For example, a U.S. balance-of-payments deficit occurs when Americans import more from the United Kingdom than the British import from America. Under floating exchange rates, the extra dollars chasing after pounds sterling in the foreign exchange market forces up the price of British pounds, making British goods more expensive for New Yorkers and making American goods cheaper for Londoners. A higher price for the pound sterling encourages New Yorkers to buy the MADE IN USA label, rather than ordering snobby English tailoring; and a lower price for the American dollar encourages Londoners to do the same. The U.S. balance-of-payments deficit shrivels through market forces.

Volcker considers flexible exchange rates the easy way out, a deceptively simple solution laced with long-run costs. "There is nothing to anchor the exchange rate at any particular level under floating rates. A rootless exchange rate encourages speculators to pounce on a depreciating currency, pushing it even lower."[26] Roosa had made that point during his debate with Friedman, arguing that depreciating currencies could spiral downward under a system of floating exchange rates.[27] Milton Friedman countered that when speculators sell low, hoping to buy even lower, they usually lose money. Speculators might enjoy the excitement, like a day at the races, but they run out of money before long. Roosa claimed that they could inflict considerable damage before going bankrupt.[28]

Volcker favored fixed exchange rates because it places international financial stability on a giant pedestal, and then anchors the system in fiscal discipline. "A country that runs a balance-of-payments deficit cannot sit back and relax while its currency depreciates. It must retrench and live within its means, just like everyone else."[29] The appropriate medicine, a tablespoon of tight money, would quiet an overheated economy and bring imports into line with exports. The problem is that swallowing the prescription, which includes a dose of high interest rates, leaves a bad taste.

The red-light alert from the London gold market never flickered during the first half of 1969.[30] Preserving the dollar's status had been the focus of Volcker's favorite committee—now called the Volcker Group by everyone who mattered—until April, when France took center stage. President Charles de Gaulle resigned on April 28, 1969, after losing a referendum on his proposal for constitutional reform.[31] The Paris newspaper *France-Soir* explained, "The general needs a new coronation every two or three years."[32] He left in a huff when he did not get it.

No one at the Treasury shed a tear; the French president's fetish for American gold still rankled. An earlier Treasury Department memorandum had warned Richard Nixon prior to a meeting with de Gaulle that "the basic French attitude toward the international monetary system is fundamentally different from ours."[33] But de Gaulle had lost his popular mandate because of the discipline he administered six months earlier to preserve the value of the French franc. Perhaps it was selfish, for the "Glory of France," but it was also a beachhead in the battle for fixed exchange rates—so everyone at the Treasury paid attention.

The French had been spending too much in Germany, primarily because of Prussian efficiency but also because Parisians enjoyed Hamburg night life more than Berliners liked Place Pigalle. (Prices were too high in Paris for reasonably similar services.) French francs were piling up in Germany, and the Bundesbank, the German central bank, had to buy the French currency to prevent a price decline. The exchange rate between francs and marks, or between any two currencies, remains fixed only when central banks make it so, by buying a currency that is in excess supply and selling a currency in excess demand. That was how exchange rates were maintained in the Bretton Woods System.

De Gaulle knew that the Bundesbank would absorb a temporary excess of francs in the marketplace, but would gag on a continuous influx. Prolonged purchases threatened Germany with inflation because whenever the Bundesbank bought francs with marks, the German money supply increased.[34] France would have to cut back on imports from Germany, including Hamburg's favorite attractions, or watch the franc depreciate.

De Gaulle implemented an austerity program in November 1968—fiscal discipline to prevent a devaluation of the French franc . . . just what the Fixed Exchange Rate Doctor ordered. He rallied support with a somewhat incoherent patriotic plea, "Frenchwomen! Frenchmen! What is happening in regard to our currency proves to us once again that life is a struggle, that effort is the price of success, that salvation demands victory."[35] Government budget restraint succeeded in maintaining the franc's value, but within five months it cost de Gaulle at the polls. A young worker in the Orléans railway station explained the problem: "I've no confidence in anybody. I vote my pocketbook, and it says no."[36]

Volcker knew that the absence of de Gaulle from Parisian politics would do little to alleviate America's balance-of-payments deficit and would not even solve the gold problem. More fundamental forces—domestic inflation and foreign competition—undermined the dollar. The Volcker Group had been preparing a memorandum for the president outlining American options, and Paul had been able to devote all his waking hours to the problem. He had few distractions, with Barbara, Janice, and Jimmy having remained in New Jersey until June 1969, the end of the school year.

Paul had been living in a furnished apartment on Fourteenth Street in the rundown part of northwest Washington during the first half of 1969. He did not mind the location, except that his number-three position at the Treasury carried the privilege of a car and driver. Paul worried that some of the unsavory characters lurking in the hallways would get the wrong impression, that a man with a chauffeured car had a healthy wallet as well. He tried to dress like a commoner—easily accomplished with a wardrobe of just a few worn suits that had been custom-ordered to fit his oversize measurements. When one of these antiques disappeared at the cleaner's, Volcker waited a month before accepting reimbursement. "It was a very nice suit."[37]

Paul missed Barbara's sharp banter at formal Washington social events that came with his position as undersecretary, whether it was a State Department buffet reception for the prince of Afghanistan or cocktails at the White House for the German chancellor. He recalls standing next to Barbara during his earlier stint at the Treasury, as silent as a butler, while she twitted the Irish finance minister with "I didn't know Ireland *had* a finance minister."

Others also noticed that Paul benefited from help in social situations. Cynthia Martin, wife of the Federal Reserve chairman, revised an invitation to a formal dinner party, suggesting, "We'll have another opportunity after Barbara moves into town."[38] Perhaps Miss Palmer, Volcker's favorite kindergarten teacher, had been onto something when she noted that Paul "does not take part in group discussion."

Barbara ran the Washington branch of the Volcker household long distance, often reminding her husband to deposit his last few paychecks so she could pay the rent and the telephone bill. When Paul applied his "always procrastinate" strategy to delay meeting their real estate agent, Barbara left a message. "I told Marcia Clopton of CBS Realty to get aggressive with you."[39]

On Thursday, June 26, 1969, Paul stood before the president of the United States in the Cabinet Room of the White House, pointing to a flip chart summarizing five months of work by the Volcker Group. Treasury Secretary David Kennedy, Volcker's boss, had arranged the meeting and had asked Volcker to lead off. Key international advisers flanked the president at the elliptical table, including Secretary of State William Rogers, National Security Adviser Henry Kissinger, Federal Reserve Chairman William McChesney Martin, and Counselor to the President Arthur Burns.

Volcker had worried about the meeting, like a teenager preparing for his first date, and not just because it was a center-stage performance for Richard Nixon. That was reason enough—his Democratic lineage would always mark him an outsider—but also because there had been a breach of security that could have ended his tenure with this leak-obsessed administration.

Paul knew that Nixon would not have read the forty-eight-page memorandum "Basic Options in International Monetary Affairs,"[40] which had been delivered to the Oval Office; the president viewed "the dollar problem as something we should make go away, presumably painlessly."[41] Volcker had asked Bruce MacLaury, his deputy undersecretary and a future president of the Brookings Institution, a left-of-center think tank in Washington, to prepare a few charts showing the major options under consideration, hoping the visual aids would hold Nixon's interest during the oral presentation. MacLaury sent out rough sketches to a commercial graphic arts company for production, including one showing a doubling in the official price of gold from thirty-five dollars to seventy dollars.

"What were you thinking?" Volcker had grumbled. "A speculator could have easily made a fortune buying gold on the London market and then leaking the chart to the press."[42] MacLaury had no answer, but the graphic artist had taken courses in color design rather than advanced speculation, so no damage was done.

The Volcker Group report had, in fact, dismissed the option of raising the price of gold precisely because it would have inflamed speculative interest in the precious metal. Moreover, doubling the price would have rewarded Russia and South Africa, the major gold producers, and France, the major gold hoarder. None of these three made America's Most Favored Country list. The Volcker Group wanted to deemphasize the role of gold in international finance and included the chart just for completeness.

The formal memorandum blessed a benign-sounding "evolutionary change in the existing system," as though it would be buried deep in the business section of the *New York Times*, hidden behind the weekly Federal Reserve Report (which is easily located with a compass). In fact, Volcker's recommendations would make front-page headlines when they surfaced.

Volcker knew Nixon cared most about American world power, and he presented his objective to retain "a pivotal role for the U.S. dollar as the leading reserve and vehicle currency," as though it were a nuclear warhead.[43] The main threat to this dominance, he said, came from "common recognition that attempts at large scale conversion [of dollars into gold] would be frustrated by a lack of adequate gold in U.S. reserves."[44] Volcker identified "the strong inflationary pressure in the United States over the past four years . . . [as] a major factor . . . undermining confidence in the dollar."[45] He compared the American experience unfavorably with Germany, which places "extremely high priority on resisting inflation," and suggested that we might want to "encourage greater consistency among [monetary] objectives in a framework of fixed exchange rates."[46]

Volcker's reference to "consistency among monetary objectives" reflected the vulnerability of the Bretton Woods System. He knew the system of fixed exchange rates would come crashing down without cooperation among central bankers, a victim of the triple-headed monster that would become known as the Trilemma.[47] The insight of the Trilemma, sometimes irreverently called the Unholy Trinity, is that countries committed to *fixed exchange rates* and *free international flow of capital* must pursue the *same monetary targets*. Pursuit of different interest rates, for example, unleashes what the hedge fund industry in the twenty-first century calls "the carry trade," but has been the staple diet of foreign exchange traders ever since speculation was invented in biblical-era Egypt.[48] This not-so-complicated strategy turns speculators into very wealthy arbitrageurs and would ultimately destroy Bretton Woods.

Foreign exchange speculators are not especially religious, certainly no more than the rest of Wall Street, but when they pray, they beg the Lord of High Finance to grant them two countries with fixed exchange rates and different interest rates. When German interest rates are 7 percent and U.S. rates are 4 percent, for example, speculators will borrow in dollars at 4 percent, exchange the dollars for marks, and invest in marks at 7 percent. They pocket the 3 percent differential without incurring risk as long as the exchange rate between dollars and marks remains fixed.[49] Three percent does not sound like much, but the profit is $3 million for a relatively modest-size foreign exchange trade of $100 million. Speculators will do this trade as often as they can because it is an arbitrage—riskless, profitable, and something for which they do not need capital (they can borrow whatever they need). Speculators have reached their nirvana.

All this is very good for speculators, making them fat and happy, but it is very bad for fixed exchange rates. As speculators buy marks and sell dollars without limit, they push up the value of the mark and push down the value of the dollar. Under the rules of the Bretton Woods System, the Bundesbank must intervene, buying dollars and offering marks in exchange to prevent the dollar from depreciating. But if the speculative onslaught was to continue, the Bundesbank would eventually stop buying dollars, because it would mean flooding the world with marks. To prevent the flood, they would let the exchange rate float, a victim of the Trilemma.

Fixed exchange rates are easily destroyed by such speculative attacks. Most governments defended their turf by fabricating a spider's web of capital controls to hamper speculation. Volcker had, in fact, helped design such regulations during his earlier stint at the Treasury, a "youthful indiscretion" that left him a staunch opponent of government intervention. Roosa had conceived the "interest equalization tax," a special levy on international investments to stem the outflow of dollars into higher-yielding foreign securities, and turned it over to Volcker to hash out the details. The resulting legislation produced a jigsaw puzzle of exemptions, for the Canadians, for the Japanese, and for every constituency that yelled the loudest.[50] Volcker discovered "the enormous gap between beautiful concept and practical application."[51]

Volcker expressed his antipathy toward controls during his Cabinet Room presentation, supporting the "free flow of goods . . . and investment internationally," but compounded his earlier indiscretion by conceding that "our balance of payments position will continue to require the protection of capital controls."[52] He worried about the inconsistency, and would wrestle with principle versus pragmatism during his entire career. But none of the assembled dignitaries objected to this touch of split personality disorder, an infirmity that comes with high office. Instead, they waited patiently for the plan that would guide America's international monetary policy. Everyone waited patiently, that is, except for the most important person in the room, the president of the United States.

Volcker had anticipated Nixon's lack of interest, but still felt his shoulders sag when he saw the president's eyes flit away. He had seen this Nixon before, during the first televised presidential debate with Kennedy in 1960, when Nixon's furtive glances offstage gave him the shifty appearance of a small-time crook. Now the impatient look meant that five months of work was about to get flushed down the drain.

Volcker rushed to the core of his recommendations, arguing for "a substantial appreciation of the Deutschemark" to provide immediate relief for the dollar and suggesting a limited increase in "exchange rate flexibility for the longer term."[53] He expected a "perhaps imminent . . . French depreciation" and proposed "early activation of Special Drawing Rights [SDRs]," a supplement to international reserves that would be called "paper gold." (It is neither.)[54]

The forecast for France, which devalued the franc in two months' time, elevated Volcker as a seer.[55] More important to him, the core recommendations worked within the Bretton Woods framework, delivering a "fundamental, but evolutionary, change in the existing system," as promised.[56] Germany, with a persistent surplus of exports over imports—the Volkswagen Beetle was cheaper and more reliable than anything General Motors produced—should be have been forced to raise the value of its currency to restore balance. And the proposed increase in exchange rate flexibility built on the minor daily variability already permitted.[57]

But in addition to these recommendations to sustain Bretton Woods, Volcker added a contingency plan that would rock the foundations of the system and alter the international financial landscape forever. He said the plan should be used only if "forced upon us by events," because it would be "considered by foreign countries as a U.S. power play . . . [and] it would contain the seeds of political divisiveness."[58]

Volcker's bombshell, suspending the convertibility of the dollar into gold, had been discussed before, but now took center stage.[59] He said, "the major objective and potential advantage of suspension . . . would be to strengthen [our] . . . negotiating position . . . by eliminating . . . a run on our gold stock . . . [and forcing] foreign countries . . . [to] passively hold dollars or permit a gradual appreciation of their currencies."[60] Volcker felt that foreigners would willingly hold dollars if "the United States retained reasonable price stability."[61] The dollar standard could replace the gold standard as long as America lived up to its responsibilities.

Volcker looked at Nixon for some reaction, but the president seemed distracted. And then he heard Arthur Burns, the pipe-smoking former professor with the title of counselor to the president, clearing his throat, as though preparing to give a lecture. Burns had been chairman of the Council of Economic Advisers under President Eisenhower and had tutored the then vice president, Nixon, in economics. Volcker knew that Burns was an ally who supported Bretton Woods, having already warned Nixon against freely floating exchange rates: "And whatever else we may do, let us not develop any romantic ideas about a fluctuating exchange rate: there is too much history that tells us that a fluctuating exchange rate . . . give[s] rise to international political turmoil."[62] But Volcker worried that Burns would launch into a tirade on the evils of suspension or, even worse, push for an increase in the price of gold. Nixon ended the suspense, and the meeting, with "Good job, and keep me informed about where we stand."[63]

As they rose to leave, David Kennedy came up to Volcker and said, "Well done," and then leaned closer: "At least he didn't say no." This thin endorsement made Volcker think that Richard Nixon would resist launching a financial warhead to counter an international monetary crisis. David Kennedy was not a Nixon insider and had little clout with the president. Volcker nodded and said, "I guess we have a policy by default."

CHAPTER 4

Gamble

Harry Houdini could not have conjured a more magical six months than the second half of 1969. Neil Armstrong stepped onto the surface of the moon on July 20. The New York Mets overcame one-hundred-to-one odds to win the World Series on October 16. And the free-market price of gold collapsed to $34.90 on December 9.[1]

Volcker considered the Mets victory the most unlikely of these events. The team had come into existence in 1962 and had finished last or next to last in the National League every year until then. The dislocation in the gold market ran a close second to the Mets—the price declined to the lowest level since the advent of two-tier trading, a shade below the mystical thirty-five dollars per ounce, after reaching an all-time high earlier in the year. The moon landing was exciting, of course, but it was more predictable. America had made steady progress in space exploration since JFK's challenge to the nation in May 1961 to put a man on the moon by the end of the decade.

The drop in the outlook for gold corresponded with improvement in the U.S. dollar during the second half of 1969. Volcker's personal life took a turn for the better as well, after Barbara joined him in their rambling colonial house in Chevy Chase, Maryland, in July. He was happy that she was with him. They went to a dinner party at the home of Cynthia and Bill Martin, the one Cynthia had rescheduled until Barbara could attend. Volcker recalled the time President Lyndon Johnson browbeat Martin over interest rates, and recognized the changed posture in the Federal Reserve chairman since then.

In September 1965, when Volcker was deputy undersecretary, he attended a meeting with his boss at the time, Treasury Secretary Henry "Joe" Fowler, Martin, and President Johnson.[2] Fowler began by saying, "Chairman Martin wants to raise the discount rate." Johnson interrupted and said, "You mean he wants to extract more blood from the American people." Martin ignored the bait and said, "I think it's necessary at this point in the battle for price stability."

Johnson knew that an increase in the discount rate—the rate the Federal Reserve charges for loans to commercial banks—would be announced like a financial funeral on the evening news, and would raise borrowing costs as it rippled though the banking system. LBJ tried to make Martin back down and finally said, "Bill, I'm going into the hospital tomorrow to have my gallbladder removed. You wouldn't do this while I'm in the hospital, would you?" Martin sighed and said, "No, Mr. President, we'll wait until you get out of the hospital."

Volcker had argued with Fowler privately in favor of Martin's position, but to no avail. His support for the Fed chairman cost Volcker more than he knew. After the battle over the discount rate, Johnson asked Fowler whether he had considered a replacement for Martin as chairman of the central bank. Fowler said that he considered Paul Volcker, but "we want a sure vote, not a reasonable fellow who will try to steer us down the right path."[3]

The confrontation between Martin and the president had surprised Volcker. Paul knew that Martin had taken a principled stand supporting Federal Reserve independence from the U.S. Treasury while he was an assistant secretary in the Truman administration.[4] And here was Martin, Volcker's personal hero, checking with the president of the United States about raising interest rates, which he eventually did over LBJ's objection, but it was a decision clearly within the central bank's mandate. Volcker would remember this lesson in political economy. The Federal Reserve may be independent, but so is the president, and he is elected by the American people. Better to have the commander in chief on your side.

By 1969 inflation had jumped to over 5 percent, tame by later standards but a worrisome number at the time. The Martin-led Federal Reserve Board tightened credit during the first half of the year, raising the discount rate to reduce bank lending and curtail excess spending. Martin had regretted easing monetary policy earlier, and was determined not to ease prematurely again: "The horse of inflation is out of the barn and already well down the road . . . [now we have to] prevent it from trotting too fast."[5] He kept a tight rein until his term of office expired in January 1970.[6]

Monetary restraint and high interest rates, designed to control inflation, also enhanced prospects for the American dollar. Corporate treasurers could earn 8 percent on risk-free U.S. Treasury bills by the end of December 1969, compared with less than 6 percent earlier in the year, so they kept their money at home rather than sending it abroad.[7] Gold speculators abandoned the precious metal in favor of interest-bearing securities. A London bullion dealer noted, "The question is not who's selling but who's buying. The answer to that is no one."[8] And a Zurich banker added, "There is the growing realization that there will be no increase in the official price [of gold] in the near future." With gold down to thirty-five dollars an ounce in December, speculators felt as though they had lost their pants as well as their shirts (very worrisome as winter approached). The decline of nine dollars on gold purchased at the peak of forty-four dollars a few months earlier meant a 20 percent loss.[9]

According to the *New York Times*, gold's tarnished reputation vindicated the "United States policy in establishing . . . a two-tier system for gold in March 1968" and also benefited Treasury Secretary David Kennedy. "The crowning defeat for gold speculators and victory for the pre-eminence of the United States dollar . . . is providing a favorable atmosphere for the first European tour of David M. Kennedy as United States Treasury Secretary."[10]

Volcker liked and respected David Kennedy. "[He] was the epitome of honesty and openness . . . [and] once he had settled on me as his choice as Under Secretary for Monetary Affairs he insisted on it over political opposition. I was, after all, a Democrat . . . in an administration suspicious that it had inherited far too many civil servants sympathetic to the opposition."[11] Volcker should have welcomed the favorable comments in the press. Instead, they made him nervous, like when a teammate says, "Only six more outs and we've got ourselves a no-hitter"—the proverbial recipe for disaster.

Volcker suspected that the dollar's revival might be short-lived and that the "favorable atmosphere" greeting Kennedy could easily become turbulent. He testified before the congressional Joint Economic Committee that "the United States' [balance of] payments position and domestic inflation were fundamentally more important than any other issue."[12] They were certainly more important than the short-term investments flowing into America that had buoyed the dollar and trashed gold. Capital flooded ashore when U.S. interest rates rose, but ebbed just as quickly when rates declined. And when the tide turned, foreign central banks would drown in dollars, and the free-market price of gold would sound the warning like a foghorn.

Volcker's fears were well founded.

The White House staff celebrated on two counts when Nixon nominated Arthur Burns to replace William McChesney Martin as chairman of the Federal Reserve Board effective February 1, 1970. Burns would take up residence at the central bank, where he could implement policies favorable to the president. And Burns, the imperious professor, would vacate his position as counselor to the president, where he was resented for his special relationship with Nixon.

William Safire, a Nixon speechwriter, noted that Arthur Burns took liberties that no one else would. In one particular incident, Burns had been in the Oval Office making a typically long and slow presentation on a welfare reform.[13] "As I said in my July 8 memorandum, Mr. President—" The president interrupted Burns to speed things along: "Yes, Arthur, I read that." Burns then interjected, "But you couldn't have, Mr. President. I didn't send it in yet. I have it with me here." Nixon did not miss a beat, "Thanks, Arthur, I'll read it." According to Safire, the president seemed almost amused, but his staff took umbrage for him.

Soon after becoming Fed chairman in February 1970, Burns began to ease monetary policy to counter rising unemployment, and by November 1970, Treasury bill yields had declined by two percentage points compared with a year earlier. Corporate treasurers registered their disapproval by shifting investments abroad. According to a Volcker Group memorandum, "Our overall payments position is running in very heavy deficit despite some welcome improvement in our trade and current account. This deficit reflects sharply adverse capital movements, partly reflecting easier money in the U.S."[14] And the price of gold registered its concern, jumping more than 10 percent, to over thirty-nine dollars an ounce.[15] The euphoria of 1969 had disappeared like a puff of magician's smoke.

Volcker recognized that fickle capital flows would precipitate the need for drastic action.[16] With a crisis all but certain, he dusted off the contingency plans laid out in his Cabinet Room presentation of more than a year earlier, but worried that the president would need congressional approval before launching what Volcker (and many others) considered the nuclear option. Volcker knew that only Congress could change the price of gold, and he asked Michael Bradfield, an assistant general counsel at Treasury, to determine whether the chief executive had the right to suspend gold convertibility while leaving the price unchanged.

Bradfield's eight-page memorandum made Volcker smile.[17] It confirmed that changing the "par" value of gold required congressional approval, citing the Gold Reserve Act of 1934, which had raised the price of gold from $20.67 to $35.00 per ounce. But that same legislation, the memorandum noted, conferred on the secretary of the treasury the discretion to suspend gold sales.

To anyone but a lawyer, a total suspension of gold sales seems more dramatic than a simple change in price, closer in spirit to a military blockade, the equivalent of a declaration of war, than a commercial adjustment. But the legal perspective was all that mattered, and the law gave the president and his treasury secretary the authority to act without congressional interference. Volcker felt prepared for the looming international crisis.

On November 18, 1970, Richard Nixon confided to his chief of staff, H. R. Haldeman, that he had grown impatient with his economic advisers. According to Haldeman, "They failed in the one prime objective [the president] set, to keep unemployment under five percent in October . . . and [the president] doesn't want to take *any* chance on screwing up 1972."[18]

Nixon's focus on the next election continued the following day, in a meeting with the University of Chicago economist Milton Friedman, who was an unofficial adviser to the president. According to Haldeman, "Friedman urges we stay on the present economic course," and the president said "it was nice to have someone say we're doing things right." Haldeman then reports that Nixon, still concerned about 1972, said we "can't afford to risk a downturn, no matter how much inflation."[19]

Milton Friedman surely did not propose more inflation to achieve lower unemployment. He did not believe in this Keynesian medicine that had been practiced in the Kennedy-Johnson White House, and had warned against it in his presidential address to the American Economic Association.[20] But Nixon embraced the Democratic philosophy with the enthusiasm of a convert, encouraged by an unwitting blessing from Friedman.

Milton Friedman had famously said that "We are all Keynesians now," a stunning admission by the leading opponent of activist government intervention.[21] Friedman subsequently qualified his remarks, explaining that he actually meant "In one sense, we are all Keynesians now; in another, nobody is any longer a Keynesian."[22] To an academic such as Milton Friedman, qualifying remarks are as important as footnotes, but both are ignored by politicians when it serves their purpose.

Nixon described himself as "a Keynesian in economics," and would soon name a Democrat to his cabinet to confront the emerging problem called stagflation.[23] Britain's chancellor of the exchequer, Iain Macleod, had used the term *stagflation* to describe a combination of high unemployment and high inflation.[24] And according to the *New York Times*, this British disease now threatened America's reputation. "Europeans Fear American 'Stagflation' Will Drag Their Own Economies Down."[25]

Stagflation would spread like a pandemic during the coming decade, but in November 1970 it was unprecedented and puzzling.[26] From his perch at the Federal Reserve Board, Arthur Burns complained that "We are dealing . . . with a new problem, namely, persistent inflation in the face of substantial unemployment—and that the classical remedies may not work well enough."[27]

Burns used this perceived violation of economic principles to promote wage and price controls, which he liked to call an "incomes policy" to avoid being labeled a socialist by the libertarians in the White House basement. Nixon agreed to develop "a market-oriented" incomes policy, over the objection of his economic advisers, Paul McCracken of the Council of Economic Advisers and George Shultz, now head of the Office of Management and Budget, in exchange for a promise from Burns to follow an expansionary monetary policy. "I have been assured by Dr. Arthur Burns that the independent Federal Reserve System will provide fully for the increasing monetary needs of the economy. I am confident that this commitment will be kept."[28]

No one has confirmed what the press called the "Accord of 1970," but in retrospect, Nixon's reference to central bank independence sounds as hollow as his future declaration "I'm not a crook."[29] Arthur Burns would abandon prudent monetary policy during his tenure as Federal Reserve chairman, in part under pressure from the White House, but also because he truly believed that "the rules of economics are not working the way they used to . . . even a long stretch of high and rising unemployment may not suffice to check the inflationary process."[30] Burns's printing press would lay the foundation for the Great Inflation of the 1970s.

Nixon signaled his dissatisfaction with the economic status quo by replacing Volcker's boss, Treasury Secretary David Kennedy, with John Connally. Connally had been secretary of the navy in the Kennedy administration and a former Democratic governor of Texas, and had survived the car ride with JFK on November 22, 1963, suffering serious wounds during the assassination. He worried about his new cabinet position.[31] "When I took over as Secretary of the Treasury, I did so with feelings of trepidation," he wrote later. "I was not an economist; I had really never studied monetary affairs. My experience with fiscal issues was limited largely to a familiarity with Congress in the matter of appropriation of funds."

Nixon did not care about economics, just politics, and judging by the reaction of a leading Democrat, the president had hit the bull's-eye: "It's an outrageous appointment. The Republicans are in trouble over the economy and they want to palm off the blame on a Democratic Secretary of the Treasury."[32] The *Washington Post* viewed Connally's appointment from a somewhat broader perspective. "The nomination of Texas Democrat Connally to the Nixon Republican Cabinet was a bold maneuver with great potential ramifications. In some respects it can be considered the opening shot of the 1972 Nixon campaign."[33] An unnamed Democratic strategist was more specific: "There goes Texas."[34] Paul Volcker narrowed the focus even more: "There goes my job."[35]

Paul confessed to Barbara over dinner after Connally's news conference, "This comes at the wrong time for me. We are headed for a major crisis and I won't be here."

"Don't you want to work for this guy? He seems smart, confident, he's good-looking, and he's a Democrat—even if he is a Texas Democrat."

"I'll have to resign. I am sure he'll want to bring in his own people."

Barbara raised her eyebrows. "Don't be so insecure. I think he needs your technical expertise more than your letter of resignation."

"Perhaps, but I'll prepare one anyway, just in case."

Volcker wanted to remain at the Treasury, where he could accomplish two objectives: advance his career and help rescue the country from danger. He had liked working for David Kennedy, a wise and decent man, but Nixon had not respected the former banker. John Connally, on the other hand, was a force to be reckoned with. Herbert Stein, a member of Nixon's Council of Economic Advisers, described Connally as "tall, handsome, forceful, colorful, charming . . . and political to his eyeballs."[36] According to William Safire, Nixon had fallen "in love."[37]

Volcker thought that Connally could vanquish the forces of evil at the CEA, where proposals for floating exchange rates ruled.[38] He had been concerned ever since George Shultz, a strong proponent of floating rates courtesy of Milton Friedman, was appointed director of the

Office of Management and Budget (OMB). Shultz and Paul McCracken at the CEA were powerful allies. Volcker recalled a letter he had received from Shultz, when Shultz was secretary of labor. The message still rankled: "Dear Paul, I noticed with great interest the reports of your remarks about flexible exchange rates . . . I heartily support your view and congratulate you on the effort you are making."[39]

Volcker did not like receiving a congratulatory pat on the head from Shultz, as though he were a schoolboy who had finally learned his lesson. Besides, Shultz had misinterpreted Volcker's proposal for wider bands within the Bretton Woods System of fixed exchange rates—a very different approach from the freely floating rates Shultz and Friedman wanted. Greater flexibility within the Bretton Woods framework would still require a commitment to domestic discipline, Volcker's favorite remedy for balance-of-payments deficits. Supporters of floating rates preached benign neglect—the price system would take care of everything. Paul thought that "benign neglect would work about as well eliminating the dollar problem as it did in solving racial discrimination."[40]

Volcker had so far ignored Shultz, thinking the labor secretary should busy himself with wage settlements of the Teamsters or the United Auto Workers, rather than with movements of the French franc or the German mark. But once Shultz had moved to OMB, monitoring the federal budget for the president, he could not be ignored.

Connally waved away Volcker's resignation letter when he arrived at the Treasury in February 1971, saying, "What I really want is your loyalty."[41]

Volcker, a company man by temperament, said, "I know how to do that. Is there anything specific?"

"I'll need to spruce up my background . . . some late-night reading material to bring me up to speed."

Volcker spent the next month preparing a sixty-page, triple-spaced draft entitled "Contingency Planning: Options for the International Monetary Problem."[42] He then walked the thick memorandum into Connally's office. "It's not exactly bedtime reading, but it suggests that reasonably foreseeable events—possibly in a matter of weeks—could set off strong speculation against the dollar, and it lays out the policy options at our disposal."[43]

Connally's eyes widened as he listened to Volcker. The treasury secretary took the memo and carefully placed it in his briefcase, as though he were a college freshman securing the answers to a big exam. The document would become Connally's game plan.

The memo cited a combined assault by the usual dollar-bashing suspects—a persistent deficit in the balance of payments, short-term capital outflows, and rising concern over price stability. The clear and present danger stemmed from a "massive increase in foreign official dollar holdings to approximately $24 billion . . . [and a decline in] our reserve assets . . . to $14 billion."[44] America's gold stock, amounting to $11 billion of the $14 billion of reserves, was at risk.

Volcker knew that a tighter monetary policy and higher domestic interest rates could provide a double-barreled solution—by attracting foreign capital and by controlling inflation. But he also knew that this would never pass muster with his new boss, who had slipped into contention for the vice-presidential slot on the Republican ticket in 1972. Connally may not have known much about economics, but he knew enough to recognize the liability of high interest rates in the upcoming election. Even a war hero like Charles de Gaulle did not survive tight money and a tough-love approach to defending his country's financial honor.

Volcker's memo proposed a massive 15 percent currency realignment to discourage foreign imports and to make U.S. products more competitive.[45] An upward valuation of the German mark and the Japanese yen would discourage Americans from buying the cute Volkswagen Beetle or the sexy Datsun 240Z, in favor of a Ford Falcon or Chevrolet Corvette.[46] Currency realignment would be popular in Detroit but would cause armed insurrection in Bonn and Tokyo, where the relatively cheap mark and yen were good for business.[47] Germany and Japan would need encouragement to revalue their currencies.

Volcker knew exactly how to create a cooperative international spirit. Instead of reacting defensively to a crisis, he preferred an aggressive strategy, the equivalent of an all-in bet in a game of Texas Hold-'em. He proposed a "cold blooded suspension" of gold convertibility, "justified not by a run . . . but by a conviction that the situation is increasingly untenable . . . [and] to force change by taking the initiative . . . to set forth a more or less full blown reform plan . . . [including] some lasting realignment in exchange rates."[48] The reward would be a restoration of convertibility—in some fashion—once a new, workable system was in place. The risk was that suspension would roil the marketplace—causing a calamitous collapse in the stock market and a shutdown of foreign exchange—before reaching the Promised Land.

Volcker also proposed an unusual form of shock treatment to the U.S. economy as a way to deflect international criticism of the suspension. Foreigners would have good reason to resent America's dictatorial decree—their complaint would simply mimic the uproar among American citizens after Franklin Delano Roosevelt's 1933 domestic gold suspension (and he had just been elected president of the United States in a landslide). To convince foreign governments that we were serious about controlling inflation, the root cause of the balance-of-payments deficit, Volcker suggested "a temporary wage-price freeze . . . [in] the form of a Presidential request that labor work under existing contracts . . . for a short period of time—say 90 days."[49]

Volcker viewed a freeze pragmatically, as a way to dampen inflationary expectations during a transition period.[50] He gained confidence in this judgment from his mentor Robert Roosa, who had suggested more than a year earlier that "The initial shock effect of such a Presidential request might tranquilize inflationary expectations."[51] But Volcker ignored the likely resurgence in expectations after removing the temporary freeze, unless the government embarked on a fundamental shift in monetary and fiscal policy—an error in judgment he still regrets.

Volcker suspected that Connally's experience as governor of the Lone Star State prepared him for a gunslinger's gamble. His memorandum emphasized that the "risks are very high," but added, "they are [high] with any other course suggested."[52] He urged "a prompt decision," despite having learned the high art of procrastination from his father. He had waited long enough, nearly two years since he had first broached gold suspension in the Oval Office. And he wanted America to act preemptively, to avoid the appearance of defeat at the hands of currency speculators.

It was almost too late.

The drama began during the first week of May 1971, six weeks after Volcker's memorandum predicted an imminent dollar crisis, and lasted more than three months, until August 15, 1971, when Richard Nixon stunned the world in a televised Sunday-night address. The president would turn Volcker's proposals into law.

According to a front-page article in the *New York Times* on May 5, 1971, "Europe's financial centers were buffeted . . . by the greatest wave of currency speculation in two years. Corporations, banks and others who control large sums of money exchanged unwanted dollars for West German marks . . . and other 'strong' European currencies . . . The German central bank had to intervene in the foreign exchange market, propping up the dollar to prevent it from skidding below its lower limits. The Bundesbank accomplished this by adding more than $1-billion to its already swollen dollar coffers."[53]

Speculators are often painted in ruthless colors, ready to exploit turmoil and confusion for personal gain. In reality, most resemble Harvard-educated George Sheinberg, who was the thirty-six-year-old treasurer of the Bulova Watch Company in May 1971. Sheinberg had begun worrying about the dollar two weeks earlier, because "one of the currency newsletters said there was nothing to worry about."[54]

Bulova followed the practice of borrowing marks from German banks to finance its German clock manufacturing and purchasing. The more nervous Sheinberg got about the dollar, and about repaying the marks the company owed, the earlier he left his home in suburban White Plains, New York, and headed into his Manhattan office. During the first week of May, he began arriving at seven o'clock in the morning to contact foreign-exchange dealers in London, where he bought marks with dollars "to protect us on the purchase of clocks." Unfortunately for Bulova, he did not buy enough before the Bundesbank got tired of propping up the value of the dollar.[55]

On the morning of May 5 the German central bank decided, after an hour of buying $1 billion, on top of the billion it bought the day before, that it could no longer continue its currency operations.[56] The central banks of Switzerland, Belgium, Netherlands, and Austria followed immediately. The news that each country also "closed down their foreign exchange markets in one of the gravest monetary disturbances since World War II" created special difficulties for American tourists.[57] U.S. guests could not pay their bills at the Intercontinental Hotel in Geneva because it refused to accept dollars—a galling indignity considering that the Intercontinental was American owned.[58]

Telexes describing the escalating crisis streamed across Volcker's desk in his second-floor office at the Treasury, and the anxiety sent him scurrying with alarming frequency to the private men's room located in his office. Volcker tried to exercise restraint: "My favorite lawyer, Mike Bradfield, worked in the office directly below mine, on the first floor of the Treasury Building. He had told me on numerous occasions that he could always tell when a crisis had reached the critical stage by the cascade of flushing he heard. The more I thought about that, of course, the more frequently I visited the john."[59]

Volcker's anxiety subsided after he recognized that the crisis provided cover for a policy change America needed. He urged Connally to permit the upheaval "to develop without action or strong intervention by the U.S. . . . . [and to use] as negotiating leverage . . . suspension of gold convertibility . . . to achieve a significant revaluation of the currencies of the major European countries and Japan"[60]

The loss of $400 million in gold during the second week of May—to Belgium, Netherlands, and (of course) France—had brought U.S. gold stocks to the lowest level since the years before World War II, and made the suspension of convertibility even more urgent.[61] The burgeoning crisis would legitimize the "cold blooded suspension" Volcker had proposed two months earlier, deflecting the resentments and justifying an otherwise unpalatable economic decision.

John Connally prepared for a public performance as though he had studied drama at the Actors Studio, and Volcker took notes: "At the annual meeting of the International Monetary Conference in Munich [at the end of May 1971], which brought together the leading commercial and central bankers, . . . [Connally] sat through all the meetings and the elaborate lunches and dinners, quietly sizing up his audience and their thinking before delivering the traditional closing address."[62]

Connally showed Volcker that preparation includes more than just knowing what to say; how to say it is equally important. Unlike other finance ministers, Connally took his own measure of the assemblage, and planned his words and cadence accordingly. "He taught me a lot," says Volcker.[63]

Paul had, in fact, drafted his boss's remarks, but when Connally showed him the final version, it had a very different ending than the ambiguous conclusion Volcker had written. "It was pure Connally in tone," says Paul, "and I could never do it, no matter how much I practiced."[64] Connally planned to end his speech with dramatic flair: "I want without any arrogance or defiance to make abundantly clear that we are not going to devalue, we are not going to change the price of gold, [and] we are going to control inflation."[65]

Volcker swallowed his disbelief and asked Connally if he wanted to say that so strongly. "After all, we might have to end up devaluing before too long."

Connally did not hesitate. "That's my unalterable position today. I don't know what it will be this summer."

The response stunned Volcker into silence.

Paul admired John Connally's social skills and had learned much from the master politician. He had stopped wearing socks that slid down below his ankles and switched to a dry cleaner who impressed a sharp crease in his trousers. But there were limitations. Volcker could never wear blinders like a carriage horse—they simply did not fit around his large head. He preferred to equivocate, qualify, and risk being branded a poor communicator, rather than feign certainty. His reluctance to skate near the boundary may have prevented him from ever becoming treasury secretary, but it would eventually turn him into the most trusted man in America.

Although Connally ignored Volcker's suggestion that he scale back his rhetoric, he clung to Volcker's battle plan. Not only did Connally allow the crisis to proceed unchecked, but he attacked those in the White House who questioned the strategy.

Paul McCracken, the soft-spoken former University of Michigan economist who headed Nixon's Council of Economic Advisers, lamented the dollar crisis in an early June memo to the president: "We have just muddled through another international monetary crisis . . . [but] we cannot be sure of having escaped entirely or permanently."[66]

Connally's response to Nixon sent a direct shot at McCracken. "Given our present international economic and financial position, some monetary disturbances . . . are virtually inevitable . . . [But] I must take vigorous personal exception to [McCracken's] premises and conclusions . . . Far from 'muddling through' the recent disturbance . . . [we] quite deliberately avoided a strong reaction."[67]

McCracken's memo to the president also included an argument for floating exchange rates. "A system that combines rigidly fixed exchange rates with free trade and capital movements appears to be unworkable . . . You recognized this two years ago . . . when you decided that the U.S. would . . . support a study of greater [exchange rate] flexibility . . . but it has not so far led to concrete results because . . . the attitude of some our own representatives has been lukewarm at best."

Connally recognized Volcker's image painted in lukewarm strokes, so he concluded his rebuttal with the following observation: "In view of recent developments it is hard for me to see how informed observers could think the flexibility issue is dead. But its specifics do involve difficult tactical as well as substantive questions . . . [which] are under active review within the Treasury and in the Volcker group."

The president weighed the exchange and issued a ruling, like the judge and jury he was. He sealed the fate of events to come by appointing Connally "the lead man" in making a recommendation about dealing with the crisis, with instructions that Connally "consult with Paul McCracken, Arthur Burns, George Shultz . . . and your own experts."[68]

Volcker smiled.

Paul created a briefing book about the size of a New York City telephone directory, detailing all aspects of the New Economic Policy.[69] He divided the black loose-leaf binder into two parts. Section A contained an extensive set of bogus plans in case subversives (such as a *Washington Post* reporter) managed to procure a copy. Section C contained the real plans and was divided into twelve tabs, starting with

"Suspension" and extending through "Balance of Payments Controls." Volcker had purposely omitted a section B, as another confusing diversion should the plans fall into enemy hands.

Connally had supplemented Volcker's recommendations on gold convertibility and the wage-price freeze with a proposal for a 10 percent import surcharge. Volcker had warned that the surcharge could spark a protectionist war with U.S. trading partners, but Connally insisted—precisely because it would disturb the Germans and Japanese, forcing them to bargain in good faith.

On August 2, 1971, John Connally used the briefing book's details and his considerable personal charm to convince Richard Nixon to act.[70] The 4 percent drop in the dollar against the German mark since the Bundesbank allowed the rate to float in May, and the spike in gold to over forty-two dollars an ounce, had brought matters to a head. But the president wanted to wait until Congress returned after Labor Day before implementing the plan. He had heard about the risks of suspension from Federal Reserve chairman Arthur Burns, and worried that closing the gold window "could cause a panic."[71]

Nixon told Connally to bring Paul McCracken and George Shultz up to speed, but to warn them both about leaks. "And that means tell Shultz that he cannot talk with Milton Friedman."[72] Shultz had been relaying to the president Friedman's arguments for floating exchange rates.

Volcker liked the presidential embargo on discussions with Friedman but worried about the delay. "I did not want us to wind up implementing the package out of desperation."[73] On Thursday morning, August 12, after reports from Frankfurt, London, Tokyo, and Milan that speculation had pushed the German mark to its highest level against the dollar in more than twenty years, forcing massive intervention by all the world's central banks, Volcker turned desperate.[74] He telephoned Connally at his Texas ranch, where the treasury secretary had gone for a brief vacation. The conversation made it briefer:

"I think you'd better get back here quick."

"Thanks. I'm on my way."

George Shultz had met with Nixon a number of times on August 12 and, in keeping with his training as a labor negotiator, had counseled patience. The president did not need much convincing to stick with the original timetable.

Nixon said, "We're not really ready. To get everyone ready we have to go to Camp David. September 7 seems like the right time . . . The decision should be made by you, Connally, Burns, and me. I know Connally will want to bring Volcker . . . but he's so obsessed by things international . . . I don't know."[75]

Shultz saw an opening to push his agenda. "Volcker also thinks we should solve the international problem by restricting the domestic economy . . . but I don't think you want to do that."

"Never . . . Unfortunately, I don't have a hell of a lot of confidence in Volcker."

Connally went directly from the airport to the White House at 5:30 on the afternoon of August 12, joining the president and George Shultz in the president's office in the Old Executive Office Building. Nixon was pleased to see him, greeting Connally with a loud "I'm glad you're here," but the president seemed determined to avoid being stampeded.[76]

"I don't think we should do the whole program right now, especially the freeze and the import surcharge . . . but if you think shutting the gold window must be done immediately then you can announce it yourself . . . making it sound like a temporary measure, as a prelude to a complete package."

Connally had no intention of getting out in front on this and appealed to Nixon's addiction to grand gestures. "The problem with doing this piecemeal is that people will keep worrying about what is coming next . . . especially if we just close the gold window. It will seem clear that we were forced into it. Doing the whole package at once means that you have thought this through carefully . . . You will seize the initiative."

Nixon circled back to his concerns about the gold window. "Actually, Arthur [Burns] wants just the freeze. He thinks the risks of suspension are too great."

"Arthur is talking like a central banker. You have the best man in the country down here. Why don't you talk to Volcker about this yourself."

Connally had relied on Volcker's technical expertise and thought the president should as well, but Nixon had other ideas, courtesy of Shultz. "Volcker thinks we ought to sacrifice the domestic economy to save the dollar. I'm not in favor of that."

Connally sounded surprised to hear this. "Well, I certainly don't think like that and I'm pretty sure Volcker doesn't either."

"Good. That is why we are going to continue with an expansionary policy."

"I agree . . . but the public will believe that you are serious about controlling inflation if you announce the freeze."

George Shultz had been listening to the interchange and began discussing the details needed to implement the wage-price freeze. The president interrupted him, in a clear and authoritative voice:

"What I think we should do, after hearing all of the possibilities, is this . . . We ought to do the entire program at once, announcing it this coming Monday. We'll have a meeting at Camp David starting tomorrow afternoon. I'll have it all set up. But we need total security. The fewer people the better. The three of us will be there, make sure we have McCracken, and of course, Arthur must be involved." Nixon paused, and then did a graceful pirouette. "And John, you bring Volcker."

The meeting began on Friday afternoon, August 13, 1971, at the presidential retreat at Camp David in Maryland's Catoctin Mountains.[77] It ended three days later, on Sunday morning, August 15, 1971. The president's message to the country that evening lasted a total of twenty minutes.[78]

Those twenty minutes changed Paul Volcker's life.

CHAPTER 5

Transformation

At 12:00 midnight on Sunday, August 15, 1971, Volcker boarded a refitted military transport plane on the runway at Andrews Air Force Base headed for battle with European finance ministers. Nixon had lit the fuse three hours earlier with his address to the American people on network television outlining the administration's New Economic Policy. The plan, hatched over the weekend at Camp David, invoked the Trading with the Enemy Act of 1917 to impose some of its emergency measures, and threatened global economic warfare.[1]

Most foreigners would not care about the most dramatic announcement, the three-month freeze on wages and prices imposed by the president, except to marvel that a California Republican had adopted a Social Democrat's approach to controlling inflation. But America's trading partners would resent the suspension of gold convertibility, which tarnished their dollar holdings, and the 10 percent surcharge on imports, which made their exports less welcome on American shores. Those measures were the equivalent of a declaration of economic hostilities.

The president had asked John Connally to lead a news conference the next day in Washington, a coveted spotlight for Nixon's chief economic spokesman. Connally assigned Volcker the task of conducting a private meeting with foreign central bankers and finance ministers in

London, launching Volcker's transformation from monetary technician to international financial diplomat.

Paul could not wait to embark on his mission. He felt like a wartime emissary dispatched to cool a provocation. Volcker had always regretted missing the call to action during World War II, blaming himself for failing to convince the draft board that he was short enough to fight. Now he looked forward to defending his country, to maintaining the supremacy of the American dollar as the world's premier currency, and to ensuring the stability of international trade within the framework of a revamped Bretton Woods System. It was the beginning of a new career.

Volcker replayed the whirlwind weekend in his head as he settled into the cavernous hull of the transport plane. The meeting at Camp David had been conducted in total secrecy: no reporters, no phone calls, and by order of the president, no representatives from the State Department. Nixon had been almost dismissive: "I want this kept secret . . . don't bother with the foreign relations types."[2] Volcker thought the president's distrust of the foreign affairs bureaucracy had deep roots, extending back to Nixon's days as a congressman on the House Un-American Activities Committee, and his pursuit of Alger Hiss, a State Department official accused of espionage in 1948 and convicted of perjury in 1950.

Volcker noted the president's attention to detail, especially when it bordered on the absurd. Nixon's obsession began with instructions that every person sign the guest book as they entered Aspen Cottage on Friday afternoon, August 13, and ended on Sunday morning, with detailed directions during the final picture-taking ceremony.[3] Volcker smiled, recalling how Nixon exhorted his valet, "Manolo, quick, Manolo, bring in more chairs, we need more chairs for the picture."[4] The president understood the historic significance of the unfolding events, and participated in every substantive decision.

The joust with Arthur Burns over the wisdom of gold suspension, with the president as referee, dominated Volcker's thoughts. Burns had not minced words.[5]

"Volcker and Connolly may be right about closing the gold window, but I think they are wrong. We are taking dramatic steps . . . the wage-price freeze, the border tax, and the government spending cuts. They will electrify the world. On the other hand, there are grave risks in closing the gold window. First, political . . . Pravda [the Communist Party newspaper] will headline this as a sign of the collapse of capitalism. The second risk is economic . . . world trade will suffer. Foreign exporters will clamor for action—"

Connally interjected, "So the other countries don't like it, so what . . . We'll go broke getting their goodwill."

Burns protested, "They'll retaliate."

"Let 'em. What can they do?"

Volcker cringed, having spent the better part of his professional career nurturing America's international relationships, but said, "I hate to do this. All my life I have defended Bretton Woods, but I think it's needed . . . we cannot continue this way. But let's not just close the gold window and sit. We need to negotiate a new set of exchange rates. This is an opportunity to repair a system that needs fixing."

Paul McCracken offered some balance: "People's reaction to closing the gold window could be negative. On the other hand, they could see it as part of a program of strong action on wages and prices."

Volcker tried some historical perspective, "There is a certain public sentiment about a 'cross of gold.'"

Paul realized his error too late—a misplaced reference to the denunciation of gold by presidential candidate William Jennings Bryan at the 1896 Democratic convention.

Nixon put Volcker in his place: "Bryan ran four times and lost."[6]

Arthur Burns's special relationship with Richard Nixon, extending back to the Eisenhower administration, might have carried the day. His warnings about the dire consequences of suspension worried the president. But Connally's tongue and Volcker's expertise won Nixon over. Volcker had lugged a fat briefing book to every meeting, just in case he needed to consult the black loose-leaf binder containing the plans. His preparation paid off. No one else could muster an answer when the president asked how much revenue the import tax would generate.[7]

Volcker grounded all his calculations in economic analysis, despite the skepticism he had learned from Morgenstern at Princeton.[8] He knew this precision gave him the credibility of a surgeon, but he also recognized the downside. His numerical skills left him vulnerable to being branded an idiot savant.

Not after his mission abroad.

The roar of the engines buzzed in Volcker's ears as the military transport plane, without windows, lumbered into the air. He could hardly believe that he had returned by helicopter from Camp David just a few hours earlier, had stopped at the Treasury to prepare the press release describing the new program, and was now off on a transatlantic journey. He worried about delivering the proper message, considering that the draft apology for abandoning gold he had given to William Safire, the president's speechwriter, had disappeared entirely from Nixon's televised talk. The president had written much of the speech himself and turned over detailed notes to Safire with explicit instructions to avoid "the gobbly gook about crisis of international monetary affairs . . . which seemed to be the thrust of Volcker."[9]

Nixon told H. R. Haldeman, his chief of staff, "Don't circulate the drafts of the speech. Show the other people only the sections that concern them. I want it to be a surprise." It was.

Volcker marveled at what a master politician could engineer with the proper turn of phrase, like the sweep of a magician's wand. During the first minute of his talk, Nixon had transformed three days of anxiety into victory. "The time has come for a new economic policy for the United States . . . We must create more and better jobs. We must stop the rise in the cost of living; we must protect the dollar from the attacks of international money speculators."[10]

Volcker knew that Americans would respond well to thwarting unprincipled speculators. He wondered how that would play in London.

The New York Stock Exchange greeted the president's plan with thunderous approval, jumping more than 3 percent on Monday, August 16, the first day of trading after the president's talk.[11] The surcharge on imports, raising the cost of Volkswagens and Toyotas, buoyed domestic automakers. Eager buyers pushed up the shares of Chrysler by more than 15 percent, while the larger companies, General Motors and Ford, rose 10 percent each.[12] Gold mining stocks declined, suffering from

Nixon's edict, which diminished America's need to replenish its stock of the precious metal.[13]

Nixon won new friends among investors. Clarence Netherland, a petroleum engineer watching stock prices flash across an electronic screen in a Merrill Lynch brokerage office in Dallas, said, "There's a hell of [a] lot more confidence in the economy now. We have begun to face up to realities."[14] Frederick Papolos, a retired Florida businessman, added, "Mr. Nixon has proved himself to be a real statesman. I'll vote for him in 1972, although I didn't in 1968."

Consumers went on a buying spree as well.[15] Martin Spenser, a personnel consultant in New York City, visited Sherry-Lehman, a fine wine and liquor store on the Upper East Side of Manhattan and bought a case of Château Lafite-Rothschild. "A wise decision," said the store owner, Sam Aaron. "I assume retailers and restaurants will be buying madly . . . until present supplies . . . run out." Louis Evans, the president of Evans Motor Company in the Forest Park suburb of Atlanta, reported that several people had shown up early Monday morning to buy Toyotas, and he suggested that "the surcharge announcement was the reason."

The *Wall Street Journal* delivered a lecture from its editorial page pulpit, preaching against the inflationary consequences of the wage-price freeze and the foreign exchange uncertainty triggered by gold suspension.

> President Nixon has revealed in his two and a half years in office a predilection for the grandstand play . . . So it should not come as a surprise that he responded to his growing problems with the U.S. economy as he did in his speech Sunday night . . . [But] grandstanding is . . . more likely than not to fail in meeting the popular hopes that it raises . . . A wage and price freeze could result in rather panicky return to price inflation after it is lifted . . . The import surcharge and a floating dollar will initially produce confusion; what comes out of it could be better or worse.[16]

Both were valid concerns.

The suspension of gold convertibility brought foreign exchange markets to a standstill, except for small retail transactions. In London on the day after Nixon's speech, the press reported a "bewildering variety of exchange rates for tourists . . . The London Hilton would change up to $50 for a person at $2.60 [per pound sterling] during the morning, but it switched to $2.80 a pound during the afternoon."[17] In Milan, Dr. and Mrs. Lawrence Gould from New York City "were just shocked" when their dollars could not buy them even an ice-cream cone. "Fortunately our trip was ending," they said, "and we had enough foreign currency to see us home."[18]

Confusion reigned in foreign exchange because Nixon had upended a key pillar of the Bretton Woods edifice: the link between the U.S. dollar and gold. Until Sunday night, August 15, 1971, the U.S. Treasury permitted foreign central banks, such as the Bank of England or the Bank of Japan, to exchange dollars for gold at the official rate of thirty-five dollars per ounce. And because they could exchange dollars for gold, these central banks felt comfortable using dollars as reserves to establish fixed exchange rates for world travelers.

The Bank of England, for example, would intervene in the market by buying and selling pounds versus dollars, as necessary, to maintain the exchange rate at $2.60 per pound. And the Bank of Italy would intervene in the market by buying and selling lira versus dollars, as necessary, to maintain the exchange rate at 600 lira per dollar. The fixed exchange rate between the dollar and the pound meant that American tourists knew how much they needed to pay their bill at the London Hilton. The fixed exchange rate between the lira and the dollar meant that Dr. and Mrs. Lawrence Gould could enjoy gelato for about fifty cents while on their way to the Milan airport.

Americans did not care that President Nixon had suspended the convertibility of dollars into gold, having been barred from holding the precious metal since 1933. They cared only about fixed exchange rates and what the dollar would be worth in terms of the pound, yen, and lira. But suspension flustered foreign central bankers because many held dollars as reserves, assuming they could exchange their greenbacks for gold.[19] Now that the dollar was no longer convertible, at least some members of the exclusive club might stop intervening in the foreign exchange markets, allowing the dollar to float with supply

and demand. The financiers worried that the ensuing chaos would im-
mobilize international trade.

Treasury Secretary John Connally tailored his press conference on Monday morning, August 16, to the domestic side of the president's speech.
He understood that the upcoming presidential election, less than fifteen
months away, began at the supermarket checkout counter. He promised
that the new Nixon policies would fill the shopping cart. "The programs
are designed to create more jobs and reduce unemployment . . . to stimulate car sales . . . to bring inflation under control . . . [and] to give the
American worker a chance to increase his productivity."[20]

Connally knew that George McGovern, at the time the only declared
candidate for the Democratic presidential nomination, had disparaged
Nixon's international program immediately after the president's speech:
"It is a disgrace for a great nation like ours to end in this way the convertibility of the dollar."[21] Connally deflected the criticism with a hu-
morous aside: "I am not prepared to say what is going to happen in the
international money markets . . . [but] there is no question that we
shook them up."[22]

Connally then withdrew from the fray by publicly designating Paul
Volcker as the point man for all matters international. "I want to say to
those of you who do not know, that about midnight last night, Undersecretary Paul Volcker left with Dewey Daane of the Federal Reserve
Board to go to London. A meeting will be held this afternoon at the
American embassy at four o'clock with representatives of our principal
trading partners . . . So our people are there. They are already talking.
But so far as the reaction of the central bankers in Europe, frankly I
am unable to tell you."[23]

It was past four o'clock in London when Connally made the an-
nouncement, and Volcker had already engaged a pride of financiers at
Wychwood House, residence of the American ambassador to London.
He knew most of these veterans of earlier crises, including Otmar Em-
minger of the Bundesbank, Jeremy Morse of the Bank of England,
Rinaldo Ossola of the Bank of Italy, and Claude Pierre-Brossolette of
the French Ministry of Finance. Two representatives from the Bank of
Japan who happened to be vacationing in London at the time were

pressed into service. They should have known that summer in the British capital rarely lasted more than a day.

Volcker summarized the proceedings at a press conference after the meeting, offering few details while remaining faithful to the substance.[24] "I came for consultations, not negotiations, but we want to return to a stable system as soon as possible." When asked whether he still dismissed floating exchange rates as ivory tower scribbling, he smiled. "I don't think we can object to anything as an interim solution . . . and we do not have a blueprint going forward. But long-term monetary reform will be a slow process."

Behind the closed doors of the meeting, Volcker had already embraced floating exchange rates as a means to accomplish a noble cause: a revitalized Bretton Woods System. "Letting the markets determine a credible set of exchange rates might not be entirely bad . . . We do not want to jump from one crisis to another."[25] His flexibility elicited concern from the Bank of England's Jeremy Morse; "It might be difficult to get back to a fixed parity system."[26] Volcker seemed prepared to take a calculated risk, a characteristic that would serve him well in the future. The press commented favorably: "Mr. Volcker, despite his reputation for conservatism, is open to persuasion."[27]

Volcker invoked a higher authority during the news conference when it came to gold. "The President would like to see a further diminution of the role of gold in international finance." He had been even more explicit about Nixon's preferences during the meeting with the central bankers, saying that the president did not want to raise the price of gold, even though that would be "a quick and easy solution" to the excess supply of dollars abroad.[28]

America's stock of gold would cover twice as many dollars if the Treasury set the official gold price at seventy dollars an ounce rather than thirty-five. But raising the dollar price of gold, technically called a devaluation of the dollar, required congressional approval. Nixon did not want to suffer the embarrassment of devaluation, an indignity last perpetrated on the American people in 1934, at the urging of Franklin Delano Roosevelt.

Volcker dismissed devaluation because it would reward speculators and countries such as France, which had spurned dollars in favor of the precious metal. He wanted to restore a fundamental balance in

U.S. imports and exports by depreciating the dollar against other currencies, the yen and the mark in particular. Central banks could allow the dollar to depreciate without a formal U.S. devaluation against gold simply by refraining from propping up the dollar in the foreign exchange market.

The dollar had already dropped by more than 6 percent against the mark since the Bundesbank stopped intervening in May.[29] But Volcker calculated the dollar would have to decline by an average of 15 percent to restore the competitiveness of U.S. exports in world markets.[30] Fifteen percent would make Volcker as unpopular among America's trading partners as the tax collector.

Four months of negotiations would be needed to produce a new set of exchange rates under a revamped Bretton Woods System. Japan and France were the major bottlenecks: France, because President Georges Pompidou, a protégé of de Gaulle, wanted to embarrass the United States by forcing a devaluation of the dollar against gold; Japan, because companies such as Sony and Toyota wanted the yen to remain cheap relative to the dollar to encourage their exports to America. An embarrassing press report showed the extent of Japanese inroads: "Secretary of the Treasury, Mr. John Connally decided . . . that all senior members of his staff should have television sets in their offices so that they could keep in touch with the developing world monetary crisis. A Treasury purchasing agent was sent out and he returned with several portable sets—all products of the Japanese Sony Company."[31]

Volcker dominated the negotiations from the outset, touring the major European financial centers to explain the American position.[32] A communiqué from the Paris correspondent of the *New York Times* labeled Paul Adolph Volcker "the President's Monetary Envoy" and quoted him as saying, "Mr. Nixon is facing the facts."[33]

The Paris news story carried a picture of Volcker alongside French finance minister Valéry Giscard d'Estaing, Connally's counterpart in Pompidou's cabinet. The snapshot elevated Volcker in the international hierarchy as surely as a presidential promotion. Going forward, he received royal treatment at the famed Hotel de Crillon, located on the Place de la Concorde, a few steps from the Champs-Elysées. Management at the five-star hotel, built in the eighteenth century, would reserve the same bed for Volcker as had been used by the six-foot, five-inch general Charles de Gaulle.[34]

London's *Financial Times* featured Volcker in their "Man of the Week" column with the headline "Big Man in a Big Job," and offered historical perspective. "Paul Volcker has held his present job since the Republicans came to power two and a half years ago. That he got the job at all is noteworthy since he is widely believed to be a Democrat. But the fact that he has kept his post despite the dollar's vicissitudes . . . underlines both his professional competence and his growing personal authority in Washington."[35]

The *Financial Times* elaborated on key details: "No one could miss Paul Volcker in a crowd. President Nixon's international monetary trouble shooter stands all of six feet seven inches high in his sober black socks, weighs 240 pounds and tops off his impressive frame with a pair of steely eyes, a slack jaw, and a near bald crown to his head." Volcker clearly owed John Connally more than just an opportunity to represent America in world finance. His "sober black socks" came directly from the boss's example of sartorial footwear.

The Sunday edition of the *New York Times* on August 22, 1971, confirmed Volcker's transformation from technocrat to diplomat. The front page of the business section carried a black-bordered rectangular box that ran the entire length of the page, as though it were designed for the Volcker family scrapbook.[36] The caption at the top read "Nixon Did It," with a picture of the president immediately below. At the bottom of the frame the title read, "The World Reacted," followed by a picture of Karl Klasen, head of the German central bank. In the center appeared the heading "Volcker Explained It," bordering a picture of Paul, with eyes peering out from behind a microphone.

Alma Volcker, Paul's mother, could not have done a better job.

The price reaction in gold to the suspension of convertibility surprised Volcker, teaching him a lesson in market psychology he would never forget. Arthur Burns had asked him during the Camp David meeting, "What will happen to the price of gold?" Volcker had answered, "Everybody who speculates in gold will seize on this to make a mint. We have to come up with a proposal to demonstrate that gold is not that important."[37] He added that "fortunes could be made" with the information on suspension, and joked to budget director George Shultz that, given "a free hand," he could make up the government's $23 billion budget deficit.[38]

Luckily for Volcker, and the U.S. Treasury, he never got the chance to put the speculation to work. The free-market price of gold in London had closed at forty-three dollars an ounce on Friday, August 13. The market remained closed on Monday, August 16, to let everyone digest the president's bombshell, and then reopened on Tuesday with a giant yawn. The gold price remained virtually unchanged for the entire week after suspension and declined to below forty-one dollars an ounce by the end of August.[39]

Volcker's forecasting record while treasury undersecretary had earned him the reputation of foreign exchange Nostradamus, having anticipated the French devaluation in August 1969 and the dollar crisis in May 1971. But his "fortunes could be made" observation sits on the shelf of miscalculations alongside business statistician and educator Roger Babson's 1928 prediction, "The election of Hoover . . . should result in continued prosperity for 1929."[40] The only consolation is that Volcker himself might have contributed to gold's lackluster performance.

Speculators had pushed up the free-market price of gold to forty-three dollars an ounce prior to Nixon's announcement, eight dollars above the official thirty-five-dollar price posted by the U.S. Treasury, anticipating an American devaluation. Under the bizarre two-tier market operating since March 1968, dealings among central banks took place at the official price and private transactions at the free-market price. The spread between the two reflected the ancient and honorable forces of supply and demand. Speculative demand had focused on gold as the government's key monetary asset, a legacy of a century under the gold standard and of the dwindling stock of U.S. gold relative to dollar obligations abroad.[41]

Volcker thought that Nixon's suspension of convertibility on August 15 confirmed a crisis that would inflate renewed speculation. He had not considered that his dismissal of devaluation during his London consultations the following day would puncture the balloon. He had underestimated the power of his own words because he knew that both Nixon and Connally cared more about politics than economics, and would sacrifice finance for political gain. He was right to expect devaluation to make a comeback but wrong in his assessment of market psychology.

Volcker had forgotten what he had learned on the government bond desk of the Federal Reserve Bank of New York. Traders bought and sold based on their expectations of the future, transacting at prices that reflected their best predictions of what was likely to happen. Prices respond only to surprises, and speculators had already built an expected devaluation into the price of gold. Volcker had disappointed the speculators, and they drowned their sorrows by selling their gold.

Volcker slipped into his role as international financial diplomat as though it were a custom-made suit. He wanted to negotiate a new set of exchange rates quickly, before foreign governments retaliated with their own trade barriers. He spent as much time in London, Paris, and Rome immediately following August 15, 1971, as he did in Washington, D.C. Perhaps that is why he encountered trouble on the domestic front on the morning of September 11, 1971.

Barbara called his office at eleven o'clock.[42] "Have you forgotten something?"

Paul looked at his jacket to make sure it matched his pants. "Not that I know of . . . but I assume you are going to tell me."

"Well, today we should be celebrating our trip to Maine."

He had not only forgotten their wedding anniversary but had given Barbara the opportunity to remind him of a colossal error. His planning of their honeymoon trip to Pocomoonshine Lake in Maine ranked as the low point in almost twenty years of marriage. Paul had thought that sharing his love for the Volcker family passion with Barbara would get them off to a great start. He overlooked the possibility that fly-fishing would not necessarily arouse the same romantic interest in his new bride as it had in his father and grandfather.[43] Barbara made her point by ending their trip two days early, right after they had spent an evening watching bears rummage through the garbage in the nearby village of Grand Lake Stream.

He responded with a weak attempt at humor. "Well, my only defense is that I'm not sure what day it is because I'm not sure what city I'm in."

Barbara waited, to let him squirm, and then said, "At least you have an excuse. The only reason I remembered is because the mail just arrived and your mother sent us an anniversary card."

Volcker's international financial diplomacy during the fall of 1971, as the dollar depreciated, went about as well as his conversation with his wife on September 11. The Italian Socialist Party, a key member of Prime Minister Emilio Colombo's coalition government, extended the resentment beyond simple economics. The Italians denounced the dollar's weakness as a consequence of American spending on the Vietnam War, and echoed the French position, urging "the abandonment of the dollar as an international standard and reserve currency."[44]

John Connally counseled patience from the beginning. He felt that time was on America's side as the mark and yen appreciated, and the dollar declined, under the temporary float that began with the May crisis.[45] He knew that the import surcharge irritated all America's trading partners, especially the Japanese, and the suspension of dollar convertibility bothered the French most of all. Connally was determined to exploit these irritants until the United States achieved the 15 percent depreciation of the dollar that it needed to be competitive in world markets.

Volcker had been taught restraint by his father, but John Connally added that strategic element to the art of negotiation, turning it almost into science. Volcker recalls that "while the French were buying dollars to prevent the franc from appreciating during the fall, Connally took a trip to Indonesia for no other reason than to make French finance minister Giscard d'Estaing think we did not care. I learned a lot from him, but sometimes he played his cards so close to the vest that I did not know what he really wanted."[46]

Arthur Burns, still resentful over Volcker's victory in suspending gold convertibility, memorialized Volcker's vulnerability with the following entry in his diary: "Poor and wretched Volcker—never knowing where he stood on any issue—had succeeded in instilling an irrational fear of gold in his tyrannical master [Connally], whom he tried constantly to please by catering to his fear of foreigners (particularly the

French) instead of his capacity (not inconsiderable) for straight reasoning."[47]

The meeting on Monday, November 29, 1971, of the ten richest noncommunist countries, known as the Group of Ten (G-10), took place in the Palazzo Corsini in Rome, a princely setting for a breakthrough in the ongoing financial drama.[48] The palazzo, built in the eighteenth century along the Tiber River, had served as the Roman town house of the Corsinis, a Renaissance banking family from Florence, and was now home to the Italian Academy of Arts and Sciences. Masterpieces by Rubens, de Hooch, and Brueghel decorated the walls of the makeshift press room, installed on the first floor.[49]

The rotating chairmanship of the G-10 meetings put John Connally at the head of the forum, with the remaining ministers of finance and their central bankers arrayed comfortably at the ornate rectangular table. Volcker sat immediately to the right of Connally, as the chief U.S. representative, and Federal Reserve chairman Arthur Burns sat next to Volcker. Burns's presence reminded Volcker that he was about to lose the battle on devaluation, courtesy of the French.

Arthur Burns had relayed a message from Giscard d'Estaing to Richard Nixon, saying they would accept a "five or six percent" appreciation of the franc versus the dollar if the U.S. devalued the dollar against gold by the same amount. This would maintain a constant price of gold in terms of francs, precisely the stability that gold-loving Frenchmen wanted. According to Burns, there was a "widespread and long-standing custom of the French population to hold gold as a hedge against inflation and political uncertainty."[50]

Prior to the G-10 meeting, Connally had told Volcker that Nixon had authorized a modest U.S. devaluation, despite all their denials, if that was necessary to move negotiations forward.[51] The French surely wanted to embarrass the United States, and the large holdings of gold at the Banque de France, courtesy of General de Gaulle, strengthened their enthusiasm and intransigence.[52] France's gold would gain in dollar value if they forced America to take its medicine, confirming the wisdom of Gaullist policy.

Volcker accepted devaluation against gold as the price in prestige

America had to pay for accomplishing the desired appreciation of the major currencies against the dollar. He felt better knowing that his recommendation to continue the suspension of convertibility had prevailed.[53] French gold would be worth more dollars after devaluation, but the French would not be able to capitalize on their gain—a typical French victory, putting appearance over substance.

John Connally played the role of chairman in Rome as though he wanted an Oscar. He spoke of the historical significance of their discussions, the appropriate setting in the birthplace of Western civilization, and urged everyone to renew their efforts to move toward a viable system of international cooperation. He then asked if there were new items of business, cuing Volcker with an imperceptible wink that left no doubt about what should come next.[54]

Volcker cleared his throat. "Well, suppose, just hypothetically, we were willing to discuss the price of gold. How would you respond if we increased the price by ten or fifteen percent?"

Connally interrupted. "All right, the issue has been raised. Let's assume ten percent. What will you people do?"

Volcker had purposely overreached with his 15 percent proposal, knowing that Giscard d'Estaing had suggested France would accept 5 percent. America needed a bigger move to adjust exchange rates. Now Paul worried that his exaggeration, combined with Connally's correction, advertised dissension within the U.S. Treasury. Unsure of how to set the record straight, Volcker said nothing, recalling a favorite quote attributed to Mark Twain: "Better to remain silent and be thought a fool than to speak out and remove all doubt."

For the next hour, no one spoke. Most of the central bankers smoked, while the finance ministers looked at their shoes, probably checking whether they needed a shine.

Germany had always been the most flexible of America's trading partners, so it was no surprise when Finance Minister Karl Schiller spoke first. The export powerhouse could afford to be generous because of its balance-of-payments surpluses. Moreover, preserving America's commitment to defending Western Europe against Communist aggression carried great weight in West Germany. In March 1967, Karl Blessing, the then president of the Bundesbank, had written to Fed chairman William McChesney Martin pledging that Germany would refrain from demanding gold from the U.S. Treasury in consideration of American defense commitments in Europe.[55]

Schiller said Germany could live with a 10 percent U.S. devaluation "and would probably add some percentage to it."[56]

One of the bankers asked, "What do you mean by 'some'?"

Professor Schiller, a former academic at the University of Hamburg, responded with a brief linguistics lesson. "In the German language, 'some' does not mean 'one.' It means 'two.'"

Volcker knew that Schiller's proposed 12 percent appreciation of the mark had put Germany's European partners on the spot. Everyone wanted the United States to remove the import surcharge and recognized that the price for that relief was a major realignment of exchange rates. But France could not afford anything close to a 12 percent appreciation of its currency. Most Americans loved the Volkswagen, but probably thought Peugeot, the pride of the French automobile industry, was a miniature poodle.

Nevertheless, Giscard d'Estaing remained silent. Nixon and Pompidou were scheduled to meet the following week. The French finance minister knew the final negotiations would take place then. And so did everyone else.[57] The press anticipated "The Coming Devaluation of the Dollar."[58]

The Azores Islands, a Portuguese archipelago in the mid-Atlantic, home to a U.S. air base and less than a thousand miles from continental Europe, served as the neutral meeting point for the American and French presidents on Monday, December 13, 1971. Georges Pompidou arrived prepared with a lecture on the centrality of gold to a stable international monetary system. He knew far more finance than Richard Nixon, having been an investment banker at Rothschild, and he recognized an opportunity to capitalize on France's position in European economic affairs. French intransigence had paid dividends ever since de Gaulle withdrew from NATO in 1966.

Nixon, for his part, wanted to skip the economics and talk politics, in preparation for his scheduled visits to Peking in February 1972, and to Moscow the following May.[59] He delegated the monetary discussions to Connally and Volcker. Pompidou, after his pitch to bury the dollar as the premier reserve currency, assigned the task of planning the greenback's funeral to finance minister Valéry Giscard d'Estaing.

Two days of negotiations produced a compromise "Framework for Monetary and Trade Settlement," signed by both presidents.[60] Among the key items, the United States agreed to remove the import surcharge and to devalue the dollar by raising the price of gold from thirty-five dollars to thirty-eight dollars per ounce. France agreed to allow the franc to appreciate against the dollar by roughly the same 8 percent as the jump in the price of gold and, as an interim step toward monetary reform, would permit some flexibility around the newly established exchange rate.[61]

The presidents agreed to defer discussions of longer-term issues to a broader forum. The items on this "too hot to handle" list included the division of responsibilities among countries for defending stable exchange rates, the proper role of gold, and a timetable for resuming dollar convertibility into gold. However, Nixon committed the United States "to assist in the stability of the . . . newly fixed structure of exchange rates . . . by vigorous implementation of its efforts to restore price stability."[62] This benign pledge that every Boy Scout could support would become a source of conflict between the two presidents.

John Connally viewed the Azores agreement as a blueprint for the meeting of the G-10 scheduled for the following week in Washington. He chose the precise venue with purpose: the Commons Room of the Smithsonian Institution Castle, a 116-year-old red sandstone structure designed by James Renwick, architect of St. Patrick's Cathedral in New York City. A crypt just inside the castle contains the remains of James Smithson, the illegitimate son of an English duke who left his fortune to the U.S. government and bestowed his name on the complex of museums and research centers now known as the Smithsonian.[63] The Gothic architecture and forty-foot-high vaulted ceiling of the cathedral-like Commons Room conferred an aura of high purpose on the assembled ministers of finance and central bankers.

After two days of deliberations, on Saturday, December 18, 1971, the conclave unveiled a new structure of prices and arrangements in international finance. The dollar would be worth less against everything. An ounce of gold would now cost $38 rather than $35. A dollar would buy 3.22 German marks rather than 3.66 and would exchange for 308 yen rather than 360. Even the lowly Italian lira became more expensive: a dollar would buy only 581.5 lira rather than 625.0.[64]

Central banks would still intervene to maintain fixed exchange rates, but those rates could vary by $2\frac{1}{4}$ percent around their central values rather than the 1 percent leeway permitted under Bretton Woods.[65] Dollar convertibility into gold remained suspended, meaning central banks could not exchange greenbacks for gold even at the higher price of $38. The international financial system had become a de facto dollar standard despite France's success at embarrassing the United States.

Volcker should have been happy. He had engineered the depreciation of the dollar against all the major currencies, making American goods more competitive in world markets. He had shored up the Bretton Woods framework of fixed exchange rates by adding a built-in safety net of modest fluctuations around central values. He had avoided the freely floating exchange rate system advocated by Milton Friedman, George Shultz, and the Council of Economic Advisers. And he had had to swallow only a small devaluation of the dollar against gold.

President Nixon surprised the gathering of financiers by appearing at the Smithsonian to celebrate the accomplishment. The president hailed the agreement as inaugurating a new era of international finance. "It is my great privilege to announce on behalf of the finance ministers and the other representatives of the ten countries involved, the conclusion of the most significant monetary agreement in the history of the world."[66]

Volcker, standing off to the side, muttered under his breath, "I hope it lasts three months."[67]

Paul made a living as a professional skeptic, but his doubts about the newly minted Smithsonian Agreement were well founded. The realignment of exchange rates fell far short of the 15 percent adjustment needed for a new sustainable system.[68] The dollar would remain under pressure.

CHAPTER 6

Compromise

A letter of protest from French president Georges Pompidou to Richard Nixon landed for comment on Volcker's desk on February 4, 1972.[1] He did not like what he saw. The free-market price of gold had risen to a record high of fifty dollars an ounce, a 15 percent jump less than two months after the Smithsonian Agreement.[2] Gold speculators were betting on another upheaval.

Pompidou began his note to Nixon with "Our conversations of December 13 and 14, 1971, were characterized by frankness and mutual understanding that were particularly useful."[3] This means anything but what it says, of course. A frank discussion is diplomatic speak for a fistfight. Pompidou actually meant "Our argument ended in *mis*understanding."

After the opening bow, the French president rolled up his sleeves. "I am not confident that the combination of a large budgetary deficit and a policy of low interest rates [in America] can strengthen the confidence of the international community . . . nor do I believe that such a course affords . . . for the defense of the new parity for the dollar which you yourself have fixed."

Pompidou scolded Richard Nixon, but in fact blamed Federal Reserve chairman Arthur Burns for dollar weakness. The head of America's central bank had allowed a half-point decline in U.S. interest rates since Nixon hailed the monetary agreement in December as the second coming of Bretton Woods. The decline in rates had encouraged investors to transfer money abroad to earn higher returns, leaving the dollar more than 2 percent lower.[4] The French president had expected Nixon's handpicked chairman of the Federal Reserve to support the president's objective. Burns was doing precisely that . . . but it was not the same as Pompidou's objective.

Nixon had been pressuring the Fed to ease monetary policy in preparation for the 1972 elections.[5] As early as October 10, 1971, the president had told Burns, "I don't want to go out of town fast." A month later, Burns signaled progress in keeping the president in office with a brief telephone call: "I wanted you to know that we are reducing the discount rate today." He called Nixon again on December 10, 1971, to report a second decline in the discount rate. This time Nixon replied, "Good, good, good."

But the president wanted more. The day before Christmas, he told his budget director, George Shultz, "If I have to talk to [Burns] again I'll do it. Next time I'll just bring him in." Shultz, a soft-spoken labor negotiator in real life, confirmed that he knew how to play rough. "I'm sure we'll have to keep after him on it . . . It was good to have that discussion about the procedures for appointment [to the Federal Reserve Board] so that he sees that he doesn't have complete control."[6]

Shultz, the former dean at the University of Chicago business school, minimized any qualms Nixon might have had about the impact of an easier monetary policy on exchange rates. "Why worry about interest rates going down? . . . We want low interest rates. What's the problem there? So, we don't have a return flow of money from Europe? So what?"

Shultz knew that lower U.S. interest rates would reduce value of the dollar internationally and undermine the newly repaired system of fixed exchange rates agreed to at the Smithsonian. Milton Friedman, who supported floating exchange rates as the free-market solution to international finance, would have been pleased with his former colleague.

In his letter to Nixon, Pompidou broadened his concern about the dollar. "You must no doubt be impressed to see the extent to which we Europeans are directly interested in the strength of your currency. This is true because . . . it would be disastrous for the international monetary system and thus for the entire free world should the accords of last December . . . become only a precarious pause along the path to a new crisis."[7] The French hated the exalted status of the greenback, but could not help pleading for the dollar to remain the hub of international finance. Perhaps a split personality is the real French disease.

Volcker knew that Pompidou had identified a serious problem. The absence of an American commitment to sound money would weaken the dollar and torpedo the Smithsonian Agreement. He recalled the meeting he had in London on August 16, 1971, with the finance ministers of America's trading partners to explain the New Economic Policy. Johann Schoellhorn of the West German Ministry of Economics had led off the questioning with whether "there had been any decisions on monetary policy."[8] Volcker had responded, "Since the president was announcing a [wage-price] freeze, he would not want to flaunt this by raising interest rates." But after the recent drop in rates, Volcker had run out of excuses. He expected the Smithsonian accord to collapse sooner rather than later.

It did, but the country that led its downfall surprised him.

Volcker could not fight the president, so he battled the Federal Reserve chairman instead. On Friday, May 12, 1972, in Montreal, Arthur Burns gave the keynote speech before an international monetary conference sponsored by the American Bankers Association. He confronted the assembled financiers from twenty countries with an apocalyptic threat: "It is an urgent necessity to start the rebuilding process [of the international monetary system] quite promptly . . . If cooperative efforts . . . are long postponed . . . we might then find the world divided into restrictive and inward-looking blocs . . . a world of financial manipulation, economic restrictions, and political friction."[9]

Burns presented a Ten-Point Program to avoid disaster, including a call for responsible domestic economic policies, a confirmation of greater exchange rate flexibility in a revised Bretton Woods System, an endorsement of a diminished role for gold as a monetary asset, and a plea for greater international cooperation. None of these was considered confrontational, except perhaps for the last comment on cooperation, which was a swipe at Connally for his aggressive negotiating style. The treasury secretary had been referred to as "Typhoon Connally" during his fall 1971 trip to Japan.[10]

Burns then stuck his nose where it did not belong by suggesting that America restore "some form of dollar convertibility into gold" as part of the total package of reforms. Volcker, who represented the Treasury at the conference in Connally's absence, was not pleased. He believed (at least at this point in his career) that U.S. international financial policy was made at 1500 Pennsylvania Avenue, next door to the White House, in the building fronted by a statue of Alexander Hamilton, the first secretary of the treasury, and not in the marble edifice on Constitution Avenue that housed the Federal Reserve Board. "The Treasury was in charge of America's gold, and we had not yet decided what to do about convertibility, except that it was best to say nothing. Arthur had gotten too far ahead. We could never resume convertibility without running a sustained surplus in our balance of payments. And for that we would need further concessions on exchange rates."[11]

Volcker held a news conference repudiating the authority of the Federal Reserve chairman in terms that would have made John Connally proud. He assured everyone that Dr. Burns "is not speaking for the United States government" and added that Burns's statement "certainly wasn't any kind of a model for reform."[12] The press described the Treasury's view of Burns's Ten Point Program as "not being in quite the same class as the Ten Commandments that Moses brought down from Mount Sinai."[13]

Arthur Burns did not like having his authority challenged, although the reference to Moses probably fed his ego despite the negative context. When asked why he had spoken out on convertibility when the administration had refrained from putting forward any specific proposals, he said, "In the United States we have an independent central bank. This was my decision."[14] Apparently Burns believed in an independent central bank when it came to gold but not interest rates.

On Tuesday, May 16, less than a week after Arthur Burns launched his guided missile at the U.S. Treasury, John Connally dropped a bombshell of his own. He resigned as secretary of the treasury. Connally had been saying that he "was tired after his eighteen months of service in

Washington," but no one had listened.[15] The *New York Times* political columnist James Reston speculated that this was a prelude to the national elections in the fall, designed to "give the Republicans Texas in November . . . on a Nixon-Connally ticket."[16] But that prediction never materialized. Spiro Agnew remained Nixon's running mate, and Connally returned to Texas to practice law.[17] No one in Washington missed him more than Volcker.

"It was a great personal loss," Volcker deadpans. "I had already thrown out all of my argyle socks." And then he adds, "I learned how to get things done from a master tactician. His tough talk produced results because he had the political clout to back it up. And that was because he not only ran the Treasury but was also the chief economic spokesman for the administration. He sat at the head of the table, a position that promotes success . . . if you follow through."[18]

Connally's rough negotiating style had won grudging admiration abroad. Britain's national daily newspaper the *Guardian* called him "a political superstar, the Nixon administration's John Wayne."[19] His record at Treasury also garnered qualified praise from a not-so-friendly domestic press. The *New York Times* editorialized: "History has still to decide whether his tough tactics did more harm or more good. Unquestionably, his threats and pressures did produce a realignment of exchange rates more advantageous . . . than had been anticipated."[20] And the *Washington Post* reported, "European finance ministers with whom he came in contact stood in positive awe of him, and found him a shrewd and tough bargainer."[21]

The president coupled the announcement of Connally's resignation with the appointment of George Shultz to succeed him. Nothing could have been more threatening to Volcker, except perhaps if Milton Friedman himself had set up a classroom inside the Treasury Building. Shultz had tried to convince Nixon to accept floating exchange rates and had denigrated Volcker's earlier support for the status quo. Moreover, Volcker had thrived under Connally's bare-knuckle diplomacy, perhaps because foreign finance ministers were pleased when Volcker showed up to talk instead. He would not enjoy that advantage compared with Shultz, who was as conciliatory in public as Connally was confrontational.

Volcker should have worried, but he had grown since the last changing of the guard at Treasury, when John Connally replaced David Kennedy. Serving as the president's international envoy had boosted his self-confidence. He did not even think about tendering his resignation to Shultz, and the new treasury secretary did not ask for it.

George Shultz and Paul Volcker needed each other. Shultz had a doctorate in economics from MIT but had focused his entire career on the domestic economy and labor negotiations. Moreover, he was the proverbial invisible man to America's trading partners across the Atlantic, despite his influence with the president. The *Washington Post* commentator Hobart Rowen said, "The trickiest problem for Shultz may be in the international area. He is almost unknown to the financial men in Europe and Asia and for a while is sure to rely heavily on the irreplaceable technician's brilliance of Under Secretary Paul A. Volcker."[22]

Volcker, of course, needed Shultz to complete what he had started: establishing a firm foundation for international finance. The Smithsonian Agreement was a fragile structure that could be easily wiped out by another financial hurricane. Volcker knew how vulnerable the system was and began to consider compromise.

The gold market wasted no time registering concern after the May 16, 1972, announcement that Shultz would replace Connally. The free-market price in London jumped to an all-time high of $57.50 an ounce on the news.[23] A U.K. bullion dealer said, "Speculators are moving into gold in some force," and a Montreal coin dealer added "Gold coins are just disappearing from the shelves, everybody wants to hold them to see what happens."[24] The speculators did not have to wait long to cash in.

On Thursday, June 22, 1972, Volcker testified before the House Banking and Currency Committee on the future of the international monetary system, offering a surprisingly flexible vision. He said that "the reform must have a wide agenda, including the related issues of trading rules, investment and development . . . it must be deep and not just a patch-up of Bretton Woods . . . and there is widespread agreement that the future system of exchange rates must provide for greater flexibility than in the past."[25] Volcker set a generous two-year timetable to complete the process.

He also said, in response to a question triggered by weakness in the pound sterling, "I certainly have no expectation that Britain would devalue the pound." He pointed out that "Britain still has a surplus in her balance of payments and nations with a surplus are in no position to devalue their currency."[26] Volcker meant that only countries with a balance-of-payments deficit should be allowed to gain a competitive advantage through devaluation.

A day later, Chancellor of the Exchequer Anthony Barber announced that the United Kingdom would allow its currency to float, rather than adhere to the bands agreed to at the Smithsonian. Britain had effectively devalued the pound sterling by refusing to buy the excess supply of pounds in the market.[27]

"Those SOBs hung me out to dry," Volcker recalled. "I was embarrassed."[28]

Britain's defection displeased Volcker but bothered almost no one else. When H. R. Haldeman, Nixon's chief of staff, asked the president if he wanted to see presidential assistant Peter Flanigan's report on the British devaluation, his immediate response was "I don't care. Nothing we can do about it."[29] When Haldeman added that Flanigan said the devaluation showed the wisdom of our refusal to resume convertibility, Nixon responded, "Good. I think he's right. It's too complicated for me to get into." Finally, Haldeman tried to stoke Nixon's interest with a message from Arthur Burns, saying that the Federal Reserve chairman was concerned about follow-up speculation against the Italian lira. Haldeman's effort clearly backfired when Nixon snapped, "I don't give a shit about the lira."

This infamous remark cannot compete with other Nixon gems, but it seems strange coming from the man who hailed the Smithsonian Agreement on currency values "the most significant monetary agreement in the history of the world." Of course, Nixon had other things on his mind on the morning of June 23, 1972, having just finished a discussion with Haldeman to cover up the break-in at the Democratic headquarters at the Watergate hotel and office complex.[30] He had simply lowered his diplomatic guard and said what most Americans would have said.

The British float upended Volcker's two-year timetable for reform. Six months earlier, in January 1972, he had assigned a review of long-range planning to George Willis, a career civil servant who had just retired but refused to leave. Willis had been at the Treasury longer than anyone could remember, most recently serving as the director of the Office of International Affairs, and then continuing as a consultant. He firmly denied rumors that he had worked on the charter for the Bank of the United States with Alexander Hamilton, but he only smiled when the topic of Bretton Woods came up. Willis had joined Treasury in 1941, the same year that Harry Dexter White, America's technical expert at the New Hampshire conference, wrote the first draft of the U.S. proposals.[31]

Volcker asked Willis to survey all the recently proposed reforms and to report back. He received little encouragement from Willis's memorandum. The problem for reform was to maintain stability by retaining central values for exchange rates, while forcing countries with balance-of-payments surpluses, such as Germany and Japan, to reduce their surpluses while allowing those with deficits, such as the United States, to reduce them. Willis told Volcker, "The United States can expect to encounter resistance from all other countries when it tries to reduce its deficit. No country wants us to do this."[32]

Whenever Volcker promoted the wisdom of a specific scheme with Willis, he received the answer "It just won't work."[33] Sometimes Willis varied the refrain by saying, "That won't work, either." After one lengthy exchange, Volcker exhaled, turned his palms upward, as though checking for rain, and said, "Okay, George, what *will* work?"

Willis thought for a while and said, "Nothin'." And for emphasis: "Absolutely nothin' will work."

Willis was right, of course, but Volcker was not ready to admit defeat.

George Shultz ended the foot-dragging on monetary reform after the British withdrawal from the Smithsonian Agreement. The new treasury secretary planned to make his debut on the world stage at the fall 1972 meetings of the International Monetary Fund and wanted to put forth an American proposal.

Shultz asked Volcker, "Where do we stand on planning?"[34]

"We're not that far along," Volcker replied.

"Well, I'd like to have something for the IMF meetings."

"Are there any guidelines?"

"Yes, something that has a chance to work. A consensus."

Shultz's directive surprised Volcker. "I saw another side of the man I had considered a potential adversary. Now that he was in charge of international monetary reform, his instincts as a labor negotiator took over. He wanted to build a consensus on a practical proposal—an approach that I believed in."[35]

Shultz and Volcker shared a commitment to pragmatism, a devotion to implementing a workable solution that advanced a cause. Their relationship benefited from another common bond: Princeton basketball. Shultz had played for the Tigers before graduating in 1942, a few years before Volcker arrived at Nassau Hall. Shultz refuses to confirm or deny that he has a Tiger tattooed on his gluteus maximus.[36]

Volcker spent the summer of 1972 mixing fixed and floating exchange rate ingredients to get the right proportions. The outcome, designated Plan X (perhaps to preserve some mystery), allowed currencies to bend but not break in response to forces of supply and demand.[37] The proposal specified "central values" for exchange rates, resembling the par values of Bretton Woods but renamed to reflect increased bands of fluctuation around those values. The scheme required countries with persistent balance-of-payments surpluses to raise the central values of their currencies, and countries with deficits to lower their central values. Limited convertibility of accumulated reserves into gold would be permitted to promote compliance with the rules. For example, surplus countries such as Germany and Japan would be allowed to convert dollars into gold if they raised the value of the mark and yen to make their exports less attractive.

Volcker was quite proud of the design and sent it for comments and suggestions to select members of the Volcker Group. Robert Solomon, a senior staffer at the Fed and an expert in international trade, pointed out that it was a great idea—so great, in fact, that John Maynard Keynes had proposed almost the same thing thirty years earlier, while planning for the Bretton Woods conference.[38] Volcker did not mind retracing the steps of the great British economist but worried how a monetarist sympathizer such as George Shultz would react to a Keynesian initiative.

On Tuesday, September 26, 1972, George Shultz began his address to a standing-room-only audience at the International Monetary Fund conference with a message straight from the University of Chicago's free-market playbook. "We can now seek a firm consensus for new monetary arrangements that will serve us all in the decades ahead . . . Our mutual interest is encouraging freer trade in goods and services and the flow of capital to the places where it can contribute most to economic growth."[39] But when it came to outlining the details, Shultz laid out Volcker's Plan X, emphasizing that "a workable international agreement will . . . take as a point of departure that most countries will want to operate within the framework of specified exchange rates."[40]

Volcker had thought that Shultz would adopt Milton Friedman's scheme for freely floating exchange rates. The treasury secretary had reviewed Volcker's draft with Friedman a few days before his talk.[41] Instead, Shultz put his Chicago colleague's proposal on the back burner, knowing that the finance ministers of the world were not ready for truly radical reform. The treasury secretary was not a monetarist ideologue like his former colleague. He was a consensus builder who had learned that patience paid dividends. Besides, he did not have to wait long to get what he truly wanted.

Willy Brandt, chancellor of West Germany, concerned over renewed speculation against the dollar in favor of the German mark, sent a classified cable to Richard Nixon on Friday, February 9, 1973.[42] "If we do not succeed in stabilizing the present situation on exchange markets by joint and rapid action, the future development would lead to dangerous political consequences. The cohesion of the Free World would be endangered economically, psychologically, and finally, also politically, at a moment when . . . it is of utmost importance to negotiate on the basis of unity of the Western countries."[43]

Brandt makes it sound as though controlling foreign exchange ranked alongside nuclear nonproliferation in the survival kit of a democratic world. Perhaps he exaggerated, but the devaluation wars in Europe during the 1930s still haunted politicians. And the German chancellor knew firsthand about international crises, having been the mayor of West Berlin in 1961, when the Soviet Union sanctioned the construction of the wall separating East Berlin from West. Brandt had also hosted JFK's visit to the divided city on June 26, 1963, when Kennedy gave his "Ich bin ein Berliner" speech, in defiance of the Communist regime. Now he wanted something narrower, more specific, but apparently worthy of his personal attention. "I would appreciate if the American monetary authorities would, in the future, do everything in their power to support the [dollar-mark] exchange rate."[44]

Nixon responded to Brandt within a day—after all, this was about the German mark and not the Italian lira—but he sidestepped the technical details and emphasized a broad diplomatic effort he had already initiated. "I appreciate your constructive message on international monetary developments . . . I had come to the same conclusion as you on the importance of our authorized representatives working together immediately to find solutions. It was for this reason that I dispatched Paul Volcker on his trip to Tokyo and Europe on Wednesday [February 7]. He is fully cognizant of my thinking on these matters."[45]

Nixon had been paying attention to foreign exchange, which at the time competed with the Watergate scandal for front-page news.[46] Speculators were shifting funds out of dollars and into the mark and the yen because Americans continued to spend too many greenbacks abroad. The president had sent Volcker to Japan after cabling Prime Minister Kakuei Tanaka, "Because the continued Japanese–United States [trade] imbalance is so central to the problem [of disturbances in the currency markets] . . . I have asked Mr. Paul Volcker, Under secretary of the U.S. Treasury for Monetary Affairs, to fly to Tokyo to relate the reasons for our conclusion that action must be taken immediately in the exchange rate field if we are to remain in command of the situation."[47]

Volcker had arrived in Tokyo on Thursday evening, February 8, the first leg of his secret globe-trotting mission to stabilize world finance— again. He went directly to the home of Finance Minister Kiichi Aichi, a venue with less press surveillance than the ministry office, and outlined a U.S. proposal to make American products more competitive. Volcker suggested a 10 percent devaluation of the U.S. dollar against gold and a 10 percent upward valuation of the yen, for a combined 20 percent appreciation of the Japanese yen versus the dollar.

Aichi recoiled at the size of the proposed revaluation, which would exceed the Smithsonian adjustment. "That is a shock."[48]

Volcker asked, "Is that a big shock or a little shock?"

"It is a big shock . . . a Volcker shock . . . big like Mr. Volcker."

Paul smiled. "There would be no purpose talking to the Europeans if it were anything less."

Aichi suggested floating the yen, allowing the exchange rate to move freely with supply and demand without interference from the Bank of Tokyo, but the finance minister could not commit to a formal revaluation until he saw what Germany was prepared to do. "Fixing a new rate would be a highly political decision."

Volcker had hoped for more but suspected that temporarily floating the yen would lead to a substantial appreciation versus the dollar. Paul thought he had enough leeway to continue his journey, and boarded a military transport taking him to Europe. The plane was a converted Boeing KC-135 tanker, outfitted with full accommodations for the overnight journey.

After Volcker was airborne, he received a final communiqué from Aichi through Roger Ingersoll, the U.S. ambassador to Japan. Ingersoll telephoned Jack Bennett, Volcker's deputy at the Treasury, with the following message: "The Japanese finance minister asked me to express his concern about the publicity of 'our travelling friend's' visit to Tokyo, and of his strong hope that no word would leak out of his visit, especially since the finance minister was questioned about whether the United States had pressured Japan into closing the foreign exchange market . . . If there were any publicity the finance minister would say it was a visit by 'the travelling friend' to his very old friend, the Japanese finance minister, on his way to Europe."[49]

Aichi's amateur cryptography, like a schoolboy slipping a concealed note to a classmate, amused Volcker. He did not mind the label "travelling friend" as an alias, but doubted it would jump-start a second career as a spy. The *New York Times* disparaged the weak undercover effort when Volcker arrived in West Germany. "At six feet seven inches and 240 pounds, Paul Adolph Volcker, the Under Secretary of the Treasury for Monetary Affairs, has certain obvious problems as a secret agent in foreign capitals."[50] The *Times* headline encouraged Volcker not to give up his day job as a monetary diplomat. "Mr. Volcker has come to be thought of as the Henry Kissinger of monetary diplomacy—the intellectual master of arcane international affairs . . . who often speaks abroad for the United States government . . . The Nixon Administration confirmed his globe girdling search for means of resolving the new monetary crisis."[51]

Volcker made Bonn the first stop of his European tour, to consult with Helmut Schmidt, the German finance minister. Schmidt, who would soon succeed Willy Brandt as chancellor, was staunchly pro-American and spoke flawless English. He surprised Volcker with an opening harangue: "The United States does not understand how much damage the last ten days has done to European-American relations . . . It seems as though the U.S welcomed the monetary crisis . . . You believe this is a good development."[52]

"I can assure you that's not the case," Volcker said, realizing that he could not have given that response prior to August 15, 1971. Back then, he had urged John Connally to exploit the foreign exchange crisis to justify suspending gold convertibility. "My trip here is in part a response to Chancellor Brandt's request to the President. The major problem is Japan, but Europe too—"

Schmidt interrupted, as though he was cross-examining a hostile witness. "How great is your basic deficit with Europe?"

"Four billion dollars with Japan and a half billion with Europe, but Japan has been shuffling out of the dollars it receives from us and they wind up in the Bundesbank. It is a multilateral problem."

"The problem is a dollar problem . . . And do not make the mistake of underestimating the political repercussions."

"I came to Bonn to work things out."

"We should have sat together a week ago . . . It is late."

"The time is ripe for resolving the crisis."

Finally, Schmidt softened. "Okay, let us do it this weekend."

Volcker paused before proceeding with a concrete proposal toward floating exchange rates. He suspected that unless they acted now, it would take years of international negotiations to implement. And he had already accepted the compromise. "One possibility would be a common European float against the dollar, and a separate float of the yen versus both—"

Schmidt interjected, "This would not be the worst solution, but it isn't feasible . . . time is very short."

Volcker knew that only another upheaval could precipitate the change. "The difficulty is that no one is ever prepared to move except in a crisis."

At a late night news conference on Monday, February 12, 1973, the day Volcker returned from the weekend of negotiations that concluded his global tour, Treasury Secretary George Shultz announced a 10 percent devaluation of the U.S. dollar against gold. Shultz said that the increase in the official gold price from $38.00 an ounce to $42.22 an ounce was "a technical change" with "no practical significance," considering that this official price differed so much from the free-market price, now quoted at $68.95.[53] Shultz had a point, but this did not prevent the American devaluation from making front-page headlines in the *New York Times* and the *Washington Post*. Even the *Times* of London, the standard-bearer of British understatement, could not resist the temptation.[54]

Newspapers need provocative headlines to entice readers, but they were right to feature the U.S. devaluation. It was the second time in fourteen months that the dollar had been devalued after remaining stable at thirty-five dollars since 1934. The devaluation advertised America's culpability in the crisis and served to lubricate the engine of international financial negotiations.

Volcker had spent the previous four days traveling thirty-one thousand miles from Washington to Tokyo (for his friendly chat with Aichi), to Bonn (for Schmidt's lecture), to London (for a conference with Chancellor of the Exchequer Anthony Barber), to Paris (where Valéry Giscard d'Estaing played host), to Rome's Leonardo da Vinci airport (Finance Minister Giovanni Malagodi was waiting for him), back to Paris (with Malagodi in tow), and finally home (to get a clean shirt and a cheap cigar).[55] Along the way, he engineered a depreciation of the dollar against the mark and the yen. A day after the announcement of the devaluation against gold, the dollar purchased only 2.96 marks and 270.0 yen compared with 3.15 marks and 308.0 yen prior to the talks.[56]

Volcker succeeded by enabling foreign politicians to use the devaluation against gold as cover for dollar depreciation. Japanese prime minister Kakuei Tanaka denied any involvement. "We should appreciate that the United States . . . felt its responsibility deeply and devalued the dollar." Tanaka avoided saying that the Bank of Japan would allow the yen to float up in value in the foreign exchange market. German finance minister Helmut Schmidt described the American devaluation as "vindicating" Bonn's policies because the mark would remain stable relative to its European trading partners.[57] The Italians disapproved of the entire process because Britain, Germany, and France had negotiated as an exclusive clique with the United States, rather than working through the European Common Market. The daily *Il Tempo* in Rome carried a front-page editorial with the headline "The Snubbed Lira."[58] The Italians were right (even more than they knew at the time).

Dollar depreciation would defuse the crisis by making U.S. exports more competitive on world markets, with the resulting incentive to "buy American" reducing the glut of greenbacks abroad. Perhaps even the U.S. Treasury would switch allegiance from Sony to Motorola. Unfortunately, these shifts in consumption would take time, and no one knew this better than Volcker.

At a February 16, 1973, news conference, Volcker warned that the "full effects" of the devaluation would take more than two years.[59] "If there is anything we've learned it's that exchange rate changes . . . can only work their way through the system and restore the flows in the balance of trade over a period of time . . . And that period of time seems terribly long as you wait for it to happen." More ominously, he added, "An exchange rate action almost inevitably has a perverse impact in the short run. It is going to make imports more costly in particular, and the trading pattern in the short run is set . . . You may go backwards before you go forwards."[60]

The press memorialized Volcker's globe-trotting by labeling the new structure of exchange rates the "Volcker Agreement."[61] The arrangement lasted less than three weeks, making Volcker wish they had ignored his exploits. By March 1, 1973, gold had jumped by more than 25 percent, to $86.00 per ounce, and the dollar had declined 5 percent against the mark, to 2.82 marks per dollar. The frenzied speculation confirmed Volcker's suspicion: a giant step backward.

The glut of dollars for sale forced central banks in Europe and Japan to suspend their dollar purchases to avoid domestic inflationary pressures, referred to as "the dollar peril" by a European banker.[62] The official closing of foreign exchange markets began on Friday, March 2, but this did not eliminate private transactions at commercial banks and at airport kiosks. It simply meant that currency values would be allowed to float with supply and demand, unfettered by central bank intervention.[63]

Volcker knew it was just the beginning.

French finance minister Valéry Giscard d'Estaing invited an American delegation, consisting of Treasury Secretary George Shultz, Federal Reserve chairman Arthur Burns, and Volcker, to Paris for an emergency conference on Friday, March 9, 1973, with representatives of the countries belonging to the European Common Market—Belgium, Denmark, France, Germany, Ireland, Italy, Luxembourg, Netherlands, and the United Kingdom.[64] Volcker suspected a formal proposal by the Europeans for a joint float of their currencies versus the dollar, along the lines he had suggested to German finance minister Helmut Schmidt in February. With Britain floating since June 1972 and Japan floating since the February devaluation, a European float would represent a final break with fixed exchange rates.

The Friday morning meeting on March 9, 1973, amused Volcker. The Europeans had not seen George Shultz up close before and they knew relatively little about his views. Shultz did not help them. He listened more than he talked, true to his training as a labor negotiator.[65] Right before the lunch break, Helmut Schmidt broached the possibility of a joint European float. "How would the United States respond?" he asked, as though he were handling a vial of nitroglycerin. Shultz answered even more delicately: "It is something we would consider sympathetically."[66]

Volcker felt as though he were watching a scene from *Masterpiece Theatre*. Shultz had masked his support for floating exchange rates during his tenure as treasury secretary, and now, like a professional athlete on the brink of victory, he remained under perfect control. Volcker recognized the contrast with a John Connally performance and knew that each method had its place. As much as he admired his former mentor, however, his instincts placed him squarely in the Shultz School of the Performing Arts.

During the lunch break, Arthur Burns, who feared floating rates with a passion, cornered Shultz and Volcker. He warned them that abandoning fixed exchange rates risked currency wars among nations, accompanied by political suspicion and the loss of domestic discipline. And he emphasized that "the exchange rates that emerge in a free market [are not] an infallible indication of what is the fundamental equilibrium."[67]

Volcker had heard these arguments before—and had made some of them himself, while defending the Bretton Woods System. He, too, believed in the virtues of fixed exchange rates, but his pragmatism had taught him that time had expired on America's options. Only a permanent change in economic fundamentals could save the system he had worked so hard to sustain. And only Arthur Burns could do it. Volcker turned to the Federal Reserve chairman and said, "Arthur, if you want a par value [fixed exchange rate] system you had better go home right away and tighten money."[68]

Burns sighed. "I would even do that."

Volcker suspected that Burns would not deliver. A week later he knew it. At a press conference the following Friday, March 16, 1973, Shultz, flanked by Burns and Volcker, stood before a roomful of reporters at the American embassy in Paris to answer questions about the European initiative that had just been announced.[69] Germany, France, Belgium, the Netherlands, Luxembourg, and Denmark had agreed to jointly float their currencies versus the dollar, like a miniature precursor to the euro. Britain, Ireland, and Italy had decided to sink or swim on their own.

A reporter asked Shultz, "Mr. Secretary, what does this all mean for American monetary policy?"[70] It was a reasonable question that Shultz viewed as radioactive, knowing how sensitive Burns was (at least publicly) about Federal Reserve independence. He turned the microphone over to the Fed chairman, who delivered a clever response in his most authoritarian voice: "American monetary policy is not made in Paris; it is made in Washington."[71]

Burns's answer made good press, but disappointed Volcker, more than anyone knew. He felt his shoulders sag while the consequences sank into his brain. "We were at a turning point in American economic history. Inflation was well under way in the United States, and the international monetary system was about to become less stable. Burns's reluctance to factor international considerations into monetary policy was misplaced. We were ignoring our responsibility as custodian of the international medium of exchange, a responsibility that coincided with our obligation domestically to control money and credit. I was convinced that pursuing a monetary policy imprinted with the label 'Made in Washington' was a mistake."[72]

Volcker resigned as undersecretary of the treasury for monetary affairs on Monday, April 8, 1974, three weeks after George Shultz announced his resignation. Richard Nixon had chosen Deputy Treasury Secretary William Simon, a former partner at brokerage firm Salomon Brothers, to succeed Shultz. Simon's appointment had been delayed by a political power struggle, and Volcker had waited while he thought there was an outside chance he might be named secretary.[73]

Others in the administration had felt the same way. Donald Rumsfeld, at the time the U.S. ambassador to NATO and a future secretary of defense under Gerald Ford and under George W. Bush, sent a note to Volcker: "Given your unique experience, many years of service and your well known competence and skill, there was a good possibility that you would succeed George Shultz."[74]

Volcker knew that foreign finance ministers would have supported his promotion by acclamation. He recalled with pride an incident during a Group of Ten meeting, chaired by French finance minister Valéry Giscard d'Estaing, who would become president of France in May 1974.[75] Giscard d'Estaing, a favorite Volcker sparring partner during Franco-American negotiations, had announced a meeting of principals only, meaning that only finance ministers and central bankers themselves—no deputies—could participate. George Shultz turned to Giscard d'Estaing and asked, "How about Paul?" Giscard d'Estaing looked surprised and then said, "Of course, we never considered Paul a deputy."[76] A headline in the *International Herald Tribune* summed up Volcker's status abroad: "Volcker No. 4 at Treasury, No. 1 in European Capitals."[77]

Volcker should have known that Richard Nixon would never appoint him secretary of the treasury. Despite his public status as the president's monetary diplomat, he was not part of the inner circle. Nixon had told

Prime Minister Tanaka of Japan and Chancellor Willy Brandt of West Germany in February 1973 that he had sent Volcker as his personal emissary. But during Volcker's news conference after his thirty-one-thousand-mile global trek, a reporter asked how often he had spoken with the president during his trip. Volcker did not hesitate to take himself down a peg by answering, "Not at all. I spoke with Secretary Shultz and he spoke with the President."[78]

Nixon enjoyed surprises. He had stunned the establishment by appointing John Connally, a prominent Texas Democrat, as treasury secretary. And Connally had tutored Volcker, a conservative Democrat, in the art of Washington politics. But Volcker could never make a point without qualification, and Nixon could never trust him to toe the party line. Volcker accepted the consequences. He did not know any other way.

PART III

Fighting Inflation, 1979–1987

CHAPTER 7

Prelude

Arthur Burns exploited Paul Volcker's fixation with public service to persuade him to accept, as of August 1975, the presidency of the Federal Reserve Bank of New York, the second most important position in America's central bank. Burns occupied the most powerful slot, chairman of the Board of Governors of the Federal Reserve System, having been reappointed to a second four-year term by Richard Nixon in January 1974.

As Fed chairman, Burns was the final authority on appointments within the system and was its chief spokesperson. The New York Fed is the most important of the twelve regional Federal Reserve banks that serve as branches of the central bank. During the 1920s, Benjamin Strong, president (then called governor) of the Federal Reserve Bank of New York, dominated the system. Even more recently, during the 1950s, the president of the New York bank had challenged the authority of the Washington-based chairman. Volcker occupied a front-row seat in that battle.

To promote an independent central bank, congressional legislation mixed public and private authority in designing the Federal Reserve System, with built-in checks and balances to prevent any one person, including (especially) a sitting president, from gaining undue influence.[1] There are seven members of the Board of Governors, who are appointed to fourteen-year terms by the president of the United States, with the advice and consent of the Senate. The fourteen-year terms are staggered so that, absent resignations or deaths, the president gets to appoint only two new members. The president designates the chairman from among these seven members of the board, but the chairman's term of office does not coincide with the president's. Although each member of the board has the same vote in all deliberations, the chairman dominates by virtue of his role as the central bank's representative before Congress, with the president, and at international meetings.

There are twelve regional Federal Reserve banks dispersed geographically throughout the country, including the Federal Reserve Bank of New York, of San Francisco, of Philadelphia, and of Atlanta. These banks are technically owned by commercial banks, such as JPMorgan Chase and Bank of America, but they are supervised closely by the Board of Governors in Washington and amount to little more than branches of the central bank. The president of each Federal Reserve bank is selected from a slate of candidates approved by Washington.

The key policymaking arm of the system is the Federal Open Market Committee, often referred to as the FOMC. All seven members of the Board of Governors serve on the FOMC, along with five of the regional bank presidents, who rotate membership—except for the president of the Federal Reserve Bank of New York, who is a permanent member.

The special status of the New York bank stems from its location and from its role in executing the purchase and sale of securities for the entire system, called open market operations, the Fed's main weapon of monetary control. The chairman of the Board of Governors is the chairman of the FOMC, and the president of the New York bank is the vice-chairman. Meetings of the FOMC are held eight times a year and end in a formal vote (jacket and tie required) on a directive to chart the course of monetary policy until the next meeting, with concurrences and dissents recorded for posterity.

Volcker wonders to this day why Arthur Burns wanted him at the New York Fed. "I respected Arthur, especially his expertise in business cycle analysis, but we had battled throughout my years at Treasury."[2] Perhaps Burns wanted to neutralize an adversary by making him an in-house critic.[3] Volcker knew that antagonism between the board and New York defined earlier relationships. "I watched New York president Allan Sproul challenge the authority of Chairman William McChesney Martin in the early 1950s over who controlled open market operations. I was rooting for Sproul, of course, since I was working in New York."[4]

Allan Sproul lost the argument and resigned as president of the Federal Reserve Bank of New York in 1956, but the antagonism continued to tug beneath the surface, like an ocean undertow.[5] It erupted in 1970, when Burns became chairman of the Board of Governors. Alfred Hayes, who had replaced Sproul as president of the New York Fed, greeted Burns with a dissent in the formal vote at Burns's first meeting of the FOMC on February 10, 1970, wanting a tighter monetary policy to fight inflation.[6] Philip Coldwell, president of the Federal Reserve Bank of Dallas, also dissented, for the same reason, and recalled, "For the next five meetings Al Hayes and I would be brought into Arthur's office [for] . . . a lecture from Arthur on the importance of consensus."[7]

The reprimand did not end Hayes's dissents. The *New York Times* headlined the ongoing battle in 1972 with "Rift in Federal Reserve: Board Versus the Bank Here," and compared the confrontation with Sproul's earlier insurrection.[8] Burns had retaliated in many small ways, including questioning the New York bank's travel budget, and then began a very public search for a successor to Hayes more than a year before Hayes's scheduled retirement in August 1975.[9]

Headhunters had been chasing Volcker well before he left the Treasury, with offers that would have guaranteed a lifetime supply of Cuban cigars. A letter from recruiter Russell Reynolds in November 1973 proposed that Volcker consider a position at a leading investment banking firm with compensation in the low seven figures.[10] A million-dollar investment banking salary package may sound pedestrian by twenty-first-century standards, but back then, when George Steinbrenner had just bought the New York Yankees for $10 million (yes, the entire team), and the highest-paid major leaguer was Cy Young Award–winner Jim "Catfish" Hunter, earning $750,000 a year, a million dollars was real money.[11] "It certainly got my attention,"[12] Volcker recalls.

A story in the *New York Times* heralded the seduction of Paul

Volcker, and the proverbial funeral of Alfred Hayes, on the day after the Treasury announced Volcker's resignation. "A Treasury spokesman said that Mr. Volcker had reached no decision yet on his future plans . . . [but] there were rumors . . . that [he] . . . might be in line for the presidency of the Federal Reserve Bank of New York. Mr. Volcker spent four years at the bank in the nineteen-fifties."[13]

Volcker was also pursued by his former bosses.[14] Henry "Joe" Fowler, the treasury secretary who had told President Lyndon Johnson not to consider replacing the then Fed chairman William McChesney Martin with the independent-minded Volcker, wanted Paul to join him as a partner at Goldman Sachs, the investment banking money-making machine. And Robert Roosa offered a partnership with the old-line Brown Brothers Harriman, including the promise of a coveted private office off the partner's room like his own.

But Burns knew how to lure Volcker. He waited until after Paul actually left the Treasury in June 1974 before inviting him to his apartment for a friendly dinner.[15] Burns could not help lecturing Volcker while puffing on his professorial pipe.[16] "I need you with me on the FOMC."

"I'm flattered, Arthur, but I have to make some money. Barbara has just been diagnosed with rheumatoid arthritis, and Jimmy, well, who knows what he will be able to do in the future."

"We will pay you more than a living wage. The New York president earns more than twice my salary."[17]

"I understand, but—"

"Hayes is making ninety-five thousand and you know how I feel about him. I'll get them to pay you that to start."

"Look, Arthur, I've been working for the government for more than five years. I'm tired, and it's time for a change."

Burns shook his head in dismissal. He had a rectangular face topped with distinguished-looking white hair (almost too much hair for a central banker). He spoke very slowly. "You belong in public service, Paul, nowhere else."

Volcker delayed his response to Burns for two weeks, until after he had left with friends on a salmon fishing trip in Canada. "My father would have let that kind of decision sit even longer." He stopped at a gas station with the very last public telephone along the route, according to their guide. He squeezed his frame into the wooden phone booth and called Burns at the Federal Reserve Board, reversing the charges, of course.

"I'll do it," he said without preamble.

"Good. I knew you would . . . Enjoy your vacation."

In 1974 the Gallup organization, a private company which conducts surveys to track public opinion, reported that Americans considered inflation their biggest concern. Eighty-one percent of those polled cited the high cost of living as the nation's paramount problem, far exceeding the next-highest category, lack of trust in government, mentioned by 15 percent.[18] Watergate had uncovered deception in the White House, forcing the president of the United States to resign, but people still cared more about rising prices cheating their pocketbook.

Some respondents to the Gallup Poll described how inflation had changed their lifestyles. Barbara Reese, a thirty-year-old housewife who had just moved to Charlottesville, Virginia, said that the $3,000 salary increase her husband received the previous fall had been swallowed up by inflation. She began working at a store at night as a way of meeting some local people, but says, "Now it's a necessity. We need the money for groceries."[19] Susan Ostrander from Chicago, a travel consultant married to an investment banker, said that she had used her salary for personal expenditures, but "now it goes into the checking account, not the savings account." And Tony Zengel, a New York artist, said, "No matter how fast I paint I just can't make enough money . . . I've been living without a telephone. It's very depressing . . . I can't afford to be a full-time artist anymore."

The public's resentment made sense, considering that consumer prices surged by 12 percent during 1974.[20] The unprecedented jump reflected, in part, the earlier quadrupling of oil prices by OPEC, the Organization of the Petroleum Exporting Countries.[21] More troublesome was an emerging trend that had bubbled to the surface. The double-digit rate of price increase in 1974 topped off a ten-year period, beginning in 1965, when the average rate of inflation exceeded 5 percent per year. By way of contrast, the annual rate of inflation over the previous ten years had been less than 2 percent.[22] What is now called the Great Inflation was well under way.[23]

The simplest explanation of inflation—too much money chasing too few goods—tells the truth in the long run. Without cash, people cannot spend, and without spending, prices cannot increase. The money supply in the United States grew twice as fast in the decade after 1965 compared with the decade before, corresponding to the jump in inflation.[24] And the turning point came when President Johnson signed a bill lifting the gold cover against bank reserves in March 1965, severing the connection between money and gold.[25] The responsibility for anchoring the domestic money supply shifted to the discretion of the Federal Reserve System. Thus far the central bank had failed the test.

But there was some hope. Ten years after dropping gold from the monetary police force, Congress made amends by voting to end the forty-year-old ban on investing in the precious metal by U.S. citizens.[26] After December 31, 1974, Americans could protect themselves against monetary irresponsibility by buying gold, just like their French cousins. Banks and retail establishments throughout the United States prepared in advance to meet investor demands.

The Sterling National Bank and Trust Company in New York and the First AmTenn Corporation, with bank branches in Tennessee, Alabama, and southern Kentucky, readied gold bars in sizes ranging from one ounce to forty ounces.[27] Alexander's, Inc., a department store with twelve branches, and the Finlay jewelry outlets, in more than one hundred retail stores, prepared to take orders. They promised to deliver bars in "skintight plastic wrappings . . . so that a gold bar or wafer could not be shaved or tampered with before delivery."[28] The free-market price of gold responded to the anticipated demand by reaching a peak of $197.50 on December 30, 1974, an increase of 75 percent during the year.[29]

It was the beginning of a speculative roller coaster.

Volcker had been responsible for monitoring the price of gold and managing America's stock of the precious metal during his tenure as undersecretary of the treasury for monetary affairs from 1969 through 1974. When he took office at the Federal Reserve Bank of New York on August 1, 1975, he became a permanent member of the FOMC, joining the group responsible for managing the supply of credit and the level of interest rates in the United States. The *New York Times* labeled him a

"Monetary Pragmatist," citing his role as midwife in the birth of floating exchange rates despite his earlier support of Bretton Woods.[30] The *Times* added that Volcker was "philosophically sympathetic with Dr. Burns, which means . . . that he leans toward tight money policies and high interest rates to retard inflation."[31]

Arthur Burns had not yet lost his reputation as an inflation hawk. He had testified before Congress that the Federal Reserve is "determined to follow a course of monetary policy that will permit only moderate growth in money and credit . . . [which] should make it possible for the fires of inflation to burn themselves out."[32] He also instructed members of the FOMC behind closed doors of the Fed's boardroom that "No other branch of government . . . has anything approaching an articulate policy for bringing down the rate of inflation."[33] He maintained that "the Federal Reserve System had the power to abort the inflation . . . [by restricting] the money supply."[34]

And yet Burns is justly criticized for failing to control prices, which increased at 6½ percent per annum during his eight years as Fed chairman, an unprecedented inflation rate for peacetime.[35] Ticket prices to major-league baseball games, for example, increased by an average of 50 percent between 1970 and 1978.[36] In a 1979 lecture, Burns admitted that under his leadership the central bank had failed "to maintain its restrictive stance . . . long enough to end inflation."[37] He said that restoring price stability would frustrate "the will of Congress" by creating unacceptable levels of unemployment.[38]

Volcker wasted little time asserting his independence after occupying the wood-paneled presidential suite on the tenth floor of the Federal Reserve Bank of New York. A sick-looking potted plant stood on the floor near the corner entrance to his office, greeting him each morning like an aging butler. After a few days, he told his secretary, "Get rid of that thing."[39] A week later it was still there, so he said, "Does that plant have a lifetime retainer?" She said, "Sort of. They had an officers' meeting and concluded that if they removed yours they would have to take away all of the other plants . . . They're still discussing what to do about it."

Volcker recalls, "That is why I left for Chase in 1957."

He had more success making his mark in Washington. In November 1975, after just three months on the job, he dissented from Burns's position at the FOMC, saying that he felt "strongly that the right approach to policy today [is] to hold interest rates fairly steady. The system had [eased substantially] in recent weeks to stimulate growth in monetary aggregates and [I do] not like the idea of encouraging further declines that might have to be reversed in the . . . near future."[40] Eight months later, in July 1976, he did it again. "I wouldn't like . . . the federal funds rate going down to 4.75 percent and I wouldn't want to see [Burns's] range specified unless things really went haywire . . . the market is going to interpret it as a strong signal and I don't think this is the time for strong signals."[41]

Burns said nothing to Volcker on either occasion, having anticipated his behavior. A reporter had written that Burns claimed he would not have supported Volcker's appointment if he had been "seeking rubber stamps."[42]

Volcker had a reputation to uphold, but neither dissent measured up to New York standards. He had proposed somewhat higher interest rates within a narrow target range, almost like Clarence Darrow making a procedural objection in the courtroom. Volcker recalls: "They were modest and restrained attempts at tightening. I just wanted to show Arthur, and perhaps everyone else on the committee, that I would back up my tough talk on inflation with action."[43]

There was, in fact, little to dissent about at the time. High interest rates and tight credit in 1974, before Volcker had arrived at the Fed, had triggered a sharp recession. As a result, inflation declined from 12 percent in 1974 to 5 percent in 1976.[44] Investors celebrated by punishing the gold speculators for their lack of faith in America. The price of the precious metal dropped from the peak of $197.50 an ounce on December 30, 1974, to $103.05 on August 31, 1976, a decline of nearly 50 percent in less than two years.[45]

Citibank's *Economic Newsletter* attributed the price rout to a "softening of private demand for gold coins and gold bars by individuals for hoarding or investment."[46] Just when Congress had decided to allow American citizens to hold gold, people said, "Thanks, but never mind." The drop in demand for gold reflected more than just the measured progress on inflation; it meant that inflationary expectations had stabilized as well.[47] Homestake Mining Company, listed on the New York

Stock Exchange, confirmed the new outlook by suspending its gold mining operation in Western Australia.[48]

It did not last.

The challenger, Jimmy Carter, beat the incumbent, Gerald Ford, in the presidential election of November 2, 1976, for many reasons, but high unemployment and high inflation head the list.[49] The country had gone through a sharp recession the previous year and had almost nothing to show for it, except for WIN buttons—red letters on a white background—commemorating the "Whip Inflation Now" campaign launched by President Ford during 1974, after Richard Nixon had resigned the presidency.

Inflation was 5 percent during the Bicentennial election year, less than half its 1974 level, but almost the same as was considered embarrassing in 1969.[50] And the unemployment rate averaged almost 8 percent in 1976, more than in any year since World War II, except for 1975.[51] Stagflation—the lethal combination of high unemployment and high inflation—enveloped the American heartland in a giant pincer movement and squeezed the Republicans from office.

The persistence of inflation, despite the unemployment, reflected a change in people's behavior. Tessie Rogers, a divorced mother of two in Atlanta, said, "I just finished buying a house and the biggest reason I did it was inflation. I was afraid that if I didn't do it now, tomorrow might be too late."[52] Judy Frank of Des Moines, the wife of a high school teacher, went back to work part-time and used her income to keep the family in extras, "a new carpet and a color television." Arthur England, chief judge of the Florida Supreme Court, said he had "borrowed to the hilt" on his insurance policies. And Kathy Neuhas, whose husband served on the East Hampton police force, confessed they had borrowed money to take their two girls to an amusement park in New Jersey. "We just felt we had to." She sounded less certain when adding, "Something's got to give. The whole bottom's going to fall out soon and I'm afraid it'll fall on us."

An inflationary virus had wormed its way into people's brains and altered their consciousness.[53] The resulting "buy now, pay later" philosophy for people with jobs overwhelmed the spending restraint of the unemployed, resulting in higher prices. Mainstream economists had to rework their thinking to take account of Milton Friedman's warning that gains in employment would disappear once inflationary expectations caught up with reality. That time had arrived in America.

Volcker understood the power of expectations better than most, having watched traders trying to anticipate future bond prices during his earlier stint on the New York Fed's trading desk. At his very first FOMC meeting on August 19, 1975, he had warned the optimists seated around the table not to be encouraged by the projections "for reduced inflation emanating from some econometric models."[54] He pointed out that these mathematical-statistical formulations "did not take adequate account of the important factor of expectations." University of Chicago economist Robert Lucas would win the 1995 Nobel Prize in Economics for promoting the concept of rational expectations and for showing the limitations of econometric models that ignored them.[55]

The rational expectations model gives more credit to people such as Tessie Rogers and Kathy Neuhas than the standard formulations of the day. Consumers and investors from Atlanta to East Hampton would incorporate all the available information in their inflation forecasts according to Lucas's view, including whether the Federal Reserve was increasing the money supply at an inflationary rate. They did not simply extrapolate past history, as Keynesian econometricians assumed. Rational expectations undermined the trade-off between unemployment and inflation that had ruled economic policy since the early 1960s, because Tessie Rogers and Kathy Neuhas could not be consistently duped by the Fed. The ultimate logic of rational expectations turned the central bank into an inflation machine, without any redeeming features.[56]

Volcker never joined the extremists, but he publicly embraced the wisdom of rationality in a speech to the Boston Economic Club in December 1976.

It is no historical accident that the past few years have seen the rise . . . of so-called rational expectations . . . in effect arguing that the ultimate inflationary consequences [of economic policy] will be promptly taken into account in today's actions . . .

Some versions . . . actually seem to imply that systematic demand policies will be wholly impotent to affect the real economy. I would not go nearly so far, but I do think . . . that what
people think and expect . . . is a fact of economic life that we
cannot escape . . . The moral is that concern about the inflationary consequences of policy cannot be postponed until the economy approaches its reentry to full employment.[57]

Volcker had sprinkled numerous handwritten edits throughout his
speech but left the moral of rational expectations untouched. The need
to consider the inflationary consequences of monetary policy even with
unemployed resources was not yet the conventional economic wisdom,
but had already claimed Volcker as a fellow traveler.

Keynesian economic models ignored inflationary expectations, but
the market for gold bullion did not. Trading in gold futures at New
York's Commodity Exchange, then located in the newly constructed
4 World Trade Center, would surpass all previous records during 1978,
and exceed the combined bullion volume in London, Frankfurt, and
Zurich.[58] On July 28, 1978, the price of gold passed its previous peak of
$197.50, and would trade as high as $243.65 later in the year.[59] According to Andre Sharon of the brokerage house Drexel Burnham Lam-
bert, "The pressure seems to be coming from the bottom . . . Customers
are asking their brokers, 'Why don't [we] try this thing?' "[60]

Sales of gold jewelry also skyrocketed. Bill Tendler, a jeweler on
MacDougal Street in New York City's Greenwich Village, reported a
dramatic rise in orders. "It seems to be psychological. The more expensive it gets, the more it is a mystique. People say, 'Yeah, I know it has
gone up, but I sure like it.' "[61] Andre Sharon offered a test. "If you believe, given the history of the past seven or eight years, that [Ameri-
cans] will tolerate the pain of disinflation, then the price of gold will go
down. If you believe that we will panic at the first sign of pain—a rise
in the unemployment rate, say—gold will go up."[62]

Volcker suspected that America could not tolerate the pain needed
to combat a jump in inflation. "I think this may create a severe dilemma for monetary policy. I myself do not think it's something that
monetary policy can very adequately handle by itself, unaided by new

policies elsewhere in the government."[63] He did not specify what those other policies might be, because something else bothered him more.

G. William Miller, President Jimmy Carter's first appointment to head the central bank, had replaced Arthur Burns as chairman of the Federal Reserve Board in March 1978. Miller had been president of Textron Corporation, an aerospace conglomerate, before becoming Fed chairman. His experience in banking and economics was limited to the largely ceremonial position of serving as a director of the Federal Reserve Bank of Boston. Fed chairmen do not need a doctorate in economics—Burns was the first—but Miller's lack of experience in finance would hurt his credibility on Wall Street.

A week before the White House disclosed Miller's appointment, the *New York Times* listed Paul Volcker, Robert Roosa, and Bruce MacLaury (Volcker's former deputy at Treasury) as the leading candidates to replace Arthur Burns.[64] After the surprise announcement of William Miller, the *Times* quoted the first reaction of a banker who preferred to remain anonymous: "G. William *who*?"[65]

Volcker, who had not expected to be appointed—no New York Fed president had become chairman before—greeted the news diplomatically. "I'm not surprised that [the president] picked someone from the business community. It might be a good thing."[66] And Milton Friedman, the leading monetarist critic of the Fed, welcomed a practical man of affairs running the central bank: "Money is too important a matter to be left to the bankers."[67]

Volcker quips, "The wisdom of Miller's appointment is one of the few things that Milton and I ever agreed on."[68] And they both were wrong.

William Miller brought a CEO's penchant for efficiency to the Board of Governors. He grew impatient with the collegial spirit of FOMC meetings, where everyone seated at the twenty-seven-foot-long mahogany table had a chance to speak. Most participants showed about the same restraint as a politician working a fund-raising breakfast. After six months on the job, Miller had had enough. He brought hourglass egg timers to the board meeting on Tuesday, August 15, 1978, and told his colleagues,[69] "I'm going to try to set them up when each of you starts to talk and [board secretary] Murray [Altmann] is going to show a mean streak—since I'm a gentleman—[and tell you when your time is up]."

Charles Partee, who had been a top staffer at the Fed before becoming a board member, wanted more details. "What are they—three minutes?"

"Yes. And when your three minutes is up, he's going to say 'next speaker.'"

Volcker sensed a loophole. "How many times can you talk, though?"

Altmann, who had just become the board secretary, recognized trouble. "I'm not sure yet whether you're serious."

The chairman smiled. "We are having a lot of fun but we are serious."

Members of the FOMC dismissed William Miller's egg timers as an ill-conceived practical joke, just as they ignored the THANK YOU FOR NOT SMOKING sign he had placed on the boardroom table.[70] Everyone talked and smoked, led by Henry Wallich, the board's resident expert in international finance, who considered it his constitutional right to enjoy a fine cigar. Meanwhile, Volcker puffed away on his favorite ten-cent stogie and lamented the plight of the dollar in the foreign exchange market.

Volcker had watched gold reach a new high during the last week of July 1978, so he was not surprised, during the first half of August, when the U.S. dollar sank to new lows against the German mark, seconding the vote of no confidence in America.[71] On August 15, 1978, he told the FOMC, "I think it's important particularly in view of the international situation that we correct the misapprehensions about our lack of concern over inflation. I do think it would be wise to put a specific mention of the international situation in the directive at some point."[72]

Volcker thought "domestic and international price stability went hand in hand," and he wanted this reflected in the FOMC Directive, the instructions for monetary policy voted on at the end of each meeting. During his tenure as undersecretary of the treasury, he had urged Arthur Burns to protect the dollar with high interest rates. Now that gold and fixed exchange rates had become the dinosaurs of international finance, Volcker believed that the dollar's role in world trade depended even more on price stability than it had before. Americans could no longer consume more cars and televisions than they produced if foreigners were unwilling to hold dollars as international money. According to Volcker, "Our moral obligation to prevent a debasement of our currency coincided with our self-interest."[73]

Volcker championed America's international responsibilities, but had to shoulder some of the blame for the greenback's decline. He had voted with the majority of the FOMC, slowly pushing up the federal funds rate, the overnight interest rate on loans of reserves between banks, to discourage excessive spending and inflation. If banks had to pay more for reserves, the raw material needed to make loans, they would charge more to consumers and businesses. But the FOMC operated with a delicate touch, mimicking a team of brain surgeons, raising interest rates in quarter-percent increments at each meeting. According to Volcker, "I don't think we could be accused of not having been prudent and cautious and gradual."[74]

Mark Willes, a member of the FOMC by virtue of his position as president of the Federal Reserve Bank of Minneapolis, wanted to use a sledgehammer rather than a scalpel in tightening credit. He would leave the Fed in 1980 to become president of General Mills, the food conglomerate most famous for bringing Cheerios to the breakfast table, but in mid-1978, Willes had urged Volcker privately to "push up rates more aggressively to convince people that we are serious about controlling inflation."[75]

Volcker said, "The FOMC doesn't operate that way."

Willes, who dissented eight times during the year, said, "Perhaps we should."[76]

Volcker recognized in himself the tendency to procrastinate. Staffers at the Federal Reserve Bank of New York joked that he never made a decision before its time, and the hereafter counted in the calculation. He recalled that dawdling in London had destroyed his doctoral dissertation. But he dismissed those thoughts when answering Willes. "Maybe, but I can do more by building a consensus within the committee."

He would change his mind before long.

The FOMC increased the federal funds rate to 9 percent in October 1978, a jump of more than two percentage points over a six-month period, but Mark Willes was not impressed, and lectured the group.[77] "I'd just make one comment . . . since there seems to be so much concern about rising interest rates. We seem to accept easily the notion that if we want to look at real wages we adjust for inflation, and that if we want to look at what is happening to profits and depreciation, we adjust for inflation. Most of the economic theory that I know says that if you want to look at the real bite of interest rates, you also adjust for inflation. And interest rates adjusted for inflation are not high at all."

The "buy now, pay later" philosophy of people such as Tessie Rogers and Kathy Neuhas confirms that an interest rate of 9 percent is not high if wages and prices are increasing at about the same rate. It pays to borrow and buy something tangible, such as a big house, a small diamond, or a tightly wrapped bar of gold, to reap the capital gain and repay the loan in cheaper dollars.

The rate of inflation averaged over 9 percent during the three months prior to the FOMC meeting of Tuesday, October 17, 1978, and Volcker began to think that Willes had been right.[78] He said openly at that meeting, "I do have some question about whether we pitched it at the right level in the last year. I suppose . . . having looked back, that we've been a little too easy . . . and meanwhile inflation has gotten worse."[79]

No one commented, except for William Miller. "I don't think inflation has accelerated since I've been at the board, to put it bluntly."

"I was thinking of a period of probably fifteen or eighteen months."

Miller smiled. "Well, you fellows fouled it up before!"

Volcker had not been trying to assign individual blame, but he admitted without excuse, "There is something to what you say." And then added, "But I also think inflationary expectations have hardened . . . And that is a problem. I do think this is a critical period."

The foreign exchange market noticed. On October 30, 1978, one dollar purchased 1.72 German marks, an all-time low, representing a decline of more than 20 percent in a year.[80] A currency analyst in Frankfurt said, "It's the same old story—lack of confidence in U.S. government policies."[81] And a London financial analyst concurred: "It will take a lot to change sentiment and a long time to restore confidence."[82] But a taxi driver in Frankfurt hurt the most: "I would rather not take any dollars at all. If somebody offered me dollars, I would drive him to the nearest bank to check the rate . . . I don't know what it's going to be tomorrow, do I?"[83]

A massive dollar-rescue operation launched on Wednesday, November 1, 1978, delayed Volcker's first substantive FOMC dissent for five months. Treasury Secretary Michael Blumenthal, the former president of Bendix Corporation, a company that made home washing machines and antilock braking systems for cars, convinced President Jimmy Carter of the need for drastic measures, including a significant increase in U.S. interest rates.[84]

Anthony Solomon, who held Volcker's old position as undersecretary of the treasury for monetary affairs, then orchestrated a $30 billion intervention in the foreign exchange market, the equivalent of total warfare on anti-dollar speculators.[85] Solomon implied that the Treasury would abandon the policy of benign neglect toward the dollar that had ruled since floating exchange rates had replaced Bretton Woods. "The point has come where Adam Smith had to be curbed."[86] Adam Smith was not a speculator, of course, but he took the blame as the founder of modern economics.

Volcker participated in the dollar rescue by requesting an increase from 8½ percent to 9½ percent in the discount rate charged by the Federal Reserve Bank of New York for lending reserves to its member banks. Unlike most changes in the discount rate that occur after a fundamental shift in policy by the FOMC, the November 1 increase signaled a new initiative. Establishing the discount rate is one of the few prerogatives left to the regional Federal Reserve banks, but the Board of Governors in Washington must approve all changes. Volcker recalls, "I was only too happy to conduct a special telephone meeting of my directors to vote for an increase once I knew Washington would approve."[87]

Foreign exchange markets painted a new outlook. On the day the rescue package was announced, the dollar rose by 6 percent against the German currency, and a month later it had jumped to 1.93 marks.[88] Had the Frankfurt cabbie not spurned the greenback, he would have earned a profit of more than 10 percent during November.[89] The program also punished gold speculators. An ounce of the precious metal declined from its peak of $243.65 on October 31, 1978, to $193.40 at the end of November, a decline of more than 20 percent.

The rise in U.S. interest rates restored a shine to the tarnished dollar, but Volcker expected the gains to fade without follow-through, especially if inflation accelerated. He had good reason for concern. Corporate borrowing showed no signs of tapering off with the increased cost of funds. The controller of R.H. Macy, Mortimer Leavitt, said that the department store's "aggressive capital spending program hasn't changed in light of any recent events. The company . . . will just go along with interest rate increases. If you want to eat . . . you pay the price. You don't stop eating."[90] A spokesman for St. Joe Minerals Corporation, the largest producer of lead and zinc in the United States, added, "Much of our spending is on a long lead-time basis and we certainly wouldn't leave things sitting there half or three-quarters finished."[91]

By the March 20, 1979, meeting of the FOMC, almost five months had elapsed since the Treasury's rescue of the dollar, and the annual rate of inflation had moved into double digits.[92] Volcker sounded the alarm.

> I think we're in retreat on the inflation side; if there's not a complete rout, it's close to it. And in my view that poses the major danger to the stability of the economy . . . It's an obvious danger for international stability [especially] . . . if the dollar . . . should [return to] the panicky situation we had earlier . . . There's no doubt in my mind that . . . this is the time for some firming rather than the reverse. I think we are at a critical point in the inflation program, with the tide against us.[93]

Volcker faced a battle.

Frank Morris, a friend of Paul's ever since they shared an office at the Treasury when JFK was president, served on the FOMC in his capacity as president of the Federal Reserve Bank of Boston. Morris had been on the committee for over ten years, more than twice as long as Volcker. He had been appointed president of the Boston Fed in 1968 from a select list of candidates that included one six-foot, seven-inch financial economist from Chase Manhattan Bank. Volcker recalls: "They chose well. Frank is a first-rate economist and a devoted central banker . . . but it did rankle at the time. It is the only job I was ever turned down for, unless I count when the Federal Reserve Board refused to hire me right after I finished Princeton in January 1949."[94]

On Tuesday, March 20, 1979, Morris staked out a position diametrically opposed to Volcker's. "I think we're facing an emerging conflict between the domestic and international requirements of monetary policy . . . I think we're approaching a cyclical peak in the economy sometime around midyear . . . If it's our objective to avoid a recession, I think we have to [ease] today; I don't think we can wait for another month . . . I think the issue is whether we seriously are concerned about avoiding a recession or not."[95]

Frank Morris knew from his long experience on the FOMC that members responded more to the domestic economy than to international finance, in keeping with its congressional mandate to "promote full employment . . . and reasonable price stability."[96] In 1913, Congress conferred its constitutional right "to coin money and regulate the value thereof" on the Federal Reserve System. The central bank's obligations have changed over the years, in response to economic circumstance and political pressure, but the Full Employment and Balanced Growth Act of 1978, also known as the Humphrey-Hawkins Act, formalized the goals of full employment and price stability. Foreign exchange remained in the Senate cloakroom.[97]

Morris argued that Volcker's recommendation to tighten credit was inconsistent with those priorities. "Paul, I think, is resigned to a recession; I think the international constraint may be more of a factor in his thinking than he let on."[98]

Volcker felt cornered. He had gone on record with an incriminating message a few months earlier, in a speech at the University of Warwick in Coventry, England, that received considerable attention.[99] "It has been a difficult matter to bring . . . exchange market stability to bear on a Congress . . . preoccupied with the domestic economy . . . In retrospect the case can be made that . . . more forceful response to pressures on the dollar would have ultimately been helpful in promoting domestic as well as international stability . . . Today, a stronger and stable dollar is plainly in the interest of the United States and the rest of the world."[100]

Volcker tried to navigate a response to Morris that would salvage the case for tighter credit while avoiding perjury. "Inflation is a factor in my thinking."[101] He told the truth, but Morris's speech carried the day.[102] The FOMC refused to tighten, and Volcker, with three others, voted against the decision. The press labeled the FOMC dissenters "the Volcker minority."[103]

In the three months ending June 1979, prices increased at nearly 13 percent per annum, a relentless acceleration in the rate of inflation that caused both resignation and resentment across the country.[104] Terry Grantham, a college student and painter's helper in Lubbock, Texas, said, "Every day that goes by it seems like the money I have doesn't buy as much . . . I was raised as a steak and potatoes boy, but now it ain't that way no more. Forget the steaks and go with hamburger or bologna."[105] But Ron Gordon, a baseball fan in San Francisco, rebelled. He refused to accept the nickel increase in the price of hot dogs and beer at Candlestick Park, where the Giants played their home games.[106] Gordon assembled an inch-thick folder of statistics and protested before the San Francisco Recreation and Park Commission, which had approved the five-cent price increases. His effort attracted the attention of Alfred E. Kahn, President Carter's chairman of the Council on Wage and Price Stability, who praised his "heroic and unflagging campaign."[107]

Ron Gordon prevailed on hot dogs—the price increase was rescinded—but he lost on beer. His batting average, a respectable .500, exceeded Jimmy Carter's by a wide margin. The president's approval ratings declined to 30 percent in June 1979.[108] At a meeting of the National Association of Broadcasters in Dallas, he had been asked whether the federal government was not the main cause of inflation.[109] It was the same question he had gotten earlier, in Elk City, Oklahoma. The president smiled and said, "That seems to be the most popular question." Wayne Hardrow, of the North Carolina Association of Broadcasters, summed up the mood with "Where do we go from here?" as if inflation were a mysterious fourteenth-century plague.

On Sunday evening, July 15, 1979, President Jimmy Carter delivered his diagnosis to the American people in a televised speech from the Oval Office. The president had spent the previous ten days at Camp David discussing the country's problems with industrialists, labor leaders, economists, pastors, and ordinary Americans (not necessarily in that order). His thirty-three-minute talk addressed the details of the country's dependence on foreign oil, but his broader message focused on "the crisis of confidence" that he considered "a fundamental threat to American democracy."[110] Carter lamented that "for the first time in our history a majority of our people believe that the next five years will be worse than the past five years." He recognized that "the phrase 'sound as a dollar' was an expression of absolute dependability until ten years of inflation began to shrink our dollar and our savings."

Two days after his speech, Carter requested the resignation of his entire senior staff, a housecleaning to signify a fresh start. Instead, it created confusion. The president removed five of his cabinet members, including Treasury Secretary Michael Blumenthal, who had run afoul of the so-called Georgia Mafia in the White House.[111] In November 1978, Blumenthal had convinced Carter to support the discount rate increase that had accompanied the dollar rescue package. He compounded his offense in April 1979, by publicly calling for an increase in interest rates soon after the "Volcker minority" had urged a tightening of credit conditions.[112] When asked at his final news conference whether he had jumped or was pushed, Blumenthal answered, "I took advantage of an opportunity to get paroled with time off for good behavior."[113]

Blumenthal's firing provided fodder for talk show hosts such as Johnny Carson on *The Tonight Show*. "Treasury secretary Blumenthal did not handle his job too well. He asked for his severance pay in Krugerrands."[114] No one had to tell the late-night television audience that the Krugerrand was South Africa's gold coin. Carter's cabinet shakeup had triggered an overnight jump in gold to over $300 an ounce, a new record.[115] The *New York Times* commented that the resignations "significantly intensified European worries" and quoted a specialist at Samuel Montagu & Company, a leading London gold trading firm: "Seen from over here this looks pretty awful."[116]

The president replaced Blumenthal with Fed chairman William Miller, considered by Carter's political advisers more of a team player. The switch delighted Miller, who was pleased to bequeath his egg timers to the next Fed chairman, whoever that might be. The vacancy at the central bank worried America's trading partners.

Gilbert de Botton, general manager of Zurich's Bank Rothschild, said, "My feeling is one of gloom. Washington is becoming more politically organized."[117] A European finance minister who preferred to remain anonymous said, "I hope that whoever now becomes dominant will pursue a conservative monetary policy and not delude themselves into thinking that they can float the United States . . . by adopting an inflationary policy." The press reported, "Several European officials and bankers suggested that Paul A. Volcker . . . would be an ideal choice" for Federal Reserve chairman.

Volcker met with the president on Tuesday, July 24, 1979, in the Oval Office. They were joined by William Miller, the new treasury secretary, who had called Volcker at the New York Fed the day before to set up the meeting. The discussion lasted less than an hour, and Volcker knew it had not gone well. He returned to New York that same afternoon.

On the flight back, he thought about the other names appearing publicly on the short list to succeed Miller.[118] He knew them all well. Bruce McLaury, Volcker's former deputy at Treasury and now president of the Brookings Institution, the liberal Washington think tank, had been mentioned as a possible candidate. David Rockefeller, the chairman of Chase Manhattan Bank, had also been listed. Volcker had worked for Rockefeller during his two stints at the bank. And A. W. (Tom) Clausen, the CEO of Bank of America, a third name in the hopper, had offered Volcker the number-two job there when he left the Treasury. It was an impressive group, and Volcker wondered whom the president would pick, now that he had talked himself out of the job.

After landing at LaGuardia Airport, Volcker called his two best friends, Larry Ritter and Bob Kavesh, and asked them to dinner for a postmortem. They met at Parma, a neighborhood Italian restaurant around the corner from Volcker's Seventy-ninth Street apartment on the East Side of Manhattan. Ritter and Kavesh, about the same age as Volcker, were professors at NYU's Graduate School of Business. Volcker had gone to Harvard with Kavesh and had overlapped with Ritter at the New York Fed. "They would not bullshit me about anything," Volcker says. "Barbara liked them for the same reason."[119]

"Well, I blew it," Volcker began after they had sat down.[120]

"What do you mean?" Ritter asked. He had learned the art of listening while recording the stories of players from the early days of baseball. He had turned the oral history into a bestselling book, *The Glory of Their Times*, sharing the royalties with the old-timers because he thought it was the right thing to do.

"I was sitting alongside the president, who sat in a wing chair,"

Volcker growled. "I said that I attached great importance to the independence of the Federal Reserve and that I also favored a more restrictive monetary policy. And just for emphasis I pointed at Miller, who was sitting in a chair next to me, and added that I wanted a tighter policy than him."

"The Volcker charm at work," Kavesh said. "What did Carter say?"

"Nothing. He just listened."

Ritter lit a cigarette and tried some humor: "Were you smoking one of your El Cheapos?"

"He just said that Miller was there," Kavesh interjected. "Of course he was smoking."

They laughed together, and then Volcker continued. "You know it might be for the best. I would have to take a fifty percent cut in salary if I were offered the job. I don't know how we could mange . . . I don't know if I have the right to ask my family to make that kind of sacrifice."

Volcker looked at both men for a response. Neither one spoke, until Ritter said, "If the president calls, you cannot turn him down."

Kavesh asked, "What did Barbara say?"

"The same as him." Volcker nodded toward Ritter.

Paul knew that they had given him the answer he wanted. This was the job he had trained for his entire professional life. This was the job that provided the opportunity to rescue his country from crisis. He wanted it more than he cared to admit.

"Did Barbara say anything else? Kavesh continued.

Volcker looked down at his plate. "Yes. She said we'd manage."

At 7:30 the following morning, the sharp ring of the telephone woke Volcker. It was the White House.

CHAPTER 8

Challenge

Volcker sat at the oversize desk in the chairman's office at the Federal Reserve Board in Washington, D.C., inhaling the aroma of his favorite A&C Grenadier cigar. The smoke irritated his eyes. A cigar aficionado had once told him that Grenadiers were little more than "horse manure sprinkled with tobacco," but Volcker did not care. Macanudos had never fit his pocketbook, so he had learned to like what he could afford. Now that he would be earning $57,500 a year rather than the $110,000 salary as president of the Federal Reserve Bank of New York, the Grenadiers tasted even better.

Volcker waved away the fumes and stared at the postcards, letters, and telegrams piled neatly in front of him. There must be at least two hundred, he thought, and it was only August 7, 1979, a day after he was sworn in as chairman of America's central bank in the East Room of the White House. He had read a few of the messages and they made him nervous.

Not all of them, of course.[1] Some made him smile, such as the one from Dave McGrath, which read, "I felt like a big shot just telling people I was once your college roommate. I was also happy to hear that you refused to pay $5 for a lousy drink in Zurich." Others raised a lump in his throat, like the one from Judge Waesche reminiscing, "Your father was highly respected for his honesty and ability . . . I know he would be proud of your appointment." And some gave sound advice, such as Doc Wolk's suggestion "To please keep the cigars under five a day, if not for your own sake then for the dollar."

But too many old friends, including Tom Rees and Ed Hamilton, delivered the identical message: "I called my broker and sold short gold and went long dollars." Volcker worried that lawyers and consultants, like Tom and Ed, expected immediate success in the battle to control inflation, as though he could say the magic words and erase a decade of futility. He knew the euphoria was premature, a recipe for disappointment. Volcker preferred skepticism.

And then he saw a glimmer of hope: an envelope sticking out of the pile with a Vermont postmark. This one, he thought, could deliver a pessimistic message that would buoy his spirits. He knew that Milton Friedman summered in Ely, Vermont.

Volcker's history with Friedman, the Nobel Prize–winning University of Chicago economist, went back more than twenty years, to Volcker's first job at the Federal Reserve Bank of New York. He recalled Friedman coming to the bank in 1957 to explain his research indicting the Federal Reserve for causing the Great Depression. Friedman had presented his case like a prosecutor, offering evidence that the central bank had allowed the money supply to decline by one third between 1929 and 1933, which in turn caused the economic collapse. "Milton was convinced he had found the gospel truth. I was skeptical of anyone so confident—whether from Chicago or Cambridge."[2]

Volcker slid the envelope from the middle of the pile and smiled. The accompanying letter was written in Friedman's barely legible longhand, covered a single page, and was dated July 31, 1912 (Friedman's birthday). It greeted him with "Dear Paul":

> My condolences to you on your "promotion." I am delighted for the country at your accession to the chairmanship but sympathize with respect to the difficulties you are doomed to face. You have, however, a great advantage and consolation. Your predecessors have, most unfortunately on every other count, left records that it will not be difficult to improve on. The years 1930–1933 aside, and perhaps also 1920 and 1921, there has never been both a greater need and greater opportunity for the [Fed-

eral Reserve] System to render service to the nation by coura-
geous and steady policy of monetary restraint, experienced
gradually and moderately. As you know, I do not believe that
the System can rise to that challenge without major changes in
its method of operation. My very best wishes to you for success
in pushing those changes and those results.[3]

Volcker wanted Friedman's message broadcast throughout the country. He thought about a discreet leak to a favored reporter but decided
instead to write a letter that would accomplish the same result. It began
with "Dear Milton":

It's taken a little while to get out from under and to respond to
those special letters of congratulations or condolences—and
I recognize that the latter may be more apt than the former. I
don't know whether I have simply been elected the fall guy in
most difficult circumstances, but some of the broad directions
of necessary change seem clear enough. And as you point out,
the past record has not exactly been perfection. I am perfectly
confident you will find plenty to criticize but I also suspect
you know I will not be unhappy to have you preaching the
doctrines of monetary rectitude as we move ahead . . . In any
event, the test will come soon enough, and we will, as always,
be following your comments with interest.[4]

Milton Friedman had won the 1976 Nobel Prize in Economics as an
agent provocateur, subverting the foundations of the establishment.
Some contemporaries dismissed his ideas as though they were funda-
mentalist doctrines of a midwestern preacher. Friedman often sounded
like a true believer, but he rarely lost a debate. His friend and former
colleague at the University of Chicago, George Shultz, Nixon's treasury
secretary, once quipped, "Everybody loves to argue with Milton, particularly when he isn't there."[5] Friedman's advice to Richard Nixon,
Margaret Thatcher, and Ronald Reagan gave prominence to his views.

Friedman argued throughout his career that the Federal Reserve
should restrain inflation with steady and slow monetary growth. In
an especially provocative article, he proposed that a modest rate of

deflation, a decline in the price level, serve as the central bank's objective.[6] Volcker's obsession with inflation should have made Friedman a natural ally. Instead they went to war, like the biblical clash between David and Goliath, with the five-foot, three-inch Friedman battling the six-foot, seven-inch Volcker over how to conduct monetary policy. And it was not always cordial.

Milton Friedman is most famous for saying, "Inflation is always and everywhere a monetary phenomenon," in the sense that inflation cannot occur without increases in the money supply that exceed the growth of output.[7] Months before Volcker took office, Friedman used his *Newsweek* magazine column to advertise the Federal Reserve's responsibility for the inflation of the 1970s.[8] "From April 1975 to September 1978, the quantity of money . . . grew at the rate of 10 percent per year. Since the end of World War II [the money supply] grew that fast during only one prior period of equal length—from February 1970 to July 1973." Friedman predicted that "the current inflation is not likely to reach its peak until late 1979 or early 1980, by which time it may challenge the earlier record."

Friedman should have held Arthur Burns accountable for the Federal Reserve's dismal performance. Burns governed the Federal Reserve System from January 1970 through March 1978. The chairman is the public face of the Federal Reserve in congressional hearings and he manages the secret deliberations of the FOMC. His final word on appointments within the system makes him more than just another vote at the table, just like the legendary King Arthur. And Burns knew as well as Friedman that inflation comes with excess growth in the money supply. Friedman, a former student of Burns, said, "Outside of my parents and my wife, there is nobody else who had as much influence on my life as Arthur Burns did. And that major source of influence started exerting itself during a course I took [from him]."[9]

The *New York Times* identified Burns as the culprit in the recent inflationary surge: "Although Mr. Burns was critical of the economic policies of the Carter Administration, he permitted an uninterrupted expansion of the money supply in 1977 to finance the economic stimulus that many now hold at least partly responsible for current inflationary woes."[10] But Friedman turns his former teacher into a victim rather than a perpetrator.[11] "Arthur Burns . . . [had] been informing Congress . . . that the Fed has reduced its target rates of growth of the monetary aggregates as a gradual step toward a steady reduction of inflation . . . In sharp contrast, the actual rates of monetary growth [had] risen rather than decreased . . . Duplicity? Not at all. Simply another example of how an individual may be unable to bend an institution, subject to many pressures and forces, to his will . . . It has occurred time and again in the Fed's sixty-four-year history."

Friedman excused Burns, perhaps out of loyalty, but he knew that a strong personality at the central bank could make a difference. In his influential *A Monetary History of the United States*, written with Anna Jacobson Schwartz, he laments the death of Benjamin Strong, governor (president) of the Federal Reserve Bank of New York in 1928, and writes that Strong's guidance could have avoided the fatal mistakes of the Federal Reserve during the Great Depression. "If Benjamin Strong could have had twelve months more of vigorous health, we might have ended the depression in 1930."[12]

By the time Volcker occupied Strong's position at the New York bank, the locus of power had shifted to Washington. Volcker's dissents in March and April of 1979 failed to sway the FOMC majority, but he would be more persuasive as chairman.[13] The press expected Volcker's leadership to make a difference. "Paul A. Volcker isn't going to be another G. William Miller, or Arthur Burns, or William McChesney Martin Jr. in his new post as chairman of the Federal Reserve Board— even though on the surface, all Fed chairmen sound alike. They don't like inflation, big government spending, excessive regulation . . . Mr. Volcker, a skilled market technician . . . and monetary diplomat, . . . [will] be more rigorous in the application of orthodox monetary policies than . . . Mr. Miller."[14]

William Miller had been chairman for only eighteen months before Volcker's appointment, too short a time to measure his direct impact on inflation, but he undermined the Fed's role as guardian of the currency. He opposed a discount rate increase approved by a majority of the board in July 1978, registering a dissent that the *Washington Post* labeled " 'political'—an attempt to assuage the Carter administration fears that higher interest rates would be dangerous to the country."[15]

Richard Adams, executive vice president at Chemical Bank (now merged into JPMorgan Chase), said, "I think Mr. Miller's image has been tarnished . . . The economy is still operating at a strong level . . . We've got excessive money growth and excessive inflation . . . We feel better when we have a Federal Reserve chairman who is in command of the Board."[16] And the *New York Times* complained, "How does [Miller] justify his vote in light of the acceleration of the growth of the money supply and the sharp rise in consumer prices?"[17]

The press counted on Volcker's international stature to make an impact.

> The remarkable speed and enthusiasm with which European governments have welcomed Mr. Volcker . . . testifies to the pivotal role they see him playing . . . The key is the long personal involvement Mr. Volcker has had with men who have become heads of state . . . The President of France, Valéry Giscard d'Estaing, and the Chancellor of West Germany, Helmut Schmidt . . . are both former finance ministers who dealt with Mr. Volcker . . . and who trust him. Volcker will stand out in an otherwise rather undistinguished Washington scene as the one man they already know and respect.[18]

The newspaper references to Giscard d'Estaing and Helmut Schmidt reminded Volcker of his thirty-one-thousand-mile dollar-rescue trek in February 1973. Paul cringed when recalling that this final effort to maintain fixed exchange rates collapsed a month later, ushering in the era of floating exchange rates championed by Milton Friedman. He suspected that the years spent shoring up the doomed system had been a waste. The run on the dollar in October 1978 offered bittersweet comfort. It demonstrated American vulnerability but also negated Friedman's claim that a floating system would put an end to international currency crises. And that had been his main consolation—until now.

The European response to Volcker's appointment meant that his failed efforts to preserve Bretton Woods had served a higher purpose. He had earned the "trust" and "respect" of his former sparring partners. And nothing mattered quite so much to the new chairman of the Federal Reserve Board as trust and respect. He needed all the help he could get.

Volcker prepared extensive notes for his first meeting as chairman of the FOMC, scheduled for Tuesday, August 14, 1979, a week after his formal appointment.[19] He squeezed fifty tightly scripted lines onto two yellow legal-size pages as though he were cramming information onto a crib sheet. He wrote near the top of the page, "This meeting has more symbolic importance than ordinarily." It was his first test as chairman, and he viewed the agenda as a blueprint for action. He hoped to have more success convincing the FOMC to join him than he had had with Barbara.

Paul had spent the previous weekend trying to change his wife's mind about her remaining in New York while he went to Washington. He had tried every angle, including the truth.[20]

"I need you to show me which fork to use at those state dinners, and to put the bigwig ambassadors in their places."

Barbara had always downplayed her influence. "They talk to me only to get to you."

"It's not true. But that should not matter if I say I need you with me."

"I'll come when it's really important."

"Is that always?"

"I came for the White House ceremony."

"Jimmy, Janice, and your parents were there."

"Well, it was clearly important."

And then she added, "You go, I stay."

Paul accepted the verdict, unable to address the real problem. Barbara needed the proximity of Dr. Michael Lockshin, the physician who was treating her rheumatoid arthritis, and Jimmy, who had moved back home, needed Barbara's attention.[21] Paul rented an inexpensive one-bedroom apartment in a building that served almost like a dormitory for students at George Washington University. He furnished it with a king-size bed, a bridge table, and a ten-inch black-and-white television. He controlled expenses further by folding his six-foot, seven-inch frame into a coach seat every Friday afternoon on the Eastern Airlines shuttle to New York.

A letter to Volcker from Douglas Dillon, President Kennedy's treasury secretary at the time of Volcker's first apprenticeship in Washington, acknowledged the hardship: "Your willingness to take on [the chairmanship] at such great financial sacrifice is typical of you and a great service to the nation. With you at the helm I feel confident about our monetary policy for the first time since the departure of Bill Martin."[22]

Volcker appreciated Dillon's sentiments but knew that the chairman of the Dillon, Read international banking house could not fathom the depths of the Volcker family finances. Barbara had to take a part-time job as a bookkeeper and rent out a room in their New York City apartment to help balance the budget. Volcker thought the *National Enquirer* could splash a provocative headline across its front page: "Fed Chairman Turns Family Apartment into Boarding House: What Next?"

Volcker's bachelor status from Monday through Friday paid an unexpected dividend. He spent more time with Janice, who had just graduated from nursing school and lived in the Washington suburb of Alexandria, Virginia. Paul would ask her to serve as his escort when Barbara could not make a formal Washington dinner. He recalls, "I thought it was only fair. After all, Janice was the rebel . . . I think she might have even smoked pot in high school."[23] He pauses to roll his eyes in mock horror. "But what I remember most was when she slapped an IMPEACH NIXON bumper sticker on my car while I was undersecretary." Paul did not think it was as funny back then. Now he smiled. "I guess that's why I thought it was okay to bring my laundry to her apartment every week."

The Federal Reserve System's headquarters, on Constitution Avenue and Twentieth Street in the nation's capital, covers an entire block and faintly resembles a rectangular Taj Mahal. The four-story building with a white marble façade was completed in 1937 and elicited approval from the then first lady, Eleanor Roosevelt. "I think the building's exterior is very beautiful and have admired it often, but I was equally impressed by the interior."[24]

Volcker also liked the inside of the building, perhaps because it was built for his dimensions. The boardroom, which serves as the meeting place for the Federal Open Market Committee, sets a spacious tone. The two-story enclosure measures almost half the size of a regulation basketball court, with floor-to-ceiling curtained windows lining the longer wall.[25] A twenty-seven-foot-long mahogany table, accommodating twenty upholstered chairs, with a generous brass chandelier hanging overhead, makes the room look like the formal dining quarters of an English manor house—except that an oversize map of the United States, identifying each of the twelve regional Federal Reserve districts, covers the back wall. A private entrance connects the chairman's office directly to the boardroom, offering him access like that of a judge to his courtroom.

Volcker opened his first FOMC meeting on August 14, 1979, with an awkward announcement. He had been appointed chairman of the Board of Governors by the president of the United States, but the FOMC has its own procedures requiring a separate confirmation. "I might say for the benefit of those who have just come in that we had a little executive session to do some important business, the first item of which was to elect a chairman. I'm not sure whether it's entirely appropriate that I announce my election, but it proceeded."[26]

After listening to a report on economic conditions, Volcker began his prepared remarks with a friendly poke at his predecessor. "I am conscious that without an egg timer time has been passing. But . . . it might be useful if I just set out a few thoughts . . . I don't intend to make it a habit particularly, but this is a meeting that is perhaps of more than usual symbolic importance [and] . . . I thought I'd just lay out a strategy . . . so you can have something to shoot at."[27]

He then articulated his perception of the main economic problem, sounding more like a psychiatrist than a Keynesian or a monetarist. "When I look at the past year or two I am impressed myself by . . . the degree to which inflationary psychology has really changed. It's not that we didn't have it before, but I think people are acting on that expectation . . . much more firmly than they used to . . . The dollar externally obviously adds to the dilemma . . . Nobody knows what is going to happen to the dollar, but I do think it's fair to say that the psychology is extremely tender."[28]

Volcker had learned the importance of market psychology at the

New York Fed's trading desk and had absorbed the rational expectations theories of economists in Chicago and Minnesota.[29] He combined those lessons into a warning to the FOMC: "Economic policy . . . has a kind of crisis of credibility."[30] Nevertheless, he felt constrained about acting precipitously. "We don't have a lot of room for maneuver and I don't think we want to use up all our ammunition right now in a really dramatic action . . . Dramatic action would not be understood without more of a crisis atmosphere . . . where we have a rather clear public backing for whatever drastic action we take."[31]

Volcker had followed this script before. He let the May 1971 foreign exchange crisis simmer for four months before recommending the suspension of gold convertibility in August 1971. He would not wait that long in 1979.

A public squabble erupted after a meeting of the Federal Reserve Board on Tuesday, September 18, 1979, that stunned everyone, like a fistfight among cardinals in the Sistine Chapel. The morning began with Volcker's second FOMC meeting as chairman and ended with the committee ratifying his recommendation "to make a little move [up] in the federal funds rate."[32] The vote was 8 in favor and 4 against, with 3 of the 4 dissenters urging greater tightening.[33] Volcker wanted tighter credit and higher interest rates to fight inflation but knew that some members of the FOMC were worried about a recession, so he emphasized caution. "I am not particularly eager to make a major move now or in the foreseeable future."[34]

No one but Wall Street professionals would have recognized the slight increase in the federal funds rate, the interest rate on overnight loans of reserves between commercial banks. The New York Fed's trading desk implements the FOMC Directive by selling government securities from its holdings to withdraw reserves from the banking system. These transactions push up the federal funds rate by forcing banks to scramble for reserves, but the action occurs far from the public spotlight. However, a follow-up meeting of the Board of Governors on the afternoon of September 18 broke the silence.

Volcker convened the seven-member board to discuss raising the discount rate charged on loans of reserves to commercial banks. Unlike movements in the obscure federal funds rate, discount rate decisions are announced immediately and are reported on the evening news with the gravity of a declaration of war. But most financial market professionals ignore the rhetoric. Banks borrow reserves at their regional Federal Reserve banks as a safety valve, after reserves have been drained from the market at the behest of the FOMC, and the discount rate increase is a defensive parry to block the escape route. The Board of Governors controls the discount rate by legal statute, but it usually follows the lead of monetary policy established at the FOMC.

September 18 was no exception to the norm. The Board of Governors voted to approve an increase in the discount rate to a record high of 11 percent, a jump of half a percent, and explained in its press release that the increase was taken "against the background of increases in other short term interest rates . . . and to discourage excessive borrowing by member banks from the discount window."[35] The vote was 4 in favor and 3 against.

The half-point increase in the discount rate, the second since Volcker took office in August, pleased him.[36] "It confirmed publicly our commitment to tight money to control inflation."[37] He went to bed on September 18 with a smile but awoke the following morning with a headache.

The September 19, 1979, front page of the *New York Times* described the prior day's discount rate decision as though it were an armed insurrection among the rank and file. "In an unusual 4–3 split, the seven-member Federal Reserve Board voted yesterday to raise the discount rate . . . The vote left uncertain whether Paul A. Volcker . . . could continue to command a majority for his high [interest] rate policies. The split was seen as indicating a fundamental division within the Board over whether inflation remains a more pressing problem than recession."[38]

The divided board had not bothered Volcker until then. Two of the dissenters, Nancy Teeters, appointed by Jimmy Carter as the first woman member of the Federal Reserve Board, and Charles Partee, the former Fed staffer famous for his hand-tied black bow ties, had actually voted that morning with the FOMC majority in favor of raising the federal funds rate before voting against the discount rate increase. Teeters explained that "we haven't always kept [the discount rate] in alignment" with other short-term rates.[39] Only board member Emmett Rice, also appointed by Jimmy Carter, had dissented at both the FOMC meeting and the follow-up meeting of the Board of Governors.

Volcker felt confident he could marshal the same four votes on the board to raise the discount rate again. "Henry Wallich grew up in Weimar Germany with hyperinflation as a tutor. He always wanted higher interest rates. Phil Coldwell had been chastised by Arthur Burns for joining the anti-inflation crusade of Al Hayes in the early seventies. He was not about to defect now. And although [board vice-chairman] Fred Schultz was a Carter appointee, he had a strong anti-inflation streak and was loyal."[40]

Volcker might have managed the bad publicity, but a second front-page article on September 19 delivered a knockout punch. The headline "Gold Price Soars at Record Pace in Wild Trading" received top billing in the *New York Times*.[41] The newspaper reported that transactions during the day on the New York Commodity Exchange, located at 4 World Trade Center, had become "chaotic," and at times "there were temporarily no sellers, only would-be buyers."[42] Gold jumped more than $25.00 and hit a new record price of $376.25 per ounce.[43]

Volcker recalls, "I knew we had a credibility problem beforehand, but the combined weight of the split decision and the increase in gold brought the problem to a head. The 4–3 majority suggested to some that I was one vote away from repeating Bill Miller's mistake. And the jump in gold was a clear symptom of hardening in inflationary expectations."[44]

Gold had humbled Volcker in the past. He had doubted the report on October 20, 1960, when speculators pushed up the price of the precious metal by 14 percent in one day, to forty dollars an ounce, shattering the thirty-five-dollar ceiling imposed by the U.S. Treasury. And he had miscalculated prior to the gold suspension in August 1971, when he told George Shultz that he could wipe out the Treasury deficit by buying gold. Speculators had driven up the price beforehand, leaving Volcker and others in the dust.

Volcker respected the warning from gold, and public commentary from those he respected confirmed the message. Wall Street economist Henry Kaufman, who had apprenticed with Volcker at New York Fed in the 1950s and had been predicting higher interest rates since the beginning of 1979, sounded the alarm: "In effect, it is a vote against the established economic and financial system."[45] Undersecretary of the Treasury Anthony Solomon, who was the first to recommend Volcker as Fed chairman to President Carter (Carter responded, "Who's Paul Volcker?"), said the gold boom "cemented inflationary expectations," and if it continued it could be "very damaging."[46]

The alarmist quotes from Henry Kaufman and Anthony Solomon caught Volcker's attention. A week earlier, Volcker had written a note to Kaufman after reading his monetary policy pronouncements in the *New York Times*: "Dear Henry: I never thanked you for writing after [my] appointment, but don't think you have to give all your advice through the newspapers—pick up the phone now and again."[47] Kaufman had clearly not taken his old friend's suggestion, but Volcker would forgive him.

Kaufman and Solomon confirmed the crisis Volcker needed for drastic action.

At the morning FOMC meeting on Tuesday, September 18, before the board conflict erupted into public view, Lawrence Roos, president of the Federal Reserve Bank of St. Louis, prodded Volcker.[48] "Well, Paul . . . maybe I am out of order to raise this now, but couldn't there be a discussion again of whether or not our traditional policy of targeting on interest rates . . . is appropriate? Shouldn't this be given another look . . . in view of everything you've said and the less than happy experience that the FOMC has had over the past years in achieving its goals?"

Roos had been urging the FOMC to mend its ways ever since joining the committee in 1976, continuing the monetarist tradition of the St. Louis Fed that had begun with its former president, Darryl Francis. Roos had invoked the mantra "focus on money supply and allow interest rates to find their own way" so often that many members of the FOMC thought his remarks sounded like a recorded announcement. Volcker did not. "My feeling would be that you're not out of order in raising that question . . . I presume that today, for better or worse, we have to couch our policy in what has become the traditional framework. But I think . . . we should be exploring it again in the relatively near future. And I would plan to do so."

The future arrived when the crisis made front-page headlines the following day. Volcker responded by asking FOMC economist Stephen

Axilrod and System Open Market Account manager Peter Sternlight to outline the plan that would revolutionize the Federal Reserve's operating procedures. The two career Federal Reserve employees complemented each other perfectly, and based their report on earlier work done at the Fed. Axilrod provided the research perspective as the FOMC's staff director for monetary and financial policy, and Sternlight provided the practical input as manager of securities transactions in the New York Fed's trading room.

On Thursday, September 27, 1979, the day before Volcker's scheduled departure to Belgrade for a meeting of the International Monetary Fund, he reviewed a confidential three-page memo from Axilrod and Sternlight. A single sentence on the second page of their draft captured the essence of the plan Volcker would present to the FOMC after he returned from Europe: "The Federal Open Market Committee . . . would seek to hold increases in the monetary base and other reserve aggregates to amounts just sufficient to meet monetary targets and to help restrain growth in bank credit, recognizing that such a procedure could result in wider fluctuations in the shortest term money market [interest] rates."[49]

Volcker knew that focusing on the monetary aggregates would turn monetary policy on its head. The so-called aggregates referred to measures such as the money supply (checking accounts plus currency), or total bank reserves, or bank reserves plus currency (called the monetary base), that influenced total spending and inflation. The famous quantity theory of money, which Volcker had studied at Princeton, taught that increases in the money supply meant higher prices and inflation. Modern monetarists, led by Milton Friedman, resurrected the lessons of the quantity theory and urged the Federal Reserve to control money and the related monetary aggregates—hence the name "monetarists."

Volcker believed that controlling the aggregates could help restrain inflation in the long run, but this strategy would also produce wide fluctuations in interest rates in the short run, disturbing traditionalists on the FOMC. The new plan would be considered a monetarist takeover of the Federal Reserve System, and would create turmoil in credit markets, just as a strategy shift at De Beers, the South African diamond cartel, would cause chaos in diamond prices. During the 1970s both De Beers and the Federal Reserve had operated in similar ways.

The mystique of a diamond comes from its beauty and scarcity, but neither occurs naturally in nature. Diamond cutters engrave facets into raw stones to make them shine, and De Beers restricts the supply to jewelers to keep engagement rings in precious demand. During much of the twentieth century, the Diamond Trading Company, the marketing arm of De Beers, controlled the world's supply of uncut stones offered to the wholesalers of New York, Antwerp, Tel Aviv, and Bombay (now Mumbai).[50] These merchants were invited every five weeks to a so-called sight at 2 Charterhouse Street, the London headquarters of the Diamond Trading Company. Monty Charles, a longtime senior manager of the firm, determined the number and size of uncut stones released each month. His job was to keep prices high and stable so that diamonds were profitable for the company but marketable on Main Street.

Charles consulted with economists and industry analysts employed by De Beers. These experts tracked the world demand for diamonds and the inventory of unsold gems in jewelry store windows, examining trends in income, spending, and celebrity fads that might cause the demand for diamonds to rise or fall. Monty then distributed the uncut stones (with a polite request to the wholesalers for payment) that he judged would keep the price of diamonds firm and steady. He would accommodate an expected jump in the public's demand by releasing more uncut stones from the company's underground vaults, and he would neutralize a drop in demand by withholding the raw material from the market and adding them to inventory.

De Beers was not above the law of supply and demand, but it could manipulate supply to prevent shifts in demand from affecting price. If De Beers had pursued a different strategy, such as rigidly increasing mine production every year, it would have had to allow prices to fluctuate with shifts in demand. For example, if De Beers increased diamond output by 5 percent a year, then diamond prices would rise when demand rose by more than 5 percent and prices would fall if demand rose by less (or actually fell).

Volcker had never visited Tiffany or Cartier, but he understood as well as anyone that the Federal Reserve behaved just like De Beers, except that it controlled a different, but no less desirable, scarce resource: the supply of dollars. Commercial banks are legally required to hold dollars as reserves against checking accounts, and individuals need dollars to pay for things they buy. A $100 bill is worth more than the paper it is printed on because the Federal Reserve System restricts the available supply, just as the value of a polished diamond exceeds the industrial use of the stone because De Beers restricts supply. Unlike De Beers, however, the Fed controls supply to promote economic activity rather than to make a profit. The New York Fed's trading room in Lower Manhattan serves as the system's control center.

When Volcker became chairman, he had promoted Peter Sternlight to manager of the trading desk at the Federal Reserve Bank of New York, replacing Alan Holmes, who had just retired. Volcker had known Sternlight, a thin man who walked three miles to work each day from his Brooklyn apartment, since they served together on the trading desk in the early 1950s. Sternlight was a technical expert, having remained on the eighth floor of the New York Fed's headquarters on Liberty Street for most of his career.

Peter Sternlight manipulated the supply of dollars available as currency and reserves by buying and selling securities in the government bond market. These so-called open market operations occur quietly, via telephone contact between Sternlight's traders and Treasury securities dealers at commercial banks, rather than on the noisy floor of an organized exchange, where trading sometimes resembles a barroom brawl. But these obscure transactions have a profound impact on the FOMC's target federal funds rate, the overnight interest rate on loans of reserves between banks. When Sternlight sells securities and reduces reserves, for example, commercial banks are caught short of their legal requirement, so they scramble to borrow reserves in the federal funds market. This buying pressure drives up the overnight interest rate.

Peter Sternlight aims his transactions at the federal funds rate specified by the FOMC at the end of each meeting. For example, on September 18 the FOMC wanted a slight increase in the rate, so Sternlight engineered a drop in reserves until he hit the new higher target. He would then add reserves if the rate went up too much and would withdraw reserves if the rate went down, just as Monty Charles adjusted the supply of raw diamonds to keep prices steady.

Volcker recognized that this technical procedure, which had served since the Treasury–Federal Reserve Accord in 1951 to maintain orderly conditions in the money markets, now undermined the Fed's credibility as guardian of the currency. Controlling the federal funds rate by adding or subtracting reserves meant that the Fed lost control over reserves made available to banks, just as when De Beers varied the amount of diamonds it distributed to keep prices steady.

Monty Charles did not mind the loss of control over his inventory, especially when he was releasing more stones than expected, because that made money for De Beers. But Volcker knew it was a disaster for the Federal Reserve continuously to expand reserves and other monetary aggregates to keep the federal funds rate from rising too quickly. The Fed had done precisely that during much of the 1970s, and the end result had been that banks made more loans and created more deposits than the Federal Reserve had promised. The excessive growth in the monetary aggregates—total bank reserves, the monetary base, and the money supply—had fueled inflation and inflationary expectations, destroying the Fed's credibility.

Volcker and other members of the FOMC had rejected the monetarist approach of focusing on the monetary aggregates and permitting greater fluctuations in interest rates many times before. The committee devoted much of the meeting on March 29, 1976, while Arthur Burns was still chairman, to considering placing more emphasis on aggregate reserve measures. The FOMC rejected the plan, in part, because of opposition by Burns. Volcker flirted with the proposal but then concluded, "Mr. Chairman, . . . maybe this will make you feel a little better . . . I think I can . . . give you categorical assurance of not a monetarist in the group."[51] Burns, a diplomat in victory, responded, "Well, that fills me with deep regret."

In 1978, Volcker dismissed the tight link between money and prices articulated by the quantity theory and put forth by monetarists to keep inflation under control. "I believe there are in fact a variety of nonmonetary . . . factors that can affect the rate of inflation in the short—and not so short-run . . . My own support of the use of monetary 'targets' does not start from a 'monetarist' perspective."[52]

He based his support for targeting the monetary aggregates, as described in the September 27, 1979, Axilrod-Sternlight memorandum, on the favorable impact on inflationary expectations and central bank credibility, an approach closer to rational expectations than to mainstream monetarism. "The announcement of the so-called [monetary] growth ranges . . . sets a general framework for expectations about inflation . . . This role in stabilizing expectations was once the function of the gold standard, the doctrine of the annually balanced budget, and fixed exchange rates. I view the monetary targeting approach as . . . a new . . . comprehensible symbol of responsible policy."[53]

He wanted to restore the gold standard without gold.

Volcker's commitment to controlling the aggregates would require a drastic shift for the FOMC: abandoning the "prudent and cautious and gradual" approach to interest rates. He knew that anything less would fail to establish the Fed's credibility. He thought the crisis that had exploded on September 18, 1979, justified the risk, and he would exploit that event to persuade the FOMC to implement an experiment it had thus far resisted. But a visit with his Board of Governors colleague Henry Wallich to discuss the draft memo gave him pause.

Volcker and Wallich had much in common, including a dislike of inflation, an attachment to cigars, and a shared history at the Federal Reserve Bank of New York, where they were attracted to the same woman. Volcker recalls, "Henry stole our coworker, Mabel Brown, and married her before I could catch my breath. Actually, he didn't really steal her. It was no contest whatsoever. I was so self-conscious about my looks and height, and she was so pretty, that I never worked up the courage to ask her out. Henry clearly had more confidence."[54]

Henry Wallich still had the confidence to defy Volcker, even though Paul was now the chairman of the board. "It's a pact with the devil," Wallich said when Volcker dropped by his office to discuss the new procedures.[55] Wallich's hatred of inflation resembled a childhood phobia, but he worried more about losing control of interest rates. "The existing methods have the advantage that we know the interest rate and we don't run the risk of the rate going in the wrong direction and creating dollar problems."[56]

Volcker shared Wallich's concern about the dollar, but felt that the inflation-fighting credibility of the new operating procedures would win support abroad. He would learn the truth on his way to Belgrade, during a private lecture from his old friend Helmut Schmidt, now the chancellor of West Germany.

CHAPTER 9

The Plan

Volcker sounded like James Bond during a telephone conference call with the FOMC on Friday, October 5, 1979. He had already stressed the confidential nature of the final Axilrod-Sternlight memorandum they would be discussing at the emergency meeting in Washington the following day. The increased gyrations in interest rates under the new procedures could mean millions in profits or losses for financiers and bankers throughout the world. Volcker also wanted to avoid leaks about the meeting itself. "I think there is a need to come in here as inconspicuously as possible . . . [and to stay] at diverse hotels . . . I imagine you do know that the Pope is coming in [to Washington] which may be good cover . . . [but] it may not be [enough]."[1]

A report at the beginning of the conference call by Peter Sternlight would have been amusing under different circumstances.[2] "There has been word from our [trading] desk—I think [it] . . . actually started in the foreign exchange markets—about a rumor that Chairman Volcker has resigned. And this is having a downward effect on the securities market."

Volcker clarified his position only half jokingly, having been shadowed by reporters since the crisis began. "The answer is 'not yet.'"

Joseph Coyne, the board's public information officer, added, "We will be saying 'absolutely ridiculous.'"

Volcker knew that such denials could be counterproductive, and he wanted to avoid fanning the speculative fever that had erupted during the week. He concluded with "I'm asking for a Papal blessing of this meeting . . . I will see you all in the morning at nine-thirty. Thank you."

The pontiff must have been listening.

The events of the previous seven days had erased any lingering doubts Volcker had about the need for drastic measures. He had returned the three-page draft memo to Stephen Axilrod and Peter Sternlight on Friday, September 28, with instructions to add numerical details for a special meeting of the FOMC on his return from Europe. That evening, he boarded an air force jet, along with Treasury Secretary William Miller and Charles Schultze, chairman of Jimmy Carter's Council of Economic Advisers, to attend a meeting of the International Monetary Fund in Belgrade. They had a scheduled stopover the next day in West Germany to meet with Chancellor Helmut Schmidt. Volcker took the opportunity to brief the president's two top economic aides about his plans. They were not pleased.

Shultze, a traditional Keynesian who had been at the Brookings Institution, the liberal Washington think tank, before joining the administration, complained, "We're not against raising interest rates, but the monetarist links are unproven and inflexible."[3] Volcker said, "Rest assured that I will not put monetary policy on automatic pilot." Schultze worried about an exit strategy. "Once you go down this road, it will be difficult to go back." Volcker emphasized, "Let's take one step at a time. This is an opportunity we cannot pass up."

Volcker had checked the foreign exchange market before they boarded the plane and reported that the dollar had fallen to 1.74 marks, capping a 4 percent decline since the September 18 discount rate debacle. The U.S. currency had dropped to its lowest level since the record of 1.72 marks reached prior to the dollar-rescue operation in November 1978.[4] Volcker worried about a repeat performance. "That is not an eventuality I would like to see and it's important that it not happen."[5] Schultze considered the dollar a sideshow, having cut his teeth on domestic problems as director of the Bureau of the Budget (later Office of Management and Budget) in the Kennedy administration. Volcker knew that he would gain reinforcements in Hamburg. The U.S. currency would take center stage under the direction of Helmut Schmidt.

The German chancellor did not disappoint. He hosted a lunch for Volcker, Miller, and Schultze, with Otmar Emminger, head of the German central bank, attending as well. While everyone ate, the chancellor talked.[6] "The world needs stability much more than anything else," he said, repeating a message Volcker had heard from him in February 1973, when the dollar was worth three marks. Now Schmidt had to be content with a more modest objective, one that reflected America's diminished status. "I would like to get back into a world in which the dollar would be two marks and stable."

Schmidt's lecture cheered Volcker but irritated Schultze. "He was at his egotistical worst," the chairman of the Council of Economic Advisers said.[7] Volcker almost concurred: "He was at his egotistical best."[8] A scheduled news conference at the end of the four-hour meeting was canceled, but a joint press release stated, "Both sides agreed [that] . . . exchange rate stability . . . and a strong dollar are in the interests of both countries." A reporter asked Schmidt about the significance of the meeting as he departed in his limousine. The chancellor smiled. "We had a good lunch."[9]

A very public lecture by Arthur Burns in Belgrade saddened Volcker as much as Schmidt's private sermon had pleased him. On Sunday, September 30, as a prelude to the gathering of the world's central bankers and finance ministers for the IMF meetings, Burns delivered the annual Per Jacobsson lecture entitled "The Anguish of Central Banking."[10] William McChesney Martin introduced Burns with "I am proud to say [he] was my successor at the Federal Reserve," but that was before Burns's message.[11]

Volcker arrived late and had to sit on the floor, cross-legged, with his back to the wall. He flipped through a copy of the talk while listening to the former chairman explain why "central bankers, whose main business . . . is to control inflation, have been so ineffective in dealing with this worldwide problem."[12] Burns blamed inflation on the "political currents that have been transforming economic life in the United States and elsewhere since the 1930s."[13] In particular, "budget deficits have become a chronic condition of federal finance . . . [and] when the government runs a budget deficit it pumps more money into the pocketbooks of people than it withdraws . . . [and] that is the way . . . inflation . . . has been raging since the mid-1960s."[14]

Volcker recalled how Milton Friedman had told that same story in his *Newsweek* article "Burns on the Outside," after Carter replaced Burns as chairman. "We have been having inflation not because evil men at the Fed have been willfully turning the printing press, but because John Q. Public has been demanding inflation [by] . . . asking Congress to provide us with ever more goodies—yet not to raise our taxes."[15] The root cause of inflation was excessive government spending, according to Friedman and his former professor, plus the political reality that prevented, in Burns's words, "the Federal Reserve . . . [from] frustrating the will of Congress to which it was responsible—a Congress that was intent on providing additional services to the electorate."[16]

Volcker knew that government deficits made life difficult for the central bank, forcing a Fed chairman into the role of a Marquis de Sade tightening interest rates to painful levels to restrain private spending to make room for Uncle Sam. But blaming the inflation of the 1970s on government deficits ignored the Federal Reserve's timidity under Burns's leadership.

Volcker recalled a conversation between Nixon and Burns during the weekend of August 13, 1971, at Camp David that came closer to the truth. Nixon had suggested labeling his proposed tax relief for business an employment tax credit.[17] "The businessman will not give a damn what it's called as long as he gets it." Burns thought for a moment and said, "I would add in [a] personal tax break." The president smiled. "You are too softhearted, Arthur, to be a banker." Burns sighed. "I have not been at it long enough."

Nixon may have been a crook, but he was a perceptive crook.

The press attending the Belgrade meeting painted Burns's talk as an "insider's view of the relations between the Fed and other parts of the Government."[18] The *Wall Street Journal* concluded that "Arthur Burns . . . contributed to the uneasy mood here . . . [His] main conclusion was that given the political and economic forces feeding inflation in the industrial nations 'it is illusory to expect central banks to put an end' to the wage price spiral by themselves."[19]

The reaction in the marketplace suggested that Burns had irritated the speculators as well as the central bankers. On Monday, October 1, the day after the former Fed chairman's speech, gold rose to $414.75 an ounce, a jump of 4 percent from the previous close on Friday, September 28.[20] The new speculative burst convinced Volcker to cut short his stay in Belgrade and return to Washington to complete work on the Axilrod-Sternlight memorandum. William Miller and Charles Schultze urged him to remain a little longer to avoid the appearance of a panicked departure. The delay did not help.

Volcker's exit the following day from Belgrade created more confusion than Burns's apologia. The London gold fixing, normally a fifteen-minute negotiation to find a consensus price to clear the market, took more than two hours on Tuesday, October 2, 1979.[21] The price of the yellow metal hit an all-time high of $442 an ounce, up more than 6 percent from the previous day, before settling at $426 at the close of London trading.[22]

The *Wall Street Journal* explained: "Gold skyrocketed . . . and then plummeted . . . all touched off early in the European business day when it was learned that Paul Volcker . . . had left a meeting of the International Monetary Fund . . . while the session was still under way."[23] Rumors that "South American central banks were dumping their dollar reserves . . . for gold . . . and Arab oil producing countries also were giving up the United States currency" fed the gold-buying spree.[24] Speculation that Volcker's departure meant that "a new dollar-defense program would be initiated" triggered the subsequent sales of the precious metal.[25]

The speculative gyrations convinced Volcker to meet on Thursday, October 4, with members of the Board of Governors in the Special Library, an intimate setting down the marble hallway from the boardroom in the Fed's headquarters. It was the day before the conference call inviting the entire membership of the FOMC to their clandestine gathering, and he wanted to build a consensus beforehand. "I had to avoid a repetition of the September 18 division over the discount rate, when Partee, Teeters, and Rice dissented."[26]

The smell of leather-bound books and furniture polish give the Special Library, a wood-paneled room resembling a formal den, a sense of

Federal Reserve history. The original board table from the Fed's early home in the U.S. Treasury dominates the center of the room, and built-in bookshelves filled with Annual Reports since 1914 line the walls. Fixed to the lip of the mahogany tabletop are brass nameplates about two inches wide, each identifying a member of the original Federal Reserve Board.[27] It is as though the seats along the sides of the rectangular table are reserved for the ghosts of Adolph Miller, Charles Hamlin, and Paul Warburg. Only the nameplate at the head has disappeared, leaving two well-lacquered tiny holes as a reminder of the vanishing.

The missing nameplate belonged to the secretary of the treasury, the ex officio chairman of the Federal Reserve Board until 1935, who sat at the head of the table whenever he chose to attend meetings.[28] Resentment toward the Treasury runs deep within the Federal Reserve bureaucracy, dating back to 1914, when the board became a reluctant tenant on the second floor of the Treasury Building, and continuing through the accord in 1951, when the Treasury finally freed the Fed from its obligation to maintain a ceiling on U.S. interest rates.[29] The Special Library celebrates Federal Reserve history by honoring the original board table and by suppressing the treasury secretary's nameplate. Volcker's plan to focus on the monetary aggregates and set interest rates free would bury the remnants of the Treasury's influence.

The meeting in the Special Library identified "speculative activity in the gold market which appeared to be spilling over into other commodity markets."[30] Charles Partee, a dissenting troublemaker back in September, sounded the alarm.[31] "I was extremely bothered by the market developments of the last two weeks. I think the spreading of the gold [market psychology] into the more remote metals is very bothersome. Silver we understand and platinum we understand, but the spreading to copper, zinc and lead is very bothersome . . . It leaves one with the thought that because of a run from currency—a desire to get into goods and out of money—we might have now a new development in our economic experience."

The touch of panic in the Special Library pleased Volcker.

"We wouldn't be here today if we didn't have a problem with the state of the markets, whether international or domestic," Volcker said to the

FOMC shortly after ten o'clock on Saturday morning, October 6, 1979. "I think the rumors that were floating around in the market yesterday— first that I had resigned and then that I had died—are symptomatic . . . that the psychology . . . is ready to crack open, depending upon what decisions they see coming out of here."[32]

Volcker recalled his admiration for former treasury secretary George Shultz, who built a consensus for floating exchange rates with an even-handed approach, suppressing his preferences to promote an exchange of views. The crisis atmosphere encouraged Volcker to follow suit and present the alternatives to the committee like a judge instructing a jury. "I think there are broadly two possibilities. One is taking measures . . . thought of as the traditional type . . . a discount rate move . . . a significant increase in the federal funds rate . . . some reserve requirement changes . . . The other possibility is a change in . . . our operations as outlined in the memorandum that was distributed . . . with a greater effort to . . . achieve a money supply target . . . recognizing that would require a wider range for the federal funds rate."[33]

Volcker paused to assess the somber mood at the table and then continued to underplay his hand, like a poker player holding a pair of aces.

> As I look at these two approaches there are advantages and disadvantages . . . to both of them . . . My feeling was that by . . . changing operating techniques . . . and thereby changing psychology a bit, we might actually get more bang for the buck . . . [But] we run a risk almost whatever we do . . . If we are lucky, this change [in technique] will improve our chances of reaching our money supply targets . . . [but] it has some built-in pressure to move interest rates downward . . . if money supply begins running low . . . [and] that would be unsettling internationally.[34]

Volcker then related the reservations of CEA chairman Charles Schultze and Treasury Secretary William Miller. "I discussed the whole problem . . . with the Administration . . . They are ready for a strong program [but] . . . they shy away very strongly . . . [from] a shift in technique at this point because . . . that is the more risky course for a variety of reasons . . . [especially] concern about locking ourselves into a technique . . . that might not be suitable in light of all the circumstances."[35]

Volcker concluded his overview with a qualification that made him sound like a reluctant bride planning a divorce: "I am prepared . . . to go with whichever way the consensus wants to go as long as the program is strong, [but] if we adopt a new approach [it should be understood that] we are not locked into it indefinitely . . . And . . . early next year . . . we would have a thoroughgoing ground up decision as to whether we wanted to maintain . . . it . . . [or] return to our more traditional practices."[36]

Volcker knew he had disappointed the confirmed monetarists on the FOMC hoping for a permanent conversion to their doctrine, but they were not the ones who worried him. Lawrence Roos, president of the St. Louis Federal Reserve Bank, had been waiting so long for a trial run that he would vote in favor of anything with a monetarist fragrance. "I assume that my credibility with you and my colleagues would be severely jeopardized if I came out in opposition to this proposal. I also was told by my father to keep my mouth shut when things are going well."[37] He followed the old man's advice.

The Keynesians were cause for greater concern. Volcker wanted to avoid dissents that would damage the credibility of the new procedures. Charles Partee provided a glimmer of hope, repeating his earlier alarm over the speculative excesses in the base metals. But Volcker worried about Frank Morris, who had opposed his call to arms earlier in the year because of a weak economic outlook. Morris had accused Volcker of sacrificing the domestic economy to promote the dollar internationally.

Morris spoke up right after Partee. "I agree with Chuck . . . Despite my view that the recession is going to be sharp, I think we are in a situation where we have to be willing to do something dramatic today . . . And I think our credibility will really suffer if we announce a change in procedure and then fail to have the guts to go through with it."[38]

Volcker never felt comfortable showing affection, but he thought (for a nanosecond) about kissing Frank Morris, even though Morris was halfway down the twenty-seven-foot-long table. Instead, he praised his old friend by repeating (twice) the most important word Morris had said, just in case anyone had missed it. "If I may just interject, Frank, I agree with what you are saying . . . But presumably the guts will have to have a number on it—the degree of our guts on the upside [for interest rates]."[39]

Morris jumped back in. "Well, that's right. But it's got to be a pretty big number."[40]

"I understand."[41] Volcker nodded in agreement, just like the elder Roos would have advised.

Volcker thought that Henry Wallich's academic pedigree gave him license to buck the consensus. The former Yale economics professor had disparaged the monetarist links between money and economic activity and had warned Volcker away from its satanic influence. Volcker listened carefully when Wallich spoke. "I think the main argument in favor of the [new] reserve strategy is that it allows us to take stronger action than we probably could by the other technique. We are much more constrained in the [traditional approach] by the appearance of very high interest rates. In the new strategy interest rates become almost a by-product of a more forceful pursuit of the aggregates . . . [In fact] there is that risk of interest rate uncertainty involved in the new strategy. We would have to guard against interest rates going in the wrong direction."[42]

Partee interjected: "Which is what direction—up or down?"[43]

"It is quite clearly down . . . It involves a signal that we've switched policy and the markets are going to respond accordingly . . . But we need to watch this [new] strategy . . . for interest rates and for the exchange market so that we don't get surprised by interest rate movements when they could be harmful."[44]

Volcker should have let them fight it out, but he could not permit the discussion to pass unchallenged. Wallich had irritated a nerve that would remain exposed for years to come. Volcker would be accused of pushing the new program as political cover for dramatically higher interest rates. He denied the premise. "I'm not sure it's self evident that in interest rate terms the new technique is stronger. It may or may not be, depending on what happens to the money supply. I think that is inherent in the new technique . . . I don't think at this stage . . . we know the answer . . . We'll never know the answer no matter how long we talk."[45]

The press conference at six o'clock on Saturday evening, October 6, 1979, in the Federal Reserve's boardroom drew an unhappy crowd of more than fifty reporters, many still wearing their weekend golf shirts. The informality of the assembled journalists contrasted with the majesty of the great seal of the United States embossed on the front wall of the cavernous boardroom, with the eagle's ten-foot wings spanning the crowd below. America's coat of arms framed Volcker preparing to announce the central bank's most important decision in its history.

The unusual timing, Saturday evening on a Columbus Day holiday weekend, made the press conference feel like an emergency military briefing by the chairman of the Joint Chiefs of Staff. Volcker had asked his special assistant, Joseph Coyne, to call the media immediately after the FOMC had adjourned at four o'clock, to offer full disclosure to all. A delay would risk the leak of sensitive information into speculators' hands, lining their pocketbooks when markets opened Sunday night in Asia. The head of the CBS Washington bureau asked Coyne whether to send his only TV crew, which was covering the pope.[46] The Fed's public relations chief answered that he would "remember the press conference long after the Pope had left town."

Volcker began with a disclaimer: "I will tell you that the major purpose of this press conference is to show that I have not resigned—the way the early rumor had it yesterday—and I'm still alive—contrary to the latest rumor. We have been busy during the day . . . developing a series of actions that is reflected in the release in front of you . . . I think in general you know the background . . . the inflation rate has been moving at an excessive rate . . . and the anticipations of inflation have been unsettling to markets both at home and abroad."[47]

The press release highlighted the FOMC's decision to concentrate on controlling the level of bank reserves and permitting greater variability in short-term interest rates. It also announced the decision to increase the Federal Reserve's discount rate by a full percentage point, from 11 percent to 12 percent, and the introduction of a special reserve requirement on bank borrowings that had eluded Fed control.[48] Volcker had managed to forge a monetary policy sledgehammer without dissents and was pleased to entertain questions from reporters.

The decision to increase the discount rate by a full percentage point provoked a question related to the September 18 dissents. "The Board split four to three in raising the discount rate by just a fraction. What has happened since then to change the Board's mind?"[49]

Volcker replied, "What has changed since then is quite clear ... business data [have] been good and better than expected, the inflationary data [have] been bad and perhaps worse than expected, and we have had developments in markets [suggesting] ... the dangers of instability and inflationary expectations." He paused, and then allied himself with the earlier minority. "I was not voting for more than a half percent discount rate increase two weeks ago. In that sense I changed my mind too."

The consequences of the new operating procedures garnered the most attention, with some questions triggering friendly banter.

"Are you saying hands off altogether on the federal funds rate?"

"Cautious central bankers never talk in extremes but I think the banks will have to learn ... how to make reserve adjustments."

"But [the rate] still won't be completely free to go as high as it might?"

"I don't know what you think is 'as high as it might.' There will be substantial freedom in the market."

Other questions created more controversy, both contemporaneously and going forward.

"Mr. Volcker, what domestic economic effects would you anticipate from this series of actions? Would you expect it to further slow the economy or deepen the recession?"

"I would hope ... and expect that these actions would ultimately have a settling effect on financial markets. I think it is basically good for longer term interest rates ... because they are sensitive to inflationary expectations."

The reporter followed up: "But in immediate terms does it have an effect that will tend to slow down economic growth ... in this country?"

"Well, you get varying opinions about that. I don't think it will have important effects in that connection. I would be optimistic about the results of these actions. But we're in an area dealing with economic events that are not fully predictable."

William Greider, a columnist for *Rolling Stone* and formerly with the *Washington Post*, disparaged Volcker's response to the reporter's question in a retrospective on the October 6, 1979, news conference:

"Volcker evaded the point and concealed his real expectations."[50] Greider should have checked the record.

Volcker had been grilled about the same issue at his public confirmation hearings more than two months earlier, by Wisconsin senator William Proxmire, chairman of the Senate Banking Committee. Proxmire understood money and finance better than most members of Congress, having received an MBA from Harvard Business School, and he was not shy about displaying his expertise. "Dr. Arthur Okun . . . a former CEA [Council of Economic Advisers] Chairman and a highly respected economist . . . found that when the Fed had tightened the money supply . . . [it caused] a terrific price in the loss of jobs and loss of production . . . [And] this may not be the way to cope with inflation. What is your response to that?"[51]

Volcker respected Proxmire's intellect as well as his reputation as a maverick. The Wisconsin senator irritated the Washington bureaucracy with his monthly Golden Fleece Award for "frivolous government spending."[52] Proxmire had conferred the honor on the Federal Aviation Administration for spending $57,800 on a study of the physical measurements of 432 airline stewardesses, paying special attention to the "length of the buttocks" and how their knees were arranged when they were seated. A $27,000 study by the Justice Department on why prisoners wanted to get out of jail received the Golden Fleece Award as well.

Volcker expected the independent-minded senator to understand an unconventional perspective on monetary policy. "I think we have to be very careful about the implications of studies [like Okun's] . . . Part of the difficulty . . . [is] that the prolonged nature of the [current] inflation has changed expectations, it's changed the way people look at their personal lives . . . I think it's fair to say the economy probably doesn't react the same way you, and certainly I, were brought up to think . . . It's perhaps symptomatic of some of the new problems . . . that we find some evidence recently that actions [such as tight monetary policy] that are interpreted as dampening the inflation rate have a favorable impact . . . the long term interest rate will decline instead of going up—whereas . . . easier money . . . [has] a rather perverse effect . . . that is counterproductive."

Volcker's observation that tight money would lower long-term interest rates found little support in the reigning econometric models;

those models' flawed view of expectations made them useless props in the discussion. But he had made this same point, reflecting a rational expectations approach to monetary policy, at his first FOMC meeting as chairman: "I think we are in something of a box—a box that says that the ordinary response one expects to [monetary] easing actions may not work . . . They won't work if they're interpreted as inflationary . . . On the other hand, a tightening action obviously has risks too . . . But to some degree the perversity of reactions can help us there. I think there is some evidence, for instance—if a tightening action is interpreted as a responsible action . . . that long-term rates tend to move favorably."[53]

Volcker never identified himself with the extreme rational expectations theorists, and would privately refer to "those crazy economists up in Minnesota" (including future Nobel Prize winner Thomas Sargent), who warned everyone about the impotence of a fully anticipated monetary policy.[54] But Volcker had accepted an even more controversial tenet of their doctrine when it was still a newborn, "that concern about the inflationary consequences of policy cannot be postponed until the economy approaches . . . full employment."[55] Belief in the favorable response in long-term interest rates to tight money required even less of a religious commitment to rational expectations than worrying about inflation with unemployed resources.

Volcker hoped that the credibility conferred by the new monetary procedures would produce two different interest rate effects. Federal Reserve operations dominate the overnight interest rate on loans of reserves between banks, but inflationary expectations dominate longer-term interest rates. Volcker expected the new procedures to increase the volatility of the federal funds rate but reduce the interest rate on long-term bonds. He would be disappointed.

CHAPTER 10

Sticking to It

"Mr. Volcker is a gambler. He is betting high with a poor hand. The entire nation needs to hope that he beats the odds," warned an editorial with the title "Mr. Volcker's Verdun," published in response to the October 6, 1979, announcement.[1] The editors at the *New York Times* likened Chairman Paul Volcker's attack on inflation to Marshal Philippe Pétain's battle near the city of Verdun, France, the longest and bloodiest encounter of the Great War. "By forcing interest rates to shoot up like a signal flare, Mr. Volcker, like France's Marshal Pétain at Verdun, seeks to assure his own forces that the enemy 'shall not pass.' Marshal Pétain did hold the fort—at the cost of 350,000 casualties. No lives are directly at stake in slamming the gates on credit but the risks are nonetheless substantial."

Economists on the left and right expressed their concern as well. John Kenneth Galbraith, a Harvard Keynesian and popular author with an acerbic wit, spoke at a dinner commemorating the fiftieth anniversary of the 1929 Crash, and recalled the escapades of some white-collar criminals. He warned the assembled that "trust in people who owe their intelligence to association with large sums of money . . . may be misplaced."[2] Noting that the Fed chairman had access to the vast financial resources of the central bank, he added, "The moral is that you hadn't better trust Paul Volcker either."

Allan Meltzer, a monetarist from Carnegie Mellon University who would write a monumental three-volume history of the Federal Reserve, withheld approval of the October 6 initiative from a very different perspective: "I didn't send them a congratulatory telegram. I'm going to hold my breath and hope they don't mess it up."[3]

Volcker never expected to win a popularity contest, but he resented being labeled a gambler. "The only time I ever rolled the dice was playing Monopoly with Janice and Jimmy—and I didn't like losing."[4] He was, of course, experimenting with an unproven strategy, but the old methods had failed, and doing more of the same would have gambled on the status quo. Risks prevailed either way.

The verdict in the marketplace on the Federal Reserve's announcement troubled Volcker more than newspaper editorials or professorial pronouncements. The government bond market in the United States was closed for the Columbus Day holiday on Monday, October 8, the first trading day following the Fed's announcement, but favorable responses in gold and foreign exchange, which trade worldwide, offered initial encouragement. The dollar rose to 1.794 marks, a significant jump of 2 percent from the previous Friday, and gold declined to $372 per ounce, a drop of 3.3 percent from its Friday close.[5]

Gold and the dollar confirmed the favorable European commentary on the American initiative. The manager of Zurich's Bank Rothschild said, "After all its past quarrels with the Fed, it now looks as if the White House may finally have bitten the anti-inflation bullet."[6] A foreign exchange dealer in Brussels added, "The United States has put its finger right on the spot this time."[7] And a report from a correspondent in Bonn summarized the sentiment: "The Fed actions bolster the reputation of Federal Reserve Chairman Paul Volcker as 'a tough guy.'"[8]

Meg Greenfield, a Pulitzer Prize–winning columnist at the *Washington Post*, made "tough" synonymous with leadership, "in the sense of being serious and consistent and aggressive," and claimed that Americans also valued that trait.[9] "A great deal of admiration has been expressed for Volcker's unambiguous and painful action to get hold of the runaway inflation—damn the side effects and cost, it had to be done. I happen to agree. But I also think there is something truly disturbing about the fact that . . . we are all sitting around hailing one among us who was obliged to take harsh measures to restrain our undisciplined ways." Leslie Pollack, chief investment officer of the brokerage firm Shearson Hayden Stone, concurred. "Volcker is the first Fed chairman in twenty-five years who's doing what he's paid to do."[10]

The resumption of government bond trading on Tuesday, October 9, took the chairman down a notch. He had sanctioned the unprecedented two-percentage-point increase in the overnight federal funds rate, to 13.86 percent, but had not expected the ten-year bond rate to follow suit. Volcker thought the favorable effect of the new procedures in dampening inflationary expectations should have pushed down long-term interest rates, even if the actual rate of inflation remained high. Instead, the ten-year bond rate jumped from 9.6 to 9.93 percent, a huge one-day increase in that maturity range.[11] And it was about to get worse.

Historical precedent had encouraged Volcker to believe he could raise the federal funds rate and simultaneously decrease the ten-year bond rate. He knew that the two rates usually move in the same direction because they both represent the price of lending dollars over different time horizons—one day for the federal funds rate and about 3,650 days for the ten-year bond. But the ten-year bond rate is more complicated than the overnight rate because bond buyers have to worry about inflation eroding the value of their investment over ten years. Lenders for one day do not worry about inflation because the price level does not change that much overnight, at least not in the northern half of the Western Hemisphere.

Volcker recalled observing a dramatic shift in long-term interest rates versus short-term interest rates during 1975, before he became president of the Federal Reserve Bank of New York. The federal funds rate declined to an average of 6 percent in July 1975, down from 13 percent a year earlier, while over that same period, the ten-year government bond rate rose from an average of 7.8 percent to over 8.0 percent.[12] Short-term interest rates declined because the Fed tried to cushion the emerging recession, and long-term rates rose because investors worried about the inflationary consequences of the easier monetary policy.

Volcker thought the procedures announced on Saturday evening, October 6, could work in reverse. Higher short-term rates to fight inflation and lower long-term rates because investors believed the Fed's new look would succeed. This twist in the yield curve would have confirmed the Fed's credibility. The market delivered a sobering message, and not just to Volcker.

The ten-year bond rate had spiked to over 10¾ percent when the FOMC gathered in the boardroom in the Fed's headquarters on Tuesday, November 20, 1979, the first meeting since the October 6 announcement.[13] John Balles, president of the Federal Reserve Bank of San Francisco, sounded befuddled: "The only bad result I see from our October 6 actions is the very sharp rise in long-term interest rates. Maybe the school of rational expectations has an answer . . . because I can't get [one] from anybody else . . . To the extent that those rates are influenced by expectations of inflation I'm still wondering why . . . they went up instead of coming down."[14]

During his confessional, John Balles had queried Mark Willes, seated at the long mahogany table in his capacity as president of the Federal Reserve Bank of Minneapolis, the hotbed of rational expectations thinking.[15] Willes remained silent, but Balles solved the expectations puzzle himself. A decade of failed promises by the Fed to control accelerating inflation had promoted skepticism among rational bond investors. Balles urged his fellow members not "to rock the boat by any major change in the posture that we adopted . . . because I think we're right in the midst of a great credibility test . . . Our impact on long-term interest rates and inflationary expectations . . . will be messed up if we don't meet those goals that we've announced."[16]

Volcker understood the power of credibility and had embraced monetarism to promote the cause. He had forsaken control over interest rates and adopted a "monetary targeting approach as a new . . . comprehensible symbol of responsible policy," and told his colleagues on November 20, 1979, "When I appear in public or in private the first question I get is, 'Are you going to stick with it?' "[17]

The question jogged Volcker's memory of Arthur Burns's mea culpa in Belgrade, when the former chairman lamented, "The Federal Reserve was willing to step hard on the monetary brakes at times—as in 1966, 1969, and 1974—but its restrictive stance was not maintained long enough to end inflation."[18] Volcker knew that failure to maintain monetary restraint nurtured inflationary expectations, and he pledged to avoid making the same mistake he had observed in July 1975, when the economic downturn convinced the Fed to loosen credit and allow short-term rates to decline. The error may not have been obvious back then, before the Great Inflation had gathered force, but the accompanying rise in long-term interest rates was like a darkening sky before a storm.

The history of the past decade would haunt the Federal Reserve. In the meeting, Volcker warned the FOMC that their "sticking to it" under monetary aggregate targeting, which allowed interest rates to fluctuate with supply and demand for credit, might be misinterpreted.[19] "I was at a lunch yesterday where there were some presumably sophisticated people . . . I went through my song and dance [about how] we are going to stick with it in terms of the money supply but that doesn't mean interest rates can't come down. I no sooner got finished with this ten to fifteen minute discussion when . . . a member of the Washington economic press . . . says, 'Now, what I want to know is when are you going to change policy?' I said, 'What do you mean by changing policy?' He says, 'The first time interest rates go down.'"

Volcker could have questioned the intelligence of all financial journalists, or just those gathered in the nation's capital, but instead he simply raised his palms in surrender. "There we are."

Henry Wallich had told Volcker that he would regret the day he left interest rates to their own devices, and that he would have to pay for this Faustian bargain with the monetarists. Volcker had responded, "Sometimes you have to deal with the devil."[20]

The bill from below would arrive shortly.

The price of gold hit an all-time high of $850 an ounce on Monday, January 21, 1980, a record that would last almost thirty years.[21] International tensions in Iran and Afghanistan—it all started back then—combined with a worsening of inflation to an annual rate of 13½ percent during the last quarter of 1979, contributed to the speculative outburst.[22]

The more than doubling in gold prices between the November 20 FOMC meeting and the peak on January 21, 1980, created an uncommon interest in the precious metal.[23] Harry Yaruss of the Rodman and

Yaruss Refining Company in New Jersey said that people want to "sell their gold before someone steals it," and Jack Brod, owner of the Empire Diamond and Gold Buying Service in New York, hired an extra security guard to control the crowd outside his sixty-sixth-floor establishment in the Empire State Building.[24] Inside Brod's office, a woman by the name of Anne Dawson exchanged several gold chains, a pin scarf, a gold locket, and a 1962 high school ring for $305. Another customer, Ernest Harvey, an employee of a textile company, offered four of his extracted teeth containing gold inlays, and walked away with $160. Jack Brod recalled, "We had a dentist come in with gold inlays and silver fillings . . . They were worth $3,000."

J. Cantor Shoes in Yonkers, New York, had a small stamp and coin exchange in a corner of the shop. "Until four months ago you could sit and do nothing" in that end of the store, said the owner, Bob Cantor, "But now it's become positively wild."[25] A Yonkers widow handed Cantor several pieces of gold jewelry and said, with a touch of sadness, "Here are my husband's gold cuff links and tie clip. I know they are fourteen-karat gold." A well-dressed woman in a fur hat and blue wool coat chimed in: "There's no sense keeping old jewelry lying around in drawers. And from everything I've heard lately, this is the right time to sell."

The woman in the hat was right (making berets and derbies fashionable among Wall Street forecasters). The supply of antique jewelry and old dentures overwhelmed the speculative demand for gold and contributed to a collapse in price to $500 an ounce by April 1980.[26] The decline would have buoyed Volcker's spirits, but a downward spiral in both the economy and the money supply tempered the celebration. A recession had taken hold that would test Volcker's commitment to the monetary aggregates, just as Henry Wallich had predicted.

Volcker had come under attack from enemies and friends, and sometimes it was hard to tell them apart. Donald Regan, the head of investment giant Merrill Lynch, explained that "we talk about B.V. and A.V., Before Volcker and After Volcker," to measure the diminished profitability of the brokerage business.[27] Regan would exact some revenge after becoming treasury secretary under President Ronald Reagan. Henry Kaufman, chief economist at Salomon Brothers, bypassed Volcker's earlier invitation to "pick up the phone every now and again," and turned to the press to describe members of the Federal Reserve Board as "reluctant gladiators," fearful of fighting inflation by taking decisive action to retard the growth of credit.[28]

Kaufman's complaint would have surprised most Americans. The prime rate charged by commercial banks to their most creditworthy borrowers hit a record 20 percent in April 1980, making the previous peak of 12 percent during July 1974 seem like a summer romance. Arthur Okun, the former chairman of the Council of Economic Advisers under President Johnson, said a month earlier, only weeks before his untimely death at age fifty-one, that he expected to see interest rates climb to peaks that "will never be surpassed in my lifetime or the lifetime of anyone now alive."[29] Okun died before the surge, but everyone else noticed, and anger spilled into the streets.[30]

In mid-April, Gale Cincotta, a consumer activist from Chicago and head of the National People's Action coalition, led a five-hundred-person protest to the Federal Reserve's doorstep in Washington.[31] Volcker met with the leaders in his office and then confronted the crowd at the C Street entrance to the Fed's white marble building. Mrs. Cincotta repeated the main message: "We are very upset about interest rates. They are killing us."[32] A man dressed in a shark outfit stood nearby wearing a sign indicating he was a loan shark, in case anyone missed the point.[33] Volcker responded with "I'm with you, but we have to lick inflation first."[34]

Inflation had increased to an annual rate of 15 percent when Volcker arranged an FOMC conference call on Tuesday, May 6, 1980.[35] Six weeks earlier, President Jimmy Carter had enlisted Volcker's help in administering a program of consumer credit controls designed to curtail spending while avoiding still-higher interest rates.[36]

Trouble followed.

Volcker had objected to controls because he believed that temporary measures to suppress spending would not reduce underlying inflationary expectations. The wage-price freeze in August 1971 had taught a painful lesson. Nevertheless, he went along with the White House request despite his reservations. "I found it impossible to resist . . . the

President [who] had publicly supported . . . our risky and unprecedented monetary policy."[37] Volcker recalled Carter's very public response to a question of whether he would support tight money policies even if it hurt him politically: "The number one threat to our economy is inflation."[38] William Miller, Carter's treasury secretary, confirmed the message: "The President is very supportive of these actions because he's determined to carry on the war against inflation."[39] And Charles Schultze, the chairman of the Council of Economic Advisers, added, "The basic thrust of what the Fed did was needed."[40]

Volcker felt he owed the president, but he encountered resistance from a jealous Congress always guarding its monetary powers from encroachment by the executive branch. Republican senator Jake Garn questioned the precedent when Volcker testified on credit controls before the Senate Banking Committee. "As you may remember from your confirmation hearings, I have always been very concerned about the independence of the Fed."[41]

Volcker justified his pragmatic compromise with the White House while puffing like a reluctant witness on a progression of cigars.[42] "In no sense have we surrendered our independence. There are probably varying views within the Federal Reserve, but our actions were taken [because] . . . they would provide some supplementary usefulness in terms of what we're trying to achieve."

Garn respected Volcker, so he let it pass. "Well, my time is up."

Volcker escaped further public recrimination, but the economy did not. Compliance with restrictions on consumer credit curtailed spending beyond what anyone had expected.[43] Chase Manhattan and Citibank announced they would not issue new Visa or MasterCards, and Bank of America suspended applications for second mortgages.[44] Janice Fried, a real estate agent in Brooklyn, had borrowed the $1,500 maximum on her Citibank Ready Credit checking account to help pay for a renovation on her home. Citibank had then increased her limit to $3,500, and she used the balance to help pay for a new Peugeot. After the controls were announced, Citibank sent her a letter reducing her credit line to $500. "That really got me," said Mrs. Fried. "They trained us one way and now they are changing the rules."[45]

The imposition of credit controls cut Mrs. Fried's checking account and her spending, and similar effects throughout the country sent the money supply and the economy into a tailspin.[46] The drop in money violated Volcker's monetarist pledge to control the monetary aggregates. He had adopted the new procedures to prevent excessive money growth from feeding inflation, and that remained the Fed's main priority, but he had to address the flip side of the monetarist coin: avoiding anemic money growth to prevent an economic collapse. Compounding the problem, the overnight interest rate had dropped to less than 12 percent from more than 19 percent a month earlier, signaling by conventional measures that the Fed had eased policy.[47] Volcker organized the FOMC telephone conference call on Tuesday, May 6, 1980, to confront the bill of particulars that Henry Wallich had warned about.

"I think we're in danger of making a great mistake,"[48] Wallich began, after hearing the plan to jump-start the money supply by expanding bank reserves, a process that would force down the federal funds rate even further. "The real policy action is on interest rates, not on the money supply. Whatever happens to the money supply over a period of a month has next to no effect on the economy. But these [lower] interest rates—not only internationally but domestically—convey an impression of a drastic shift in policy and create expectations that we're all for inflation as soon as we work out of this difficulty."

Lawrence Roos took the other side, reminding everyone of the monetarist compact they had signed: "I think we recognize that the most important objective of the Federal Reserve today is to restore credibility . . . And I know of no way to destroy that credibility more quickly than to start dancing back toward the stabilization of interest rates after . . . all . . . of us have said that we're no longer targeting on the fed funds rate."[49]

Volcker saw merit in both points of view, having kept an eye on interest rates throughout the monetarist exercise.[50] He tried to mediate: "Well, I think there is some question as to how credibility gets defined in these circumstances which I suppose is what the argument is about."[51] He meant that the credibility of the Fed's commitment to controlling the money supply clashed with its commitment to maintaining high interest rates, and both served as ammunition in battling inflation.

Nancy Teeters had been a reluctant convert to monetarism on October 6, 1979, succumbing only because the new procedures promised a swift decline in interest rates if the economy faltered.[52] She chided

Volcker like a Sunday school teacher. "You know, Paul, I'm a little disturbed by the fact that when [the funds rate was] going up nobody was concerned about the speed at which it went up . . . If we are really going to follow this policy, then we're going to have to let the market determine how rapidly it comes down. It seems to me we should give ourselves some leeway and if we're wrong, the market will turn the rates around and they will go back up again."[53]

Volcker thought Teeters made a good point. He had promised to control the money supply and inflation, and had pledged his *guts* to *stick to it*. He knew those words were easy to say and hard to do, as with diet and exercise, and he worried with Wallich that declining interest rates might signal a shift toward monetary ease. The drop in rates would be misinterpreted by the same reporters he had encountered before. But he had embraced the monetary aggregates on October 6 and had argued back then that interest rates under the new procedures might be higher or lower "depending upon what happens to the money supply."[54] On May 6, 1980, he upheld his end of the bargain. "We may be in a situation where literally in order to get the [money supply] turned around [the funds rate] has to go very low and then go right up again, which bothers some people, including me. But I don't know how to avoid that either."[55]

He paid for keeping his word.

By July 1, 1980, the prime interest rate collapsed to 12 percent from its peak of 20 percent in April, almost matching the 50 percent drop in the federal funds rate over the same period.[56] Maury Harris, an economist for the brokerage firm Paine, Webber, Jackson and Curtis, and formerly with the Federal Reserve Bank of New York, said, "The evidence increasingly suggests that the Fed has eased."[57] More disappointing, speculators showed their lack of faith in the central bank by placing their bets on more inflation. The price of gold increased to $660 an ounce by July 1, a jump of 30 percent since the beginning of April, and the dollar declined by 10 percent against the German mark during that same three-month interval.[58]

Volcker had hoped for a more nuanced response to the decline in interest rates, along the lines of a *New York Times* op-ed article that he had admired back in May: "Will sharply declining interest rates signal an end to the anti-inflationary posture that we so desperately need to sustain? This will not be the case as long as the Federal Reserve sticks to its guns and keeps control over bank reserves and the money supply. The sooner than expected upturn in economic activity will push up interest rates . . . In the past this is when the Federal Reserve caved in to political pressure to keep interest rates from increasing . . . But [that] . . . can be successfully resisted if rates have been allowed to fall freely during the contraction phase."[59]

Speculators drowned Volcker's hope for nuance in a sea of skepticism. They turned the decline in the monetary aggregates recorded during the first half of 1980 on its head, considering the drop a signal that further monetary ease was forthcoming.[60] Henry Kaufman confirmed this belief by saying the "weak growth in the monetary aggregates . . . would leave the Fed little leeway."[61] The decline in interest rates between April and July reminded everyone of the past, when Arthur Burns abandoned high interest rates before curing inflation. Volcker would have to deliver a second installment of higher interest rates before the economy recovered to erase those earlier sins.

The market's distrust of the Fed's commitment to control inflation was the second setback for Volcker during his first year as chairman. The absence of a decline in long-term bond rates after the October 6 announcement had been his first disappointment. History had suggested otherwise. Evidence that introducing a new monetary regime could deliver a knockout punch to inflationary expectations came from the battle during the 1920s in central Europe to control hyperinflation.

Runaway price increases after the Great War had reached disastrous proportions in Austria, Germany, Hungary, and Poland. Employers paid workers twice a day so they could spend in the afternoon what they had made in the morning, before the value of their cash evaporated. And then a radical reform of monetary institutions—an exchange of new currency for old and the establishment of an independent central bank—cured the hyperinflations within months.[62]

A close reading of the past, however, showed that supporting fiscal discipline, rather than just a money makeover, explained the revival of central European monetary credibility during the 1920s. Thomas Sargent, the rational-expectations expert at the University of Minnesota who won the Nobel Prize in Economics in 2011, explained that "The essential measures that ended [those] hyperinflations . . . were, first, the creation of an independent central bank . . . and, second, a simultaneous alteration of the fiscal regime . . . Once it became widely understood that the government would not rely on the central bank for its finances the inflation[s] terminated."[63]

Sargent went on to emphasize, "It goes without saying that the credibility that is essential under the rational expectations theory cannot be manipulated by promises or government announcements . . . [only a] once-and-for-all, widely believed, uncontroversial, and irreversible regime change . . . can cure inflation at little or no cost in terms of real output."[64]

Volcker recognized that "there were no shortcuts."[65]

CHAPTER 11

New Territory

Jimmy Carter ended his honeymoon with Paul Volcker on October 2, 1980, a month before the presidential election, by describing the "strictly monetarist approach" of the Federal Reserve chairman as "ill advised."[1] The president, speaking to a crowd of supporters in a backyard gathering in Lansdowne, Pennsylvania, a suburb of Philadelphia, added, "I think that Paul Volcker is an outstanding Chairman and is highly qualified and very brilliant," but the Federal Reserve put "too much of their eggs in the money supply basket."

Former Fed chairman William McChesney Martin led the counterattack. He termed Carter's comments "deplorable . . . a serious and unfortunate thing," and added a philosophical note: "Partisan politics ought not to be around the dollar."[2] Former chairman Arthur Burns said, "The President's criticism of the Federal Reserve is regrettable," and explained the problem: "The basic reason for the rise of interest rates is that fears of inflation are increasing. If the Federal Reserve acted on the President's advice . . . interest rates would almost certainly rise sharply further."[3]

Volcker refused to join the chorus, and instead, while talking with reporters at the annual meeting of the International Monetary Fund, almost apologized for the increase in interest rates that had preceded Carter's remarks. "The prime rate is a little more jumpy on the upside than it is on the downside . . . and you wonder whether it hasn't jumped and anticipated too much."[4] Volcker knew the Federal Reserve had caused the uproar by raising the discount rate a week earlier, an event he considered "a rather forceful move" even under the new operating procedures.[5] Moreover, tightening monetary policy like that during an election campaign was unprecedented.[6]

It marked a turning point for the central bank.

On Thursday, September 25, 1980, the Federal Reserve Board had approved by unanimous vote a one-percentage-point increase in the discount rate to 11 percent. The discount rate is the interest rate charged to commercial banks for borrowing reserves from their regional Federal Reserve banks. The individual Federal Reserve banks must petition for a rate change to the seven-member board chaired by Volcker. On September 25 the board rejected a proposed one-half percent increase as "too cautious, particularly in light of the excessive monetary expansion that had occurred recently," and favored a one-percentage-point increase because "inflationary expectations were worsening."[7]

Most changes in the discount rate occur after a fundamental shift in policy by the Federal Open Market Committee, but the September 25 increase signaled a new initiative. The press quoted Henry Kaufman: "The Federal Reserve tightened monetary policy this week."[8] The *New York Times* cited earlier conflicts between presidents and the central bank, including complaints by Harry Truman in 1951 and Lyndon Johnson in 1965, when the Federal Reserve increased interest rates. The *Times* contrasted those incidents with allegations of Federal Reserve favoritism toward Richard Nixon in 1972. "In a twist on the usual theme, Mr. [Arthur] Burns was attacked in 1972 from outside the Administration for allegedly boosting the money supply to help insure Mr. Nixon's re-election, a charge he strongly denied."[9]

Volcker's willingness to raise the discount rate six weeks before the election confirmed that the Federal Reserve had broken with the past and had changed more than just its technical procedures since the days of Arthur Burns. The *Wall Street Journal* advertised the Federal Reserve's new look on the paper's editorial page: "To anyone willing to draw the moral, Mr. Carter's assault on Mr. Volcker provides an unwitting lesson on why we need an independent Fed."[10]

Volcker recalls an unusual backdrop to the entire episode: "The timing of the discount rate increase was unfortunate, right in the middle of the presidential campaign, and it might have contributed to Carter's defeat. The economy had begun to rebound rapidly from the brief recession that began in January of 1980, and we could not afford to wait. It was among the most difficult things I've done in my professional life. Jimmy Carter had appointed me, and I voted for him in 1976, and would do so again in the upcoming election. But no matter what I thought or felt, there was no choice other than to increase the discount rate. I had a job to do."[11]

Volcker switches gears: "But it is ironic that the president accused the Federal Reserve of being preoccupied with the money supply while prominent monetarists criticized us for not following the party line and for allowing the money supply to grow erratically during 1980. I suspect that most of them choked on Carter's description of our approach as 'strictly monetarist.'"[12]

Earlier in the year, Milton Friedman had disparaged the Fed's record as a "particularly egregious example of the contrast between talk and action," and complained that the Fed under Volcker has not given up on "manipulating interest rates" and that it paid only "lip service" to controlling money supply growth.[13] Friedman, the leading monetarist of the day, was also Governor Ronald Reagan's "favorite economist," according to George Shultz, the chairman of Reagan's Coordinating Committee on Economic Policy during the presidential campaign.[14]

Volcker never denied that the Federal Reserve monitored interest rates. The October 6, 1979, announcement shifted attention toward reserves but did not remove interest rates from consideration.[15] And the FOMC Directive combined a desired path for reserves and an associated range for the federal funds rate.[16] Volcker accepted a mixed strategy, and imperfect control over bank reserves and the money supply, just like Monty Charles at De Beers juggled his objective of price stability in the diamond market with periodic inventory adjustments to avoid accumulating too many or too few raw stones.[17] Volcker liked the quip attributed to Nobel Laureate Paul Samuelson: "Central bankers were born with two eyes so they could use one to watch the money supply and the other to watch interest rates."[18]

To the journalists asking for a response to Friedman's criticism, Volcker sidestepped a confrontation by commenting, "Oh, Milton."[19] But behind the closed doors of the Federal Reserve's boardroom he had encouraged freewheeling debate, almost like a college seminar.

For example, at the FOMC meeting on September 16, 1980, Lawrence Roos led the monetarist complaint with "I hate to belabor this, but . . . I don't think [the quarterly] rates of growth [in 1980] in any way reflect any . . . policy or directive that we gave."[20] Lyle Gramley, a recent Carter appointee to the Federal Reserve Board, took the other side: "Our . . . objective is . . . to achieve a longer-run path of monetary and credit expansion . . . I don't see the system as working out unfavorably just because the quarterly pattern is so erratic." Volcker saw merit in both arguments. "These are all matters that we have to look at . . . I don't particularly like what has been happening . . . we have put all this money [on] the money supply and have had these quarterly fluctuations which don't seem to be particularly controllable . . . The most optimistic view is that these quarterly movements are not very significant."

A week after the internal debate, Volcker had discarded the cloak of optimism like an ill-fitting hand-me-down. He led the board in its unanimous decision on September 25, 1980, to raise the discount rate to "underscore the Federal Reserve's resolve to continue its policy of discouraging excessive monetary growth."[21] And less than a month after that, on October 21, 1980, the FOMC tightened further to achieve "a sharp reduction in monetary aggregates."[22] The federal funds rate rose by three percentage points, from 11 percent to 14 percent, in the six weeks before the nation went to polls.[23] On November 4, 1980, Ronald Reagan defeated Jimmy Carter to become the fortieth president of the United States.

Carter lost the election because Americans were tired of inflation, tired of gasoline lines, tired of American hostages in Iran, and tired of paying taxes, of course. Ronald Reagan had promised to reduce taxes.

But Jimmy Carter blamed Paul Volcker. Carter recalled that his "advisers were very concerned" when he appointed Volcker as Federal Reserve chairman.[24] They warned him about "putting someone as strong, independent, and as outspoken as Volcker in charge of the Federal Reserve." Carter concluded, "Our trepidation about Volcker's appointment was later justified, when the Federal Reserve under his leadership . . .

raised interest rates to very high levels—which ultimately achieved his goal of reducing inflation but also brought about a severe recession." And finally: "These economic restraints . . . were a negative factor in my 1980 reelection campaign."

Volcker apologized by following through on his plan.

Arthur Burns sat in a wing chair in front of the fireplace in Volcker's office. A few feet away, Volcker sprawled his six-foot, seven-inch frame across the couch while lighting up his six o'clock cigar, number eleven for the day.[25] He could see a wisp of smoke curling upward from number ten in the ashtray on his desk. It was not the first time he indulged two cigars at once, and he acknowledged the extravagance "especially now that each cost a quarter." Volcker waited while Burns lit his pipe, and enjoyed inhaling the tangled smoke.

It was Wednesday, November 19, 1980, and Burns had asked for the meeting with an urgency usually reserved for an international crisis. He had just returned from Los Angeles after the drafting of a report by members of Reagan's Coordinating Committee on Economic Policy.[26] The group was chaired by former treasury secretary George Shultz and included Milton Friedman, future Federal Reserve chairman Alan Greenspan, Congressman Jack Kemp, former treasury secretary William Simon, and Citibank chairman Walter Wriston.[27]

"Milton wants to abolish the Fed," Burns said with an uncharacteristic tremor in his voice. "He wants to replace you with a computer."

"It's a metaphor, Arthur."

"I understand, Paul, but it's more than that."

"What is that supposed to mean?"

Burns thought for a moment. "I don't think I can show you our report but I can describe what it says."

"Are you sure you want to do that?"

"Under the circumstances . . . yes."

Burns cleared his throat and spoke as though he were delivering a eulogy.[28] "The key message is that while the Federal Reserve is an independent agency, in practice, independence does not mean that the Federal Reserve is immune to Presidential and Congressional influence. The problem for the new administration is to assure accountability . . .

while preserving independence." Burns adjusted his glasses. "I convinced them to conclude with those last three words."

"I appreciate your efforts, Arthur, but this battle over the Fed's independence is nothing new. I've heard all of this—"

Burns raised his hand like a traffic cop. "Milton has allies within the group, especially Wriston and Simon. But most important, he has direct access to the president-elect, and you know how persuasive he [Friedman] can be." Burns then paused and thundered a warning. "Do not forget that for as long as you are in this office."

Volcker recalls never having seen Burns quite so agitated. "He had gotten so red at the end of the conversation that I thought he was going to have a stroke."[29] But Volcker tried to separate fact from rhetoric. He had heard Friedman's jibe about replacing the Fed with a computer at a conference earlier in the year.[30] He also knew that Walter Wriston had staffed Citibank's Economics Group with more monetarists than at a University of Chicago cocktail party.[31] An alliance with Friedman made sense. And Burns was certainly right about Friedman's power with words. Volcker recalled how convincing he was in past debates with Robert Roosa over fixed exchange rates.[32]

A debate with Milton Friedman resembled mortal combat, a duel to the death, and Friedman always emerged unscathed. Volcker did not think this necessarily proved his case. "Burr vanquished Hamilton in America's most famous duel, but that did not make him right."[33] Nevertheless, he recognized Friedman's skill and took Burns's warning to heart. Volcker was not surprised when Ronald Reagan wondered, "Do we really need the Fed?"[34]

After the election, the Federal Reserve continued what it had started during the presidential campaign, tightening credit to restrain inflationary expectations. The economic upturn from the brief recession of 1980 had begun. Volcker warned members of the FOMC at their first post-election meeting about the likely consequences of their actions, especially if Reagan's promised tax cuts increased the government's budget deficit. "When I speak of collisions next year, I think you ought to be aware . . . of the potential for the Federal Reserve to be left out there hanging alone in extremely unsatisfactory economic circumstances . . .

The danger that I see . . . is that everybody will be committed to an attack on inflation but it's entirely up to the Federal Reserve to perform."[35]

John Balles, president of the San Francisco Federal Reserve Bank, added, "I have a hunch that [nothing is] . . . really going to change unless or until the size of that budget deficit comes down, however it may be done. Until then, we're under awful pressure."

Actions by the Federal Reserve over the next month promoted a confrontation. The board increased the discount in two steps to 13 percent, and the FOMC pushed the federal funds rate to over 20 percent, the highest levels to date.[36] Commercial banks responded by raising the prime rate to an all-time record of 21½ percent. The FOMC had taken a sledgehammer to inflation, and in the process, at the last meeting of 1980, Volcker articulated guidelines for monetary policy that eclipsed the changes he had made on October 6, 1979.

Volcker liked to doodle while listening to the discussion at the FOMC. Nothing fancy: a mindless row of triangles inside triangles that resembled a cubist's rendition of the Grand Tetons. But on Friday morning, December 19, 1980, he stopped etching and took notes on what he was hearing.

Board member Lyle Gramley, who had spent most of his career as a Fed staffer, said, "We have adopted targets for growth of the monetary aggregates that . . . just don't provide any room for real growth. And I don't think we ought to back away from that. That's what we've been trying to achieve . . . I'm prepared to accept a weak economy."[37]

Charles Partee, who matched Gramley's experience at the Fed, complained, "Traditionally . . . we wanted . . . to keep pressure off markets so as not to have excessive demand . . . It seems to me now we have gone far, far away from that. We now say . . . we are going to work to reduce inflation through monetary policy . . . In that context, I think we need to have a view of how weak an economy we are prepared [to accept]."[38]

Volcker saw an opportunity to turn Partee's complaint into a new mantra for the Federal Reserve, but he waited until everyone had spoken before expressing his views.[39] He then confessed his innermost thoughts in a soliloquy worthy of the lead character in a Shakespearian drama, perhaps with the title *To Be or Not to Be a Central Banker*:

> Partee's point . . . deserves reiteration. We are in completely new territory for the Federal Reserve [and] economic policy. An implicit assumption that we are just avoiding excess demand is not the present policy. We have . . . taken the position . . . that we are going to do something about inflation maybe not regardless of the state of economic activity but certainly more than we did before . . . It is a very important distinction.
>
> We obviously have a credibility problem—by "we" I mean the United States . . . The Federal Reserve is only part of that larger problem. But when we talk about credibility, I think far, far, too much emphasis is put on these monetary targets. When I listen to people talk about credibility and their discouragement about inflation—and they are plenty discouraged—what I hear [is] . . . "You brought us to the brink . . . and we got a little worried. [But] we have been through that kind of experience before and . . . it all evaporated and nothing happened" . . . and they said: "We shouldn't have worried."
>
> Maybe I'm getting discouraged . . . but . . . when we take on this inflation fighting job—taken on by ourselves or taken on in a broader context—we should not look around for much of a constituency. If we . . . go to the brink or let some . . . things happen that we have not allowed happen during the entire postwar period, people . . . are not going to be very happy . . . And I'm not at all sure that we can change inflationary expectations without it happening. That, I think, is the nature of our problem.
>
> I was out in Chicago yesterday and [asked a banker a question that illustrates the point.] "What do you fellows think you're doing? You're expanding your assets like crazy in the middle of interest rates rising; you're eroding your capital positions; you're getting more extended on liquidity; and you have every lending officer out there on the road." His answer: "I sure do. If we get in trouble, the government will protect us."

These are attitudes that go a little beyond whether we made or missed our monetary targets. In effect, one way of putting it is that they think if there's a clash between the monetary target and a real problem in the economy, we are going to give way, whether we are inside the target or outside the target.[40]

Volcker ended his December rant from the heart with the usual FOMC practice of setting targets for various measures of the money supply, but that objective now took a backseat to the ultimate goal of reducing inflation. His belief that dousing inflationary expectations justified pushing the economy "to the brink" represented a break with the past. He accepted this painful objective to counteract the moral hazard problem he had described.[41]

Concern with moral hazard had started in the insurance business. Liberty Mutual Insurance Company, for example, worries that its automobile insurance policies make some drivers less vigilant about avoiding accidents. The company insists on a deductible in their policies so that drivers share in the damage and reduce their *immoral* behavior accordingly. Shakespeare's rendition of moral hazard was more eloquent, of course. In his play *Timon of Athens*, he phrases a character's support of capital punishment as a deterrent with "Nothing emboldens sin so much as mercy."[42] Shakespeare pinpoints why businessmen behave badly unless they worry about bankruptcy.

Before Volcker's soliloquy on December 19, 1980, Lyle Gramley indicated he would tolerate "a weak economy" to bring inflation under control, but Volcker never specified how close to the edge he would go. He did not know but recognized that only a scary glimpse of the precipice would discourage inflationary behavior. He admitted to this unpopular perspective during the ABC network news program *Issues and Answers*.[43] Interviewer Dan Cordtz said, "I don't want to put any words in your mouth, but you seem to be saying that we really have to suffer a great deal . . . to get out of this." Volcker responded, "People have to change their expectations and their behavior and that is always an uncomfortable process . . . we've got to affect people's behavior . . . that we will all be better off to conduct ourselves in a non-inflationary way."

Volcker defined the objective of price stability as "a situation in which expectations of generally rising (or falling) prices over a considerable period are not a pervasive influence on economic and financial behavior."[44] In December 1980, Americans found themselves far from that circumstance. Inflation stood at 12 percent per annum, and the economy had already recovered from the brief recession of 1980, setting the stage for another round of double-digit price increases.[45] The best professional judgment among leading economists was that Americans should view the problem of inflation as being as intractable as urban graffiti.

Paul Samuelson, the MIT Nobel Prize winner, said, "In economies such as ours . . . the system is biased toward upward price creep."[46] Stanford University Nobel Laureate Kenneth Arrow saw "a self-perpetuating core of inflation" that would make it "very difficult to see any set of policies" to escape from it without forfeiting prosperity.[47] And financial forecaster par excellence Henry Kaufman said that he had "considerable doubt" that the Fed could accomplish its ultimate objective, which is to tame inflation.[48] He added for good measure that the Fed no longer had "credibility in the real world."

But the marketplace supplied a glimmer of hope.

Volcker met Ronald Reagan on Friday, January 23, 1981, three days after the inauguration. Martin Anderson, the president's assistant for policy development, had suggested to Volcker that the president visit him at Federal Reserve headquarters on Constitution Avenue.[49] Volcker rejected that friendly gesture because it was too friendly. "I might have been overly sensitive about keeping the president out of the Federal Reserve building because of my earlier conversation with Arthur Burns, but it would have been unprecedented for a sitting president to visit the Fed chairman. The normal protocol was for me to pay a courtesy call at the Oval Office, but that was not what they wanted."[50] Instead, Anderson scheduled a lunch meeting for Volcker and the president on neutral ground, at the U.S. Treasury.

Volcker reviewed the disappointing record on inflation before he arrived at the meeting. Consumer prices had increased at an annual rate of over 12 percent during 1980, a decline from the more than 13 percent rate of 1979, but an embarrassing record for his first calendar year as chairman.[51] However, two of Volcker's favorite psychological indicators, gold and the dollar, offered some hope.

Gold had declined steadily after the discount rate move on September 25, 1980, dropping by 17 percent by the end of the year, to $589 an ounce, compared with $711 on the day before the rate increase. The dollar rose by 10 percent against the German mark over the same period, ending the year worth 1.97 marks per dollar, compared with 1.79 on September 24, 1980. Volcker had been especially pleased when the dollar hit 2.00 marks during mid-December, recalling Chancellor Helmut Schmidt's plea for stability at that level during his harangue against America's weak currency before the Belgrade meetings. Volcker had checked earlier in the day on January 23, and the dollar was worth 2.02 marks.

The jump in the federal funds rate engineered by the FOMC during the last three months of 1980 had gained a measure of credibility for the central bank among international investors. In Volcker's mind, these favorable votes in the marketplace counted far more than the negative newspaper quotes of economists. But the increase in the ten-year government bond rate to almost 12½ percent, a jump of three-quarters of a percentage point over the same period, tarnished the glow.[52] Evidently America's bond investors remained more skeptical of the Federal Reserve's resolve than the international set—unless something else worried them more.

The president sat at the head of the table in the wood-paneled conference room pressed into service for the lunch. Volcker sat to Reagan's left, and Donald Regan, the secretary of the treasury, on the right. Volcker had already met Regan, a former chairman of brokerage giant Merrill Lynch, and knew other members of the president's economic entourage, including Murray Weidenbaum, chairman of the Council of Economic Advisers, who had worked for Volcker in the Nixon Treasury; David Stockman, a thirty-four-year-old former congressman who had been appointed budget director; and Martin Anderson, who had brokered the meeting. The president knew exactly where to begin.[53]

"You know," said Reagan, "I was very pleased to read a prediction that the price of gold will nosedive below three hundred dollars an ounce. If that's true, it would mean we've made great strides against inflation."

"I could not agree with you more, Mr. President. In fact we're well below the peak price of $850 an ounce of last January."

"Well, I expect we'll make even more progress going forward."

The clutch of reporters and photographers was then ushered from the room, and the president continued: "But I do have a question that I'd like you to help me with."

"If I can."

"I've had several letters from people who raise the question of why we need the Federal Reserve. What do you suggest I say to them?"

Volcker suppressed a smile and would later thank Arthur Burns for the early warning. "Mr. President, there have been concerns along those lines, but I think you can make a strong case that we've operated quite well. Unfortunately, we are the only game in town right now fighting inflation . . . and I'm just quoting the treasury secretary. Once the budget gets under control we'll have a better shot at taking the pressure off prices."

Donald Regan nodded. He had gone on record saying, "When this administration takes over we'll . . . deal with inflation in several ways at once rather than just one way."[54]

They failed to deliver.

CHAPTER 12

The Only Game in Town

Ronald Reagan, wearing a dark blue suit and blue-and-red tie, stood behind a lectern embossed with the presidential seal on Tuesday, January 19, 1982, the eve of his first anniversary in office.[1] The news conference would highlight the performance of the U.S. economy during the past year, with Paul Volcker center stage. Reagan had complaints about both topics.

Congress had passed the president's key legislative initiative during the summer of 1981, a tax-reduction bill sponsored by Representative Jack Kemp and Senator William Roth, which reduced the top personal income tax rate from 70 percent to 50 percent, among other changes.[2] The rise in inflation during the 1970s had pushed up both wages and prices, leaving many middle-income Americans in higher tax brackets. The legislated decline in marginal rates, a centerpiece of Reaganomics designed to stimulate economic incentives, was long overdue. But a recession had begun about midyear that brought bad news. The unemployment rate had increased to 8.6 percent when the president addressed reporters in the White House Press Briefing Room, compared with a rate of 7.5 percent a year earlier, an increase of more than one million people without work.[3]

Progress on inflation, which had dropped substantially compared with a year earlier, was overshadowed in the president's mind by the failure of interest rates to decline.[4] High borrowing costs would impair the road to economic recovery. Reagan had written in his diary, "[I] dropped in on a meeting of [my] economic advisors—a roomful of our country's greatest economists. None of them could explain why interest rates are so high."[5] President Reagan was not the only politician to complain. West German chancellor Helmut Schmidt said that real interest rates were at their highest levels "since the birth of Jesus Christ."[6]

The ten-year government bond rate had increased to more than 14 percent when the president held his anniversary meeting with the press, an increase of more than two percentage points compared with when he took office.[7] Two percentage points may not sound like much, but the jump in mortgage rates, which move in tandem with the Treasury bond rate, would raise the annual payments on a $100,000 twenty-year mortgage by more than $1,700.[8] Volcker had promised that interest rates would drop after inflation declined. So far the reverse had occurred.

Helen Thomas, the dean of the White House Press Corps, began the questioning by lamenting the plight of the jobless, and other reporters followed with questions about sanctions against Russia and relations with the press. Reagan managed to avoid controversy, until a reporter asked, "Would you agree with those people on Capitol Hill who have called for Mr. Volcker's resignation?" The president said, "Well, I can't respond to that because the Federal Reserve System is autonomous . . . the members of that commission are term employees, they're not serving at anyone's pleasure . . . there's no way that I can comment on that."[9]

Reagan's modesty, which he wore so well, belonged in the closet with his old cowboy hats. Volcker's term as Federal Reserve chairman would expire in eighteen months, and Reagan would then have the pleasure of designating a new chairman. The president's "no comment" response in January 1982 compared favorably with Congressman Henry Gonzalez's earlier threat to impeach Volcker, but not by much. Gonzalez, a Democrat from Texas, had accused Volcker of "legalized usury beyond any kind of conscionable limit."[10] The congressman showed it was nothing personal by introducing two bills of impeachment, one for Volcker and the other for the rest of the Federal Open Market Committee.[11]

Soon after Gonzalez's attack, Reagan had told a California audience, "The Fed is independent, and they are hurting us, and what we're trying to do, as much as they're hurting everyone else."[12] The White House rushed to explain that "they" referred to high interest rates and not the Fed itself, but that made Reagan sound like Jimmy Carter, who respected Paul Volcker but not his policy of high interest rates.

Reagan should have looked in the mirror for the scapegoat.

The mystery of high long-term interest rates in January 1982 begins with the remarkable drop in the rate of inflation during the immediately preceding three months compared with a year earlier. Inflation measured 4 percent per annum in the most recent quarter, versus 12 percent in the earlier period.[13] And the Survey of Professional Forecasters reported a decline in expected inflation as well.[14] The drop in inflationary expectations should have reduced long-term interest rates. Lenders prefer higher interest rates, of course, but competition whittles away the premium whether they like it or not. The ten-year bond rate should have mimicked the direction of the federal funds rate, which dropped from 20 percent to 12 percent during the year. Instead, the bond rate went its own way, rising from 12 to 14 percent.

The expected jump in the federal deficit following the 1981 tax cut could have caused the high long-term interest rates in January 1982. An increase in government borrowing to cover the revenue shortfall from the tax cut would drive up interest rates. And the structural budget deficit as a fraction of economic activity, in fact, almost doubled in the years after the tax legislation compared with earlier.[15] But Treasury Secretary Donald Regan dismissed any connection between federal deficits and interest rates.

In the beginning of 1982 Regan testified before the Senate Finance Committee, "There has been considerable concern that our projected deficits will put extreme pressure on credit markets and thus drive up interest rates. However . . . the historical record shows no such direct association of deficits and interest rates."[16] Instead, he shifted the blame for high interest rates to money creation by the Federal Reserve. "Interest rates are determined by the real rate of return on capital, the expected inflation rate and a premium for risk. Although deficits could conceivably influence expected inflation and risk, this would not happen . . . unless they were accompanied by excessive money creation."

Allan Meltzer, the prominent monetarist from Carnegie Mellon University, confirmed Regan's indictment of monetary policy. He had said during the summer of 1981 that bond rates would remain high as long as there was "skepticism about the rate of inflation and whether it is going to be reduced permanently."[17] In February 1982, Meltzer wore a bow tie and a friendly smile while testifying before the Senate Finance Committee, and gave Volcker a failing grade:

> I enjoy hearing Mr. Volcker speak. I enjoy reading his statements. I agree with most of what he says but with little of what he does . . . While he has been making clear and definite statements about the need and the desirability of slow money growth . . . neither he nor previous Federal Reserve chairmen have remained within their target bands . . . And Mr. Volcker's experience . . . in the last two years . . . [is] even worse. Not only is money growth highly uncertain, it is highly volatile . . . Is it any wonder that there is uncertainty in the financial markets? . . . The risk premium in the United States is extremely high . . . because one cannot be certain from the experience of any three-month period what the growth rate of the money stock will be in the next three-month period or for the year.[18]

The record confirms Meltzer's claim that the Federal Reserve failed to control money supply growth, but the marketplace ignored his concern.[19] The price of gold averaged $384 an ounce during January 1982, compared with $557 a year earlier, a decline of more than 30 percent over twelve months. The dollar bought an average of 2.29 German marks during January 1982, compared with 2.01 marks a year earlier, an increase in the value of the U.S. currency of 14 percent. Meltzer's alleged fear and uncertainty over American inflation should have pushed the dollar down and gold up, not the reverse, especially given the precipitous drop in the overnight interest rate.

The price of gold and the value of the dollar endorsed the Federal Reserve's credibility, a delicate concept more closely related to raising real interest rates despite countervailing political pressure, as before the 1980 election, rather than adhering to rigid control over short-term money supply growth.[20] The market's confirmation of the Fed's anti-inflation credentials left high long-term interest rates and the Bermuda Triangle as the leading unsolved mysteries of the day.

Volcker had always considered gold a favorite barometer of inflationary expectations and had been pleased to learn that Ronald Reagan felt the same. The president had suggested to him immediately after the inauguration that a drop in price below $300 an ounce would confirm "great strides against inflation." The decline during his first year in office achieved two-thirds of the objective, but failed to bring down borrowing costs. In fact, the rise in long-term interest rates coupled with the decline in inflationary expectations meant an increase in the expected real return on bonds, pleasing wealthy lenders but making poor borrowers even poorer. Volcker blamed the deficit, a polite euphemism for Reaganomics.

Volcker had not endeared himself to the new president. He had worried about Reagan's proposed tax cuts during the presidential campaign and had discussed the "inevitable collision" with monetary policy behind the closed doors of the FOMC immediately after the election.[21] Increased government borrowing to cover the revenue shortfall combined with tight credit would drive up interest rates. The Wall Street nugget "The government always gets its money" tells the story. Volcker had testified at the Senate Appropriations Committee and proposed "concrete actions on spending cuts before a final decision is taken on a tax program."[22] Treasury Secretary Donald Regan had told the same committee that tax cuts "can't wait until budget outlays are reduced."

Volcker thought that presidential adviser Milton Friedman would have better served the republic by railing against Reagan budget deficits, even though Friedman said they were "not as large as in many past years," than by undermining the Federal Reserve's independence.[23] Friedman famously said that inflation is always a monetary phenomenon, but he attributed the root cause of inflation to government deficits.[24] The connection, according to Friedman, is politics. "Financing government spending by increasing the quantity of money is often the most politically attractive method to both presidents and the members of Congress."[25] In particular, when citizens complain about the high cost of borrowing, Congress pressures the Federal Reserve to minimize the impact of deficits by buying government bonds with newly created money, a process known as monetizing the deficit. The "independent" Federal Reserve usually responds because it is a creature of Congress, which can change its operating mandate at any time.

Volcker had testified before the Senate Budget Committee after the president's tax cut was enacted in mid-1981, urging restraint on spending to repair the damage. Senator Lawton Chiles, a Florida Democrat, listened patiently to the Fed chairman and then raised eyebrows among those assembled in the hearing room with the following observation about central banker vulnerability.[26]

"The realities are that we are stuck with a tight monetary policy . . . Right now, you are the only person with a finger in the dike . . . [but] we are going to have an explosion . . . [and] we will have to knock out the Federal Reserve Board altogether . . . You have given us a good lecture about how much we should cut in spending. I just do not think, however, that . . . is in the realm of possibility."

"You are the political expert," Volcker responded. "What I am saying . . . is that the challenge before the Congress and the Administration now is to do what cutting they can do . . . [But] shooting the messenger or the head of the Federal Reserve is not going to do anybody any good."

"But it is going to be a lot easier to cut the head off the Federal Reserve System," Chiles interjected, "than to make these huge cuts, [and] that is what I am afraid is going to happen."

Volcker elaborated in self-defense: "Let me just clarify the point. It may be easier to cut the head off the Federal Reserve, but even when the Federal Reserve is running around headless you will still have exactly the same problem you started with."

Everyone laughed, except Paul.

Volcker had shown a nonpartisan distaste for budget deficits. He had testified on the impact of the deficit on interest rates in April 1980, when Jimmy Carter was still president, and the shortfall in government revenues resembled a rounding error compared with deficits during the Reagan years.[27] He did not get much numerical help from his fellow economists.

Senator John Chafee, a Republican from Rhode Island, had asked Volcker during hearings of the Finance Committee,[28] "As you mentioned, we have had home builders and road builders, real estate agents, everyone in Washington deeply concerned about interest rates. You said the best thing we can do to lower interest rates is to end the federal deficit on the theory that interest rates and inflation march along together pretty much."

Volcker interrupted. "On that theory and also on the theory—it is clearly more than a theory—that by removing the government borrowing demand from the market you have a direct impact on interest rates."

"No question," Chafee continued, "but on the other hand we have respected economists who say if we balance the budget . . . then interest rates would only go down [by] one-third of one percent, and how much better off are we."

"Not much if that analysis is correct," Volcker said, "but I do not accept that analysis. I think that kind of statement is based on econometric equations that do not reflect and cannot pick up the dynamics of the process."

Volcker wanted to tell a simple story. The government runs a deficit when it spends more than it receives in taxes, and to cover the shortfall it must borrow by selling bonds. Basic economics teaches that additional bond sales will drive down prices and push up interest rates. But opponents argue that a potential offset to the increased supply is that people may save more to cover higher future taxes needed for the deficit. And that means people buy more bonds in the interim, leaving the interest rate almost unchanged in the process.[29] Resolving the net impact of the deficit on interest rates requires formal statistical estimates, which makes Volcker very unhappy.

Volcker never trusted econometricians, especially since the rational expectations revolution in the mid-1970s gave him formal justification, but statistical answers involving the budget deficit were doubly suspect. The measured numbers for the deficit do not correspond to the concerns of bond investors.[30] At the simplest level, the government can spend without selling bonds by running down its cash balance, and can sell bonds without spending by adding to the Treasury's cash. Budget forecasters smooth out these timing discrepancies, but their craft ranks alongside astrology in precision, creating chronic insomnia among potential investors in government bonds. Rudolph Penner, a director of the Congressional Budget Office, wrote, "Budget forecasts are always wrong, and often they are wrong by a lot."[31]

Bond buyers worry about unpleasant deficit surprises, rather than simply focusing on the best guess of budget projections, and each circumstance is unique.[32] In January 1982, President Reagan's budget outlook suffered from two sets of uncertainties, whether revenues would grow as fast as projected and whether unspecified cuts in government spending would materialize. Sanford Weill, chairman of the brokerage giant Shearson/American Express and a future chairman of Citibank, said, "If they come with a deficit that is substantially larger than what they projected in the first year, no one will believe the projections for the second and third years."[33] And Gilbert Heebner, an economist with Philadelphia National Bank, added, "Summing up, 1983 and 1984, not 1982, are the problems on the policy front. In those years something will have to give, if we are to reduce budget deficits and to avoid high interest rates."[34]

David Stockman, Reagan's budget director, undermined the administration's already diminished credibility with a series of ill-conceived confessions to a Washington reporter. Stockman had authored the projections reconciling the 1981 tax cut with Reagan's promise to balance the budget by 1984, and had dazzled everyone with his command of the details, but then had second thoughts about the exercise. Stockman's mea culpa appeared in the December 1981 issue of the *Atlantic Monthly* magazine: "None of us really understands what's going on with all these numbers. You've got so many different budgets out and so many different baselines and such complexity now in the interactive parts of the budget . . . and all the internal mysteries of the budget, and there are a lot of them. People are getting from A to B and it's not clear how they are getting there. It's not clear how we got there."[35]

Stockman had confirmed the market's worst fears.

In the beginning of 1982, Donald Regan and Allan Meltzer had correctly identified risk as the key to high interest rates, but they focused on the wrong risk. Gold and the dollar confirmed that financial markets believed Volcker's pledge to extinguish inflation and recognized his progress. The jump in long-term interest rates did not come from an inflation scare but instead reflected a recurring budget nightmare.[36] Higher real interest rates help investors sleep better at night.

Meltzer himself testified to anxiety over the budget before the Senate Finance Committee: "Let me turn briefly to the fiscal side . . . There is great uncertainty about the budget problem and how it will be resolved. We are, I believe, on the verge of a fiscal crisis. Not in 1982 and 1983, the years which receive so much attention . . . but on out as far as we can project, we do not see the size of the budget deficits coming down relative to GNP [national output] or saving. That's a problem which I think hangs over the economy and creates uncertainty . . . we have very uncertain outcomes."[37]

Meltzer saved the scariest prediction for last: "We run the risk of sliding into the . . . instability characteristic of modern Italy or of moving to some other less desirable solution that no one can now foresee."

The collision between Volcker's tight monetary policy and Reagan's budget deficit resembled cold war brinksmanship, like Kennedy confronting Khrushchev over missiles in Cuba.[38] The stakes were not nearly as ominous as world conflict, but the fallout of high interest rates clouded America's economic landscape. The press reported that Alan Greenspan, at the time a member of Ronald Reagan's outside economic advisers, contends that "if the Administration doesn't act to convince the markets that the deficit will be down to around $80 billion by 1984, the resulting rise in interest rates will make the Reagan economic recovery 'feeble.'"[39] An $80 billion deficit violated Reagan's campaign promise to balance the budget but would divert Wall Street from thinking about instability worse than Italy's.

Robert Lucas, the future Nobel Laureate in economics at the University of Chicago, turned the confrontation between Volcker and Reagan, and the deficit-increasing tax cut of 1981, into a moral conflict in a *New York Times* essay: "Can a resolutely 'monetarist' central bank, restraining monetary growth no matter what else is happening, insulate the economy from the effects of this fiscal dishonesty? The [Reagan] Administration has boldly wagered all of Paul Volcker's chips on this possibility, but it is buying only time . . . it is not within the abilities of any central bank to make things work out right in a society that insists that the real resources spent by its government can exceed, on a sustained basis, the resources that government extracts from the private sector via taxes."[40]

Who would fold his cards first, Volcker or Reagan?

The first meeting of the Federal Open Market Committee in 1982 began at 2:30 on Monday afternoon, February 1. Before joining the group, Volcker had sat in his office staring at a fifty-dollar box of Partagas cigars perched at the edge of his desk. Treasury Secretary Donald Regan had sent these exquisite Dominican exports as a peace offering, having denigrated Volcker's "erratic" money growth and addiction to "cheap" cigars a week earlier.[41] Paul could not smoke them. His father would turn over in his grave if he knew his son was inhaling a two-dollar cigar, and besides, they were far too rich for his taste. He would offer one to Henry Wallich's more refined palate after the meeting, depending on how it went.

Credibility dominated the discussion. A jump of 15 percent in the money supply since December surprised just about everyone, considering that the deep recession that began in mid-1981 should have withered the demand for cash.[42] Regulatory changes allowing banks to pay interest on checkable deposits had reduced the reliability of these numbers, making it possible to discount the increase as an aberration.[43] But the Fed's reputation remained fragile to many of those seated around the table, and they worried about appearing soft.

Gerald Corrigan, a voting member of the FOMC as president of the Federal Reserve Bank of Minneapolis, who had served as Volcker's special assistant when Paul first arrived at the board, emphasized history: "The message that seems to be coming through both from [Capitol] Hill and the Administration is that it's time to change [our] monetary policy . . . [But] I think we run the risk that credibility will be affected in a more amplified way because of the perception that the Fed has buckled under again—[everyone will say] 'they always have and they always will.' "[44]

Board member Emmett Rice, not known as an inflation hawk, made a similar point: "As you know, I've been one of the people who have been worried . . . that the money supply . . . has not grown fast enough . . . [but] my instinct is . . . that to change the targets for the aggregates at this point would probably damage our credibility."[45]

Volcker sounded more flexible than his colleagues: "I will make one more comment . . . All this worry about our credibility is there, but . . . we do not build up credibility for the sake of building up more credibility. We build up credibility to get the flexibility to do what we think is necessary. If I were convinced now—more convinced than I am that change is appropriate—I would say the heck with that point."[46]

Frederick Schultz had been appointed to the Federal Reserve Board by Jimmy Carter a month before Volcker, and had been Paul's most reliable ally during the previous two years. His term was about to expire, and Reagan had appointed Preston Martin, a California mortgage executive, to replace him. Schultz chose his last meeting on the FOMC to challenge Volcker, and he emphasized politics:

"I disagree with your comments on credibility. I think there is an enormous sense out there that we are still the only game in town in the fight against inflation . . . We are right back in the situation we have been in before, particularly now that the President will not do anything about the deficits . . . If we give an indication that we are caving in and if we start making some changes, there are some really serious costs in terms of credibility, Paul. I think that the credibility factor is more important than you just gave it credit for."[47]

Schultz knew that the specter of uncontrolled deficits would deflate Volcker's trial balloon to avoid further restraint. Volcker did not need much convincing to remain silent. At the end of the February 1, 1982, meeting, the FOMC voted to take account of "the recent surge in growth of the [money supply]" and to seek "no further growth" during the first quarter of 1982. The committee raised the target federal funds rate to 14 percent, compared with a 12 percent objective in December 1981.[48]

The Federal Reserve's purposeful increase of two percentage points in the overnight interest rate six months into a major recession was unprecedented. It seemed belligerent to some, including Massachusetts senator Edward Kennedy, who wanted to end the Fed's independence.[49] But it also confirmed the central bank's determination to uphold its responsibility as "the only game in town" and to overturn its image as "the same old Fed."

It meant the Federal Reserve would not fold.

Within days of the February FOMC meeting, Volcker initiated a détente with the president. The escalating rhetoric with the administration had troubled him, and not because of the newspaper headlines—he was used to that—but his protégé Jerry Corrigan had shown how the brewing controversy could manipulate policy.

Corrigan understood politics as well as Lyndon Johnson did and had warned his FOMC colleagues about the clash between monetary and fiscal policy. "We are sitting here looking at a fiscal situation that is just untenable. And one of the concerns I have—and maybe it is tilting at our windmills a little—is that if the perception is that we really are easing, any prospect of being able to do better on the fiscal side is weakened . . . because that creates the impression that we are going to sit here and monetize all that debt . . . I must say I would be troubled at [that] prospect."[50]

Using monetary policy as a weapon to promote responsible fiscal policy fit Volcker's battle plan, but he also wanted the flexibility to ease monetary policy sooner rather than later to avoid an economic collapse. He asked Murray Weidenbaum, chairman of the Council of Economic Advisers, to set up a one-on-one meeting with Reagan, without subordinates.

Weidenbaum was stunned by the request: "Paul had never asked me for a favor in all the time we knew each other. He had been my boss and was now a friend. I went out of my way."[51]

The meeting between the president and Volcker took place on Monday afternoon, February 15, 1982. It was Washington's birthday, an informal day in the nation's capital, and the president wore a striped golf shirt and tan slacks.[52] The relaxed atmosphere paid immediate dividends, according to Reagan's diary entry at the end of the day: "Met with Paul Volcker. I think we've broken ground for a new & better relationship aimed at getting interest rates down. He thinks we *can* get short term rates down 3 or 4 points by June. Long term will take longer."[53]

Three days later, on February 18, Ronald Reagan embraced Paul

Volcker publicly. Not physically, of course—neither man was cuddly. But Reagan's remarks at his news conference in the East Room of the White House confirmed the new relationship, and a new commitment to restraining budget deficits.

> I have met with Chairman Volcker several times during the past year. We met again earlier this week. I have confidence in the announced policies of the Federal Reserve Board. The Administration and the Federal Reserve can help bring inflation and interest rates down faster by working together than by working at cross-purposes. This Administration will always support the political independence of the Federal Reserve Board . . . At the same time, I am sensitive to the need for a responsible fiscal policy to complement a firm anti-inflationary monetary policy. I will devote the resources of my Presidency to keeping deficits down over the next several years.[54]

After the news conference, Weidenbaum telephoned Volcker: "Congratulations. You made quite an impression."[55]

"We'll see what happens."

"No, already."

"What's that supposed to mean?"

"I just spoke with the president. He now refers to you as Paul rather than Chairman Volcker."

Republican senator Paul Laxalt of Nevada was Ronald Reagan's closest friend in Congress, having served as manager of his presidential campaigns in 1976 and 1980. He could whisper in the president's ear, "Hey Ron, you've messed up, this one isn't working."[56] Laxalt urged Reagan at the end of March 1982 that "time is running out" on a budget compromise.[57] Republican senator Robert Dole of Kansas, the Senate Finance Committee chairman, delivered the same message. Dole had proposed a tax increase to help restore a measure of budget sanity, and said, "We're right on the threshold of a [budget] breakthrough," but the compromise must come in a matter of "days and weeks, not months."[58]

Laxalt was not optimistic. He knew the president best and thought that "he will play his cards right to the end."[59]

Reagan waited.

The president did not want to raise taxes; it went against everything he stood for. It would also alienate the Republican Party's conservative coalition, which had supported his program of less government. Jack Kemp, the Buffalo, New York, congressman who had cosponsored the 1981 tax-reduction bill, reminded the press that Reagan wanted to reduce government spending by strangling it off with lower taxes.[60] The president had said it was like curing our children's "extravagance simply by reducing their allowance."[61] Kemp objected to "the dramatic U-turn" on economic policy.[62]

By August 1982, Reagan knew that unless he acted, the Republicans would face a rout at the ballot box in the November congressional elections. On August 6 the White House press secretary said that the president had postponed his California vacation to help get the pending tax and expenditure legislation through Congress. "The president has brought 75 House Republicans to the White House over the last three days to emphasize his support for the tax bill."[63]

Reagan told his fellow Republicans, "We are beginning to see some real relief on interest rates with a somewhat dramatic decline over the last several days. Interest rates are going in the right direction. They must continue if we are to have economic recovery. If we do not get spending cuts and reduce the deficit, this downward trend on interest rates could be reversed. While I am reluctant to raise taxes, the price is not excessive to get the deficit down and to ensure the continuation of economic recovery."[64]

In August 1982, Ronald Reagan sounded like Paul Volcker. On August 19, 1982, the tax increase was passed.[65] It was a rare victory for the central bank. There would be more.

CHAPTER 13

The End of the Beginning

Volcker stared at the sentences on the lined pad on his desk while holding a sharpened number-two pencil like a carving knife. He had hoped to write this letter to Jimmy Carter two years earlier, but it was premature. Even now, Wednesday, August 18, 1982, while poised to slice words from the draft like excess fat, he worried about putting his sentiments on paper. He edited the letter one last time before handing it to his secretary.[1]

Dear Mr. President:

I have been about to write to you on any number of occasions over the past couple of years but always decided it might be more diplomatic to stay my hand. But I won't resist the current temptation.

I spent a day fishing with Don Daughenbaugh in Jackson Hole a week or so ago and I understand he was also a tutor of yours on a couple of spring creeks that ended up frustrating me. Don is a wonderful fellow, and I take it you have been fishing with him in Pennsylvania as well. I assume they bite a little more freely there.

I won't begin to recite all the turbulence and difficulties of the past couple of years economically and otherwise. I do often think of those days in '79 and '80 when we tried to come to grips with the problems. Somehow it always seems to turn out more difficult than you think at the start. The problems have not disappeared, but I do have the feeling that maybe we are turning the corner—certainly on inflation and maybe on the economy too.

With best wishes.

Sincerely,
Paul

Inflation had been cut in half during the most recent twelve months compared with the year before Jimmy Carter's defeat, but it was an incident during Volcker's trip to Montana and Wyoming that had encouraged him to write to the former president.[2] He had paused because of the financial fallout from Mexico but decided that Carter deserved to hear some good news on inflation. After all, he had paid the price.

Volcker and Jerry Corrigan had slipped away together during their fly-fishing trip and stopped to eat in a log cabin restaurant tucked away in the backwoods near Bozeman, Montana. The place looked as though it belonged in the nineteenth century, except for the parking lot filled with motorcycles and pickup trucks.[3] Corrigan led the way like a bodyguard as they entered the establishment, and chose an empty table in the corner that was dwarfed by surrounding wooden beams. Large men wearing flannel shirts occupied the nearly dozen other wooden tables in the room, and Volcker noticed that the patrons talked among themselves while glancing in his direction. Corrigan, who was just learning the art of fly-fishing under Volcker's tutelage, whispered, "I'm not real comfortable here." Volcker laughed a little too loudly. "Welcome to the United States of America."

Volcker viewed the menu on the chalkboard behind the bar, hoping to find his favorite dessert, lemon meringue pie, listed among the specials of the day. Before he got very far down the list, movement at two adjacent tables distracted him. Three men, each about the size of a Coke machine, stood and headed toward his table. He saw Corrigan's eyes widen as each man dug his hands into his pockets while approaching.

Volcker wondered what he had done to attract them, until the first man took out a ten-dollar bill and extended it to him. "Excuse me, sir, but I was wondering whether you could sign this . . . considering that it's still worth something only because of you."

Volcker had graced the cover of *Time* magazine a few months earlier and, more important, was featured in a photo spread in *People* magazine.[4] Now he signed autographs like a rock star.

The prospect of a Mexican default dimmed the celebration. Volcker had warned the FOMC about emerging risks as early as the May 18, 1982, meeting: "We face the possibility of surprises and uncertainties along the line . . . I'd like to get interest rates down, [and] it wouldn't hurt my feelings at the very least to give the market a little sense of a lead in that direction."[5] The warnings were an understatement.

The weakening economy had taken its toll. The unemployment rate exceeded 9.5 percent by mid-1982, the highest level since the beginning of World War II, corresponding to more than 10.5 million people without work.[6] And it would get worse before it got better.[7] The interest-sensitive construction industry had been especially hard hit. New housing starts during the first half of 1982 fell below one million units, less than half the number of homes started four years earlier.[8] Construction workers protested by cutting unused two-by-fours into block-size sections and attaching mailing labels and postage stamps; the U.S. Postal Service delivered them to the Federal Reserve's headquarters on Constitution Avenue in Washington, D.C. A typical message scrawled on the side of a wooden stub read, "I need my job, don't stop housing."[9] Senator Edward Kennedy accused the Federal Reserve of doing the "[Reagan] Administration's dirty work" by following a "strategy to savage the housing industry."[10]

High real interest rates hurt everyone, even those with jobs. Thomas Fisch, head of a building supplies firm in the small town of Barnesville, Minnesota, listed several local businesses that had recently closed, including a radio-TV shop and a Ford dealership, and worried that his might be next.[11] "Because of high interest rates, people can't afford to remodel homes, and I can't afford to carry my inventory."

The economic slowdown combined with the decline in inflation squeezed businesspeople. Dennis Gedzuin, manager of the Riverboat, a women's clothing store in Boston, estimated that charge-card purchases dropped by one third during 1981, and as a result, during the spring of 1982, the store offered discounts as high as 90 percent to move last year's stock. Durward DeChenne, who ran a marine equipment business in Clarkston, Washington, saw high interest rates cut his sales volume to $600,000 in 1981, down from $2 million a few years earlier. No longer able to cover the expense of carrying inventory, DeChenne began liquidating in mid-1982 at prices so low that he lost almost all his accumulated savings from twenty-one years in business. "I had hoped to succeed and retire with a reasonable income. Now I'm just trying to retire."

Volcker had observed the unwinding of inflation firsthand during 1982. Before the summer, Barbara altered their normal routine and came to Washington to stay at Paul's apartment for a while. The day she arrived, they decided to eat dinner at a local restaurant. Volcker recalls leaving the apartment first and waiting for her in the Federal Reserve car parked out front.[12] "I sat behind the driver and noticed he was reading a book with the title *How to Make Inflation Pay*. I could hardly believe it, after all my battles with Congress and presidents . . . a traitor in my own backyard. I said, 'Mr. Peña, how can you be reading a book like that?' He turned toward me and answered, 'I didn't think you would mind, especially since it was on sale in the bookstore . . . marked down from $10.95 to $1.98.'"

Volcker smiles. "A small step."

Mexico ran into the same problem as Mr. Peña's favorite bookstore: too much inventory, maybe not of books but certainly of oil. America's neighbor to the south had borrowed heavily from banks in the United States and Europe to develop capacity as an oil-exporting country. American bankers, led by Walter Wriston of Citibank, could not lend them enough, and reaped the rewards during the inflationary surge of the 1970s. But by the middle of 1982 the price of crude oil had declined by 15 percent from its previous peak.[13] The *Wall Street Journal* headlined the problem: "Mexico Reduces Mayan Oil by $2, to $26.50 a Barrel: Cut in Price Reflects Glut"[14] By the first week of August 1982, Mexico had run out of foreign exchange and was about to default on its dollar-denominated loans to U.S. banks.

Volcker understood the consequences better than anyone did. He thought that a default by Mexico would damage the biggest names in banking, the backbone of American finance, and could lead to a run on the banking system like that of the 1930s.[15] Banks differed from other firms because they facilitated payments among millions of individuals and businesses, allowing the economy to run like a well-oiled machine. Volcker shared a belief in the uniqueness of banks with his sometime combatant, Milton Friedman, who considered deposit insurance the most important innovation emerging from the Great Depression because it prevented "banking panics" from grinding the economy to a halt.[16] But deposit insurance did not protect all bank accounts equally. In 1982, federal insurance covered a maximum of $100,000, making the system vulnerable to a loss of confidence by big depositors.[17]

The World Financial Crisis of the twenty-first century, still in the distant future, would testify to the fragility of a financial system weakened by an epidemic of undisciplined lending.[18] In 2007, unqualified mortgage borrowers were the problem; in 1982, Mexico and other Latin American countries hurt lenders. But there was one big difference: In 1982 the risks were concentrated within the banks, so Volcker had a chance to limit the damage and avoid widespread disaster if he acted boldly. He recalled a guest lecturer in Professor Richard Sayers's banking seminar at the London School of Economics saying, "There will always be financial crises, but they can be managed if the problems are contained within the banking system."[19] It was good that he went to class that day.

According to Volcker's detailed list of the banking industry's exposure to Mexico, the five largest institutions in terms of total assets— Bank of America, Citibank, Chase Manhattan, Manufacturers Hanover, and Morgan Guaranty—would lose between 35 percent and 73 percent of their capital to a Mexican default.[20] The next five in rank—Chemical, Bankers Trust, Continental Illinois, First National Bank of Chicago, and Security Pacific—would lose between 26 and 50 percent of their capital.

Continental Illinois, located in Chicago, resembled a bloodied boxer on wobbly legs. It was the eighth-largest bank in the United States at the time and held more than $1 billion of "nonperforming loans," a polite euphemism for loans in default.[21] The Chicago bank had participated in too many loans originated by Penn Square, a small Oklahoma City bank specializing in oil and gas lending that was now in liquidation.[22] Continental could not survive another jolt.

Volcker had watched Mexican finances deteriorate since the devaluation of the peso in February 1982, but he was not without resources to deal with the problem.[23] He bought time by providing "window dressing" for the Bank of Mexico, making it seem as though it had enough dollars available until they could find a permanent solution. The Federal Reserve exchanged pesos for dollars with the Bank of Mexico for twenty-four hours at the end of April and again at the end of June, under existing lines of credit between the two central banks, called swap lines.[24] Mexico's end-of-month balance sheet improved as a result.

In retrospect, Volcker regrets the window dressing because it "disguised the full extent of the pressures on Mexico from the [American] bank lenders and from the Mexicans themselves."[25] He would have forgiven himself had it worked . . . and he had thought it would, of course. Mexican finance minister Jesús Silva Herzog, the personable forty-seven-year-old Yale-trained economist, known as Chucho to his friends, had met with Volcker at the Federal Reserve Board during the spring and early summer, usually for lunch on Friday afternoon, when they served lemon meringue pie in the board's dining room. During those luncheon meetings, Chucho outlined a strategy for raising money through the International Monetary Fund. The plan (and the pie) satisfied Volcker. He recalled how the IMF had solved Britain's foreign exchange problem during the 1970s.[26]

But Mexico ran out of money before the IMF rescue.

Volcker flourishes under pressure. His methodical reasoning slows everything down inside his head, the way a professional quarterback dissects the defense at the line of scrimmage. Crisis control is his favorite pastime. In August 1982 he needed to balance the unwavering goal of taming inflation against the safety of American banking.

On Friday, August 13, 1982, the eleventh anniversary of the Camp David meeting suspending gold convertibility, Volcker launched a secret rescue of Mexico.[27] Using his Rolodex as a tourniquet, he called on his network of central bankers, including Gordon Richardson of the

Bank of England, Fritz Leutwiler of the Swiss National Bank, and Haruo Mayekawa of the Bank of Japan, to arrange bridge loans to Mexico to stop the hemorrhaging. He spent the rest of the weekend working with Tim McNamar, Donald Regan's deputy at Treasury, to accelerate U.S. payments to Mexico for oil imports.

On Wednesday, August 18, before composing his letter to Jimmy Carter, Volcker gave his list of private telephone numbers of American commercial bankers, all major creditors of Mexico, to his friend Chucho.[28] Silva Herzog spent the remainder of the day calling Volcker's contacts in the banking establishment at their summer vacation homes, proposing a not-so-secret creditors' meeting to begin two days later, on Friday, August 20.

Volcker asked officials at the Federal Reserve Bank of New York to invite the more than one hundred participants to use the bank's auditorium for the negotiations. Conveniently located in the heart of the Financial District at 33 Liberty Street, the New York Fed is just two blocks from 23 Wall Street, which had served as headquarters of J.P. Morgan and Company.

During the Panic of 1907, J. P. Morgan Sr. had arranged the rescue of the giant Trust Company of America from insolvency by locking his fellow financiers in the Morgan Library until an agreement was reached to provide financial support to the beleaguered institution.[29] Volcker did not have to implement Morgan Senior's strategy to persuade the bankers to accommodate the Mexicans. The invitation was enough, especially when supplemented by an opening statement from Anthony Solomon, president of the Federal Reserve Bank of New York, that "there was some expectation of some private new money as part of this [negotiation]."[30]

"We are in a very sensitive period," Volcker said at the Federal Open Market Committee meeting in Washington on Tuesday, August 24, 1982, a few days after the Mexican negotiations at the New York Fed. "And not just economically, but in terms of the markets . . . and in fact concern—and I'm afraid to some degree justified concern—about the stability of the banking system. I am sure that this is the time to be delicate and sensitive . . . I don't think we can be overly mechanical."[31]

Volcker had pursued inflation like a religious zealot, but recognized that the Federal Reserve also had responsibility for the integrity of the financial system, to serve as a lender of last resort in times of crisis. The Mexicans had gotten a reprieve from the bankers but would have to put their house in order to qualify for assistance from the International Monetary Fund. And so would other Latin American countries, especially Brazil and Argentina, which were also heavily indebted to American banks. Defaults by these three countries could wipe out the capital of the nine largest banks in the United States.[32] Volcker had to strike a balance.

Interest rates had already dropped substantially since the last FOMC meeting, in the beginning of July, a consequence of the slowing economy, the gains against inflation, and the recent tax legislation to contain the growing deficit. The overnight federal funds rate had declined from about 15 percent to nearly 9 percent, and even the stubborn ten-year bond rate showed promise, declining a full two percentage points over the same period.[33] The ten-year rate remained above 12 percent, high by historical standards, but the drop confirmed progress.

Henry Wallich issued a familiar warning: "I think we are in some danger of doing what we have done very often at the depth of a recession, at the trough, which is to stimulate more strongly than turns out . . . to have been wise."[34]

Volcker disagreed: "I have said [on] a number of occasions that the way we have lost this game [in the past] is by staying with an expansionary policy too long during a recovery period . . . the mistakes were not made at the bottom of a recession."[35] But Volcker liked to worry, of course, so he said, "Well, I'm not very happy about the speed with which [rates] went down . . . because I think it raised some questions. But it was at least in the direction that was acceptable. I'd be more disturbed if they suddenly went bouncing up again."[36]

Volcker knew that the recent tax increase had not cured the structural deficit that would remain even if the economy reached full employment. He expected this persistent nemesis to torment him later, and it would, but for now he had altered his priorities. At the following FOMC meeting, on Tuesday, October 5, 1982, he confirmed the shift with an appeal to history that alarmed his colleagues. "There is a substantive need for a relaxation of pressures in the private markets in the

United States . . . Extraordinary things may have to be done. We haven't had a parallel to this situation historically except to the extent 1929 is a parallel."[37]

Board member Preston Martin added, "And 1931," referring to the year that Milton Friedman and Anna Schwartz called the "second banking crisis in the United States," and the year that Kreditanstalt, Austria's largest private bank, failed.[38]

Charles Partee echoed: "Nineteen thirty-one."

Volcker usually treated hyperbole with the same disdain he had for flashy neckties, but this time he had deviated. His qualifying remark, "I think this situation is manageable," added gravity rather than comfort.[39] Failure to prevent the Great Depression during the 1930s was the Fed's greatest blunder until the runaway inflation of the 1970s. Volcker suspected that invoking 1929 under such circumstances would unify the FOMC behind his proposed shift to defense (protecting the banking system by lowering interest rates) and away from offense (fighting inflation by controlling the monetary aggregates). And he was right.

At the October 5, 1982, FOMC meeting, the vote was 9 to 3 to target lower interest rates as the goal of monetary policy.[40] Uncertainty over the stability of money demand tipped the scales away from the monetary aggregates, but Volcker minimized the extent of the change.[41] "This need not be taken as strikingly as some people either fear or hope. I don't consider anything in here very inconsistent with what we've been doing. We have said we are going to interpret the [monetary] aggregates somewhat loosely . . . in the light of . . . unusual precautionary demands for money and liquidity. The market has assumed we are operating that way quite comfortably and this is an extension of that idea."[42]

Volcker had adopted the monetary aggregates to guide FOMC decisions between October 1979 and October 1982 because they conferred the credibility needed to harness inflationary expectations. But he kept one eye on interest rates and the other on money supply even during this period, allowing the money supply to prevail when it really mattered. Now that inflation had been tamed and the money supply numbers had become suspect, Volcker could return to "business as usual," which meant guiding interest rates more closely.[43] The money supply would never regain its prominence because Volcker no longer needed a crutch for credibility.[44]

Four days after the October 5, 1982, FOMC meeting, Volcker signaled the changed emphasis in monetary policy at a news conference.[45] The *New York Times* blessed the new strategy with an editorial titled "Credit for Mr. Volcker," an improvement over the hard line that had greeted him in October 1979: "Mr. Volcker's Verdun."[46] The *Times* apologized for its earlier skepticism.

> Three years ago, Mr. Volcker announced that the Fed would henceforth set goals for the growth of the money supply rather than aim at target interest rates . . . That policy was arguably justified at the time. With prices climbing at thirteen percent, a panicky public needed reassurance that policy makers would not turn fickle. The reassurance arrived and then some. The inflation rate has fallen to five percent . . . faster than most economists thought possible . . . Cynics suspect that Mr. Volcker wants to ease up a bit to appease a Congress fearful of high interest rates near election time. But . . . years of tight money have changed the Fed's image. Few doubt Mr. Volcker's willingness to get tough the moment inflation shows signs of getting out of hand.[47]

Allan Meltzer remained a skeptic: "Here we go again. It used to be that we would have bulges in the money supply every Presidential election year, but now we're getting them every two years for the Congressional elections as well."[48]

The *New York Times* got it right . . . for a change.

During formal hearings in February 1983, Congress took Volcker to task over Mexico.[49] Not because of what he did in August 1982, but because of what he had not done beforehand. He had spent four years between August 1975 and August 1979 as president of the Federal Reserve Bank of New York sharing responsibility with the Treasury Department's comptroller of the currency for supervising the largest banks in the United States, including some of those with the greatest exposure to South America.[50] Since becoming chairman of the Federal Reserve Board in August 1979, he was responsible for the safety and soundness of the entire banking system. And yet, as he had admitted publicly, in August 1982 the banking system faced an "unprecedented threat" that thus far "we haven't had to deal with during the postwar period."[51]

Congress had good reason to complain.

Republican senator John Heinz of Pennsylvania, chairman of the Senate Subcommittee on International Finance, greeted Volcker's appearance at the hearings with an accusation: "The U.S. bank debt problems would not have gotten to their present dangerous stage had our bank regulators not been asleep at the switch."[52] William Proxmire, a member of the same subcommittee, added his own welcoming sting: "Even though danger signals were apparent to all but the willfully obtuse, U.S. banks increased their exposure in Mexico during the first half of 1982 by $3.8 billion."[53]

Volcker hid behind a protective wall of cigar smoke and would have enjoyed Proxmire's "willfully obtuse" description had it not been aimed in his direction. He absorbed the reprimand as though he deserved it, which he did.

Proxmire asked Volcker, "I said in my opening statement that the regulators are not unaware of . . . the overexposure of foreign loans of the banks . . . they advised, they monitored, and they cajoled . . . and they didn't get any results . . . [But] were the regulators forceful enough . . . Were they?"[54]

"I suppose, in retrospect, probably not."

"Well, you say 'probably not.' Let me tell you what the General Accounting Office found. 'The U.S. banking regulatory authorities have adopted a uniform examination system for evaluating . . . country risk to U.S. banks . . . its impact is questionable.' Now you say 'probably not.' What should have been done?"

"That's what we are looking at right now."

Volcker could have curried favor with Proxmire's fiscal conservatism by saying that as president of the Federal Reserve Bank of New York he had cut the total number of employees from 5,292 to 4,655.[55] The only area within the bank that increased significantly in size was bank supervision, which went from 315 employees to 356. Unfortunately, the additional manpower had failed to do its job.

Volcker explains why: "Commercial bankers understand when a bank examiner gives them a green light to lend. They also respond to a red light, whether they like it or not, but most ignore the cautionary yellow. Sometimes it seems as though bankers even accelerate their lending when they see yellow, to avoid getting left behind, like drivers flooring the gas pedal before the light turns red."[56]

Bank supervision sits on the back burner of Federal Reserve operations compared with the more glamorous responsibilities of monitoring interest rates. The fiftieth anniversary edition of the Fed's popular publication *The Federal Reserve System: Purposes and Functions* devoted a total of 10 pages (out of 277) to supervisory functions.[57] This did not prevent former chairman William McChesney Martin from saying that Volcker's performance at the Fed was "very good on monetary policy, [and] a complete flop on bank supervision."[58] Martin, who was Fed chairman when the fiftieth edition of *Purposes and Function* was published, began his career as a bank examiner in St. Louis before coming to Washington.

Volcker says, "A complete flop is a little harsh, but it hurts all the more because Bill Martin is a personal hero of mine. I clearly had more work to do on supervision—but also on monetary policy."[59]

On Saturday, May 28, 1983, during Memorial Day weekend, Volcker read a softcover briefing binder while sitting in the faux-leather recliner in the green room, a lime-colored office in his East Side apartment in New York City. The floor-to-ceiling bookshelves were jammed with old volumes spilling out of every open space, like a backyard trellis overgrown with dense ivy. Barbara sat in an adjacent armchair thumbing through a magazine. Paul knew he had to reopen a topic they had discussed before. He had told Senator Paul Sarbanes, in response to a query of whether he was a candidate for reappointment, "I think that is a question I discuss only with my wife."[60] His four-year term as chairman would expire in two months, on August 6, 1983, and they needed to finalize the decision sooner rather than later. He would be leaving the next morning for an all-day fishing trip in Williamsport, Pennsylvania, best known as the home of the Little League Baseball World Series, but also famous for its streams stocked with bass and trout.[61] He wanted to get an early start.[62]

"I am asking for a meeting with the president next week."

Barbara perked up. "Are you going to submit your resignation? You know that is what they would like. Everything I read says they still don't trust a Democrat."

"Not exactly . . ."

Paul stared as a tear trickled down Barbara's cheek.

She finally spoke. "I thought you said you would think about that. We have no money and I have no life . . . I have never stood in your way and I am proud of what you have accomplished. But now that you've beaten inflation your job is done."

"For now."

"What is that supposed to mean?"

"It's just the end of the beginning . . ."

She interrupted: "You really think you're America's Churchill."

Winston Churchill celebrated Britain's defeat of Field Marshal Erwin Rommel at El Alamein in 1942 with the statement "It is, perhaps, the end of the beginning."[63] The victory marked the end of Germany's early dominance in World War II. Paul thought "the end of the beginning" described his three-year battle against inflation, and he said, "I hope I'm not Churchill. The Brits kicked him out of office after he saved their country."

"Stop trying to be so clever."

Volcker knew he deserved that, but he also believed that the real test lay ahead. The inflation numbers released during the first five months of 1983 had averaged less than 4 percent per annum, a remarkable performance that exceeded even his expectations, but price pressures would gain traction as the economy recovered.[64] The Fed had been in this circumstance before, winning a battle against inflation in 1975 by causing a sharp recession, only to lose the war by remaining accommodating for too long during the upturn.

Interest rates had declined across the board since the confirmation of easier monetary policy in October 1982, with the overnight funds rate below 9 percent and the ten-year bond rate dipping to nearly 10 percent in early May 1983.[65] In 1975 the drop in short-term rates had been accompanied by an increase in long-term rates because of a surge in inflationary expectations, an early warning that had been ignored.[66] Interest rates had behaved thus far, since the FOMC meeting last October, but he worried about remaining too easy for too long.[67] America's suffering had been too great to squander.

Volcker thought this would be his last chance to make a difference. He was fifty-five years old and knew that Barbara was right: They had nothing except this huge apartment they had bought in 1975, when no one wanted to live in Manhattan except multimillionaires and junkies. They fit neither category. He did not mind living like a graduate student in D.C., but he was embarrassed that Barbara, suffering from crippling arthritis and diabetes, had to take in a boarder to help pay the monthly bills.

Volcker had always thought that by age sixty he would have enough to retire, perhaps to teach those who were similarly foolish enough to devote their lives to public service. He did not have much more time to complete his professional goals or to meet his personal responsibilities. But he could not step aside. Instead, he proposed a compromise, one that he expected would provide time to put inflation to bed and then to repay his debt to Barbara. "I will tell the president that if he chooses to reappoint me I will leave midway through—after two years."

It did not happen that way.

The battle over Volcker's reappointment as Fed chairman had begun even before Ronald Reagan took office. In November 1980, soon after the election, the press reported that Edwin Meese III, head of Reagan's transition team, who would be named counselor to the president with cabinet rank, had said that "Mr. Reagan was committed to keeping William Webster as Director of the Federal Bureau of Investigation in his job but he would not make the same commitment to asking Paul Volcker to remain in his."[68] Meese added for good measure that it would be "difficult" to conceive of a Democrat as part of Reagan's cabinet, since a Democrat would not be "committed" to all the president-elect's beliefs.

Volcker certainly had lived up to Meese's suspicions. Even after his détente with the president in February 1982, Volcker continued to rail against the structural budget deficits that stretched well into the future. At the outset, Ronald Reagan had no choice but to accept Volcker until his four-year term as Federal Reserve chairman expired in August 1983.

Congress had installed this misalignment with the presidency as a speed bump when it created the Fed, to slow the executive branch's influence over the central bank. But now the president could chose his own chairman, someone less outspoken, someone more committed to his program.

Not all Republicans agreed with the strategy. Reagan had campaigned on two economic principles, eliminating inflation and balancing the budget. Neither objective seemed feasible at the time, especially price stability. Keynesians had labeled inflation intractable, and monetarists distrusted Volcker's pragmatism. And yet, two years after Reagan's election, Volcker had reduced inflation by two-thirds. Moreover, he served the higher purpose of absorbing complaints like a giant lightning rod.

Reagan's support for the "Kemp-Roth Tax Cut" in 1981 and his buildup of military spending doomed his promise to balance the budget. But Volcker's refusal to monetize the deficits by buying up government bonds shielded Americans from the most extreme consequences. High real interest rates sanctioned by monetary restraint had forced Reagan to increase taxes during the summer of 1982 and to return to greater fiscal discipline than would otherwise have prevailed. The renewed credibility had gained stature for the U.S. dollar in world markets. The greenback bought 2.5 German marks at the end of May 1983, a jump in value of 25 percent since Reagan took office.[69]

The high-flying dollar delivered more than just a boost to national pride. Reagan could now finance his unprecedented $200 billion deficits in Europe and Asia, softening the impact of the deficit on U.S. interest rates.[70] Real rates remained high by historical standards, but would have been even higher without the huge foreign appetite for American securities. Conservative columnist George Will teased French president François Mitterrand over the "flight of French capital to America."[71] The French franc had declined by a staggering 60 percent against the dollar since the end of 1980.[72]

Will, brimming with Republican genes, supported Volcker's reappointment. "For their finest accomplishment, reduced inflation, [the Republicans] are deeply indebted to a Democrat appointed by Jimmy Carter. The Democrat—Paul Volcker—may be more important than

Ronald Reagan this summer [of 1983] when the recovery hangs by a thread of confidence worn thin by congressional paralysis and exploding deficits."[73] Will blamed the Dump Volcker campaign on the "West Wing (of the White House) . . . trying to wring every imaginable political advantage . . . out of every decision." The influential Ed Meese occupied a corner office in the West Wing.[74]

Reagan apologized to Volcker for leaks about successors to the chairmanship. The press advertised the leading candidates, including Alan Greenspan, who ran his full-time economic consulting firm in New York, and Preston Martin, who served with Volcker at the Federal Reserve, having been appointed vice-chairman of the board by Reagan in 1981.[75] Milton Friedman was mentioned as a dark horse candidate— probably just to irritate Volcker.

Friedman had belittled Volcker's record during a meeting of the President's Economic Policy Advisory Board, a group of mostly outside consultants, in April 1983. According to the *New York Times*, Friedman "laced into the Fed Chairman for steering the country towards the rocks," while the other attendees listened, including Arthur Burns, who took a few extra puffs on his pipe during the harangue.[76] *Newsweek* reported that Friedman had "leveled a finger at Volcker" and told the president that "because of the policies of the Fed under that man we have had an inflationary surge in the money supply that is going to have to be corrected."[77] Volcker, who usually attended these advisory sessions as a guest, remained silent through "the savaging."[78]

At the end of the meeting, the president sidestepped the verbal bullying and said to Volcker, "I'm sorry about this spate of stories. I want you to know that I have simply not addressed [the chairmanship] issue yet."[79] Friedman's attack certainly did not improve Volcker's prospects.

Volcker had requested a meeting with the president scheduled for Monday, June 6, 1983, after his discussion with Barbara and after he had nearly lost a vote at the FOMC meeting a week earlier. He had favored a slight "snugging up" of interest rates to signal an end to the easy-money period, but after a lengthy discussion within the FOMC, the vote was tied.[80] He was not pleased, recalling how William Miller had lost control of his committee after voting with the minority on a discount decision in 1978. He would not make that mistake, and said to his colleagues, "Well, someone's going to have to change [their] vote . . . we will sit here until somebody has a better idea." Theodore Roberts, who had just succeeded Lawrence Roos as president of the Federal Reserve Bank of St. Louis, finally said, "Okay, Mr. Chairman, I give in." Volcker then rewarded everyone: "Now we can go eat, if we don't have any other business."

Volcker knew he had to end the speculation over the chairmanship. He was pleased that the appointment on June 6 was late in the afternoon in the White House residence, where he had met privately with Reagan before. He waited for the president in the West Sitting Hall, which serves as an informal living room for the first family, but was caught by surprise when Nancy Reagan entered wearing an elegant red evening dress. Volcker said, "Madam First Lady, you look quite beautiful."[81] The president, out of sight but right behind her, responded to the uncharacteristic flirt. "Congratulations on your good taste, Mr. Chairman."

After an exchange of pleasantries, Nancy Reagan left, and Volcker turned to business: "Mr. President, we are in a sensitive period, both domestically and internationally, and you do not need a lame duck as Fed chairman right now. But there is something I should tell you before you announce a decision, whatever it is. I think I've been here long enough, so if you choose to reappoint me, I would expect to stay for only the next eighteen months to two years. I thought you should know this before you decide."

"Paul, I will be in touch shortly."

Reagan's shorthand entry in his diary at the end of the day confirms that he had still not decided. "I met with Paul Volcker—Do I reappoint him as Chmn. of the Fed Aug. 1 or change? The financial mkt. seems set on having him. I don't want to shake their confidence in recovery."[82]

Reagan's budget director, David Stockman, and Martin Feldstein, the well-known Harvard economist who had replaced Murray Weidenbaum as chairman of the president's Council of Economic Advisers, had been early supporters of Volcker within the White House. They shared

Volcker's concern with the federal deficit and valued his inflation-fighting credentials. Treasury Secretary Donald Regan had become a more recent convert, saying the "financial markets seem to favor him . . . by an overwhelming majority."[83] Senator Paul Laxalt, Reagan's first friend on Capitol Hill, had called the president during his meeting with Volcker and urged him to reappoint the Fed chairman.[84] And so did Senate Majority Leader Howard Baker. "It's tough to argue against the success," said an unnamed White House staffer.[85]

On Tuesday, June 7, 1983, the day after Reagan met with Volcker, the president wrote in his diary, "I think we'll re-appoint Paul Volcker for about a year & a half. He doesn't want a full term."[86]

Reagan had no choice—on two counts. He had no real alternative to compete with Volcker's stature and respect. And he would have to make the congressionally mandated four-year appointment—nothing shorter—and hope for the best.

Alan Greenspan wrote to Volcker afterward. "The President's indecision was unfortunate. But in the end—as he seems usually to do—he came out on the right side."[87] Reagan certainly decided correctly, but he added insult by waiting almost two weeks to make the announcement, and even then it sounded like an afterthought.

At noon on June 18, 1983, during Reagan's regular Saturday radio address, the president deviated from his prepared remarks and inserted a "news flash," like an old-time reporter calling in a story to the newsroom.[88] He told his listeners, "Well, I'm not wearing a hat or clutching a phone [like you see in the movies]. But before getting into today's broadcast, I'd like to make an important announcement . . ."

Reagan had surprised many of his staff with the impromptu release of such an important appointment. He had delivered his radio address live from the presidential retreat at Camp David, Maryland, and had written the announcement in longhand on the paper containing his prepared remarks. Volcker knew an hour before, when the president called him in New York to confirm the offer as chairman for a second term.[89]

The informality of the proceedings did not bother Volcker. He knew that such announcements were normally made by the president in the White House, with the appointee at his side. But he had achieved his goal, so he swallowed his pride. Besides, there was some precedent for doing it this way. Lyndon Johnson, miffed at the Federal Reserve's tight monetary policy, had reappointed William McChesney Martin with a simple press release.[90]

Volcker felt that he was in good company, and that he could finish what he had started. It would not go smoothly.

CHAPTER 14

Follow-Through

An obsession as thick as harbor fog smothered Volcker's confirmation hearings on Thursday, July 14, 1983. Republican Jake Garn of Utah, chairman of the Senate Banking Committee, welcomed Volcker to the Caucus Room of the Russell Senate Office Building, a formal space with crystal chandeliers that had hosted the Watergate hearings a decade earlier, and began with a peculiar compliment: "Under your leadership the Federal Reserve certainly has acted more responsibly in redirecting monetary policy than the Congress has acted in redirecting fiscal policy . . . I'm amazed at how well Congress has been able to get away with placing a majority of the blame [for our economic difficulties] on the Federal Reserve Board . . . Congress . . . has not worked very closely . . . to match fiscal policy with monetary policy. The proof of that is the ever-increasing deficits that we face, and Congress['s] unwillingness to significantly cut those deficits."[1]

Garn alternated chairmanship of the Senate Banking Committee with William Proxmire of Wisconsin, depending on whether the Republicans or Democrats controlled the Senate. He urged Congress to "face up realistically to those budget deficits and send the proper signals to the financial markets of this country."

Garn's rant against the deficit during Volcker's confirmation seems misplaced, considering that neither the Senate Banking Committee nor Volcker had any direct control over federal expenditures and taxation, but Proxmire followed Garn's opening remarks with the same obsession. The Wisconsin Democrat greeted Volcker like an old friend. "I think we owe you . . . a rousing vote of thanks for your great job in bringing inflation down . . . Meanwhile between the Congress and the administration, two administrations, we sharply increased spending [and] reduced Federal revenues . . . and created . . . the assurance that we will . . . explode the national debt to more than two trillion dollars . . . We have created a mammoth, ponderous, and fire-eating dragon . . . And all this is just another way of saying that . . . the time is coming . . . when inflation or high interest rates or both will choke off this recovery . . . So, good luck, Paul, you poor devil."[2]

Everyone laughed except for Volcker.

He knew the deficit had obscured the progress he had made on inflation, forcing interest rates higher than they should have been. Foreign investors had softened the blow by investing in U.S securities, but that had left Middle America's mortgage payments hostage to international financiers. Volcker had tangled with the administration over the budget since the 1981 tax cut, but now he sensed bipartisan congressional support. His new lease on the chairmanship would help the cause.

The Senate Banking Committee confirmed Volcker's reappointment on July 21, 1983, by a vote of 16 to 2, with Democrats James Sasser of Tennessee and Alan Cranston of California voting against.[3] Sasser explained his negative vote: "The Federal Reserve Board . . . has stymied the economic growth of this country and seriously damaged our economy . . . Unemployment still stands at ten percent . . . Eleven million Americans are unemployed."[4] A letter to Volcker from W. B. Greene, one of Sasser's constituents, dulled the criticism: "I was extremely disappointed when I realized that one of our Senators from Tennessee . . . had voted against your re-nomination . . . He seems to forget the last ten years . . . Congratulations, I am glad you're back."[5] Another Sasser constituent, from Ellendale, Tennessee, penned a mixed message: "On September 11, 1981, I wrote a note to criticize your policy. Today I write to thank you . . . It took guts to stand up to the problem and not take the easy way out. It looks as though your ideas are working . . . Hang in there."[6]

On July 27, 1983, the entire Senate voted on Volcker's reappointment.

Senator Garn urged approval with "I doubt any chairman has served during a more difficult time."[7] Dennis DeConcini, an Arizona Democrat, led the opposition with the complaint that Volcker had "almost single-handedly caused one of the worst economic crises" in American history.[8] The Senate voted 84 to 16 to confirm Volcker for a second term as chairman of the Federal Reserve Board.

By February 1984, six months after Volcker's reappointment, the economy had rebounded significantly from the 1982 recession. Unemployment had declined a full three percentage points from its peak in November 1982, although it was still high by historical standards.[9] Volcker worried about the clash between the government and the private sector in the bond market. He told the Senate Banking Committee during his report on monetary policy on February 8, 1984, "I hardly need to remind you that inflation has tended to worsen during periods of cyclical expansion . . . [and that] the structural deficit in our Federal budget . . . [carries] implications for the prospects of reducing our still historically high levels of interest rates . . . We still have time to act—but, in my judgment, not much time."[10]

Volcker's view gained support from the just-released annual report of the president's Council of Economic Advisers. The CEA was chaired by Martin Feldstein, an outspoken professor on leave from Harvard University who wore the unfashionable black-rimmed glasses of an academic. The CEA warned that the deficit would not disappear as the economy approached full employment; it was built into the structure of expenditures and taxes, and that "federal borrowing to finance a budget deficit of five percent of GNP . . . means that the real rate of interest must rise until the demand for funds for private investment is reduced to the available supply."[11]

Feldstein's prediction put him at odds with Treasury Secretary Donald Regan, who said of the CEA report, "You can throw it away."[12] Regan did not believe that deficits provoked high interest rates, and he had considerable support among professional economists.[13] The next few months would help resolve the dispute.

Congress and the administration battled over responsibility for the deficit. President Reagan said in early February 1984, "My most serious economic disappointment in 1983 was . . . the failure of the Congress to enact the deficit proposals that I submitted last January . . . We cannot delay until 1985 to start reducing the deficits that are threatening to prevent a sustained and healthy recovery."[14] Congressional Democrats countered that the president promoted the deficit by promising increased defense spending and by lobbying for tax cuts for the rich.

Senate Banking Committee member John Heinz, a critic of the Federal Reserve during the Mexican crisis, sensed a hidden agenda in Volcker's testimony on February 8. He began his questioning of the Fed chairman with a preamble: "Now I don't want to be the skunk at the garden party, but it seems to me there's no party and there's not a lot of leadership . . . We've agreed that the deficit is bad . . . That's the good news. The fact is, however, that in terms of an action plan, we don't have one . . . And if our experience in [Congress] is anything to go by, before there's going to be leadership or compromise there's going to have to be a crisis."[15]

Volcker's ears perked up with the word *crisis*.

Heinz continued: "We will have a crisis in this country if, and only if, the Federal Reserve maintains its . . . policy of making sure the money supply grows at a steady and slow rate . . . And my question is, are you prepared to help bring about the necessary crisis through your continued restrictive monetary policy so that we deal with the deficit?"[16]

Volcker heard Heinz but could not believe his words. The Federal Reserve would commit political suicide with a home-cooked crisis, the last meal before Congress imposed a death sentence on its not-so-favorite creation. He knew that the Republican senator from Pennsylvania was something of an outsider, and had been a skeptical supporter of Reagan's 1981 tax cut because of its implications for the deficit, but Heinz could not be serious.[17]

Heinz almost sounded as if he knew Volcker's history of exploiting crises as a policy weapon. Volcker had delivered that message at his very first FOMC meeting as chairman: "Dramatic action would not be understood without more of a crisis atmosphere . . . where we have a rather clear public backing for whatever drastic action we take."[18] But the transcripts of FOMC meetings were secret and would not be disclosed publicly for another decade.[19] And Heinz certainly never saw

Volcker's confidential memo to Treasury Secretary John Connally urging that a foreign exchange crisis be allowed to simmer to pave the way for the suspension of gold convertibility on August 15, 1971.[20]

Volcker concluded that Heinz was on a fishing expedition and that he was the prizewinning catch, a nice fat 240-pound Atlantic salmon.[21] He answered with the appropriate dose of incredulity: "Let me say, as a matter of general philosophical approach—and I feel very strongly about this—it is not our job to artificially provoke a crisis. We are not going to go out there and conduct a tight money policy for the sake of trying to bring leverage on the Congress or the administration."[22]

Heinz interrupted: "Mr. Chairman, I never intimated that that was a part of your thinking."

Volcker forced a smile. "I wasn't absolutely positive about that."

And then Heinz edged closer to the truth: "[But] it might be an inevitable consequence."

"All right," Volcker said, confirming that high interest rates on the federal debt could galvanize public opinion and force Congress and the president to reduce the deficit. He then continued his disclaimer: "I just wanted to make . . . absolutely clear . . . that we adhere to a policy that we think is in the best long-term interests of the country to avoid a resurgence of inflationary pressures."

Heinz would have the last word.

On Monday, April 9, 1984, the Federal Reserve Board raised the discount rate, the first increase in nearly three years.[23] The half-point jump in this politically sensitive rate confirmed a gradual tightening of monetary policy by the Federal Open Market Committee between February and May 1984, as the economy expanded. During that same four-month period, the ten-year rate on Treasury securities rose by more than two percentage points, to within a hair of 14 percent at the end of May.[24] The ten-year rate had been at 14 percent during 1981, when investors worried that double-digit inflation could persist forever.

The increase in the bond rate as the Fed tightened credit disappointed Volcker, just as it had after October 6, 1979, when the Federal Reserve's credibility was at an all-time low. Back then, bond holders had good reason to mistrust the Fed's commitment to controlling inflation, and they demanded high nominal rates as compensation. Now, almost five years later, after inflation had been cut to a third of its peak level, he thought the Federal Reserve deserved better.

Tight monetary policy by a central bank that suppresses inflationary expectations should raise short-term interest rates but leave long-term rates almost unchanged.[25] Volcker knew that the Federal Reserve had lost the war against inflation during the 1970s by remaining too easy for too long during economic recoveries, and he had admitted this publicly: "We haven't passed the test of maintaining control over inflation during a period of prosperity."[26] But he was disappointed just the same.

Fed watchers confirmed the bond market's apparent skepticism. The Shadow Open Market Committee (SOMC), a group of monetarist economists who monitor the behavior of the Federal Reserve on a regular basis, reported, "The Federal Reserve has failed repeatedly to conduct a responsible non-inflationary monetary policy, and is failing again."[27] Allan Meltzer, a cochairman of the SOMC, confirmed that judgment retrospectively: "Apparently the public regarded the risk of inflation as very high."[28]

Some members of the FOMC agreed. Lyle Gramley, a former Fed staffer during the 1970s, warned the committee in March 1984 about repeating past errors. "I think we're in very serious danger of losing credibility as an agency that is trying to hold down inflation . . . [and] we are doing so in the second year of a recovery when expectations [for the economy] have been greatly exceeded."[29] Henry Wallich, the perennial inflation hawk, said, "It seems clear . . . that inflation expectations have increased over the last few months."[30] Marvin Goodfriend, an economist at the Federal Reserve Bank of Richmond, would later call the jump in long-term interest rates during this period "an inflation scare."[31] The marketplace delivered a very different message.

The price of gold shoots up like a distress signal when investors get a whiff of inflation. Gold almost doubled during the second half of 1979, after an inflation rate of 12 percent had taken hold.[32] Speculators worried that monetary policy could not cure the problem despite a jump in short-term interest rates. Gold increased 30 percent during the summer of 1980, when short-term interest rates declined with a weak economy.[33] Speculators thought that the Fed had gone soft in its battle against inflation. But during the so-called inflation scare of 1984, the price of gold actually declined, from an average of $385 in February 1984 to an average of $377 during May.[34] Speculators evidenced great confidence in the Federal Reserve's inflation-fighting credentials—certainly more than that expressed by economists, both inside and outside the central bank. And speculators had real money at stake.

The failure of gold to confirm inflationary expectations leaves a more prosaic explanation for the increase in the ten-year bond rate. Investors expected that increased borrowings by businesses to finance economic expansion would clash with continued government borrowing to cover the structural deficit. Competition for credit would push up "the real rate of interest . . . until the demand for funds . . . [equaled] the available supply," just as Martin Feldstein had warned at the beginning of 1984. The jump in interest rates represented an increase in the real cost of credit and reflected deficit phobia rather than an inflation scare, a repeat performance of what had happened in the second half of 1981.[35]

The increase in interest rates surprised investors. Michael Steinhardt, the stout forty-three-year-old manager of Steinhardt Partners, a successful hedge fund, lost $15 million on the purchase of $400 million Treasury securities during the spring of 1984.[36] He had expected interest rates to decline with the dramatic drop in inflation and suffered the consequences of his mistake. "I don't sleep too well at night . . . [and] I'm fatter than usual . . . it's a miserable time for me."[37] He explained what had gone wrong: "The Administration's economic credibility has sunk to an absolute low." According to Steinhardt, not one person in a million could have conceived that a conservative administration such as Reagan's would have allowed the deficit to explode as it had.[38]

Volcker did not know Michael Steinhardt, and his antipathy toward speculators would later blossom into distaste for hedge funds, but his commitment to price stability mitigated Steinhardt Partners' losses. Volcker's refusal to monetize government debt as the economy expanded suppressed a nascent inflation premium and avoided even higher interest rates.

Steinhardt benefited also from the healthy appetite of international investors for U.S. securities.[39] Foreigners dulled the impact of the deficit on interest rates in spring 1984 by buying Treasury bonds, in part because of the Federal Reserve's credibility, but this left America vulnerable to a flight of international capital. Volcker had warned the Senate Banking Committee in February, "We are . . . increasingly dependent . . . upon this inflow of foreign capital . . . [and] if the Federal Reserve is interpreted as following irresponsible policies, we face a potential for a bigger disturbance, to use a polite word, on the international side."[40]

Volcker was only partly right. International investors caused a disturbance in May 1984, but not because of irresponsible Federal Reserve policies. Nevertheless, the crisis would reverberate into the twenty-first century.

On Wednesday, May 9, 1984, at eleven o'clock in the morning, local time, the Japanese news agency Jiji released a story saying, "A bank source in New York disclosed that one of three Japanese financial institutions . . . is negotiating for the acquisition of . . . Continental Illinois Bank."[41] The rumor might have started a bidding war if Continental, with $40 billion in assets, had been a healthy bank worthy of a takeover battle. Instead, it conveyed the message that the seventh-largest bank in the United States, with too many nonperforming loans on its books, needed a cash infusion.[42]

Although it was ten o'clock at night on May 8, in Chicago, and Continental's Greek-columned home on LaSalle Street was shut for the night, the story triggered a run on the bank typical of nineteenth-century America. Federal deposit insurance, introduced in 1934 to short-circuit banking panics, was limited to $100,000 per account, and covered less than $3 billion of the total $30 billion in deposits at Continental.[43] Electronic communications permitted bank withdrawals at the speed of a computer keystroke even in 1984, making Continental Illinois the poster child for a modern banking panic.

Japanese money market traders, who normally lent funds to Continental by purchasing its short-term liabilities, started selling rather than buying soon after the news release on the morning of May 9. Investors in Europe followed suit when trading began there a few hours later. The Chicago institution was known as a "hot money bank," according to Donald Wallace, a vice president in the bond department at the investment bank Goldman Sachs.[44] More than 40 percent of its liabilities,

$16 billion, arrived from overseas, and $8 billion had to be renewed every day.[45] Wallace turned philosophical in describing Continental's problem: "Banking is all about rolling over funds, and once this money stopped being rolled over it was *gonzoed*—gone."[46]

No bank can survive a run on its own. Bankers owe money payable on demand or on very short notice but extend loans to businesses over longer time horizons. Bank loans cannot be liquidated (sold quickly) without incurring substantial loss, and any attempt to call loans to repay all depositors at once ends in failure. The core function of a central bank is to serve as a bank for banks, to provide funds when no one else will, to spread a safety net beneath the banking system. Commercial banks in the United States turn to the Federal Reserve as the lender of last resort, tendering securities as collateral at the discount window (now done electronically, like everything else), in exchange for cash reserves.

The Federal Reserve Bank of Chicago, one of the twelve regional branches of the system, threw a lifeline to Continental by lending it $3.6 billion on Friday, May 11, 1984.[47] Continental's borrowing that day was nearly four times larger than the average indebtedness to the Fed of all 5,800 member banks during the previous eighteen months.[48] Borrowing reserves at the Fed telegraphs a bank's weakness, but no one outside the system knew the extent of Continental's indebtedness. Nevertheless, the run gathered steam after the Chicago Board of Trade, Continental's longtime customer and neighbor on LaSalle Street, withdrew $50 million from the bank, including funds held for its commodities traders.[49]

Volcker thought that the signal to abandon ship from sophisticated customers at Continental could sink the seventh-largest bank in the United States. No depositor wants to stand last in line, especially those with more than $100,000 in their accounts. And he worried that the damage could swamp other banking giants with weak balance sheets that relied on foreign funds to remain afloat. He told the FOMC, "Continental is probably manageable with difficulty . . . Having two or three $40 billion institutions [in trouble] is a horse of a different color."[50]

Volcker needed a plan to raise capital for Continental to bolster public confidence—but he could not do that alone. The structure of bank supervision in the United States resembles a Byzantine mosaic, with responsibilities splintered among a variety of independent federal agencies and fifty different state banking authorities. Volcker turned to two men with little exposure outside the world of commercial banking, even though they were both presidential appointees. The outcome of their discussions confirmed the emerging doctrine of Too Big to Fail, and firmly implanted moral hazard into the DNA of American finance.[51]

Volcker would object, but not strongly enough.

Todd Conover, William Isaac, and Paul Volcker crafted a plan to rescue Continental Illinois. Conover was the comptroller of the currency, appointed by Ronald Reagan to head the Office of the Comptroller, an independent agency within the U.S. Treasury that dates back to the Civil War.[52] The comptroller supervises and regulates nationally chartered banks such as Continental Illinois. Isaac was chairman of the Federal Deposit Insurance Corporation, appointed to the three-person board by Jimmy Carter in 1978 and becoming chairman after Reagan was elected in 1981. The FDIC, established as an independent government agency during the Great Depression, insures deposit accounts in virtually every bank in the country, including Continental.[53]

On Tuesday, May 15, 1984, these three men gathered at ten o'clock in the morning in Volcker's office at the Federal Reserve Board.[54] Isaac later summed up the case for a rescue. "The system could not withstand the failure of Continental. Virtually every money center bank in the country was loaded up with loans to less-developed countries and had a lot of other problems. Bank of America, First Chicago, Manufacturers Hanover, Chemical Bank, and Chase Manhattan were among the [most vulnerable] . . . Moreover some 2,500 small correspondent banks had billions on deposit . . . If we allowed Continental to go down, a number of those banks would fail."[55] Volcker added an additional concern: "A default by a top-ten bank would have hurt us abroad. And we needed the inflow of international capital."[56]

Conover assured his colleagues, based on the most recent examination reports, that Continental was solvent, with assets worth more than liabilities.[57] Isaac proposed that the FDIC invest $2 billion in the form of a subordinated loan to shore up Continental's capital, thus signaling to depositors and other creditors that the bank would survive.[58] And Volcker agreed that the Fed would continue to lend money, on a secured basis, to replace lost deposits until the situation stabilized. No one knew how long that would take.

Volcker turned to his Rolodex, as he had during the Mexican crisis, and asked Lewis Preston, chairman of Morgan Guaranty Trust Company, which later merged into JPMorgan Chase, to assemble the country's leading financiers for a meeting with the three regulators the following morning at nine o'clock. The capital infusion would carry more weight with private banker participation.[59]

Volcker knew that secrecy was crucial. He hoped the discussions at Morgan would end before graduation exercises at Columbia University, scheduled for Wednesday, May 16, in the afternoon, at which he was to receive an honorary degree.[60] Failure to show at that event would fan the rumors circling Continental and turn deposit outflows into a raging flood. He had agreed to keep a low profile when arriving at Morgan Guaranty's branch office on Fifth Avenue by entering the building through the armored car loading dock. "The plan brought back memories of my undercover efforts in Tokyo and Bonn in 1973. I hoped it would be more successful."[61] It was.

On the morning of May 16, Volcker slipped in undetected, joining Connor and Isaac in a Morgan boardroom.[62] He noticed the Morgan humidor on a sideboard and vowed to stay away—Lewis Preston's cigars were too rich for his taste. Also present were senior officers of the top seven banks in the United States, including Thomas Lebrecque, president of Chase Manhattan; John McGillicuddy, chairman of Manufacturers Hanover; and Thomas Theobald, vice-chairman of Citibank.

After opening remarks by Preston to welcome the group, Volcker, seated on one side of the highly polished long table, urged the bankers "to act quickly and decisively to demonstrate to the world at large that we had the ability to cope with a major problem."[63] Isaac then said that the FDIC planned to invest $2 billion in Continental but suggested that the capital infusion would carry more weight if the banks picked up $500 million of it, reducing the FDIC's investment accordingly.[64]

Isaac's proposal drew mixed reviews. McGillicuddy of Manufacturers Hanover praised the FDIC's initiative, but Theobald of Citibank said, "Why would I want to help a competitor?"[65] Citibank advocated free enterprise, especially when it applied to others. The remaining bankers at the table expressed a more practical concern: Would a capital infusion be sufficient to save Continental? The bankers left the meeting without reaching a consensus.

Isaac then told Volcker that "the FDIC wanted to issue a statement that no creditor . . . would suffer a loss at Continental."[66] Volcker was not pleased. "That would set a bad precedent. It means depositors no longer have to monitor their bank's risk exposure. Frankly, I think that between your capital infusion and our loans at the discount window we should be able to stabilize Continental."[67]

"That's easy for you to say," Isaac responded. "All your exposure is collateralized, but we're on the hook for two billion dollars if Continental is forced into bankruptcy. I can't afford to let that happen."[68]

Volcker knew Isaac was right on both counts. While the Federal Reserve's lending at the discount window was fully collateralized by loans on Continental's books, the FDIC's $2 billion investment was subordinated to other claims. Still, Volcker worried about the problem of moral hazard and thought they should withhold the blanket guarantee to preserve some ambiguity in the safety net. He had always liked the notion that borrowing at the discount window was a privilege and not a right for precisely the same reason: Bankers behave more responsibly if they worry.

"Well, I've got to go and get that damn honorary degree or people will start thinking that we've really got a problem," Volcker said. "Just try to keep the wording of any release as vague as possible."[69]

He left by the loading dock, of course, went uptown to the Columbia campus for his degree, and returned at the end of the day, greeted by the following draft announcement:

> In view of all the circumstances surrounding Continental Illinois Bank, the FDIC provides assurance that, in any arrangements that may be necessary to achieve a permanent solution, all depositors and other general creditors of the bank will be fully protected and service to the bank's customers will not be interrupted.[70]

He liked it even less in print.

Volcker lost the argument to temper the doctrine of Too Big to Fail.

Perhaps he did not try hard enough. And he squandered the moral high ground two months later by supporting the FDIC's plan to pay the creditors of the bank holding company, rather than limiting the rescue to the bank itself, over objections from the U.S. Treasury.[71] According to Volcker, "The holding company was mostly a shell, so it had little practical consequence."[72] More important, the FDIC's guarantee of all deposits at the bank had made immediate headlines: "U.S. Throws Full Support Behind Continental Illinois in Unprecedented Bailout to Prevent Banking Crisis."[73] And that was the policy decision establishing the broad safety net. Volcker reaped immediate collateral benefits.

The rescue plan for Continental announced on Thursday, May 17, 1984, stopped the run before it snowballed into a panic. At the FOMC meeting five days later, Volcker protégé Jerry Corrigan persuaded the committee to omit the crisis-qualifier "while taking account of [unusual] financial strains" from their final policy directive. Corrigan said that inserting that phrase "would perhaps elevate even further the concerns . . . that the basic course of monetary policy is going to be undone by these developments."[74] The Record of Policy Actions for the May 22, 1984, FOMC meeting, released with the usual delay, omitted any reference to Continental Illinois.[75]

The Fed was free to pursue its anti-inflationary policies.[76]

Fifteen months later, on August 6, 1985, Volcker treated himself to an extra helping of dessert, two slices of Boston cream pie, to mark his sixth anniversary as chairman of the Federal Reserve Board. He could afford it. Inflation had declined to 3.4 percent during the previous twelve months, compared with more than 12 percent during his first year on the job.[77] No one had expected that kind of progress. Keynesians such as Samuelson said it was impossible, monetarists such as Friedman said the Fed was doing it all wrong, and the politicians complained about high interest rates.

Volcker had suppressed inflation even as the economy expanded from the recession of 1982. It was now almost three years into the economic upturn, unemployment had declined to its lowest level in more than five years, and inflation remained subdued.[78] The price of gold, a carbon monoxide detector for inflationary expectations, had actually declined since 1982.[79] Volcker had avoided the Federal Reserve's nemesis of the past, remaining too easy for too long, and he felt justified in having persuaded Barbara two years earlier to accept his reappointment as chairman.[80]

It would have been the right time to resign. He had told Senator Proxmire during his confirmation hearings that he might not complete his second term as chairman.[81] He had been more specific in private conversations with Ronald Reagan, saying he planned to stay for two years or less.[82] And, most important, he had promised Barbara. He owed her in more ways than one. She had sacrificed, she was sick, she had begged, and he had made a deal. But he could not do it. He could not leave while a blemish as large as his size-twelve shoes stained his legacy.

Volcker had told anyone who would listen—including Mr. Peña, his favorite driver—that interest rates would decline once inflation came down, and he had succeeded to some extent. The ten-year bond rate on August 6, 1985, was well below the level of May 1984, but remained more than 1½ percentage points higher than on August 6, 1979, the day he had been sworn in by Jimmy Carter.[83] The increase in long-term interest rates since 1979 would have raised the annual interest payment on a $100,000 twenty-year mortgage by more than $1,300.[84] And by that measure Volcker had failed.

He had already done enough to bring the ten-year bond rate below the level of August 1979. Actual inflation, inflationary expectations, and short-term interest rates were all lower in August 1985 compared with six years earlier.[85] Of all the familiar suspects affecting long-term interest rates, only the expected federal deficit was higher, leaving a puzzle as big as Alaska for those who believed that deficits did not matter. The expected deficit of 5 percent of national output had offset the benefits of reduced inflationary expectations, leaving long-term interest rates higher than before.[86]

But that was about to change, with an assist from Volcker.

In October 1985, Republican senator Philip Gramm, a forty-three-year-old Texan who carried the burden of the deficit on prematurely stooped shoulders, began a crusade to balance the budget in the United States.[87] He joined forces with fellow Republican Warren Rudman, from

New Hampshire, and Democrat Ernest Hollings of South Carolina, to sponsor legislation requiring a zero deficit by 1991. They linked the bill, known as Gramm-Rudman-Hollings, to legislation lifting the national debt ceiling that would eventually have to pass to prevent a government shutdown.

No one liked Gramm-Rudman-Hollings—which required mindless across-the-board cuts in most federal programs if Congress fell short of predetermined targets—not even its sponsors. Warren Rudman said it was "a bad idea whose time had come."[88] Deficit reduction had become an antidote to the embarrassment of raising the debt ceiling above $2 trillion, the fire-eating dragon that haunted Proxmire. When the controversial legislation finally passed on December 11, 1985, Congressman Richard Gephardt of Missouri, a future majority leader of the House, voted in favor, but said, "It could be disastrous. But the question is not if this is good policy. The question is can you let this [deficit] madness go on."[89]

Members of Congress worried, but bond traders celebrated, snapping up Treasuries even before the final tally in the House and Senate. Prices on the ten-year bond rose with improved prospects for passing the legislation, forcing down yields by a full percentage point from the day the bill was introduced until it passed.[90] The drop in yields continued during the first two months of 1986, as investors discussed how Congress would implement the law, until the ten-year rate fell below 8 percent, a level not seen since early 1978, before Jimmy Carter fell from grace.[91]

The decline of more than two percentage points in long-term interest rates during this period surprised everyone, including Volcker. "I was more skeptical than the marketplace, as usual."[92] The drop in the ten-year bond rate occurred without an easier monetary policy and without a drop in inflationary expectations. The overnight interest rate remained about the same during this five-month period and the price of gold rose slightly.[93]

Market participants confirmed the power of Gramm-Rudman, as the bill is often called, to lower the level of interest rates. Allen Sinai, chief economist at the brokerage giant Shearson Lehman, said that because of the new budget procedures, "for the first time in this decade

financial market participants can look ahead to declining deficits."[94] Lyle Gramley, who had resigned from the Federal Reserve Board earlier in the year and served as chief economist of the Mortgage Bankers Association, said, "I expect to see the bond market move up and down this year, depending on the latest signals from Washington about Gramm-Rudman."[95]

Gramley was only partly correct. Traders continued to buy bonds despite a federal district court ruling that certain provisions of Gramm-Rudman were unconstitutional.[96] Robert Dederick of Northern Trust Company explained: "Congress will be moved to reduce deficits because of the fear that, if they don't do something . . . voters will say 'throw the rascals out.'"[97] And Richard Kelly, president of government securities dealer Aubrey G. Lanston, echoed that sentiment: "The mere passage of such a radical piece of legislation shows that Congress and the President are serious about deficit reduction."[98]

According to the *Wall Street Journal*, Rudolph Penner, the director of the Congressional Budget Office, offered muted good cheer: "A major implication of the new budgetary outlook is that the danger of a fiscal catastrophe now appears remote."[99] Penner suggested later that Congress passed the Gramm-Rudman legislation knowing it would impose military spending cuts on the president. "Astute Republicans understood this point . . . [and] many were eager to discipline the President for abandoning them on the Social Security issue."[100]

Credit for the decline in long-term interest rates between October 1985 and March 1986 belongs to Senators Phil Gramm, Warren Rudman, and Ernest Hollings, the field generals who managed the legislative process. But recall that almost two years earlier, Senator John Heinz uncovered the blueprint that guided the process. In February 1984, Heinz had predicted a budget crisis as the "inevitable consequence" of Paul Volcker's pursuit of tight money.[101] The FOMC's refusal to monetize deficits since then had forced Congress to enact what Senator Daniel Patrick Moynihan of New York called "a suicide pact."[102] Republican senator Slade Gorton said, "Reducing interest rates was one of the designs of Gramm-Rudman."[103]

Phil Gramm left nothing to chance. In a phone call the day after the legislation passed, he reminded Volcker of the Federal Reserve's role in forcing budget sanity on the country. "With a tight money policy for the

government, we can now afford an easier money policy for the private sector."[104]

Volcker responded with "Congratulations on the legislation, but you know I cannot speak for the Board or the FOMC. We'll have to see how the belt-tightening unfolds."[105]

A boardroom coup changed everything.

CHAPTER 15

The Resignations

Paul Volcker resigned twice, but only one stuck.

At 11:45 on Monday morning, February 24, 1986, he called Barbara. "I think you'll have to make dinner tonight."[1]

"That's a nice surprise. I didn't think my cooking was that good."

"Well, I'm afraid you'll be getting practice on a regular basis."

"Oh my goodness, I'm sorry to hear that . . . what happened?"

"I was just outvoted at a board meeting . . . I can't continue."

"C'mon, Paul, you don't do things like that . . . speak with Baker first."

"I will . . . we're having lunch."

He did not say that Treasury Secretary James Baker might have instigated the insurrection.

James Baker III, a successful Houston lawyer with a Princeton pedigree, had managed Ronald Reagan's 1980 presidential campaign and had served as the president's chief of staff during his first term in office. In January 1985, Baker switched jobs with Donald Regan and became treasury secretary, which led to regular meetings with Volcker.[2] The two men were pragmatists rather than ideologues, and Baker's political skills and courtly Texas exterior had softened the dialogue between the

Treasury and the Federal Reserve compared with the Irish edge that had prevailed under Donald Regan. But differences remained.

Baker's main initiative had been to negotiate the Plaza Agreement, a coordinated plan among France, Germany, Japan, the United Kingdom, and the United States, to intervene in the foreign exchange markets to depreciate the dollar. The agreement took its name from the Plaza Hotel, a New York City landmark overlooking Central Park, where the final discussions took place on Sunday, September 22, 1985.

The U.S. currency had soared in value since Volcker became Fed chairman, confirmation of America's success in taming inflation, but the cause of higher prices on U.S. exports to the rest of the world.[3] Baker said a lower dollar would improve the competitive position of American cars and trucks and avoid protectionist measures in Congress. He meant that more automobile production would boost the president's popularity in places such as Flint, Michigan, and Akron, Ohio, resulting in more Republicans elected to office.

Volcker had participated in the Plaza negotiations along with the finance ministers and central bankers of the countries involved, but he knew from his years as undersecretary in the Nixon administration that the Treasury claimed priority in managing foreign exchange. Nevertheless, during the press conference at the end of the meeting, James Baker tried to camouflage the U.S. Treasury's role.

Volcker recalls, "I was perspiring from the TV lights when Baker grabbed my arms from behind and playfully pushed me in front of him as photographers snapped a group picture. I laughed because it was amusing, but it sent the wrong message, as though this was my idea and he was just following along. He wanted everyone to think we would keep interest rates low to support the depreciation of the dollar. I had never made any such commitment."[4]

Volcker had conflicted feelings about the Plaza Agreement. He felt that foreign exchange had been too volatile during the previous decade and viewed with favor government actions to stabilize rates. He thought the Plaza Agreement would revive the spirit of Bretton Woods, the fixed exchange rate system he had championed in his early professional life, by anchoring expectations with coordinated government policies. But dollar depreciation haunted Volcker like a childhood nightmare, a legacy of the currency's freefall during the 1970s. He also thought dollar strength supported the inflow of much-needed foreign capital to the United States. Volcker confided to members of the FOMC soon after the agreement, "The one thing I really worry about is the dollar getting out of hand on the down side."[5] He was right to worry.

By the beginning of February 1986, less than six months after the Plaza Agreement, the U.S. currency had depreciated by 50 percent more than expected.[6] Volcker wanted to cushion the decline in the dollar, but his options were limited. The center of gravity on the Federal Reserve Board was about to shift toward the administration.

Recall that the seven members of the Federal Reserve Board, each appointed by the president of the United States to a term of fourteen years, form a majority on the Federal Open Market Committee, the main policymaking arm of the central bank.[7] Congress, a jealous guardian of its constitutional right to "coin money," limited the influence of the executive branch on the central bank by staggering the fourteen-year terms so that, absent deaths or resignations, any sitting president could appoint only two new members to the Board. However, a two-term president such as Ronald Reagan could engrave his political imprint on the Fed.

On February 7, 1986, two weeks before the February 24 revolt, Wayne Angell and Manuel Johnson, President Reagan's two new appointees, joined the Federal Reserve Board. They replaced the longtime Fed loyalists Lyle Gramley (who had resigned) and Charles Partee (whose term had expired).[8] Angell, a Kansas banker and farmer, had been sponsored by Senate majority leader Robert Dole, and Johnson, who had been the assistant secretary of the treasury for economic policy, was suggested by Treasury Secretary James Baker.

Wayne Angell and Manuel Johnson joined earlier Reagan appointees Preston Martin and Martha Seger to form what the press dubbed the "Gang of Four" on the board, a reference to the group of anti-Mao conspirators in China.[9] The *New York Times* commented that the new alignment "could be considered a threat to control by the Fed's Chairman, Paul A. Volcker," and that there "could be a shift of political power in Fed policy-making that could hasten Mr. Volcker's departure."[10]

The Federal Reserve Board usually meets twice a week to conduct routine business, including whether to approve requests for bank mergers and to consider proposed changes in the discount rate by regional Federal Reserve banks. Although the seven-member board coordinates its decisions with the larger Federal Open Market Committee, which includes five voting presidents of the regional Federal Reserve banks, it has the authority to raise or lower the discount rate on its own.

On Monday, February 24, 1986, Volcker knew that both the Dallas and San Francisco Federal Reserve banks had petitioned the board to reduce the discount rate by half a percent. The board had rejected numerous such requests in recent months, and Volcker now advocated the same deferral.[11] He told the board, "A discount rate cut would push the dollar even lower, unless the drop was coordinated beforehand with the Bundesbank and the Bank of Japan."[12]

Preston Martin thought otherwise. A former California mortgage banker with a salesman's disposition, Martin had designs on succeeding Volcker as Fed chairman. He found that his proposal to approve the lower rate came easily, knowing that James Baker wanted an easier monetary policy and that the treasury secretary held the keys to the appointment. "The way to get them to cut [their rates] is for us to cut."

"There is no urgency," Volcker said.

"Let's take a vote."

Volcker could have tabled the discussion to defer the battle, but more than six years of unchallenged leadership lulled him forward. He allowed the vote to proceed, expecting that concern for the dollar would trump partisan politics even on the newly constituted board. Volcker miscalculated. Preston Martin, Martha Seger, Wayne Angell, and Manuel Johnson approved the decline in the discount rate. Henry Wallich and Emmett Rice, Volcker's longtime associates on the board, joined the chairman in voting against the cut, and Volcker wound up on the losing end of a 4-to-3 decision.

Martha Seger did a verbal victory lap. "[The Federal Reserve] is not supposed to be a one-person show," she said, suggesting that the four Reagan appointees could wrest control of the board from Volcker.[13]

After the vote, Volcker rose from his place at the head of the table and said, "You can do what you want from now on . . . but without me." He left the boardroom and slammed the door leading to his office, just in case anyone thought he might change his mind.

Volcker recalls, "It was a total breach of board custom for them to force a vote without prior notice . . . not to mention bad policy. I could not believe they did it."[14]

He should have known, and probably did—deep inside.

February 24, 1986, was a fight for the heart of the Federal Reserve. A week earlier, Baker had told the Senate Budget Committee he would "not be displeased" if the dollar declined further, encouraging U.S. exports.[15] Volcker contradicted Baker a day later at the House Banking and Currency Committee: "Well, I don't know, I think it's fallen enough . . . I certainly don't think it's anything we're interested in forcing."[16] Baker's policy called for lower U.S. interest rates to weaken the U.S. currency, a policy that only the Federal Reserve could implement. The vote to lower the discount rate signaled a takeover of the Federal Reserve Board by Treasury Secretary James Baker.

Manny Johnson had told Volcker when he joined the board that he would vote to lower interest rates at his first chance, a pledge to Baker, who had promoted his nomination. This had been Johnson's earliest opportunity to deliver. Volcker had thought he could sway his remaining colleagues on the board. Instead, the board had rejected Volcker's leadership and caused an emotional outburst usually reserved for affairs of the heart—which it was for Paul.

Volcker's working lunch that afternoon with Baker and Jesus Silva Herzog, the Mexican finance minister since 1982, had been scheduled beforehand. Volcker had brought along a handwritten resignation letter that he had scribbled on a yellow lined pad after his call to Barbara, but he waited until his old friend Chucho left before confronting Baker.[17]

"I have a letter of resignation with me," Volcker began.

"What are you talking about?"

"The board outvoted me on the discount rate this morning."

"So?"

"Bill Miller was the last chairman to get outvoted."

"Who cares about Bill Miller?"

"That's precisely my point."

"Don't be ridiculous, Paul. You can't resign. Why don't you wait and see where this goes before doing something we'll both regret."

Volcker recalls,[18] "I certainly did not want to leave the board that way. And I didn't think Baker wanted me to either, even though he probably had sparked the revolt by calling for an easier monetary policy. After lunch, Wayne Angell visited my office and proposed that the board meet again that same afternoon to reconsider the decision. I still do not know for sure whether Baker orchestrated the reconciliation. Manny Johnson would have been his natural messenger, but it would be typical Baker to use Angell as cover. We agreed to table the earlier vote so that I could coordinate with the Germans and the Japanese, and that is what happened . . . with a few wrinkles."[19]

No announcement occurred on February 24, 1986, but less than two weeks later, on Friday, March 7, 1986, a day after the Bundesbank and the Bank of Japan lowered their lending rates, the Federal Reserve announced a unanimous decision to reduce the discount rate.[20] Preston Martin hailed the dramatic development like an impresario unveiling his latest act, calling it an "unprecedented" example of international cooperation.[21] An unnamed Reagan administration official offered a different version of the victory. "The coordinated reduction in interest rates was a direct outgrowth of the international consultation process set in motion by Treasury secretary James Baker III."[22]

Volcker's history of leavening monetary policy with a combination of domestic and international ingredients went unnoticed.

The stillborn rebellion of February 24 remained secret until March 17, 1986, when the syndicated columnists Rowland Evans and Robert Novak dramatized the story with the title "Backstage at the Fed."[23] They added another layer of Machiavellian icing: "[Volcker's] resignation would have solved a thorny problem for the White House. California Reaganite [Preston] Martin's term as vice chairman expires on March 31. He is not eager to serve four more years as second banana unless he is likely to become chairman when Volcker's second four-year term expires in August 1987. Although Martin is a strong possibility, the White House will promise nothing so far in advance. But he might well become chairman should an immediate vacancy occur."

The failure of the boardroom coup to create an opening by unseating Volcker led to Preston Martin's resignation on Friday, March 21, 1986.[24] Volcker delivered a fitting eulogy: "Mr. Martin has brought a wide experience and background in public and private life to the nation and to the Federal Reserve. He is a man of strong and independent views as befits the Board. He has played a leadership role in many aspects of the system's work."[25] Volcker did not add "and I am glad he is gone," but that is what he meant.

A poll of leading Americans had named Paul Volcker second to President Reagan as the most influential person in the United States, but the February 24 insurrection had made him wary.[26] He no longer trusted the Federal Reserve Board to rise above partisan politics to focus on the public interest.[27] The White House tried to soothe the wounds with favorable comments on reappointing Volcker to a third term. Donald Regan, the president's current chief of staff and Volcker's least-favorite treasury secretary (although Baker now offered competition), said, "We'll have to talk to [him] about what he wants to do."[28]

Volcker loved his job and had trained for it like a chess prodigy. John Carlock, a friend of Volcker's from his Treasury days, had written to Paul when he was first appointed chairman in August 1979, "I am absolutely delighted . . . for you, but especially for the Republic. I'm glad for you because you told me once that this was the only job you really wanted."[29] Volcker had reddened at evidence of his unbridled ambition, even though it was in service of his country, and had responded to Carlock, "I refuse to acknowledge the conversation but I must confess . . . that the vaunted Fed insulation looks more and more attractive."[30]

The independence of the Federal Reserve matched Volcker's character, but he had also mastered the power of compromise necessary for success. Lawrence Roos, the former monetarist president of the Federal Reserve Bank of St. Louis and a frequent dissenter at the Fed, had penned the following note after he retired, when Volcker's second term began in 1983: "I cannot describe how pleased all [of us] are at your reappointment. Having served under your leadership I am especially aware of your qualifications for the chairmanship." Roos then added what everyone knew but few could say with such authority: "But more impressive than the knowledge and experience you bring to the position, is your willingness to continue to serve your nation at considerable financial and personal sacrifice on your part."[31]

The sacrifice had taken its toll on Paul, but even more on his family. Barbara's crippling arthritis had limited her to part-time work for an architectural firm. She told reporters, "Before Paul took the job, you could say that we held on to our pennies. Now they just slip through."[32] And Paul knew he had cause for concern: "How much of a lurch am I leaving my family in?"[33] He dismissed considering a third term but felt the palace revolt of February 24, 1986, had foreclosed the early exit he had promised Barbara. "Leaving would give the impression that I had been pushed."[34]

It was a poor excuse, a reflection of the insecurity buried deep inside a man whom few would consider as lacking self-confidence. His intellect and professional achievements dominated in public, but his youthful doubts—such as believing that his professors had no time for him—describe a vulnerability that had never disappeared. Barbara knew it all, of course, which is probably why she acquiesced.

A year later Volcker dribbled hints of his departure like the fabled trail of bread crumbs, but the marketplace registered surprise and disappointment when the actual announcement came.

In March 1987 the *New York Times* teased, "The chairman made a major change in his policy that has gone little noticed. He abandoned his trademark Antonio y Cleopatra Grenadier cigars."[35] Volcker claims, "I got tired of hearing my doctor's lectures, so I stopped."[36] But a few days before burying his lifelong habit, a letter to the editor in the *Washington Post* from Annette Penney rebuked him with "I would like to know why the [Federal Reserve] chairman is allowed to pollute the air of the Senate Banking Committee room . . . why not put a stop to it all . . . For years I have felt sorry for those who have to be around him."[37]

Shortly after Penney's missive to the *Post*, George Muller rose to Volcker's defense with the following response: "As chairman of the Federal Reserve Board, Volcker has one of the most demanding, high-pressure jobs in the country, one that affects the economic well-being not only of the American people but, indirectly, of the free world . . . Volcker is no doubt wedded to his cigar as was Winston Churchill. If it relaxes him to puff . . . while giving testimony . . . I say let those who take offense assume similar responsibilities."[38]

Muller flattered Volcker with Churchill's name, and Volcker returned the favor by renouncing cigars before his excuse expired, or so it seems.

Volcker's dissent from a far-reaching Federal Reserve Board regulatory decision on May 1, 1987, should have telegraphed his plan to resign. A majority of the board approved applications by three bank holding companies—Citicorp, Bankers Trust Company, and J.P. Morgan and Company—to underwrite certain debt securities that had been out-lawed by the Glass-Steagall legislation of 1933.[39] Volcker dissented for two reasons. He supported a limited rollback of the prohibitions enacted during the Great Depression but thought that congressional legislation rather than regulatory fiat should lead the way. He also wanted to mini-mize conflicts of interest by preventing the underwriting subsidiaries of a commercial bank holding company from carrying names similar to the bank itself.[40]

Volcker's battle against unrestrained deregulation would turn into all-out war during the twenty-first century, but the contemporaneous press drew immediate political implications: "The vote . . . represents a rare defeat for the august Mr. Volcker by a majority of the Fed governors appointed by President Reagan. It shows that in regulatory matters the more free-market-oriented Reagan appointees are prepared to vote the chairman down."[41] To downplay the conflict, however, Fed sources de-nied "that the disagreement was as sharp as one in February 1986 . . . In the current dispute Mr. Volcker did not threaten to give up his post."[42]

And that is because he had already decided to leave.

Less than a month later, Volcker asked the president's new chief of staff, former Tennessee senator Howard Baker (no relation to the Texas Baker), to meet in his office at the Fed on Tuesday, May 26, 1987. Speculation that Volcker would be offered a third term as chairman had in-creased ever since Baker replaced Donald Regan a few months earlier. Baker had complimented Volcker with a smile, saying that he and the president had "great admiration" for the Fed chairman and that Volcker had done "an extraordinary job."[43] Volcker came straight to the point in their meeting.[44]

"It's time for me to step down. I do not want to be considered for a third term."

Baker objected: "Why don't you think it over carefully and let me know for sure on Monday."

"You'll hear from me bright and early."

"By the way, who would you recommend?"

"Either Alan Greenspan or John Whitehead."

"Okay, but think about it till Monday."

"I'll be prepared."

Baker reported the conversation to the president, who made the following entry in his diary a day later: "Paul Volcker's term winding up—to re-appoint or not. Well, he told Howard Baker he wants to leave. So we put a list of possible replacements together."[45]

Reagan was known for playing "his cards right to the end," but his advisers had prepared well in advance.[46] Their list included the names Volcker had offered: Alan Greenspan, the former chairman of Gerald Ford's Council of Economic Advisers; and John Whitehead, a former cochairman of the investment bank Goldman Sachs, then serving as the deputy secretary of state. But earlier in the spring, Treasury Secretary Baker and Chief of Staff Baker had gone a step further. They had met with Greenspan to ask about his availability for the job. Greenspan had said, "If you need me I will be there."[47]

James Baker wanted Volcker to leave.[48] He worried that Volcker's independence could threaten Republican prospects in the 1988 presidential election, just as it had derailed Carter's campaign in 1980. But he also knew that dismissing him could roil the financial markets. Moreover, Reagan could not have risked rejecting Volcker if the chairman still wanted the job, especially after the Iran-Contra affair, which had weakened his moral authority.[49] The exit would require a delicate touch.

On Friday afternoon, May 29, Howard Baker managed the press like a Madison Avenue publicist. A reporter asked for guidance on the situation at the Fed: "We're all writing that it looks as if [Volcker's] going to get reappointed." Baker said, "I wouldn't try to lead you off that . . . [but] one of the major factors . . . is what Volcker wants to do."[50]

Both the *New York Times* and the *Wall Street Journal* published articles dated Monday, June 1, 1987, confirming that "the Reagan administration is inclined to reappoint Paul Volcker as Chairman of the Federal Reserve Board."[51] That same afternoon, Volcker visited the president and delivered his letter of resignation.

Volcker wrote to Reagan, "You will recall that, upon my reappointment as chairman in 1983, I felt unable to make a firm commitment . . . to remain in office for a second full four-year term. Despite my reservations at the time, that term is in fact now almost finished. However, I do think, after eight years as chairman, a natural time has now come for me to return to private life as soon as reasonably convenient and consistent with an orderly transition."[52]

Ten o'clock the following day, Tuesday, June 2, 1987, was convenient for the president. Reagan stood before a microphone in the White House Press Briefing Room flanked by Volcker and Greenspan. He accepted Volcker's resignation "with great reluctance and regret" and praised his efforts to bring inflation under control.[53] He said, "My dedication to our fight to hold down the forces of inflation remains as strong as ever," and added that Greenspan "shares the same commitment."

Following the announcement, Volcker invoked Ecclesiastes to explain why he was resigning: "There's a time to come and a time to leave."[54] A senior White House adviser emphasized to reporters that a third term was "Volcker's for the asking, but he didn't ask."[55] In a sidebar, Charles Schumer, at the time a congressman from New York serving on the House Banking Committee, offered a different perspective. He said the president "should have been on his hands and knees begging Mr. Volcker to stay."[56]

The financial world agreed with Schumer.

Investors hold elections for stocks and bonds every day with ballots made of cash. Prices rise significantly for the winners and decline for the losers in a daily referendum on information arriving in the marketplace. On June 2, 1987, Volcker's resignation hit the newswires a little after ten o'clock in the morning, and investors bought gold and sold the U.S. dollar as though Fidel Castro had become Fed chairman. The significant jump in the price of gold and the decline of the dollar versus the German mark combined to register sharp disapproval of President Reagan's failure to reappoint Volcker.[57] In France the news was greeted with the gravity befitting the loss of a head of state; trading in Paris was suspended for the first time since a false 1982 report that Reagan had suffered a heart attack.[58]

The governor of the Bank of Japan, Satoshi Sumita, wrote to Volcker the following day: "The sudden fall of the U.S. dollar in the foreign exchange market immediately after your resignation evidences the extent to which the international financial community believes in you."[59] On Capitol Hill, bipartisan praise showed that even American politicians believed in the outgoing Fed chairman. Utah Republican senator Jake Garn had urged the president to reappoint Volcker, and said, "Chairman Volcker has enjoyed enormous respect and has served extremely well."[60] Democratic senator Bill Bradley of New Jersey, a leader in the effort to deal with third world debt, said that Volcker deserves "the Nobel Peace prize as the party responsible for keeping the world economy together . . . during a very volatile time."[61]

Wisconsin senator William Proxmire recalled bumps along the road: "We should keep in mind that it was Paul Volcker's policies, unpopular policies, that broke the back of inflation. And he persisted in those policies for three or four tough years in spite of the overwhelming criticism by both administrations and by Congress . . . We're going to miss him, miss him very much."[62]

Not everyone would miss him, of course. Texas Democrat James Wright, the Speaker of the House, said that under Mr. Volcker "we've had the longest sustained high interest rates in our history."[63] When asked to describe Volcker's term as chairman, Wright replied, "Long."

Congressman Wright would have been surprised to learn that investors linked Volcker with lower rather than higher interest rates. News of Volcker's resignation caused a fire sale in government bonds. Falling prices raised interest rates on the ten-year Treasury security from 8.45 percent on June 1 to 8.72 percent on June 2, a significant one-day jump in yields for that maturity sector.[64] The bond market warned that Volcker's departure meant that the cost of credit would rise.

The movement in gold and Treasury bonds on June 2, 1987, offers a snapshot of an inflation scare. Unlike the deficit scares of 1981 and 1984, when gold remained unchanged and bond yields rose, on June 2 gold prices rose along with the jump in yields. Investors in Treasury bonds demanded a higher inflation premium going forward now that Volcker was no longer guarding the vault.

They should not have worried. He had left a handbook.

CHAPTER 16

An Equestrian Statue

Within the first week of Volcker's resignation, letters and postcards arrived by the bagful at the Federal Reserve Board. Some came addressed formally and on recognizable stationery, including messages from former presidents Gerald Ford and Richard Nixon and from British prime minister Margaret Thatcher. But the vast majority bore the spartan address Chairman Paul Volcker, Washington, D.C., with postmarks from places such as Fredonia, Pennsylvania; Winnetka, Illinois; and Anchorage, Alaska. Volcker waited until the beginning of July 1987, his last month at the board, to read each one and to compose an appropriate response, just as his mother had taught him.[1]

Gerald Ford penned an especially flattering handwritten note, emphasizing Volcker's "magnificent service" in handling "domestic and international pressures and challenges with superb skill and unquestioned integrity." Ford summed up with: "The United States and the world as a whole are fortunate that you were at the helm during these difficult times. I thank you for a job well done and your personal sacrifices."[2]

Margaret Thatcher highlighted Volcker's international contribution. "I have very much admired your resolute pursuit of sound monetary policies, and the great skill and understanding you have brought to the complex task of . . . reducing inflation in the world's largest economy.

At a time of rapid change and considerable strain in the world financial system, the role you have played has been invaluable."[3]

Donald Regan, who had fought Volcker at every turn, tried to make amends: "Your efforts and support in dealing with the international debt crisis, starting that August weekend in 1982 . . . have been exemplary . . . I enjoyed it when our paths crossed—including your 'involuntary' participation in my 1985 birthday party . . . I know you have always been motivated by your sense of duty and commitment to public service. I respect that and wish you the best."[4]

Compliments from world leaders pleased Volcker, but admiration from the American heartland warmed him more, especially when it came from those who bore the scars of battle. Michael Pavelek of Fredonia, Pennsylvania, wrote, "Though I was unemployed for an extended period, I always understood and agreed with your policy as chief of [the] Federal Reserve. You saved my life savings from becoming worthless. While a lesser person might have caved in to political pressure, you sir, served our nation and all its people with distinction."[5]

Hans Hospes of Toms River, New Jersey, added historical perspective: "You saved me from the fate that befell my parents in the 1920s during runaway inflation in Germany. I am 79 years old but remember my father, a workingman, coming home . . . with his daily wages already spent . . . If he had waited till later in the day or [the] next day, the wages would not have bought anything . . . I hate to see you leave your position in August."[6]

And some letters focused on the future. Richard Stechert of Jenkintown, Pennsylvania, began with praise: "As a taxpayer and American citizen I have this chance to thank you for your years of service to our country. Today it has always been reassuring to feel safe because of your policies." He then asked a favor: "Hopefully you will have time to tutor Alan Greenspan so that he will be able to continue in your footsteps . . . We've all taken you for granted. It kind of scares me that you're stepping down."[7]

Greenspan took a positive step on June 2, 1987. He stood behind the microphone in the White House Press Briefing Room alongside the outgoing chairman of the Federal Reserve Board and said, "Under Paul's chairmanship, inflation has been effectively subdued. It will be up to those who follow him to be certain that those very hard-won gains are not lost."[8]

They would not be—and here is why.

Volcker delivered a surprising message at the annual Per Jacobsson Lecture on Sunday, September 23, 1990, at the Sheraton Hotel in Washington, D.C.[9] His title, "The Triumph of Central Banking?," stands in sharp contrast with "The Anguish of Central Banking," delivered by Arthur Burns in Belgrade a decade earlier to a similar international gathering of central bankers and finance ministers.[10] Volcker claims that the question mark at the end of his title negates the boast, but he began his talk with: "I realize there is great wisdom in the old adage that what you think depends on where you sit . . . Nonetheless, I am convinced there is objective reality in my impression that central banks are in exceptionally good repute these days."[11]

Volcker had much to do with the improved image, according to Sir Jeremy Morse, chancellor of the University of Bristol, who moderated the event, but Volcker counseled humility rather than hubris.[12] He said that the monetary authority cannot be "all things to all men," and that combining the goals of "growth, full employment, and [price] stability risk[s] confusion and misunderstanding about what a central bank can really do."[13] He recommended that Congress narrow the Federal Reserve's mandate. "The recurring difficulty in acting before inflation builds momentum could be reduced if . . . the main continuing purpose of monetary policy [were] the stability of prices."[14]

Congress kept the old rules, but Volcker gave them new meaning. During his eight years as chairman, he put inflation first, despite the hydra-headed congressional mandate, because both Jimmy Carter and Ronald Reagan had made inflation priority number one, and, more fundamentally, because he believed that "inflation undermines trust in government."[15] Volcker could ignore the continuous carping, especially from Reagan lieutenants in and around the White House, because double-digit inflation had galvanized public opinion behind him

Milton Friedman gave primary credit to Ronald Reagan for subduing inflation during Volcker's tenure as chairman. "There is no other President in the postwar period who would have stood by without trying to interfere . . . with the Federal Reserve . . . He understood very well that the only way he could get inflation down was by accepting a temporary recession, and he supported Volcker and did not try to intervene."[16]

Volcker acknowledges Reagan's support: "He had a strong visceral aversion to inflation and an instinct that, whatever some of his advisors might have thought, it wasn't a good idea to tamper with the independence of the Federal Reserve, which . . . was trying to restore stability."[17] But Jimmy Carter had been equally supportive until the very end, when Volcker raised the discount rate right before the 1980 election.

And Ronald Reagan had complicated Volcker's job.

The Reagan budget deficits stuck Volcker with unnecessarily high real interest rates and created damaging distractions. Congressmen targeted Volcker like a giant piñata when constituents demanded a scapegoat for the high cost of credit. Volcker absorbed the blows behind his cloud of smoke without complaint. Somewhat ironically, James Baker, a partisan Republican to the core, credited Volcker with shielding Reaganomics from the Democrats. "If Volcker hadn't persevered, hadn't [taken] the political heat, I don't think we would have gotten there."[18]

Perhaps that explains why Alan Blinder, a leading Keynesian Democrat, who was appointed by President Bill Clinton as vice-chairman of the Federal Reserve Board during the early Greenspan era, minimized Volcker's accomplishments. In a retrospective on the twenty-fifth anniversary of October 1979, Blinder praises Volcker as a "highly principled and determined inflation hawk," but trivializes his lessons for monetary policy. "Paul Volcker retaught [sic] the world something it seemed to have forgotten at the time: that tight monetary policy can bring inflation down at substantial, but not devastating cost."[19]

Blinder, a successful textbook author, skimps in his appraisal. The decline in economic activity between 1979 and 1982 was severe, as he implies, but the disinflation came with much less unemployment than anyone had expected.[20] Volcker disappointed the pessimists, which included just about everyone in the economics profession, because he tamed what was called an intractable inflation. Nothing displeases a dismal scientist more than favorable outcomes.

But Volcker's more important contribution came after 1983, during the economic upturn, a time when gains against inflation had been squandered in the past. He avoided Keynesian sins of remaining too easy for too long and of focusing on economic growth until excess capacity had disappeared. He established the practical wisdom of preemptive restraint, raising real interest rates before inflationary psychology reignited excessive spending, and furthered the goal of price stability.[21]

Volcker conquered inflation without controlling the money supply and without monetarist approval.[22] Milton Friedman and Allan Meltzer, two leading monetarists, gave the Federal Reserve failing grades on controlling monetary aggregates between October 1979 and August 1982, when Volcker tried.[23] Friedman said, "There was no monetarist experiment and there was never an intent for a monetarist experiment."[24] He is right. Meltzer added that "the inflation rate was brought down too fast" and this created "pressure [since 1984] to . . . reflate."[25] It did not.

Volcker succeeded, despite Keynesian and monetarist disapproval, by allowing real interest rates to fluctuate more freely than ever before, to rise and fall like shock absorbers to smooth bumps in the economic terrain. High real interest rates curtail spending when inflation threatens, and low real rates boost expenditures when recession emerges. Between 1979 and 1982 the money supply served as a crutch for Volcker, supporting the case for unprecedented high real interest rates, but after that, discretion ruled. Volcker's record gave license to Alan Greenspan to continue preemptive interest rate adjustments to control inflation, which he did.[26]

Years later, when Greenspan's reputation as Fed chairman had reached its height, he said, "We owe a tremendous debt of gratitude to Chairman Volcker and the Federal Open Market Committee for . . . restoring the public's faith in our nation's currency . . . Maintaining an environment of stability is simpler than restoring the public's faith in the soundness of our currency."[27] It was a nice compliment, but Greenspan had missed something big.

George W. Ball, an undersecretary of state in the Kennedy-Johnson administration, who had also served as U.S. ambassador to the United Nations, wrote to Volcker in mid-1984.[28] "Some day you will receive the recognition you deserve for halting and reversing the inflationary curve. To accomplish that purely by the use of the monetary instrument with no help from the fiscal side is a <u>tour de force</u> for which you will be long remembered."

Ball ends with a rhetorical question: "How about an equestrian statue in front of the Federal Reserve Building? It would have to be at least a Clydesdale." No such display currently exists, but the former diplomat confirmed why Volcker's sculpture belongs at the entrance to Fed headquarters on Constitution Avenue, even though Ball understates his accomplishment.

Milton Friedman's popular phrase "Inflation is always and everywhere a monetary phenomenon" obscures the link between fiscal policy and inflation that Friedman himself diagnosed.[29] Alan Greenspan shares that view, which is no surprise, since Arthur Burns taught both men and drilled that wisdom into all his students. Greenspan recalls: "Burns loved to provoke disagreements among his graduate students. One day . . . he went around the room asking 'What causes inflation?' None of us could give him . . . [a satisfactory] answer . . . Burns puffed on his pipe, then took it out of his mouth and declared, 'Excess government spending causes inflation!' "[30]

Burns blamed budget deficits in the United States for his poor record on inflation, but Volcker taught the world that a determined central bank can dominate fiscal policy, even without gold as the anchor.[31] Robert Lucas, the Nobel Laureate from the University of Chicago and a Volcker cheerleader, doubted the Federal Reserve's clout, saying, "It is not within the abilities of any central bank to make things work out right" when the government spends on a sustained basis more than it receives in taxes.[32]

Volcker proved otherwise by refusing to accommodate increases in government debt as the economy expanded after 1983. He avoided monetizing the deficit through purchases of government bonds and instead forced the Reagan budget deficits to battle corporate borrowing for investor funds. The resulting increase in real interest rates pressured Congress to enact the Gramm-Rudman-Hollings bill to tame the budget. Volcker never pushed Gramm-Rudman, but he admitted to Senator John Heinz that "an inevitable consequence" of his monetary policy might be the crisis atmosphere leading to that draconian legislation.[33]

Volcker's veiled script had been anticipated by the Nobel Laureate Thomas Sargent, who had been a consultant to the Federal Reserve

Bank of Minneapolis. Sargent had written in mid-1983 that the Fed could succeed by "foreclosing the possibility of ever monetizing the deficit [and forcing] . . . the government . . . to promise higher and higher real interest rates on its ever-increasing debt. This force would eventually, and probably quite soon, create irresistible pressures to balance the budget."[34]

Gramm-Rudman's commitment to budgetary balance succeeded in lowering interest rates even though it needed help fixing the deficit. Congress had learned a painful lesson on Volcker's knee: that fiscal irresponsibility provoked crippling interest rates. Investors at home and abroad bought U.S. Treasury securities because they believed that America would no longer tolerate reckless deficit spending.

Alan Greenspan echoed Volcker on the deficit at his own confirmation hearings: "Over the long run . . . there is just no way that you can finance ever-increasing central Government deficits without ultimately . . . [driving] interest rates sharply higher."[35] He added, "There is no question in my mind that . . . [the deficit] is the most important economic policy variable."

Congress responded to the shortcomings of Gramm-Rudman with the Budget Enforcement Act of 1990, which successfully pared the deficit until a budget surplus emerged (by surprise) in 1998.[36] Soon after, when President Bill Clinton met with Greenspan to discuss a fourth term as Fed chairman, the president said, "I have to congratulate you. You've done a great job in a period when there was no rulebook to look to."[37] Greenspan gave a politically correct response: "Mr. President, I couldn't have done it without what you did on deficit reduction. If you had not turned the fiscal situation around, we couldn't have had the kind of monetary policy we've had."

Volcker laid the foundation for restoring fiscal integrity in America and in the process anchored inflationary expectations to sound monetary policy. The years of economic stability that followed came as no accident. The so-called Great Moderation—low and stable inflation without severe recessions—began in mid-1984, when Volcker gathered his second wind, and it lasted a generation.[38]

But he thought it would end badly—which it did.

PART IV

The Twenty-First Century

CHAPTER 17

In Retrospect

On Tuesday, February 2, 2010, Paul Volcker arrived at the Dirksen Senate Office Building to testify before the Senate Banking Committee on the rule that bore his name, courtesy of President Obama. Volcker had proposed a regulation that would allow commercial banks to trade securities to serve customers but prevent the type of reckless transactions accompanying the World Financial Crisis that began in 2007.[1] The Volcker Rule would permit commercial banks to buy and sell securities with clients but prohibit high-risk speculation either directly or by the banks' owning hedge funds. It was a noble idea that displeased the bankers.

Volcker had had less than ten days to prepare his remarks after Obama's announcement on January 21, 2010, supporting his initiative, but he had testified in Congress more than forty times since his departure from the Fed in 1987 and had not lost his touch. He was still a commanding presence at age eighty-two, as tall as during his Princeton basketball days, despite carrying extra inches around the midsection, with a slight loss of hearing his main infirmity.

Two days later, on February 4, Jerry Corrigan, Volcker's former colleague and now a managing director at investment giant Goldman Sachs, would appear before the same committee to comment on the proposed legislation. Volcker had mentored Corrigan, teaching him fly-fishing and recommending him as president of the Federal Reserve Bank of New York, the powerful branch of the central bank located in the heart of Wall Street, where Corrigan grew the Rolodex that nurtured his new career. Corrigan had served Volcker as a loyal knight, protecting his back and defending his honor. But now their interests diverged, and Corrigan served a new master.

Goldman Sachs was an investment bank, also called a securities firm or broker-dealer, offering the full spectrum of financial services. Like some of its Wall Street peers, it had become a commercial bank holding company after Lehman Brothers, Goldman's smaller sister, declared bankruptcy on Monday, September 15, 2008.[2] The collapse of Lehman, the largest bankruptcy in U.S. history, triggered a run on banks and other financial firms reminiscent of those of the Great Depression, and forced the government to rescue a system on the verge of collapse. It was the darkest hour of the ongoing financial crisis that began on Thursday, August 9, 2007.

The crisis started when BNP Paribas, the French equivalent of Bank of America, suspended withdrawals from three of its investment funds because it could not value the mortgage-backed securities held in their portfolios. The shock of the suspension, and the suspicion that this was not an isolated event, forced the European Central Bank (ECB) and the Federal Reserve to provide unprecedented liquidity to financial institutions in Europe and America to restore market order. We know now that these loans by the ECB and the Fed could not correct the deterioration in the value of mortgages, especially on subprime credits, that came with declining home prices. The collapse of two major investment banks, Bear Stearns and Lehman Brothers, with too little capital and too much real estate exposure, followed in 2008.[3]

Goldman Sachs became a commercial bank holding company immediately after September 15, 2008, because it wanted the privilege of borrowing at the discount window of the Federal Reserve Bank of New York to guard against Lehman's fate. Volcker had commented to anyone who would listen, "They're just trying to hide behind Uncle Sam's skirts . . . How can we let Goldman Sachs profit from speculation until something goes horribly wrong, and then force the taxpayers to foot the bill."[4]

Goldman lit the fuse for the Volcker Rule, but Volcker had made that same point almost twenty years earlier, with the following quotation from Adam Smith, the eighteenth-century Scottish philosopher who invented economics: "Though the principles of the banking trade may appear abstruse, the practice is capable of being reduced to strict rules. To depart upon any occasion from those rules, in consequence of some flattering speculation of extraordinary gain, is almost always extremely dangerous and frequently fatal to the banking company which attempts it."[5] The Volcker Rule labeled all bank speculation unflattering.

In April 1995, more than ten years before the onset of the World Financial Crisis, Volcker foresaw the tranquil origins of the biggest financial upheaval since the 1930s. He testified before the House Banking and Financial Services Committee exploring financial reform: "It is a sheer fact of human nature that if you went along for ten or twenty years without problems, that is going to create an atmosphere in which people will go to the edge. And the regulator will not be as strict and sooner or later you will have a crisis."[6]

The Great Moderation in inflation and unemployment that began in the mid-1980s had calmed the economic atmosphere, and the congressional repeal in 1999 of the separation between commercial and investment banking sanctioned earlier Federal Reserve permissiveness in expanding bank powers.[7] Stable growth during the first few years of the twenty-first century masked fundamental risks, especially in mortgage-backed securities, and the regulatory laxity encouraged reckless speculation in housing-related investments.[8] The combination fit Volcker's script for a crisis.

But Volcker had gone even further in April 1995, describing with eerie precision the dilemma that would follow deregulation: "I will not refer to Goldman Sachs . . . but I think it is obvious that if you had a large investment bank allied with a large [commercial] bank, the possibility of a systemic risk arising is evident . . . It may be even evident with the investment bank alone. We are trying to keep them out of the so-called safety net now, but certainly you cannot keep them out if they are combined with a banking institution."[9]

Volcker was no longer the banking watchdog in 1995, and although he warned against excessive regulatory leniency, his focus lay elsewhere. He was the chairman of James D. Wolfensohn and Company, a boutique investment firm that offered strategic advice to companies such as American Express and Daimler-Benz.[10] Volcker had joined the company in 1988, a few years after it was founded by the investment banker James D. Wolfensohn, and during his tenure as chairman it grew from two to ten partners.

In March 1995 he took over as chief executive when Wolfensohn was nominated as president of the World Bank. And a year later his partners negotiated the sale of the firm to Bankers Trust Company. Volcker wanted it to remain independent and small, but they saw an opportunity to cash out, which they did. According to the press, "Perhaps the most important acquisition for Bankers Trust is the services of Paul A. Volcker . . . [He] is expected to bolster the reputation of Bankers Trust, which has been tarnished in recent years."[11]

The multimillion-dollar windfall gave Paul the opportunity to do something that was long overdue: pay tribute to Barbara, who was bedridden from complications of diabetes and arthritis. The couple endowed the Barbara Volcker Center for Women and Rheumatic Diseases at the Hospital for Special Surgery in New York City in 1996. The gift allowed the hospital to recruit Barbara's longtime physician Michael Lockshin as head of the center.[12] Paul recalls, "This was one of the few sources of comfort to Barbara before she died in 1998. She deserved it."[13]

Volcker withdrew from operating responsibilities when Wolfensohn and Company was sold to Bankers Trust, agreeing only to serve on the bank's board of directors, but his reputation for honesty and integrity drew numerous requests to rent his seal of approval. He could not refuse Fritz Leutwiler, the former head of the Swiss National Bank who had been so helpful during the Mexican crisis.

In the spring of 1996, Leutwiler asked his old friend to chair an "Independent Committee of Eminent Persons" to oversee the return of assets deposited in Switzerland by victims of the Holocaust. Swiss banks had a public relations problem that rivaled al-Qaeda's. The *New York Times* editorialized, "For decades the Swiss banking industry arrogantly thwarted inquiries about its role in the Nazi period, and effectively discouraged the relatives of Holocaust victims searching for long-dormant accounts."[14] Volcker promised justice before an investigating congressional committee.[15] "We are meeting more than fifty years after the end of the Holocaust, certainly one of the most shameful and brutal episodes in human history . . . The time has surely come for a full accounting."

Volcker's willingness to tackle incendiary material brought another request for help, this one in 2002 from Arthur Andersen, the accounting firm that had certified the fraudulent financial statements of the bankrupt Enron Corporation. According to the press, Andersen turned to Volcker because he "may be one of the few public figures with enough prestige and moral authority in the world of finance to bring the giant accounting firm back to reputable standing."[16] And in 2005, Volcker was asked by the United Nations to investigate the oil-for-food scandal that involved the son of Kofi Annan, the UN secretary-general.[17] They needed to cleanse the record and knew that only Volcker's independence could overcome the potential conflict of interest. And besides, they had heard that the price was right: Volcker charged a one-dollar fee in such cases.

Volcker avoided shades of gray and expected others to do the same, but he was usually disappointed. He had learned during his career at the Fed that color-coded signals gave bankers trouble—they understood that green means go and red says no, but they had great difficulty with yellow. And that is why he bristled when Goldman Sachs became a bank in September 2008. "The lines differentiating financial institutions had been blurred, but if Goldman wanted the commercial banking safety net it should look more like a bank, specializing in taking deposits and making loans, rather than like a hedge fund, geared to speculating on mispriced securities."[18] His opportunity to change the rules would come after the 2008 presidential election.

Volcker's presence in Washington grew when Barack Obama defeated John McCain in November 2008. Paul had endorsed the Illinois senator in February 2008, while Obama battled Hillary Clinton for the Democratic nomination. "After thirty years in government . . . I have been reluctant to engage in political campaigns. The time has come to overcome that reluctance . . . It is not the current turmoil in markets . . . that [has] impelled my decision. Rather, it is the breadth and depth of challenges that face our nation . . . Among all the candidates, it is Barack Obama who has most clearly recognized those needs."[19]

Obama capitalized on Volcker's stature during the campaign, seating the financial strongman immediately to his right, as photographers captured the moment, during a roundtable discussion in October 2008 with voters in Lake Worth, Florida.[20] Other photos followed, but Obama invoked the Volcker seal most effectively during the final presidential debate, when McCain raised questions about some of Obama's associates. The Illinois senator shot back, "Let me tell you who I associate with. On economic policy I associate with Warren Buffett and former Fed chairman Paul Volcker . . . who have shaped my ideas and who will be surrounding me in the White House."[21]

But the election changed the pecking order, despite the efforts of Austan Goolsbee, a friendly thirty-nine-year-old professor from the University of Chicago business school who had advised Obama during his 2004 Senate campaign and would eventually become chairman of the president's Council of Economic Advisers. Goolsbee, who made the trim president-elect look a little overweight, had successfully urged Obama to bring Volcker into the inner circle during the campaign and pressed for more of the same after the victory. "Immediately after the election, I urged Obama to appoint Volcker as treasury secretary, even for only a few years. He would have given us instant credibility both at home and abroad. But the transition team had been taken over by Clinton's people, and that hurt his chances."[22]

Volcker's candidacy for treasury secretary had been rumored in the press and made considerable sense, despite his age.[23] The Lehman bankruptcy in September 2008 had plunged America into a financial crisis that demanded bold initiatives, as when Jimmy Carter appointed Volcker as Fed chairman in 1979. And Volcker worked as though he were a thirty-year-old, spending nine-hour days in his Rockefeller Center office in New York City when he was not traveling the world like a financial Gandhi preaching monetary reform. When Warren Buffett recommended Volcker as treasury secretary to Obama's transition team, a young man replied, "He may be a little too old." Buffett responded, "I think he's about my age."[24]

Obama raised the topic with Volcker in a telephone conversation after the election.[25] "Paul, I'd like your reaction to some names for the top job at Treasury."

"Okay," Volcker answered, knowing this was either a courtesy call or a presidential probe of his availability. He doubted that Obama had time for courtesy calls.

"What about Tim Geithner?"

"He could do the job, but he might need some seasoning. Besides, that would leave the New York Fed without a president, and that is a big hole, especially now."

"And Larry Summers?"

"He's already shown he can run Treasury, but we both know he may have a problem getting confirmed in Congress. And that's a diversion you certainly do not need, Mr. President."

Obama then got to the point. "Would you serve for one or two years if I asked?"

Volcker relished the opportunity to confront the greatest crisis since the Great Depression and believed that "you never refuse a president's request to serve your country," even at age eighty-one. He said: "Yes, but it's probably best to keep the time limit between us."

"Of course," the president-elect concurred, "and thanks."

Volcker had said yes, but he knew that an offer was as likely as rain in San Diego. Both Geithner and Summers had worked at the Treasury in the Clinton administration, Summers eventually becoming treasury secretary with Geithner as his deputy. And Obama's transition team, which vetted all job candidates for the new administration, had become a Clinton outpost.

John Podesta, President Clinton's former chief of staff, who had joined the Obama campaign after Hillary Clinton had withdrawn from the race, served as cochairman of Obama's transition team. His staff included influential alumni from the Clinton Treasury, most prominently Michael Froman, a Harvard Law School classmate of Obama's who had been chief of staff for Robert Rubin, Clinton's treasury secretary.[26]

During his stay in Washington, Rubin, a former cochairman of Goldman Sachs, had championed financial deregulation to promote the globalization of American finance, first as a White House adviser on economic policy and then as treasury secretary, where he groomed both Summers and Geithner. His son James S. Rubin was also on Obama's transition team.

The announcements on Monday, November 24, 2008, brought no surprises. Geithner, the forty-seven-year-old career civil servant, was appointed treasury secretary, and Summers, the fifty-four-year-old former president of Harvard University, was named head of the White House National Economic Council. They had been the front-runners and were young enough to play basketball with Obama. Volcker did not fit, and not just because he was too old to compete on the court and thought deregulation had gone too far. He scared them.

Volcker's independence conferred credibility but came with a price. He would speak his mind rather than spout the party line. The press called it "straying off message," but it meant the same thing.[27] Obama echoed that sentiment: "Paul . . . is held in the highest esteem for his sound and independent judgment. He pulls no punches. He seems to be fairly opinionated."[28]

Volcker had been bypassed for the job of treasury secretary before, for the same reason, when Bill Clinton defeated George H. W. Bush in 1992. The post went to seventy-one-year-old Texas senator Lloyd Bentsen, who was later succeeded by Rubin. The *New York Times* commented that Volcker lost out because he was "unlikely to subordinate [his] own strong philosophies and ideas to the new President's."[29]

Clinton could afford to reject Volcker without great consequence; there was no crisis of confidence threatening the American financial system then. But Obama faced a far more dangerous circumstance, certainly comparable in severity to Carter's in 1979, and exceeding Reagan's problem in 1983. And yet both Jimmy Carter and Ronald Reagan swallowed the entire Volcker package rather than succumb to political expediency.

Obama chose the easy way out.

The president-elect kept Volcker close by naming him chairman of a new structure, the President's Economic Recovery Advisory Board, designed to give Obama "expert advice outside the normal bureaucratic channels."[30] Stan Collender, a former staffer in the House and Senate Budget committees and partner in a public relations firm, said, "It also rents some of Volcker's credibility until the president-elect can further establish some of his own."[31]

The PERAB, as it was called, reported directly to Obama but had no resources or staff of its own. Volcker's office (which he never used) was in the Treasury Building, and his chief economist, Austan Goolsbee, had a full-time job on the Council of Economic Advisers in addition to his PERAB duties (perhaps a punishment to Goolsbee for straying off message with Volcker). Nevertheless, Volcker succeeded, with the help of Vice President Joseph Biden, in promoting the Rule that brought him before the Senate Banking Committee in February 2010.

Congress would test his resolve.

Volcker's proposed ban on commercial bank proprietary trading, a polite euphemism for speculation, almost died at 2:45 P.M. on Tuesday, February 2, 2010, while he sat before the microphone waiting to testify. Democratic senator Christopher Dodd, chairman of the Senate Banking Committee, who would eventually cosponsor the Dodd-Frank financial reform bill that would become law in July 2010, greeted Volcker.[32] "We have a lot of work left to be done, so this debate is an important one and we welcome you today to share your thoughts."[33] He then turned the floor over to the ranking minority member of the committee, Republican senator Richard Shelby of Alabama.

Senator Shelby welcomed Volcker by recalling his own debut in the Senate in 1986, "when you were Chairman of the Federal Reserve." Shelby then lobbed a Republican hand grenade. "I am quite disturbed by the manner in which the Administration has gone about introducing their latest proposals for consideration. We are more than a year into our deliberation on regulatory reform . . . [And now] seven months after the Administration first introduced [its] broad recommendations . . . this concept that we have before us today has been air-dropped into the debate."[34]

Volcker swallowed hard and suppressed a grimace, knowing that he had proposed the ban on proprietary trading the previous June, more than eight months before, in a memo to the president.[35] He had fought with Geithner and Summers since then to get his way. Shelby, like almost all Republicans, and some Democrats, too, viewed Obama's embrace of the Volcker Rule as a political affair, an attack on the evils of speculation that would please everyone but the bankers on Wall Street. And the bankers would lobby their favorite members of Congress to avoid the proposed regulation.

Volcker knew that the Rule would need Republican support, so he took Shelby's tirade as an opportunity to push a wider perspective. "I want to emphasize . . . that the proposed restrictions . . . [are] a part of the broader effort . . . designed to help deal with the problem of 'too big to fail' and the related moral hazard that looms so large as an aftermath of the emergency rescues of financial institutions."[36]

The *New York Times* had featured the comprehensive plan two days earlier, in an op-ed article Volcker wrote touting increased capital requirements and a so-called living will, or resolution authority, for large financial institutions.[37] More capital was designed to prevent failure at the beginning, and the living will was aimed at containing the spillover damage in the event of bankruptcy at the end.

Volcker recalls: "I had thought that the decision to let Lehman go in September, 2008, was understandable at the time, to undo the moral hazard of the Bear Stearns rescue six months earlier. But it backfired almost immediately and forced the Fed to rescue AIG . . . an insurance company! After that, no systemically important institution would worry about bankruptcy . . . they knew the government would come to the rescue. And that meant they could take even more risk than before without suffering any consequence—which is exactly what we mean by moral hazard. This unfortunate reality required a radical change in financial regulation."[38]

Increased capital formed the centerpiece of the U.S. Treasury's plan to prevent future bailouts.[39] All banks and insurance companies borrow money to buy assets, leveraging their capital to enhance their returns but simultaneously laying the groundwork for bankruptcy because lenders must be repaid. Leverage—the use of borrowed funds to invest—can be toxic when asset prices decline.[40] More capital reduces the risk of insolvency by enhancing a company's ability to meet its obligations.

Senator Robert Corker of Tennessee, a Republican who had joined the Senate Banking Committee a few years earlier, wanted to know why the Volcker Rule was needed on top of more capital. The bankers wanted neither, of course, but more capital was less onerous than more regulation. "If we have a bill that . . . says that if you are going to [speculate] in these risky areas of activity, that higher capital is going to be required . . . would . . . this type of legislation even be necessary?"[41]

Volcker had argued with Geithner and Summers over precisely this point, and conceded that in theory more capital would work, even though there was never enough to eliminate all risk. But as a practical matter, he did not trust the bankers to comply with the regulations. "Over time, they will reallocate that capital the way they want to."[42] And he did not trust the regulators to remain vigilant. "Congress is [not] going to specify precisely what the capital requirement is, but they are going to give the supervisor the [necessary] authority . . . [and] it is very hard to maintain very tough restrictions when nothing [bad] is happening."[43] The facts supported Volcker's skepticism.

Bankers had been minimizing their capital requirements to enhance their profitability ever since balance sheets were invented, perfecting their methods with mathematical flair in the twenty-first century. Banks created subsidiaries called structured investment vehicles (SIVs) to house assets such as subprime mortgages that were partitioned into packages with impeccable credit ratings.[44] These bank subsidiaries eliminated the need for capital in the parent company but continued to draw on a bank's reputation and liquidity, a fact that regulators ignored before 2007. All this changed after losses on the mortgages parked in SIVs forced bank holding companies, such as the then giant Citigroup, to swallow the damaged assets, impairing what seemed like enough capital beforehand.[45]

A second line of attack on the Volcker Rule came from Republican senator Mike Johanns of Nebraska, who dispensed with the pleasantries: "I must admit I have sat through this hearing and I get more confused as you testify . . . Tell me the evil that you are trying to wrestle out of the system by this rule?"[46]

Volcker was taken aback. "I feel that I have failed you if you are more confused than before."

"That is all right."

"What I want to get out of the system is taxpayer support for speculative activity, and I want to look ahead . . . It is going to become bigger and bigger, and . . . add to what is already a risky business." Volcker had emphasized looking ahead because he knew what Johanns was going to ask.

"But here is the problem, Mr. Chairman," Johanns said, using Volcker's old title to soften the sting, "and here is where I am struggling to follow your logic . . . How would this have prevented all the taxpayer money going to AIG? . . . Would we have solved the problems with Lehman had the Volcker rule been in place?'

Volcker knew that this was not the case.[47] Lehman was an investment bank that had purchased risky assets, including commercial real estate and subprime mortgages, and had financed many of its investments by borrowing money that had to be repaid overnight.[48] The mismatch between the maturity of assets and liabilities made Lehman resemble Continental Illinois a generation earlier—both survived by renewing their borrowings in the marketplace on a daily basis. Lehman declared bankruptcy when investors lost confidence in the firm's ability to repay its debts and refused to renew their loans.

Volcker conceded the point to the senator from Nebraska: "It certainly would not have solved the problem at AIG or . . . Lehman alone. It was not designed to solve those particular problems."

"Exactly. That is the point," Johanns interjected. "You know, this kind of reminds me of what . . . [Obama's] Chief of Staff said, 'never let a good crisis go to waste.' What we are doing here is we are taking this financial reform and we are expanding it beyond where we should be. And I just question the wisdom of that."

Volcker, of course, had exploited crises long before Obama's gatekeeper, Rahm Emanuel, had even thought of the phrase, much less spoken it. And that perspective contained more truth than he would admit, as when Senator John Heinz accused him of crisis-mongering in 1984 to fix the deficit. But he believed that guarding against the last conflagration is as fruitless in finance as it was in combat. "I would emphasize that the problem today is [to] look ahead and try to anticipate . . . And I tell you, sure as I am sitting here, that if banking institutions are protected by the taxpayer and they are given free rein to speculate, I may not live long enough to see the crisis, but my soul is going to come back and haunt you."

Johanns found this amusing: "That may be. There will be a lot of people. You would have to stand in line maybe."

Everyone laughed, including Volcker, but he knew that the risks of speculation remained mostly submerged, like an alligator waiting to strike, and with the same devastating consequences when they surfaced. Speculation by Nick Leeson, a trader for the two-hundred-year-old Barings Bank, had forced the company into bankruptcy in 1995, and trading losses of $7 billion by Jérôme Kerviel in 2008 had impaired the credit rating of Société Général, the second-largest French bank.

Volcker recognized that neither of those massive speculations had unleashed a financial tsunami, because they were considered isolated events. But speculators, despite their secretive nature, often pursue the same strategies, like the famous carry trade. Traders borrow in a low-interest-rate currency, like Japan's, and lend in a high-interest-rate currency, like Australia's, and assume foreign exchange risk while trying to capture the interest rate differential. It works until losses force them to abandon the strategy, as during 2007 and 2008.[49]

Herding by speculators risks a stampede to safety, the signature of a crisis.

The most powerful Republican challenge to the Volcker Rule came toward the end of the day on February 2, 2010, when Senator Mike Crapo of Idaho, a member of the Senate since 1998, returned to Senator Shelby's opening theme: "The Administration submitted a significant proposal last summer about how to approach reform . . . [and] the Volcker rule was not in that proposal . . . I assume that part of the reason . . . was because . . . we do not have the . . . the legislation language . . . And my question, Chairman Volcker, is [can you distinguish] . . . between the permissible and impermissible [trading] activities . . . Some people say [it is] impossible."[50]

Volcker knew this called for applying Justice Potter Stewart's methodology—speculation is like pornography, you know it when you see it—but he had already blurted out that analogy, and gotten a laugh, in response to an earlier question from Shelby.[51] Now he could only say, "Bankers know what proprietary trading is and what it is not, and do not let them tell you anything different."[52]

Volcker was right, and Crapo agreed, in part. "Well . . . I suspect that that may be true, to some extent, although . . . we could find different points of view among bankers as to exactly what we are talking about."

"I agree . . . [but] I do not think it is so hard to set forward the law that establishes the general principle."

"I understand the point you are making, but . . . this Committee and this Congress need some level of specificity on which to act . . . because if we get them wrong, I think that we could be doing as much harm as good."

The Volcker Rule needed greater precision to win congressional support.

CHAPTER 18

The Rule

I came to Volcker's Rockefeller Center office on Monday afternoon, February 8, 2010, for an interview—we had been meeting twice monthly since I started this biography in mid-2008. Volcker sat in a high-backed leather chair behind his desk, as always, and wore a gray double-breasted suit, white shirt, and dull tie. He looked more unhappy than usual, perhaps because the international press had memorialized his testimony of February 2 at the Senate Banking Committee with the headline "Risky Banking Like Pornography, Volcker Tells Senate."[1]

He stared at me for a moment and then tossed a familiar-looking document across the granite desktop in my direction. "Now, why the devil didn't you show this thing to me before last week? I could have waved it in front of the Committee instead of offering up salacious material. I would have made it required reading."

I smiled at the thought. "I did not know you were going to testify, but after I read the newspaper accounts, I sent it up by messenger."

"If memory serves me correctly, we discussed trading many times and you never mentioned it."

"Well, I told you that I traded, both as a market maker and as a speculator, and that I worked for a hedge fund for a while. You didn't seem to care."

"I must have blocked out the hedge fund connection . . . But you never said you wrote an article on how to distinguish between market-making and speculation."[2]

"It's been a while," I answered.

"The publication date is 2003—that's only seven years ago."

"But I began thinking about it in 1983, when I worked for Dick Fuld. That's almost thirty years ago."

Volcker looked at me as though I had just confessed to a felony. "You mean the CEO of Lehman?"

"Yes, although that was not his job back then. Lewis Glucksman was the chief executive officer and he had just put Dick in charge of all trading."

"What did you do?"

"He hired me as risk manager."

Volcker furrowed his brow. "I didn't think they had that position back then."

"They didn't," I said, and told him the story. "It was mostly seat-of-the-pants risk controls, but Glucksman wanted to create a system because he worried about trading losses—with good reason. I'll never forget my first day. Fuld and I sat in a glass-walled booth overlooking a trading floor as big as a football field, with more than a hundred traders positioned before rows of computer terminals that extended the length of the room. I could hear the roar of muffled conversations, some spoken into headsets and others shouted across the room, with phrases like 'how many,' 'how much,' and 'you're done' rising above the confusion. Fuld said, 'Are you ready to start?' I answered, 'Sure, but what are all these people doing out there?' He raised his voice in mock anger: 'What the fuck do you think I hired you for?'"

Volcker laughed. "I guess he never found out."

"It wasn't his fault, at least not then," I said. "I left Lehman a year later, before I understood that the two varieties of trading—market-making and speculation—are very different businesses. I learned the hard way, trading for myself on the futures exchange as a market maker and then trading for a hedge fund as a speculator. I lost money only when I confused the two lines of work."[3]

Market-making in securities is like the used-car business. A used-car dealer buys Chevrolets and Hondas from owners wanting to sell and then turns around and sells those cars to drivers wanting to buy, providing a ready market for secondhand cars to its customers. Dealers make money on the price markup, the difference between the buying and selling prices, and on rapid turnover. They try to avoid a build-up of unsold cars. Market makers in stocks and bonds are also called dealers, securities dealers, because they do the same thing. They buy Microsoft stock or General Electric bonds from investors wanting to sell and then turn around and sell those same securities to others wanting to buy, providing a ready market—liquidity—to investors. They avoid holding inventory for too long because their markup, the difference between their bid (at which they buy) and offer (at which they sell) is relatively small compared with the normal price fluctuations in stocks and bonds. Inventory is risky.

Speculators in securities behave very differently. They resemble antique-car collectors more than used-car dealers. Antique collectors search for value, like a 1963 Chevy Impala, a 1965 Ford Mustang, or even a 1985 Nissan Maxima, because they expect prices to rise—and they store the cars until they make a profit. Speculators in stocks and bonds do the same thing, buying undervalued securities they think will rise in value, and holding them in inventory until they do.

But it gets much more complicated. Speculators and market makers can both disguise their intentions like secret agents. At financial institutions, speculators call themselves proprietary traders to sound respectable and often pursue mixed strategies to mask their behavior. They deal with customers when it suits their purpose, serving as ready buyers while accumulating a speculative position. They misrepresent themselves as low-risk market makers to reduce their capital requirements. And market makers often stray into speculation without permission, hoping to earn profits as prices rise by accumulating more inventory than they really need. Market makers speculate because it is more exciting, like buying a Lamborghini, and to earn a bigger bonus.

Regulators implementing a Volcker Rule that permits market-making and prohibits speculation have their work cut out for them. But they can follow the guidelines of managers at securities firms who monitor trader behavior. For example, when I traded as a market maker (called a scalper) on the futures exchange, I belonged to a clearing firm that guaranteed my transactions with other members of the exchange. The manager of the clearing firm monitored every trader on his watch and would revoke trading privileges for violations of the guidelines. He checked my transactions every day—how often I bought, when I sold, how long I held a position, even the size of my inventory at various points during the day. I did not speculate.

Volcker sat back in his chair and said nothing after I had confessed to trading for a hedge fund. He then surprised me with "Maybe we can capitalize on your past indiscretions. I'd like you to write an op-ed piece for the *Times* or the *Journal* explaining how to distinguish market-making from speculation. They'll publish it."

It was an opportunity and a distraction. "I'm flattered that you ask, but that takes time and I'm trying to write a biography, in case you hadn't noticed. I was supposed to finish a year ago."

He did not hesitate: "The op-ed piece is more important."

Volcker's preference for public over private goals forced a compromise. "I'll be happy to talk to the committee staffers and to reporters—but no writing. I want to finish this book while you can still criticize it."

He ignored the quip. "Okay, I'll send the rule makers to you—that should be good enough. I've got other plans to pressure Congress in the press."

"Like what?"

"I'm soliciting support for the Rule from former Treasury secretaries . . . a letter to one of the national newspapers."

"Anyone I know?"

"Blumenthal . . . Brady . . . O'Neill . . . Shultz . . . Snow."[4]

"Very nice," I said. "Lots of Republicans . . . and I'm sure Milton is turning over in his grave with George Shultz in your corner."[5]

Volcker smiled at the thought of Shultz defying the now-deceased Milton Friedman by supporting increased regulation.[6] And then he volunteered: "I called in some chips . . . Brady owed me."

"How is that?"

"I let him use my name for a horse."

"Excuse me?"

"He owns a racing stable and asked for permission to name a horse after me . . . I said, which end? When he said the whole animal, I gave my blessing."

I laughed. "Is he any good?"

"He came in second a couple of times at Saratoga . . . and then he got sick and died."[7]

"Ouch."

"I expect to do better."

By the end of May 2011, Volcker's persistence had paid off. He had lobbied personally in Congress for the ban on proprietary trading and then joined forces with Senators Jeff Merkley of Oregon and Carl Levin of Michigan, backing their amendment to the original bill proposed by Senate Banking Committee chairman Christopher Dodd. Volcker wrote a letter for public distribution to the two senators dated May 19, 2010: "Senators Merkley and Levin: I am fully in support of the Merkley-Levin amendment, which will clarify and enhance the proprietary trading restrictions contained within the Dodd bill."[8] Merkley suggested only half jokingly that the legislation should have been called the Merkley-Levin-Volcker amendment.[9]

Congressman Barney Frank of Massachusetts, the chairman of the House Financial Services Committee, told a reporter, "When the banks come to me opposing various things [in the financial reform bill], I say to them 'If I were you, I would go and see Paul Volcker. If you can persuade him, you might have a chance. I think you are not going to see anything in this bill that Paul objects to.' "[10]

Barney Frank told the truth, with one big exception.

The Dodd-Frank Wall Street Reform and Consumer Protection Act, signed by President Obama on July 21, 2010, devotes Section 619 to the Volcker Rule.[11] This eleven-page prescription adopts the language of the Merkley-Levin amendment, which pleased Volcker, and begins with the two main prohibitions of the Rule, which he liked even more: "A banking entity shall not (A) engage in proprietary trading; or (B) acquire or retain any equity, partnership, or other ownership interest in or sponsor a hedge fund or a private equity fund."[12] But the six words preceding these restrictions, "Unless otherwise provided in this section," gave him cause for concern.

Volcker had anticipated some exceptions to the Rule but thought the wording offered the bankers a giant escape hatch. None of the prohibitions against trading in Section 619 applied to government bonds, or to reducing risks through hedging, or to helping customers transact in any security, no matter how risky. Bankers would have little difficulty slipping their speculations through the cracks. To clarify the distinctions between permissible and forbidden activities, the Dodd-Frank bill mandated a study "not later than six months after the date of enactment . . . [by] the Financial Stability Oversight Council . . . [to] make recommendations on implementing" the statute.[13]

Dodd-Frank established the Financial Stability Oversight Council (FSOC), chaired by Treasury Secretary Timothy Geithner, as a permanent committee with broad regulatory authority "to identify risks to the financial stability of the United States."[14] Members of the FSOC included Chairman Ben Bernanke of the Federal Reserve Board, Chairman Mary Schapiro of the Securities and Exchange Commission, and other key federal regulators.[15] One of the commission's earliest responsibilities was to recommend "principles for implementing the Volcker Rule . . . including an internal compliance regime, quantitative analysis, and reporting and supervisory review."[16]

In October 2010 the FSOC called for comments from the public to guide their recommendations. Volcker prepared as though this were the final battle for financial integrity. He wanted to avoid a last-minute setback.

"I don't want to get shafted again," he said to me as we ate lunch at a corner table in a restaurant overlooking the skating rink in Rockefeller Center. He had just introduced me to David Rockefeller, seated at the adjacent table. The ninety-five-year-old retired chairman of Chase Manhattan Bank and grandson of Standard Oil founder John D. Rockefeller had been Volcker's boss during Paul's Chase Manhattan days, and had just congratulated him on the recent legislation.

"He didn't seem to think you got shafted," I said, nodding toward Rockefeller.

"But he doesn't know how close to perfection we came."

A congressional conference committee reconciling the House and

Senate versions of the Dodd-Frank bill on the final night of deliberation had diluted the restriction against banks owning and sponsoring hedge funds. After the negotiations, banks could invest up to 3 percent of their Tier 1 capital in hedge funds, rather than the $500 million maximum that Volcker had conceded.[17] JPMorgan Chase, for example, could invest about $3.9 billion, Citicorp $3.6 billion, and Goldman Sachs $2.1 billion without violating the law.[18]

"Well, perfection is a high standard," I said, "but compared with your prospects last February, you cannot complain." I showed him a *Wall Street Journal* article dated February 3, 2010, with the headline "Volcker and Reform Defeated."[19]

He laughed. "They miscalculated."

"Besides," I said, "I've always thought that the ban on proprietary trading was more important—and that went through unscathed."

"I agree." Volcker smiled like a litigator sensing an opening. "And that is why I want you to provide guidance to the committee on how to separate market-making from speculation. I've written a four-page letter in response to their call for public comments and added a footnote indicating they should expect a submission from you."[20]

"You don't give up, do you?"

"I may be old but I am persistent."

"Are there any other surprises?"

Volcker smiled. "Maybe."

"I can't wait."

On Tuesday, January 18, 2011, the FSOC released an eighty-one-page report with detailed recommendations for regulators, but the exodus of proprietary traders from banks had already begun. The press reported as far back as August 2010 that JPMorgan Chase had begun "dismantling its stand-alone proprietary trading desk and is now preparing to wind down One Equity Partners, its internal private equity business," to meet anticipated regulations, and Citigroup had sold "its Skybridge Capital hedge fund group" to comply with provisions of the new law.[21] On January 11, 2011, the *Wall Street Journal* reported that Morgan Stanley, the brokerage giant that had become a bank holding company during 2008, "reached an agreement with proprietary-trading chief Peter

Muller . . . to form a new firm . . . About 60 employees are likely to follow Mr. Muller out the door."[22]

The voluntary compliance with the Volcker Rule met with praise and
skepticism. Brad Hintz, an analyst at the brokerage firm Sanford C. Bernstein, said, "This is the real stuff . . . we really are squeezing Wall Street.
Their business models are changing."[23] But most observers thought
traders could sell the Volcker Rule short with impunity. Jeffrey Harris,
the former chief economist at the Commodity Futures Trading Commission, said, "The line between providing liquidity and proprietary
trading is very thin. If people want to trade on prop accounts, they are
going to find a way to do it."[24] And the Bloomberg columnist and bestselling author Michael Lewis wrote, "Wall Street insiders [say] . . . The
banks have no intention of ceasing their prop trading. They are merely
disguising the activity, by giving it another name."[25]

The FSOC recognized the problem and introduced its report with a
warning to institutions planning to hide speculators behind market
makers. "Although 'bright line' proprietary trading desks are readily
identifiable, in current practice, significant proprietary trading activity can take place in the context of activities that would otherwise be
permitted by the statute. Therefore, an essential part of implementing
the statute is the creation of rules and a supervisory framework that
effectively prohibit proprietary trading activities throughout a banking entity—not just within certain business units."[26]

The attention to detail pleased Volcker as he reviewed the FSOC report, especially the precise metrics recommended to regulators to separate market makers from speculators. High inventory turnover, frequent
transactions with customers, and consistent profits on a daily basis,
would classify a trader more like a market maker than a speculator.[27]
Low scores on these metrics would not prove that a trader had violated
the Volcker Rule, but they would flash a warning like the Check Engine
light on a car's dashboard, and require further investigation by the regulator. The report pointed out that regulators such as the Federal Reserve
System would need "significant new and specialized resources" to implement the law.[28]

The need for more resources had concerned Volcker all along. In
February 2010 he testified, "The banks are all going to have a lot of
twenty-six-year-olds . . . [with] a lot of fancy mathematical training and

all the rest. The supervisors need a few twenty-eight-year-olds that have had the same kind of training."[29] But he knew that talent flows to the highest pay scale, so that traders at Goldman Sachs, JPMorgan Chase, and Morgan Stanley could usually outsmart the regulators at the Federal Reserve Bank of New York. He had racked his brain to turn the tables—and had hit upon a solution only after the Dodd-Frank legislation had passed.

Volcker waited until the request for public comments by the FSOC to present his idea. It appeared as the first substantive paragraph of his October 29, 2010, letter and focused on the role of a bank's chief executive officer (CEO): "In my view, effective compliance must start with clear understanding at the top of the regulated institution. As I have repeatedly stated both in public and in conversations with banking leaders, the relevant banking supervisor's first step in their examination and enforcement process should be the 'corner office.' The CEO's understanding and his instructions to other executives and staff regarding the prohibition on proprietary trading and compliance procedures for the new rules should be carefully reviewed . . . to insure effective procedures for compliance with Section 619."[30]

Volcker emphasized that the "tone at the top" matters, and the FSOC agreed. Its report includes in its summary recommendations that regulators "Require banking entities to implement a robust compliance regime, including public attestation by the CEO of the regime's effectiveness."[31] But the report went even further, suggesting that regulators consider imposing joint obligations on the board of directors and the CEO. "For example, the Board of Directors could be made responsible for . . . approving the compliance program . . . and for ensuring that these policies are adhered to in practice . . . The CEO could be made responsible for . . . communicating and reinforcing the compliance culture established by the Board of Directors."[32]

Public reaction to the report, especially commentary on the CEO's new responsibilities, pleased Volcker. Winthrop Brown, a partner at the law firm Milbank, Tweed, Hadley & McCloy, which represents banks, said, "I would be troubled if I were a chief compliance officer. It seems to be very burdensome."[33] William Sweet, a former lawyer at the Federal Reserve and now a partner at Skadden, Arps, Slate, Meagher & Flom, said the sign-off requirement "puts the CEO in a very difficult position."[34] Paul Miller, an analyst at FBR Capital Markets in Arlington, Virginia, added, "The only real negative [in the report] is that CEOs must publicly attest to the rule in some way. CEOs will not like this—but nothing else is really a surprise."[35]

Volcker had promised a surprise and had delivered more than most CEOs wanted to see. He knew that a worried CEO could devote more resources to ensuring compliance than all the regulators money could buy. The financial columnist Floyd Norris quipped, "Certification concentrates attention."[36]

Volcker concludes, "I have strongly advocated that the CEO and board of directors of commercial banks personally attest to their firm's compliance with the legal restriction . . . To my mind bankers who contend that they cannot distinguish in practice between a continuing pattern of proprietary trading and trading in response to established customer needs cannot be considered either serious or qualified bank managers, no matter how many lawyers and layers of financial manipulation are employed to subvert the plain prohibition."[37]

He is right. CEOs of major financial institutions know the difference between speculation and market-making. They also have the internal controls to manage trader behavior. Regulators do not have the resources to restrain speculation at commercial banks by themselves. The Volcker Rule will work if regulators force bank management to make it work. Otherwise it will fail.

CHAPTER 19

Trust

Gold, the ancient monarch of world finance, lost its crown in 1971, when President Richard Nixon ended foreign central banks' right to convert dollars into the precious metal.[1] Nixon followed Volcker's blueprint in administering the coup that began in Congress six years earlier.[2] Since then the world has been on a dollar standard, a fiat currency backed only by the full faith and credit of the United States. Dollars serve Americans as "legal tender for all debts, public and private," but without a fixed link to any commodity.[3]

Milton Friedman, an apostle of monetary rectitude, supported the overthrow of gold. He testified in Congress that the "gold reserve requirement is an anachronistic survival from an earlier age."[4] Friedman echoed the famous denunciation of gold as a "barbarous relic" by the British economist John Maynard Keynes, and reflected the sentiment of most American economists alive when he testified. But he worried.

Friedman wrote that the worldwide experiment in fiat currency "has no historical precedent," and cited the warning of Irving Fisher, the great U.S. monetary expert of the early twentieth century.[5] "Irredeemable paper money has almost invariably proved a curse to the country employing it."[6] Friedman was less pessimistic than Fisher, who worried about hyperinflation, but not by much. "It is not possible to say whether Fisher's 1911 generalization . . . will hold true in coming decades." It will

297

depend, Friedman said, on whether we "find a substitute for convertibility into [gold] that will serve the same function: maintaining pressure on the government to refrain from . . . inflation as a source of revenue."

The 1970s nearly confirmed Irving Fisher's worst fears. Debate over the cause of the Great Inflation in the United States continues, but cannot dismiss as coincidence the removal of gold as the monetary anchor.[7] Congress might have prevented irresponsible monetary policy by refusing to adjust the gold reserve requirement, had it still been the law, the same way it occasionally refuses to raise the debt ceiling to extract fiscal concessions.

Volcker rescued the experiment in fiat currency from failure. His belief that price stability belongs in the social contract and that inflation undermines trust in government encouraged policies to restore monetary discipline during the 1980s. He showed that a determined central banker can behave like a surrogate for gold. But even Volcker needed help. His refusal to monetize federal deficits forced Congress to implement a plan for fiscal responsibility, reinforcing the Federal Reserve's credibility.[8] The combination brought decades of price stability to America and preserved trust in the U.S. dollar both at home and abroad.

The crisis that began in 2007 threatens that trust.

Foreigners hold dollars because America has demonstrated fiscal and monetary integrity, and because the United States is a nation of laws and markets, providing a safe haven for storing wealth. Broad, deep, and resilient financial markets that are free from manipulation and excessive regulation have allowed investors to commit and withdraw funds with ease and without challenge. Foreign appetite for U.S. securities has bestowed a gift of low interest rates on spendthrift Americans. But the need for massive government intervention during September 2008 tarnished the reputation of American finance. And the policies implemented since then harbor seeds of further damage.

The Federal Reserve, under the chairmanship of Ben Bernanke, served as lender of last resort during the fragile days and weeks following the bankruptcy of Lehman Brothers on September 15, 2008. Congress established the Federal Reserve System in 1914 for precisely that purpose, to lend when no one else would to prevent the spread of financial panic. And Bernanke deserves credit for avoiding a catastrophe like the Great Depression. But by mid-2011, though the overnight interest rate had been kept near zero for almost three years, and the banks had been provided with unprecedented liquidity, the economy had failed to recover fully and unemployment remained unacceptably high.

On Tuesday, August 9, 2011, the central bank announced that the FOMC had decided "to keep the target range for the [overnight] federal funds rate at zero to one-quarter percent [and] anticipates that economic conditions . . . are likely to warrant exceptionally low levels for the federal funds rate at least through mid-2013."[9] The Fed's commitment to maintaining low interest rates for two years disturbed Volcker. "How can they know now what is appropriate for that length of time? They may be painting themselves into a corner."[10]

The 1970s taught central bankers two big lessons: Monetary policy can lower unemployment only temporarily, while inflationary expectations remain dormant, and inflationary expectations percolate to the surface even before the economy reaches full employment. Volcker brought that message forward with an op-ed article in September 2011: "The danger is that if, in desperation, we turn to deliberately seeking inflation to solve real problems—our economic imbalances, sluggish productivity, and excessive leverage—we would soon find that a little inflation doesn't work . . . What we know, or should know, from the past is that once inflation becomes anticipated and ingrained—as it eventually would—then the stimulating effects are lost. Once an independent central bank . . . invokes inflation as a policy, it becomes very difficult to eliminate."[11]

Expansionary fiscal policy, the Keynesian recipe for combating economic stagnation, shifts concern to the exploding federal deficit. But only the structural budget deficit that would prevail at full employment poses a problem, rather than the temporary increase in the deficit during recession. The increased borrowing required by cyclically declining income tax revenues, for example, reverses itself as the economy recovers, making room for corporate borrowing when it matters. In 2011, however, the full employment budget deficit was 5 percent of national output, a number reminiscent of the Reagan-era deficits, and that signals trouble.[12] The United States has thus far escaped the high interest rates that come with such unsustainable deficit spending because the economy remains in recession and because investors in U.S. Treasury securities trust the American political system to curtail fiscal excess as in the past. But that trust demands action before it dissipates.

Long-term budgetary extravagance combined with a banking system brimming with liquidity threatens investors with inflation. Increases in real interest rates as the economy expands, Volcker's medicine during the 1980s, can preserve investor confidence by restraining private spending and by persuading Congress to legislate a balanced budget. But Volcker acted after years of inflation had galvanized public opinion behind him, while in the second decade of the twenty-first century, Americans have been weakened by recession and unemployment. The Federal Reserve may not have the public support it needs to act preemptively.

Inflation is ancient history to most Americans, like some medieval curse, but the risk of resurgence in a world of fiat currency demands vigilance. Volcker worries that the international financial system is especially vulnerable now, "when foreign countries own trillions of our dollars, when we are dependent on borrowing still more abroad, and when the whole world counts on the dollar's maintaining its purchasing power."[13]

A commitment to a full-employment balanced budget would confirm the fiscal integrity needed to neutralize the danger at the source. Nobel Laureate Thomas Sargent, Volcker's favorite rational expectations expert, said that central banks need help. "They cannot do it alone."[14] Federal Reserve chairman Ben Bernanke delivered a similar message: "A large and increasing level of government debt relative to national income risks serious economic consequences . . . High levels of debt . . . impair the ability of policymakers to respond effectively to future economic shocks and other adverse events."[15]

Bernanke did not say that long-term budget balance sustains trust in the Federal Reserve's commitment to price stability. He did not have to. History delivers that message—courtesy of Paul Volcker.

Personal Records and
Correspondence

WEIGHT AND HEIGHT RECORD

	Your Standard	Opening of Term	Middle of Term	End of Term	ABOVE STANDARD (20 per cent. and more above standard)
HEIGHT					AVERAGE WEIGHT (From 7 per cent. below to 10 per cent. above standard)
WEIGHT					BELOW STANDARD (From 7 per cent. to 10 per cent. below standard)

NOTE: Compare your record carefully with the Standard Weight and Height for your age as indicated above. If your weight is 10 per cent. or more below standard, or 20 per cent. and more above standard an examination is suggested by your family physician. Normal weight may range from 10 per cent. above standard to 7 per cent. below. Ideal weight probably ranges from 5 per cent. to 10 per cent. above standard. Attention is therefore needed if your weight ranges from 7 per cent. to 10 per cent. below the standard weight.

CERTIFICATE OF PROMOTION

Promoted to Grade ....

Retained in Grade *Kdg. I* Passed on Condition to Grade ....

Washington Irving Constance Palmer
School   Teacher's Signature

PARENT'S SIGNATURE

Paul Y. Volcker	*Mrs. Paul A. Volcker*
September	February
Paul Volcker	*Mrs. Paul A. Volcker*
October	March
Paul Volcker	*Mrs. Paul A. Volcker*
November	April
Mrs. P. A. Volcker	*Paul A. Volcker*
December	May
Mrs. P. A. Volcker	
January	June

Teaneck Public Schools

PRIMARY GRADE REPORT

Kindergarten, Grades 1 and 2

OF

Paul Volcker
Name

 # 2   *Kdg*
School   Grade

Constance Palmer
Teacher

——————o——————

To Parents

EVEN with the best effort, children do not all move at the same rate. Those who are immature, slow moving, or not robust in health, may do work that is satisfactory according to their development or strength, and yet require more than the usual time to master the subject matter of a given grade. The school aims to give each child the opportunity to progress as fast as health and ability permit.

Learning how to read is made up of more than one skill and we are attempting to measure your child's progress in some of these skills which is necessary if he or she is to become an efficient reader. This is equally true of each of the school subjects.

Kindly examine this report carefully, sign and return promptly. We hope that through this report card you will come to better understand the needs and attainments of your child. We urge you to visit the school as often as convenient.

You Will Be Welcome

Kindergarten report card, page 1.

REPORT TO PARENTS

	Showing Particular Strength in	Making Satisfactory Progress in	Having Difficulty with
Sept.			
Oct.	1-4-7.13	9-8	5
Nov.	1-4-7.13	2.10	5
Dec.	1-4-7-8.13	10-11-12	5-9
Jan.	1-4-7-8.13	8.10-11-12	5-2
Feb.	1-4-7-8.13	all other subjects	2-5
Mar.	1-4-7-8.13	2-5 and other subjects	9
Apr.	1-2-5-4 7-8-13	all other subjects	9
May	1-2-4-5 7-8-13	all other subjects	so little improvement
June	1-2-11-5 1.1.13	all other subjects	still unimproved

	Sept.	Oct.	Nov.	Dec.	Jan.	Feb.	Mar.	Apr.	May	June
Times Tardy	0	0	0	0	0	0	0	0		C
Half Days Lost	1	0	2	1	1	4	0	C	C	C
Conduct	E	E	E	E	E	E	E	E	E	
Effort—tries to do his or her best	E	E	E	E	E					
If a clock mark appears in this space an interview with parent is desired										

A few outstanding habits and attitudes that are being developed in your child's school training.

DISIRABLE HABITS AND ATTITUDES

1. Works steadily until an activity is finished.
2. Keeps to the subject under discussion.
3. Shows ability to note details.
4. Shows ability to follow directions.
5. Takes part in group discussion.
6. Not dependent on imitation in thought and action.
7. Sits quietly during group discussion.
8. Shows skill in use and care of materials and equipment
9. Works willingly and happily with others.
10. Is willing to act promptly on request.
11. Responds cheerfully to requests.
12. Receives criticism in the right spirit.
13. Restrains voice to quiet tones.
14. Accepts defeat, optimistically.

READING HABITS

15. Reading as rapidly as average pupil in his grade.
16. Mastering new words for himself.
17. Understanding material of appropriate difficulty.
18. Enjoys reading independently.
19. Reading without lip or head movement.
20. Reading without pointing.
21. Increasing the eye span.
22. Growth in reading skills.

(When the above traits are not referred to by numbers on the regular report for each month, it means that your child's status in these traits is neither much above or much below average.)

Kindergarten report card, page 2: having difficulty with numbers 5 and 9.

GRAPHIC REPORT

Grades 3 to 6 inclusive

OF

_____
Name

School #2   Grade 6

_____
Teacher

Teaneck Public Schools

Teaneck, New Jersey

SOME TEANECK SCHOOL AIMS.

1. To emphasize, promote and develope good health habits.
2. To stress thoroughness in reading, writing, arithmetic and the elements of oral and written expression.
3. To teach the pupils how to think and how to study.
4. To adapt instruction to individual needs and interest.
5. To assist in developing character traits and attitudes that make for worthy membership in the home, neighborhood, town, state and nation.

TO THE PARENT OR GUARDIAN

These reports will assist you, in determining the progress of one in whom we are all deeply interested. We hope you will examine them carefully. If the report is found unsatisfactory, visit the teacher at once, preferably after 3:15 P. M., and consider with the teacher what can be done to secure improvement. We urge you to visit the school as often as convenient in order that your co-operation will allow for the best and fullest possible development or your child.

ATTENDANCE RECORD

NOTE: Please note the absence and tardiness, if any, each month. The evil of irregular attendance is a serious one, we ask your assistance in correcting it.

PERIOD ISSUED	OCT.	DEC.	FEB.	APRIL	JUNE	Total
DAYS ABSENT				6		
TIMES TARDY						

WEIGHT AND HEIGHT RECORD

Year Standard	Opening of Term	Middle of Term	End of Term
WEIGHT			
HEIGHT			

NOTE: Compare your record carefully with the Standard Weight and Height for your age as indicated above. If your weight is 10 per cent. or more below standard, or 20 per cent. and more above standard an examination is suggested by your family physician. Normal weight may range from 10 per cent. above standard to 7 per cent. below. Ideal weight probably ranges from 5 per cent. to 10 per cent. above standard. Attention is therefore needed if your weight ranges from 7 per cent. to 10 per cent. below the standard weight.

ABOVE STANDARD (20 per cent. and more above standard) AVERAGE WEIGHT (From 7 per cent. below to 10 per cent. above standard) BELOW STANDARD (From 7 per cent. to 10 per cent. below standard)

TEACHERS COMMENT AND PARENT'S SIGNATURE

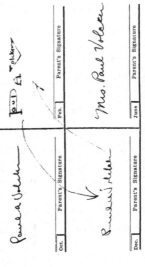

Oct. _____ Parent's Signature

Feb. _____ Parent's Signature

Dec. _____ Parent's Signature

June _____ Parent's Signature

CERTIFICATE OF PROMOTION

Promoted to Grade _____ 7

Passed on Condition _____
To Grade _____

Retained in Grade _____

_____
Teacher's Signature

Code: R.E 7

Grade six report card: fancy Volcker Sr. signature.

The following is the official report of

Paul Adolf Volcker, Jr.

for the Summer Term ending October 20, 1945

The number immediately following the subject indicates the number of the course as found in the University catalogue: the single number thereafter indicates the group attained.

Chemistry 101	1+
Economics 101	1
French 101	1
Mathematics 108	1
Psychology 101	1+
Physical Education	2

Average for Term .88

General Group for the Term 1

A student who has satisfied the requirements of a course is given one of five groups:
First, Second, Third, Fourth and Fifth, the last being the lowest passing group.
A student who has failed to satisfy the requirements of a course is given a Sixth or a Seventh Group, the latter indicating a bad failure.
When a student is absent from an examination with sufficient reason, he is marked A+ if his term grade is above passing, and A— if below passing.
When a student is absent from an examination without sufficient reason, he is given a seventh group.
The lower limit of the First General Group is 1.30; of the Second General Group, 2.30; of the Third General Group, 3.30; of the Fourth General Group, 4.30; of the Fifth General Group, 5.30; of the Sixth General Group, 6.30.

Wilbur F. Kerr

Registrar.

A Princeton semester: excellent . . . but for basketball.

Mr & Mrs Paul A. Volcker
1301 Longfellow Ave.
West Englewood, N.J.

Arrived safely but got my
first Ticket in the process.
According To the cop, I didn't
stop at a stop sign, but I think
That I did. I guess That he wins.
But if its more Than $5 I am
going To the court & complain
may be. I got iT on The Worcester
Pike. I was so innocent I didn'T
have the slightest idea why he stopped me.
I figured That it was for speeding, but
he was shocked at That idea.

Postcard home from Harvard: a traffic ticket.

Harvard Univ. Graduate School of Public Administration
Littauer Center, Cambridge, Mass. July 26, 1951.

Transcript of Harvard Record of

Paul Adolph Volcker —

Course		Grade ½	Full course
1949-50			
Ec. 201	Economic Theory		A
Ec. 241	Principles of Money & Banking		A-
Ec. 243a	International Trade	A	
Gov. 250a	Govt. Admin. & Public Policy	A	
Ec. 243b	International Trade	A	
Gov. 250b.	Govt. Admin. & Public Policy	A-	
1950-51			
Gov. 106b	History of Political Thought	A	
Ec 202	Advanced Economic Theory		Excused
Ec. 251	Public Finance		A
Gov. 112	Parliamentary Government	A	
Ec. 350	Reading & Research 1 half		Satisfactory
Gov. 300	" " " Prof. Hansen 1 half		"
Gov. 300	" " " Prof. Fainsod 1 half, Prof. Neumann		"

Degrees awarded: A. M., Harvard Univ., June 1951

The Established grades are A, B, C, D, & E.

A grade of A, B, Credit, Satisfactory or Excused indicates that the course was passed with distinction. Only courses passed with distinction may be counted toward a higher degree.

Robert G. McCloskey,
Secretary.

Handwritten Harvard transcript: two A– grades.

1. Like To set out a few thoughts — ~~not necessarily to make a habit, but~~ could be useful to lay out a few ~~things~~ reasons, write of overall strategy an I see them now, — get your reactions Thinking out loud - thinking out loud ~~recognize~~ directly relevant to central analysis

2. Won't necessarily make it a habit, but this meeting has more symbolic importance than ordinarily - people may read into it more importance than its worth in some substantive sense - but symbols important, too

3. Don't need to belabor difficulties & dilemmas for us or for economic policy generally
     A. But given we are in recession - and there is some risk it could be sizable. Energy big factor, & can't cure that by monetary policy, but recession nonetheless.
     B. I don't have to belabor inflation side of dilemma. Energy big factor, but will continue. Dubious we are going to see any ~~necessary prices actually~~ "naturally", partly because energy adjustment continuing
          1. Inflation expectation radically changed in past year or two, underlying paradoxical reaction to policy.
4. So we are in a box. "Easing" actions may not work - although difference in judgment - if interpreted as inflationary. "Tightening" action same risks, too, although "severe" with reaction on long-term rate could be favorable.
          A. Dollar adds to dilemma - trilemma. Nobody knows by but psychology tender. Ø/a will improve only with lag. So vulnerable period for months, probably until end of year. Some decline in itself no problem, but will it happen without cascading psychology.
     5. Aggregates running high. - although not so bad in longer-term perspective.
          (What do aggregates mean now?)
     6. Finally, would suggest F.R. itself (+ policy) in general has major credibility problem. - Our credentials are questioned.

Handwritten notes from first FOMC meeting as chairman, page 1.

2

Strategy—

Have to try to turn expectations + sentiment, restore credibility. Danger of wrong ~~pattern~~ guidelines, + FX crisis.

Specifically, deal with aggregates + dollar.

But "perceived" risk — not so much real, but certainly perceived.

If (and it is big if) we can restore credibility, we buy flexibility.

Sizable recession almost inevitably mean easier interest rates, but also taken pressure off at least M₁.

May or may not affect $ + inflation psychology, depending on perception.

If we succeed in turning psychology, can manage.

Don't know chances — But & also don't know consequences of failure.

Take "risks", but "risks" are balanced.

Don't have much time. Monetary policy not only instrument. Final policy also frozen now. But in ~~~~ currently rather ? ~~~~
Also don't have much ~~room — really draconian action not possible~~ argue one for long-term tax program.

Tactics—

Very little room for ~~maneuver~~ maneuver — don't want to use up all ammunitions — really draconian action not understood / would be resisted.

Impact; Ordinarily would be persuaded wait for crisis in FX or aggregates to make clear case for sizable action.

But persuaded now that some genuine useful prophylactic — potentially save us grief later. By buying credibility, we also buy "flexibility"

Leads me to believe move now, + relatively tight aggregate specification desirable. Easing usual counterproductive.

Won't define until hear discussion, but that is framework in which I approach decision.

Note we are at margin now where discount rate needs to be considered. Don't prejudice, but bear care one way or another by President. Personally, allergic to discount rate as "pure" symbol. Needs to be accompanied by something else.

Handwritten notes from first FOMC meeting as chairman, page 2.

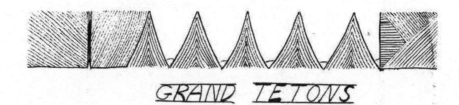

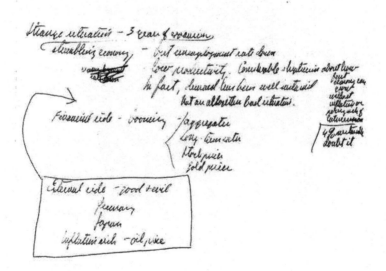

A Volcker FOMC doodle.

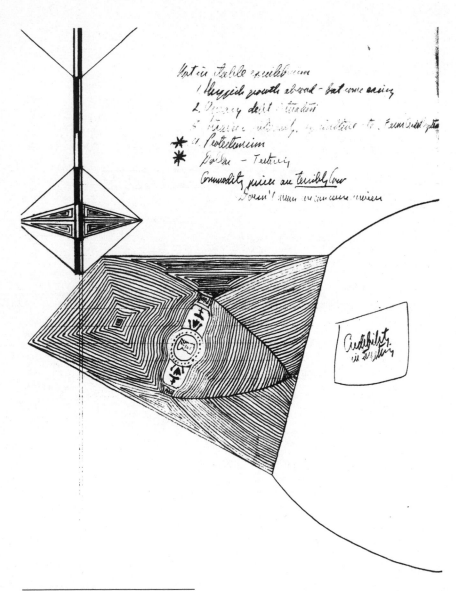

Another Volcker FOMC doodle.

HOUSE OF REPRESENTATIVES
WASHINGTON, D. C. 20515

RON PAUL
22ND DISTRICT, TEXAS

February 26, 1981

Dear Mr. Volcker:

As always, I found you to be the most impressive
witness--by far--who comes before the Banking Committee.
I want you to know that my question about the increase
in the money supply before November was not intended
to be offensive.

I have gotten many questions myself about this,
and I thought it important to have your views.

I have nothing but the highest respect for your
ability and integrity.

Sincerely,

The Hon. Paul Volcker, Chairman
Federal Reserve System
20th Street and Constitution, NW
Washington, D.C. 20551

February 26, 1981, letter from Congressman Ron Paul: on integrity.

BILL GRADISON
2ND DISTRICT, OHIO

June 5

Dear Paul,

Ever since we first met, when you were assisting David Rockefeller on the Commission on money and credit, I have followed your career with profound respect and admiration. As you move on to new challenges I just want to add my personal thanks as a citizen for what you have accomplished for the good of the country as chairman.

Hope our paths will continue to cross in the years ahead.

Sincerely,

Bill

June 5, 1987, letter from Congressman Bill Gradison: "as a citizen."

1O DOWNING STREET

LONDON SW1A 2AA

THE PRIME MINISTER   10 June 1987

Dear Mr. Volcker,

I was sorry to hear of your decision not to accept a
third term as Chairman of the Federal Reserve Board of Governors.

Over the years I have very much admired your resolute
pursuit of sound monetary policies, and the great skill and
understanding you have brought to the complex task of maintaining
monetary discipline and reducing inflation in the world's
largest economy. At a time of rapid change and considerable
strain in the world financial system, the role you have played
has been invaluable. We shall all miss you.

With warm regards.

Yours sincerely

Margaret Thatcher

Mr. Paul Volcker

---

*June 10, 1987, letter from Prime Minister Margaret Thatcher: on missing
Volcker.*

Senato della Repubblica
Carlo Azeglio Ciampi

Rome, November 28 2008

Dear Paul,

We trust you

C—

November 28, 2008, letter from Italian president Carlo Ciampi: on trust.

Photographs and Cartoons

The Magnificent Seven: members of the Federal Reserve Board as of October 6, 1979—the date that the Fed met, under Volcker's leadership, and committed to bold steps to battle inflation. Seated, from left: Henry Wallich, Paul Volcker, Frederick Schultz, Philip Coldwell. Standing, from left: Emmett Rice, Nancy Teeters, Charles Partee. (Photograph by Black Star Photo)

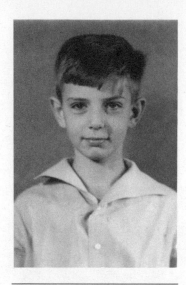

*A young Brooklyn Dodgers fan
from Teaneck, New Jersey. (Undated photograph from Volcker's
personal collection)*

*Preparing for congressional testi-
mony? Volcker demonstrates
bullfighting technique during a
visit to Madrid in September
1973 while under secretary of
the Treasury. (Photograph from
Volcker's personal collection)*

Volcker indulges in his two favorite activities while on vacation: He used a public telephone while on a fishing trip to accept the presidency of the Federal Reserve Bank of New York starting in 1975. (Photograph from Volcker's personal collection)

Judge A. Leon Higginbotham swears in Paul Volcker as chairman of the Federal Reserve Board, August 6, 1979. Barbara Volcker holds the Bible; Jimmy Carter prays. (White House photograph)

Volcker thanks Pope John Paul II. Volcker had joked during a Fed telephone conference call on October 5, 1979, that he would request a papal blessing for the committee's fateful meeting the following day. (Photograph from L'Osservatore Romano)

*Smoke signals: Volcker testifies before Congress, February 19, 1980. (George Tames/*The New York Times/*Redux)*

"Very nice, but we're going to stop printing this stuff." Volcker (right) inspects new greenbacks at the U.S. Treasury's Bureau of Engraving and Printing. As Fed chairman, he would labor mightily to convince Americans that the government was serious about restraining the money supply. (Photograph from Volcker's personal collection)

"When does the FOMC meeting start?" (Undated photograph from Volcker's personal collection)

Volcker and Ronald Reagan. Volcker came to the White House residence on Washington's Birthday, 1982, for a conversation with the president. "I think we've broken ground for a new & better relationship," Reagan wrote afterward in his diary. (White House photograph)

An honorary degree, but no umbrella: Volcker receives an LL.D. from Yale, 1984. (Photograph by T. Charles Erickson, Yale University Office of Public Information, from Volcker's personal collection)

Harvard outperforms Yale, inviting Volcker to give its commencement speech in 1985 and providing the company of an appreciative Harvard president, Derek Bok. (Photograph from Volcker's personal collection)

The man who vanquished gold offers guidance to the Iron Lady. Prime Minister Margaret Thatcher visits the Federal Reserve in February 1985. (Paul Hosefros/ The New York Times/Redux)

Where does he keep the money? Fiat chairman Gianni Agnelli at a reception with Volcker during his tenure as Fed chairman. (Undated photograph from Volcker's personal collection)

Laughter in the Oval Office: Ronald Reagan's team was relieved when the independent-minded Volcker stepped down as Fed chairman, to be replaced by Alan Greenspan. Left to right: Greenspan, Volcker, Vice President George H. W. Bush, Reagan, and Treasury Secretary James Baker. (White House photograph)

Volcker checks the president's notes: At a White House press conference, June 2, 1987, Reagan announces that Greenspan will replace Volcker. (White House photograph)

BOARD OF GOVERNORS

*Casting a long shadow: Volcker at the Federal Reserve building in Washing-
ton. (Photograph by Dennis Brack, via Black Star Photo)*

Discussing a full court press: With the U.S. economy in free fall, presidential candidate Barack Obama consults with Volcker at a meeting in Coral Gables, Florida, in September 2008. (AP Photo/Chris Carlson)

Happy days are here again? Volcker returned to government service as chairman of President Obama's Economic Recovery Board. Here he listens to an Obama address in New York City, flanked by White House Chief of Staff Rahm Emanuel and real estate executive Penny Pritzker. (Photograph by Daniel Acker/European Pressphoto Agency)

"How about we call it the Obama Rule?" Volcker was not particularly pleased at having his name attached to the rule that restricted trading at banks. He thought it sounded boastful and might narrow his legacy to two words of limited scope. (Photograph by Joshua Roberts/Bloomberg via Getty Images)

Volcker loses—but finishes in the money: a racehorse named for the financial icon, ridden by John Velasquez, is beaten at Saratoga by a half length by Forum, under Javier Castellano, August 28, 2010. (Photograph from Thoroughbred Report.com)

'It's Paul Volcker—he put me on hold!'

Cartoon by Bil Canfield. (Used with permission of PARS International)

October 22, 1985, cartoon by Draper Hill. (Reprinted by permission of the Detroit News)

Cartoon by Joe Azar, originally published in Legal Times. *(Reprinted by permission of Joe Azar)*

Acknowledgments

This project took a year longer than I expected because Paul Volcker refused to retire from public life. It would have taken even longer without the help of students at the Stern School of Business, New York University, who analyzed the documentary evidence that underpins this book. Steven Chuang, Christopher Cramer, Benjamin Harding, Chris Hemmelgarn, Elizabeth Holt, Benjamin Loveland, and Rebecca Solow listened to excerpts from the Nixon tapes, read minutes of the Federal Open Market Committee meetings covering 1975 through 1987, reviewed congressional testimony, cataloged Volcker's correspondence, and digested clippings from newspapers throughout the world. I would like to thank them for spending more energy on this project than I had a right to ask—usually with good cheer. Thanks also to Carol M. Arnold-Hamilton, research librarian at NYU's Bobst Library, for her guidance with congressional testimony.

I supplemented the written record with interviews that added a personal perspective to Volcker's public personae. I would like to thank the following for sharing their thoughts on the historical record and their insights about Paul Volcker that transcend the printed page: Stephen Axilrod, Peter Bakstansky, Ben Bernanke, Michael Bradfield, Jerry Corrigan, Joseph Coyne, Anthony Dowd, Tyler Gellasch, Austan Goolsbee, Lyle Gramley, Alan Greenspan, Henry Kaufman, Robert Kavesh, Rudolph Penner, Charles Schultze, Robert Solow, Neal Soss, Peter Sternlight, and Murray Weidenbaum.

Jimmy Volcker and Janice Volcker Zima, Paul's children, offered especially sensitive insights into their father's life. Anke Dening (Mrs.

Paul Volcker since February 2010) coordinated my visits with precision and unearthed documents that her husband did not know existed.

Archivists at the Federal Reserve Bank of New York, Joseph Komljenovich and Julie Sager, were especially helpful in providing access to documents stored there from Volcker's presidency of the Federal Reserve Bank of New York (1975–1979) and to documents shipped there at Volcker's request from his period at the Federal Reserve Board (1979–1987). Lawyers at the Federal Reserve Board raised obstacles to my seeing these documents, but Lynn Fox, a senior advisor to the board, smoothed the way. Joseph Pavel of the Federal Reserve Board's public relations office conducted two very helpful tours of the physical premises.

I have asked a number of people to comb the manuscript for errors. I appreciate their help. Kenneth Garbade applied his electron microscope to remove sloppy analysis. Rudolph Penner checked for fiscal irresponsibility. Thomas Sargent enforced rational expectations. Lillian Silber eliminated mixed metaphors and dangling participles. Richard Sylla corrected historical inaccuracies. Paul Wachtel kept me on message. My agent, Eric Lupfer at William Morris Endeavor, and my editor, Peter Ginna at Bloomsbury Press, gave wise guidance (especially in the form of Peter's squiggles) while softening the prose.

Special thanks to Ken and Lillian for listening to my complaints and responding with much-appreciated encouragement. And thanks to Paul Volcker for not meddling.

Source Material and Data

The narrative in this biography relies first and foremost on contemporary documents. These include: (1) publicly available documents, such as transcripts of the Federal Open Market Committee and the minutes of meetings released by the U.S. Treasury; and (2) private documents made available from the personal files of Paul Volcker, such as personal correspondence and memos from the U.S. Treasury and the Federal Reserve. Interviews with Paul Volcker and his contemporaries, those who worked both with him and for him, supplement the written record. Here are some details.

Documents

References to the Personal Papers of Paul Volcker are documents given to me by Volcker from his personal files. References to documents held at the Federal Reserve Bank of New York come from two sources: (1) documents from Volcker's tenure as president of the Federal Reserve Bank of New York, which are the property of the Federal Reserve Bank of New York; and (2) documents shipped in 1987 from Volcker's personal files at the Board of Governors for storage at the Federal Reserve Bank of New York. As of this writing (January 2012), both sets of materials, referred to as Federal Reserve Bank of New York Archives, are available from the Federal Reserve Bank of New York.

Minutes and transcripts of Federal Open Market Committee meetings (with exceptions noted) are publicly available documents and were sent in electronic form to me by David Small, economist at the Board of Governors. Transcripts of meetings from March 26, 1976, through January 5, 1978, not yet publicly available, were purchased in hard copy from the Papers of Arthur Burns, University of Michigan.

Minutes of the Board of Governors concerning the discount rate between

1979 and 1987, the discussion of Mexico in 1982, Continental Illinois between 1982 and 1985, and the Bankers Trust commercial paper discussions between 1979 and 1987 were all received in redacted form based on Freedom of Information Act (FOIA) requests.

Documents from the National Archives II, College Park, Maryland, were located at my request by Thomas Culbert, Aviation Information Research Corporation. David Small, economist at the Board of Governors, also provided copies of selected documents from the National Archives.

Interviews

Direct quotes in the text attributed to Paul Volcker come either from published material, in which case the document is cited, or from personal interviews I conducted with him, in which case they are labeled PIPAV (Personal Interviews with Paul A. Volcker). Forty-two interviews, which lasted between one and three hours, were conducted between August 2008 and September 2011, and were recorded. Some discussions were not recorded, and our telephone conversations were not recorded.

I conducted personal interviews with the following people to provide background information. I provide their affiliation as they relate to Paul Volcker:

Stephen Axilrod: staff director and secretary of the Federal Open Market Committee during Volcker's tenure as chairman.

Peter Bakstansky: senior vice president of the Federal Reserve Bank of New York and head of the public information area during Volcker's term as president of the Federal Reserve Bank of New York.

Ben Bernanke: chairman, Board of Governors of the Federal Reserve System, 2006–present.

Michael Bradfield: assistant general counsel for international affairs, U.S. Treasury Department, during Volcker's tenure as undersecretary; general counsel of the Board of Governors of the Federal Reserve System during Volcker's tenure as chairman.

Gerald Corrigan: vice president of the Federal Reserve Bank of New York during Volcker's tenure as president; special assistant to Volcker during his first year as Fed chairman; and member of the FOMC (first as president of the Federal Reserve Bank of Minneapolis and then as president of the Federal Reserve Bank of New York) during Volcker's tenure as chairman.

Joseph Coyne: chief spokesman and assistant to the Board of Governors of the Federal Reserve System during Volcker's tenure as chairman.

Anthony Dowd: Volcker's chief of staff, 2009–present.

Tyler Gellasch: legislative assistant to Senator Carl Levin, cosponsor of the Merkley-Levin Amendment, which incorporated the Volcker Rule as Section 619 of the Dodd-Frank legislation.

Austan Goolsbee: chairman of President Obama's Council of Economic Advisers and chief of staff of the President's Economic Recovery Advisory Board (PERAB) during Volcker's tenure as chairman of PERAB.

Lyle Gramley: member of President Jimmy Carter's Council of Economic Advisers, 1977–1980, and member of the Board of Governors of the Federal Reserve System, 1980–1985.

Alan Greenspan: chairman, Board of Governors of the Federal Reserve System, 1987–2006.

Robert Kavesh: classmate of Volcker's at Harvard and close personal friend.

Rudolph Penner: director of the Congressional Budget Office, 1983–1987.

Charles Schultze: chairman of President Jimmy Carter's Council of Economic Advisers.

Robert Solow: 1987 Nobel Memorial Prize in Economics.

Neal Soss: special assistant to Paul Volcker, 1982–1983.

Peter Sternlight: manager for domestic operations, Federal Reserve System's Open Market Account, during Volcker's tenure as chairman.

James Volcker: Paul Volcker's son.

Janice Volcker Zima: Paul Volcker's daughter.

Murray Weidenbaum: chairman of President Ronald Reagan's Council of Economic Advisers, 1981–1982; and assistant secretary of the treasury for economic policy, 1969–1971.

Data

The daily London gold fixing comes from the London Bullion Market Association, available at www.lbma.org.uk/goldfixg. Monthly data on inflation (measured by the Consumer Price Index) and the unemployment rate are published by the U.S. Department of Labor and were downloaded from the economic database at the Federal Reserve Bank of St. Louis, Federal Reserve Economic Data (FRED), available at research.stlouisfed.org/fred2/. The Survey of Professional Forecasters data on expected inflation come from the series maintained by the Federal Reserve Bank of Philadelphia and are available at www.phil.frb.org/research-and-data/real-time-center. Daily data for yields on U.S. Treasury securities are "constant maturities" as interpolated by the U.S. Treasury and made available through Datastream. The data on the discount rate and the daily federal funds rate come from FRED and are available at research.stlouisfed.org/fred2/categories/118. Data on exchange rates be-tween the U.S. dollar and the German mark, the British pound, and the Japa-nese yen are end-of-day quotes in New York for the spot exchange rate. The data on the pound and the yen come from Datastream and the data on the mark are from Bloomberg. Data on money supply growth come from the transcripts of the Federal Open Market Committee and from FRED, at research.stlouisfed.org/aggreg/. Some annual data come from the Economic History Association, available at eh.net/hmit/.

Notes

Introduction: More Than a Central Banker

1. The letter is dated summer 1987, Personal Papers of Paul Volcker. The 1970 Academy Award–winning film *Patton*, starring George C. Scott, memorialized the exploits of General George S. Patton during World War II, but Patton also served with distinction in World War I, where he first encountered the tank warfare that made him famous. The M60 Patton tank, still used throughout the world, was named after him.
2. See Ben Bernanke, "Paul Volcker," *Time*, April 29, 2010, available at www .time.com/time/specials/packages/article/0,28804,1984685_1984745_1984803, 00.html.
3. See WSJ.com, October 19, 2011, 10:27 A.M.
4. Volcker said this publicly in response to a question at the 2011 Henry Kaufman Lecture, Museum of American Finance, December 7, 2011, "A Conversation with Paul Volcker," moderated by Professor Richard Sylla.
5. *New York Times*, July 16, 1979, p. A10.
6. *New York Times*, April 1, 1982, p. D1.

Prologue: The Three Crises of Paul Volcker

1. Personal interview with Paul A. Volcker, hereafter referred to as PIPAV.
2. *Newsweek*, December 8, 2008, p. 10.
3. *New York Times*, October 21, 2009, p. A1.
4. See full text of Obama's remarks on financial reform, January 21, 2010, 11:39 A.M., WSJ.com.
5. Ibid.

6. PIPAV.

7. Volcker's testimony is in *Experts' Perspectives on Systemic Risk and Resolution Issues: Hearings Before the Committee on Financial Services*, U.S. House of Representatives, 111th Congress, 1st Sess., September 24, 2009, pp. 6–34. Biden's quote is from an interview with Volcker's chief of staff, Anthony Dowd.

8. See *Washington Post*, January 22, 2010, p. A1 continued.

9. PIPAV.

10. Ibid.

11. This quote and remainder in this paragraph are from a dinner speech at the Stanford Institute for Economic Policy Research Economic Summit, Stanford, CA, February 11, 2005, Personal Papers of Paul Volcker.

12. See Volcker's memorandum "Contingency," May 8, 1971, Papers of Paul Volcker, Federal Reserve Bank of New York Archives, Box 0108477, pp. 1–2.

13. PIPAV.

14. *The Federal Reserve's First Monetary Policy Report for 1984: Hearings Before the Committee on Banking, Housing and Urban Affairs*, U.S. Senate, 98th Congress, 2nd Sess., February 8, 1984, p. 108.

15. The 10 percent figure is based on an unscientific survey I took each academic year between 2000 and 2005 while teaching 350 first-year MBA students (average age of twenty-eight) at the Stern School of Business, New York University.

16. President Obama signed the Dodd-Frank Wall Street Reform and Consumer Protection Act on July 21, 2010. The Volcker Rule prohibitions against bank proprietary trading activities and certain relationships with hedge funds are contained in Section 619 of the act.

1. The Early Years

1. See chapter 4, Pamphlet, *Teaneck Collection at Teaneck Public Library*, available at www.teaneck.org/virtualvillage/teaneck12years.

2. PIPAV.

3. Washington's quote comes from a letter to Colonel George Baylor, warning him about the selection of officers for his brigade: "I earnestly recommend to you to be circumspect in your choice of officers . . . Do not suffer your good nature, when application is made, to say yes when you ought to say no; remember that it is a public not a private cause that is to be injured or benefited by your choice." Jared Sparks, *The Writings of George Washington; Being His Correspondence, Addresses, Messages, and Other Papers, Official and Private*, vol. 4 (Boston: Russell, Odiorne and Metcalf, and Hilliard, Gray, and Co., 1834), p. 269.

4. PIPAV. For Dick Rodda's perspective, see "Oral History of Teaneck," Teaneck Public Library, transcribed interview with Richard Rodda, July 10, 1984. Also see Joseph Treaster, *Paul Volcker: The Making of a Financial Legend* (New York: John Wiley, 2004), pp. 84–85.

5. PIPAV.

6. Ibid.

7. Ibid.

8. Ibid.

9. Ibid.

10. Ibid.

11. John von Neumann and Oskar Morgenstern, *Theory of Games and Economic Behavior* (Princeton, NJ: Princeton University Press, 1944).

12. Oskar Morgenstern, *The Limits of Economics* (London: William Hodge and Company, 1937), p. 4.

13. Ibid., p. 14.

14. Oskar Morgenstern, *On the Accuracy of Economic Observations* (Princeton, NJ: Princeton University Press, 2nd ed., 1963), p. 190

15. PIPAV.

16. Friedrich A. Hayek, *The Road to Serfdom* (Chicago: The University of Chicago Press, 1944), reprinted 1976.

17. PIPAV.

18. Ibid.

19. Ibid.

20. Ibid.

21. Ibid.

22. Ibid.

23. Robert Roosa, *Federal Reserve Operations in the Money and Government Securities Markets* (New York: Federal Reserve Bank of New York, July 1956). The author's first footnote on page 7 reads, "Messrs. Tilford C. Gaines and Paul A. Volcker must be singled out, however, because of their valiant help in steering the original draft of this booklet through the final stages of editing, checking, and printing."

24. *New York Times*, December 25, 1993, p. A37.

25. *Bid* means the dealer is ready to buy, and *offer* means the dealer is ready to sell. The 9 is short for the bid price of, say, 100 9/32, and the 10 is short for

100 10/32. The phrase "100 by 100" refers to the size of the transaction: 100 bonds with a face value of $1,000 each.

26. See the discussion in Robert P. Bremner, *Chairman of the Fed: William McChesney Martin Jr. and the Creation of the Modern American Financial System* (New Haven, CT: Yale University Press, 2004), p. 161.

27. Ibid., p. 271.

28. PIPAV.

29. Ibid.

30. Paul Volcker and Toyoo Gyohten, *Changing Fortunes: The World's Money and the Threat to American Leadership* (New York: Times Books, 1992), p. 5.

31. See Robert V. Roosa, *The Dollar and World Liquidity* (New York: Random House, 1967), p. 1. According to Arthur Schlesinger, *A Thousand Days: John F. Kennedy in the White House* (Boston: Houghton Mifflin Company, 1965), p. 654, Kennedy "used to tell his advisers that the two things which scared him most were nuclear war and the payments deficit."

32. Schlesinger, *A Thousand Days*, p. 154.

33. *New York Times*, October 31, 1960, p. 1.

34. *New York Times*, November 2, 1960, p. 25.

35. Volcker and Gyohten, *Changing Fortunes*, p. 4.

36. *New York Times*, July 2, 1944, p. 14.

37. Ibid.

38. *New York Times*, July 2, 1944, p. 14.

39. A detailed list of the participants appears in the *Christian Science Monitor*, July 1, 1944, p. 1.

40. *Washington Post*, July 28, 1944, p. 1.

41. White had earned a Ph.D. from Harvard and had been brought to the Treasury by University of Chicago economist Jacob Viner, a leading authority on international trade and finance, who had been on special assignment at the Treasury. See James Boughton, "Harry Dexter White and the International Monetary Fund," *Finance and Development* 35, no. 3 (September 1998).

42. *New York Times*, July 6, 1944, p. 1 continued.

43. See Charles Kindleberger, "Competitive Currency Depreciation Between Denmark and New Zealand," *Harvard Business Review* 12, no. 4 (July 1934), pp. 416–26; and Sebastian Mallaby, *Wall Street Journal*, Saturday/Sunday, October 25–26, 2008, p. W3.

44. *New York Times*, November 29, 1964, p. F1.

45. *New York Times*, March 22, 1954, p. 35.

46. The twice-daily gold fixing did not begin until April 1968.

47. *New York Times*, October 21, 1960, p. 1.

48. Treasury charged eight and three-quarter cents for handling (see *Wall Street Journal*, September 23, 1960).

49. Volcker and Gyohten, *Changing Fortunes*, p. 21. The date is listed there as October 30, 1960. It should be October 20.

50. Ibid.

51. *New York Times*, October 20, 1960, p. 51.

52. *New York Times*, October 22, 1960, p. 22.

53. *New York Times*, October 30, 1960, p. E10.

54. *New York Times*, October 25, 1960, p. 1.

55. Volcker and Gyohten, *Changing Fortunes*, p. 25.

56. Schlesinger, *A Thousand Days*, p. 654.

57. Ibid.

58. PIPAV.

59. The stock of gold rose from $20.0 billion in 1945 to $24.5 billion in 1949 and then declined back to $20.0 billion in 1958. See *Historical Statistics of the United States*, U.S. Bureau of the Census, Government Printing Office, Washington, D.C., 1975, p. 995. Speculators focused on deficits in America's balance of payments that began in 1958. Also see *Economic Report of the President*, Council of Economic Advisers, 1961, pp. 107–108.

60. See *Wall Street Journal*, September 23, 1960, p. 3.

61. Ibid.

62. Ibid.

63. *Wall Street Journal*, October 31, 1960, p. 2.

64. Paul A. Samuelson and Robert M. Solow, "Analytical Aspects of Anti-Inflation Policy," *American Economic Review* 50, no. 2 (May 1960): 177–94.

65. Schlesinger, *A Thousand Days*, p. 154.

66. Ibid.

67. PIPAV.

68. Volcker's appointment appears in the *New York Times*, November 18, 1963, p. 22.

69. PIPAV.

2. Apprenticeship

1. This quote and those in the conversation that follows are based on the recollection of Paul Volcker.

2. PIPAV.

3. Friedrich A. Hayek, *The Road to Serfdom*, fiftieth anniversary edition (Chicago: University of Chicago Press, 1994), p. 227. The book was published originally in 1944 in the United Kingdom by George Routledge and Sons and in the United States by the University of Chicago Press.

4. PIPAV.

5. PIPAV. David Hume (1711–1776), a contemporary of Adam Smith, articulated the link between money and prices, known as the quantity theory of money, in "Of Interest," in his *Essays, Moral, Political, and Literary* (1752). Also see Carl Wennerlind, "David Hume's Monetary Theory Revisited: Was He Really a Quantity Theorist and an Inflationist?" *Journal of Political Economy* 113, no. 1 (February 2005): 223–37.

6. PIPAV.

7. Paul A. Volcker, "The Problems of Federal Reserve Policy Since World War II," Thesis submitted to the Department of Economics, Princeton University, Princeton, NJ, Mimeograph, January 7, 1949, p. 77.

8. Ibid. pp. 233 and 235.

9. PIPAV.

10. See Peter Bernstein, *The Power of Gold* (New York: John Wiley, 2000), pp. 32–37.

11. A twenty-dollar Federal Reserve note could be exchanged for a double eagle, which consisted of .9675 ounces of pure gold.

12. A gold bar weighs 400 ounces, or 25 pounds. A regulation bowling ball can weigh between 6 and 16 pounds—with 12 pounds a reasonable size for most adults.

13. See William Silber, "Why Did FDR's Bank Holiday Succeed?" *Federal Reserve Bank of New York Economic Policy Review* 15, no. 1 (July 2009), for a discussion of the Emergency Banking Act of 1933.

14. See Executive Order 6102, dated April 5, 1933, available at www.runto gold.com/images/EO6102.pdf.

15. See "Treasury Defied on Gold Hoarding," *New York Times*, May 3, 1933, p. 1.

16. *New York Times*, May 3, 1933, p. 16.

17. The Gold Reserve Act of January 1934 legislated a number of regulations concerning gold: (1) Section 2 mandated that all gold coins be removed from circulation and required American citizens to turn in their gold coins in exchange for paper currency; (2) section 3 gave the secretary of the treasury the responsibility of controlling all dealings in gold; and (3) section 10 directed the secretary of the treasury to use gold bullion to settle international balances and to control the exchange value of the dollar.

18. Pooh-Bah is a character in Gilbert and Sullivan's *The Mikado*. The mocking title Lord High Everything Else summarizes his puffed-up image.

19. Since there are 480 grains per ounce of fine gold, the price per ounce was set at 480/13.714, equal to $35 per ounce.

20. See Federal Reserve Report, *Wall Street Journal*, January 20, 1961, p. 17.

21. The Federal Reserve held $17.2 billion in gold certificates (see ibid.), which represented 37.7 percent of the required cover against total Federal Reserve liabilities. In January 1961 the gold cover requirement was 25 percent, having been lowered from 40 percent in June 1945 (see *Wall Street Journal*, June 13, 1945, p. 3). The 25 percent minimum cover amounted to $11.4 billion in gold. Thus, only $6 billion in gold was available to meet foreign demand.

22. Official claims of foreign central banks on the United States totaled $11.1 billion at the end of 1960 (see International Monetary Fund, Annual Report, Washington, DC, 1970, p. 18).

23. Public law 93-373, which went into effect on December 31, 1974, made it legal to invest in gold in the United States.

24. Letter dated November 4, 1965, Paul Volcker, Undersecretary for Monetary Affairs, National Archives II, College Park, MD, Record Group 56, Box 4, Folder 68 (Chronological File, 1965, 1).

25. The following conversation is based on Volcker's recollection.

26. According to Roosa (*The Dollar and World Liquidity* [New York: Random House, 1967], p. 23), "The Treasury, again acting through the Federal Reserve Bank of New York, . . . set in motion the informal 'pool' through which seven other countries had initially joined with the United States on an ad hoc basis in November 1960 to help stabilize the London gold market." Charles A. Coombs, *The Arena of International Finance* (New York: John Wiley, 1976), p. 63, mentions November 1961 as the formal beginning of the Gold Pool. Roosa (*The Dollar and World Liquidity*, p. 119) evaluated the continued operation of the pool two years later: "The operations in the London gold market, all conducted by the Bank of England, have been a model of informal cooperation, renewed through frequent consultation . . . The speculative fever has largely been removed from transactions in gold."

27. Timothy Naftali, ed., *John F. Kennedy: The Great Crises*, vol. I (New York: W. W. Norton, 2001), pp. 464 and 492.

28. Ibid., p. 495.

29. Ibid., p. 496.

30. Roosa, *The Dollar and World Liquidity*, p. 44.

31. Naftali, *John F. Kennedy*, p. 496.

32. See *Reduction in Reserve Ratio for Federal Reserve Notes and Deposits: Hearing Before Senate Committee on Banking and Currency*, 79th Congress, 1st Sess., February 20, 1945, pp. 3–54. The bill was signed into law by President Truman on June 12, 1945 (see *Wall Street Journal*, June 13, 1945, p. 3).

33. Volcker's memorandum, entitled "To Establish a Committee to Study the Gold Reserve Requirement," dated February 8, 1962 (Paul Volcker, Undersecretary for Monetary Affairs, National Archives II, College Park, MD, Record Group 56, Box 11, Folder 179, Gold Cover Committee), was designed "to deflect criticism of changing the gold cover." To avoid appearing to stack the deck, Volcker included two alternative names to Sproul as chairman: John J. McCloy, former chairman of the Chase Manhattan Bank, and Henry C. Alexander, former chairman of J.P. Morgan and Company.

34. "Address to the 75th Annual Convention of the American Bankers Association," November 2, 1949, reprinted in Lawrence Ritter, ed., *Selected Papers of Allan Sproul*, Federal Reserve Bank of New York, December 1980, p. 217.

35. Memorandum to Volcker from Roosa dated February 13, 1962 (Paul Volcker, Undersecretary for Monetary Affairs, National Archives II, College Park, MD, Record Group 56, Box 11, Folder 179, Gold Cover Committee).

36. See Timothy Naftali, *John F. Kennedy*, p. 492, for Dillon explaining to President Kennedy why the gold cover legislation is controversial.

37. *New York Times*, February 5, 1965, p. 12.

38. Ibid.

39. Paul Volcker and Toyoo Gyohten, *Changing Fortunes: The World's Money and the Threat to American Leadership* (New York: Times Books, 1992), p. 42, and *New York Times*, January 7, 1965.

40. *New York Times*, March 2, 1965, p. 45.

41. France completed its withdrawal from NATO on March 14, 1967. See *New York Times*, March 15, 1967, p. 1.

42. *Repealing Certain Legislation Relating to Reserves Against Deposits in Federal Reserve Banks: Hearings Before the House Committee on Banking and Currency*, 89th Congress, 1st Sess., February 1, 1965, Washington, DC.

43. For the exact numbers on free gold, see the Federal Reserve Report, *Wall Street Journal*, January 8, 1965, p. 10. Official claims of foreign central banks on the United States totaled $15.4 billion at the end of 1964 (see International Monetary Fund, Annual Report, 1970, p. 18).

44. *New York Times*, January 7, 1965, p. 30.

45. *New York Times*, March 5, 1965, p. 45.

46. PIPAV.

47. Ibid.

48. Interview with Jimmy Volcker.

49. PIPAV.

50. Ibid.

51. According to the Member Bank Reserve Report of the Federal Reserve System, dated January 10, 1968 (*Wall Street Journal*, January 12, 1968, p. 19), the

gold stock equaled 27.1 percent of Federal Reserve notes outstanding on January 3, 1968, implying that of the $11.98 billion in gold, only $1 billion was available to cover foreign obligations.

52. International Monetary Fund, Annual Report, 1969, p. 18.

53. See Geoffrey Bell, *The Eurodollar Market and the International Financial System* (Hoboken, NJ: John Wiley, 1973), p. 20. Eurodollars were not all held by foreigners, so the $25 billion overstates the total claims by non–U.S. residents. However, the *Wall Street Journal*, January 4, 1968, p. 1, reports "an estimated $30.5 billion greenbacks that foreigners hold" could also have been turned in for gold.

54. *Wall Street Journal*, January 4, 1968, p. 1.

55. *New York Times*, January 18, 1968, p. 1.

56. *New York Times*, February 2, 1968, p. 47.

57. On March 20, 1968, the Federal Reserve reported the gold stock at $10.87 billion (*Wall Street Journal*, March 22, 1968, p. 23), compared with $11.88 billion on February 28, 1968 (*Wall Street Journal*, March 1, 1968, p. 25). During the first quarter of 1968 the U.S. gold stock declined by $1.3 billion, surpassing the total decline for 1967 (see International Monetary Fund Annual Report, 1968, p. 89). The U.S. gold stock during 1967 declined from $13.2 billion at the end of 1966 to $12.0 billion at the end of 1967 (Council of Economic Advisers, Economic Report of the President, 1970, Washington, DC, p. 282).

58. *Washington Post*, March 14, 1968, p. A1. As an aside, here are the physical characteristics of a ton of gold. A gold bar weighs 27 pounds and measures slightly smaller than a building brick: $1\frac{1}{2}$ inches high, $6\frac{13}{16}$ inches long, and $3\frac{1}{2}$ inches wide (*New York Times*, March 2, 1965, p. 45). A ton of gold, therefore, consists of seventy-four bars, which could fit comfortably on an office bookshelf (but would probably cause the bookshelf to collapse).

59. *New York Times*, March 9, 1968, p. 1.

60. *New York Times*, March 5, 1968, p. 51 continued.

61. For all quotes in this and the next two paragraphs, see *The Congressional Record*, vol. 114, pt. 5, 90th Congress, 2nd Sess., March 6, 1968–March 15, 1968, pp. 6596–98.

62. *Washington Post*, March 15, 1968, p. A1.

63. *New York Times*, January 18, 1968, p. 1.

64. *New York Times*, March 15, 1968, p. 1.

65. *New York Times*, March 17, 1968, p. E3.

66. The continuing members were Belgium, Italy, the Netherlands, Switzerland, the United Kingdom, the United States, and West Germany. France had withdrawn in mid-1967 (*New York Times*, March 31, 1968, p. SM32).

67. *New York Times*, March 18, 1968, p. 70. The managing director of the International Monetary Fund and the general manager of the Bank for

International Settlements, along with the seven central bankers, attended the meeting.

68. *New York Times*, March 16, 1968, p. 39.

69. Ibid.

70. See Friedman's testimony in *Gold Cover: Hearings Before the Committee on Banking and Currency*, U.S. Senate, 90th Congress, 2nd Sess., February 1, 1968, p. 153.

71. *New York Times*, January 18, 1968, p. 1 continued.

72. See Robert P. Bremner, *Chairman of the Fed: William McChesney Martin Jr. and the Creation of the Modern American Financial System* (New Haven, CT: Yale University Press, 2004), pp. 73–81, for a detailed description of Martin's role in the accord.

73. PIPAV.

74. Volcker and Gyohten, *Changing Fortunes*, p. 45.

75. The London gold market reopened on April 1, 1968. Beginning with that session, two prices were recorded for each day, the morning fixing and the afternoon fixing. The price of thirty-eight dollars is the morning fixing on April l. On March 15, 1968, when Queen Elizabeth closed the London market, the much smaller Paris market remained open. According to the *New York Times* (March 16, 1968, p. 1 continued), "There was more frantic buying with the price of gold driven up to almost $45 an ounce." The "almost $45" price in Paris occurred prior to the beginning of the "two-tier market" established by the communiqué from the Gold Pool that weekend.

76. A twenty-dollar double eagle sold for fifty-five dollars before March 15 and for seventy dollars on March 18 (*Wall Street Journal*, March 18, 1968, p. 6).

77. According to the International Monetary Fund, Annual Report, Washington, DC, 1969, p. 121, "The crisis of March 1968 . . . arose largely because of widespread expectation of a change in the official price of gold." The free-market price of gold reflects supply and demand from all sources. Aside from speculators, the main source of supply is newly mined gold, primarily from South Africa. The main source of demand is the jewelry industry. Table 37 in the International Monetary Fund, Annual Report, 1970, p. 125, shows that these two components are much less volatile over time than "hoarding," a residual category that includes speculation. Thus speculative demand dominates the price movement of free-market gold. As a practical matter, thirty-five dollars per ounce served as a floor because central bankers were buyers at that level to replace inventory lost to speculators. (The March communiqué did not preclude central bank buying in the free market.)

78. *New York Times*, March 18, 1968, p. 1 continued.

3. Battle Plan

1. PIPAV.

2. Recall from chapter 1 the quote from George Washington: "I earnestly recommend to you to be circumspect in your choice of officers . . . Do not suffer your good nature, when application is made, to say yes when you ought to say no; remember that it is a public not a private cause that is to be injured or benefited by your choice."

3. See "Nixon Terms Adlai Unfit for Presidency," *Washington Post*, September 7, 1952, p. M6.

4. Quote DB—Interactive Database of Famous Quotations.

5. *New York Times*, October 21, 1956, p. 193.

6. The letter is dated January 29, 1969, Federal Reserve Bank of New York Archives, Box 0108476.

7. The letter is dated January 28, 1969 (Paul Volcker, Undersecretary for Monetary Affairs, National Archives II, College Park, MD, Record Group 56, Box 2, Folder 113).

8. The memorandum (Paul Volcker, Undersecretary for Monetary Affairs, National Archives II, College Park, MD, Record Group 56, Box 13, Folder 184), dated January 21, 1969, is addressed to the secretary of the treasury, secretary of state, chairman of the Council of Economic Advisers, and chairman of the Federal Reserve Board. Volcker recalls that Treasury Secretary David Kennedy gave him the memorandum.

9. PIPAV.

10. *New York Times*, July 24, 1962, p. 12.

11. Paul Volcker and Toyoo Gyohten, *Changing Fortunes: The World's Money and the Threat to American Leadership* (New York: Times Books, 1992), p. 61.

12. Ibid., p. 36.

13. Memorandum from Volcker to Kennedy (Paul Volcker, Undersecretary for Monetary Affairs, National Archives II, College Park, MD, Record Group 56, Box 13, Folder 184), dated January 23, 1969.

14. President Johnson had established the study group chaired by Frederick Deming, who was the undersecretary of the treasury for monetary affairs in his administration. The group was then known as the Deming Group. Kissinger's memo confirmed that the study group would continue in the new administration. See Robert Solomon, *The International Monetary System, 1945–1981* (New York: Harper & Row, 1982), p. 82.

15. *Irish Times*, February 13, 1969, p. 14.

16. A version of this story appears in Volcker and Gyohten, *Changing Fortunes*, p. 68.

17. Milton Friedman and Robert Roosa, *The Balance of Payments: Free Versus Fixed Exchange Rates* (Washington, DC: American Enterprise Institute, 1967).

18. Ibid., p. 16.

19. Ibid., p. 38.

20. *Washington Post*, February 14, 1969, p. C5.

21. Ibid.

22. See Memorandum to the Secretary [David Kennedy], copy to Paul Volcker, from Undersecretary Charls Walker, February 13, 1969, Federal Reserve Bank of New York Archives, Box 108473.

23. Volcker's teachers supported floating rates as well. See Friedrich A. Lutz, "The Case for Flexible Exchange Rates," *Banca Nazionale del Lavoro Quarterly Review* 7, no. 31 (December 1954); Frank Graham and Charles R. Whittlesey, "Fluctuating Exchange Rates, Foreign Trade, the Price Level," *American Economic Review* 24 (1934): 410–16.

24. Lawrence Ritter, *The Glory of Their Times: The Story of the Early Days of Baseball Told by the Men Who Played It* (New York: Macmillan, 1966); and *Money*, coauthored with William Silber (New York: Basic Books, 1970).

25. PIPAV.

26. Ibid.

27. Friedman and Roosa, *The Balance of Payments*, pp. 47, 87.

28. In 1969 most academics dismissed destabilizing speculation as an unwarranted bogeyman, but this changed after the Bretton Woods System broke down in 1973 and the world experienced the instability of floating rates. A simple exposition of why free markets in foreign exchange can be unstable is Neil Wallace, "Why Markets in Foreign Exchange Are Different from Other Markets," *Federal Reserve Bank of Minneapolis Quarterly Review* 14, no. 1 (January 1979): 12–18. A review of the instability during the first fifteen years of floating rates is Rudiger Dornbusch and Jeffrey Frankel, "The Flexible Exchange Rate System: Experience and Alternatives," National Bureau of Economic Research Working Paper No. 2464, 1989.

29. PIPAV.

30. The London gold fixing never was below forty-three dollars during March, April, and May.

31. *New York Times*, April 28, 1969, p. 1.

32. Ibid., p. 1 continued.

33. See "Talking Paper Prepared in the Department of the Treasury, February 19, 1969," in *Foreign Economic Policy, 1969–1972*; *International Monetary*

Policy, 1969–1972, vol. 3, Bruce F. Duncombe, ed. (Washington, DC: Government Printing Office, 2002), p. 305.

34. The Bundesbank could sterilize those purchases, preventing them from increasing the money supply. But there are limits to the magnitude of sterilization given by the Bundesbank's holding of other assets (German bonds) and its willingness to hold a potentially depreciating asset such as the French franc.

35. *New York Times*, November 25, 1968, p. 1.

36. *New York Times*, April 27, 1969, p. 1.

37. Telephone logs of Paul Volcker, April 24, 1969, Federal Reserve Bank of New York Archives, Box 0108480.

38. Ibid.

39. Telephone logs of Paul Volcker, March 7, 1969, Federal Reserve Bank of New York Archives, Box 0108480.

40. Memorandum to the president dated June 23, 1969, Federal Reserve Bank of New York Archives, Box 108473.

41. PIPAV.

42. Ibid.

43. Memorandum to the president, June 23, 1969, p. 4.

44. Ibid.

45. Ibid., p. 9.

46. Ibid., p. 10.

47. See, for example, Maurice Obstfeld, Jay C. Shambaugh, and Alan M. Taylor, "The Trilemma in History: Tradeoffs Among Exchange Rates, Monetary Policies, and Capital Mobility," *Review of Economics and Statistics* 87, no. 3 (August 2005): 423–38. The Trilemma can be traced back (without the nomenclature) to Robert A. Mundell, "Capital Mobility and Stabilization Policy Under Fixed and Floating Exchange Rates," *The Canadian Journal of Economics and Political Science* 29, no. 4 (November 1963): 475–85, and J. M. Fleming, "Domestic Financial Policies Under Fixed and Under Floating Exchange Rates," *IMF Staff Papers* 9, no. 3 (November 1962): 369–80.

48. See Genesis 41: Joseph stored grain from the seven good years to prepare for the seven lean years.

49. The risk of this transaction, called uncovered interest arbitrage, is that the value of the currency in which the speculator borrows—in this case, the U.S. dollar—increases before the speculator repays the loan. That is why the commitment to fixed exchange rates is so important.

50. Volcker and Gyohten, *Changing Fortunes*, p. 34.

51. Ibid., p. 33.

52. Memorandum to the president, June 23, 1969, pp. 13, 18.

53. Ibid., Attachment A, Summary of Basic Options, p. 1.

54. Ibid. Special drawing rights are bookkeeping entries (not paper) created under the auspices of the International Monetary Fund to help settle international obligations. Unlike gold, which is generally acceptable in payment of all obligations, SDRs are usable only by central banks and have (so far) never gained the general acceptance they were designed for.

55. See *New York Times*, August 9, 1969, for reports on the devaluation.

56. Memorandum to the president, June 23, 1969, Attachment A, Summary of Basic Options, p. 1.

57. Fixed exchange rates under Bretton Woods were not quite fixed. Central bankers could allow the exchange rate to fluctuate 1 percent on either side of "parity." For example, the Bank of England could permit the dollar price of sterling, with a "par value" of $2.40 in 1969, to increase to $2.424 or to decline to $2.376 before intervening in the marketplace.

58. Memorandum to the president, June 23, 1969, p. 29.

59. On February 7, 1969, Volcker received a memo from Robert Solomon, an economist at the Federal Reserve Board, and an expert in international trade, with a covering note entitled, "Contingency Planning—U.S. Suspension of Gold Convertibility," and a document outlining the consequences of suspension written almost a year earlier, on April 8, 1968, Federal Reserve Bank of New York Archives, Box 108473.

60. Memorandum to the president, June 23, 1969, p. 32.

61. Ibid., p. 31.

62. Memorandum from Burns to Nixon, February 22, 1969, in *Foreign Economic Policy, 1969–1972; International Monetary Policy, 1969–1972*, vol. 3, p. 304fn.

63. The closing conversation in the meeting is based on Paul Volcker's recollection.

4. Gamble

1. The morning and afternoon London gold fixings were at $35 per ounce, but the *New York Times* (December 10, 1969, p. 1) reported an intraday quote by Zurich bullion dealers of $34.80 bid, offered at $35.00.

2. This conversation is based on Paul Volcker's recollection.

3. See Allan H. Meltzer, *A History of the Federal Reserve*, vol. 2, book I (Chicago: University of Chicago Press, 2009), p. 453n316.

4. See the discussion of the "Accord" in chapter 2.

5. Robert P. Bremner, *Chairman of the Fed: William McChesney Martin Jr. and the Creation of the Modern American Financial System* (New Haven, CT: Yale University Press, 2004), p. 252.

6. Members of the Federal Reserve Board who serve a full fourteen-year term cannot be reappointed. Martin was first appointed by Harry Truman in March 1951, to fill a partially unexpired term, and then was reappointed by Dwight Eisenhower in January 1956, to a full fourteen-year term. Richard Nixon announced the appointment of Arthur Burns to succeed Martin as chairman of the Federal Reserve Board in October 1969. See *New York Times*, October 18, 1969, p. 1.

7. Daily data between March 18, 1969, and March 31, 1969, show that the three-month bill fell below 6 percent. It averaged 8 percent from December 26 through the end of the year.

8. *New York Times*, November 4, 1969, p. 63.

9. The peak in the London gold fixing was $43.83 on March 10, 1969, but Zurich traded at $44.00 (*New York Times*, December 10, 1969, p. 1 continued).

10. *New York Times*, December 9, 1969, p. 93.

11. Paul Volcker and Toyoo Gyohten, *Changing Fortunes: The World's Money and the Threat to American Leadership* (New York: Times Books, 1992), p. 64.

12. *New York Times*, November 15, 1969, p. 53.

13. The following conversation is from William Safire, *Before the Fall: An Inside View of the Pre-Watergate White House* (New York: Doubleday and Co., 1975), pp. 491–92.

14. See Volcker Group memorandum dated November 4, 1970, entitled, "Options Regarding the Capital Restraint Program for 1971," International Monetary Papers, Selected Volcker Group Documents, Book No. 1, 1970, Personal Papers of Paul Volcker. Note that the overall balance of payments must always balance, but within the list of imports and exports some items are more worrisome than others, and these are highlighted by different ways to measure the deficit. For contemporary views of alternative measures, see *Economic Report of the President, 1970*, Council of Economic Advisers, Washington, DC, pp. 126–27, and Lawrence Ritter and William Silber, *Principles of Money, Banking, and Financial Markets* (New York: Basic Books, 1974), pp. 468–72. Also see International Monetary Fund Annual Report, Washington, DC, 1971, p. 198, Table 74 (United States Balance of Payments Summary, 1969–First Quarter 1971).

15. The price of gold exceeded thirty-nine dollars on October 26 and 27, and then traded between thirty-seven dollars and thirty-eight dollars during November.

16. See page 2, Volcker Group memorandum dated November 4, 1970, entitled "Options Regarding the Capital Restraint Program for 1971," International Monetary Papers, Selected Volcker Group Documents, Book No. 1, 1970, Personal Papers of Paul Volcker.

17. "Legal Aspects of Suspension of Gold Sales and Application of Option I or Option II," November 21, 1970, Michael Bradfield to Paul Volcker, Personal Papers of Paul Volcker.

18. See the entry for November 18, 1970, in H. R. Haldeman, *The Haldeman Diaries* (New York: G. P. Putnam's Sons, 1994), p. 211.

19. See the entry for November 19, 1970, in ibid., p. 212.

20. Milton Friedman, "The Role of Monetary Policy," *American Economic Review* 58, no. 1 (March 1968): 1–17.

21. See "The Economy," *Time*, December 31, 1965.

22. See "Letters," *Time*, February 4, 1966.

23. "President Nixon described himself as 'now a Keynesian in economics' according to Howard K. Smith of the American Broadcasting Company, one of the four television commentators who interviewed the President on a television show . . ." *New York Times*, January 7, 1971, p. 19.

24. See *New York Times*, July 22, 1970, p. 2.

25. *New York Times*, September 30, 1970, p. 59.

26. A search of the *New York Times*, the *Wall Street Journal*, and the *Washington Post* shows that the first article using the word *stagflation* to describe the American problem is "Money Imperils Romance: Europeans Fear American 'Stagflation' Will Drag Their Own Economies Down," *New York Times*, September 30, 1970, p. 59. An article in the *Washington Post* entitled "The Battle: Stagflation" appeared on February 25, 1971, p. A21. The term did not appear in the *Wall Street Journal* until April 23, 1973, p. 12.

27. *New York Times*, December 9, 1970, p. 93.

28. Ibid.

29. "The Accord of 1970" is the headline of the *New York Times* article by Leonard Silk, December 9, 1970, p. 93. Nixon's quote in full is: "People have got to know whether or not their President is a crook. Well, I'm not a crook. I've earned everything I've got." *Washington Post*, November 18, 1973, p. A1.

30. See Safire, *Before the Fall*, p. 491, quoting Burns in 1970. Also see Burton Abrams, "How Richard Nixon Pressured Arthur Burns: Evidence from the Nixon Tapes," *Journal of Economic Perspectives* 20, no. 4 (Fall 2006): 177–88.

31. John Connally, *In History's Shadow: An American Odyssey* (New York: Hyperion, 1993), p. 235.

32. Reported without attribution in the *Washington Post*, December 15, 1970, p. B1.

33. *Washington Post*, December 15, 1970, p. A1.

34. Ibid.

35. This comment to Barbara and the subsequent conversation is based on Volcker's recollection.

36. Herbert Stein, *Presidential Economics* (New York: Simon & Schuster, 1984), p. 162.

37. Safire, *Before the Fall*, p. 497.

38. The CEA was not, of course, really evil. Paul McCracken, Herbert Stein, and Hendrick Houthakker were first-rate economists and enjoyable to work with. I should know, because I was a senior staff economist (on leave from New York University) with the CEA during 1970-1971.

39. The letter is dated April 27, 1970, Papers of Paul Volcker, Federal Reserve Bank of New York Archives, Box 108473. It was written two days after a newspaper report (*New York Times*, April 25, 1970, p. 46) that implied Volcker would support wider bands in the existing system.

40. PIPAV.

41. The conversation is based on Volcker's recollection.

42. "Contingency Planning: Options for the International Monetary Problem," March 14, 1971, Papers of Paul Volcker, Federal Reserve Bank of New York Archives, Box 0108477.

43. PIPAV. "Reasonably foreseeable events—possibly in a matter of weeks—could set off strong speculation and strain one or more of the basic elements of the present fixed exchange rate system," appears on page 1 of "Contingency Planning: Options for the International Monetary Problem," March 14, 1971, Papers of Paul Volcker, Federal Reserve Bank of New York Archives, Box 0108477.

44. "Contingency Planning: Options for the International Monetary Problem," pp. 5-6.

45. See ibid., p. 33. The 15 percent number came from a review of statistical estimates conducted by John Auten, a Treasury economist working for Volcker (see Volcker and Gyohten, *Changing Fortunes*, p. 72).

46. Until the 1980s the Nissan brand was called Datsun in the United States.

47. China has followed the same strategy during the first decade of the twenty-first century, fixing a relatively low value for the renminbi per dollar to encourage Americans to import just about everything Beijing produces, from cotton knit shirts to steel manhole covers.

48. "Contingency Planning: Options for the International Monetary Problem," March 14, 1971, p. 59.

49. Memorandum to the secretary from Paul Volcker, March 26, 1971, page 8 of "An Economic Policy Program to Meet Domestic and International

Objectives," prepared by John Auten under the direction of Murray Weiden-baum, assistant secretary for economic policy, Papers of Paul Volcker, Federal Reserve Bank of New York Archives, Box 0108477.

50. According to Herbert Stein, at the time a member of Nixon's Council of Economic Advisers, "Connally found himself the head of a Treasury that already included a number of officials who had been leaning towards 'incomes policies' and who were in conflict with the purists—the CEA and Shultz—on that subject." See Herbert Stein, *Presidential Economics* (New York: Simon & Schuster, 1984), p. 163.

51. *New York Times*, January 11, 1970, p. 125.

52. "Contingency Planning: Options for the International Monetary Problem," March 14, 1971, p. 61.

53. *New York Times*, May 5, 1971, p. 1.

54. *New York Times*, May 8, 1971, p. 37.

55. Under the rules of fixed exchange rates administered by the International Monetary Fund, the Bundesbank was obligated to intervene to support the dollar-mark exchange rate once it declined by 1 percent below its par value. But greater adjustments were permitted if a country's exchange rate was in "fundamental disequilibrium." The *Wall Street Journal* (May 6, 1971, p. 1) reported, "Germany justifies the move as a temporary emergency measure until the mark's future can be resolved." Also see Robert Solomon, *International Monetary System, 1945–1981* (New York: Harper & Row, 1982), pp. 59 and 178–80.

56. *New York Times*, May 6, 1971, p. 1. The Bundesbank was worried about the inflationary consequences of buying dollar-denominated assets. As I pointed out in the last chapter, it could sterilize those purchases to prevent an increase in the domestic money supply, but there are limits to sterilization because the Bundesbank did not want to hold large amounts of a potentially depreciating asset such as the dollar.

57. *New York Times*, May 6, 1971, p. 1. These markets reopened within a week, while the foreign exchange markets in London and New York remained open throughout the period.

58. *New York Times*, May 11, 1971, p. 63.

59. PIPAV.

60. Memorandum "Contingency," May 8, 1971, Papers of Paul Volcker, Federal Reserve Bank of New York Archives, Box 0108477, pp. 1–2, 4.

61. See *New York Times*, May 13, 1971, p. 65. The $400 million loss is confirmed by the Federal Reserve report for the week ending May 13, 1971 (see *Wall Street Journal*, May 14, 1971, p. 26).

62. Volcker and Gyohten, *Changing Fortunes*, p. 74.

63. PIPAV.

64. Ibid.

65. See Volcker and Gyohten, *Changing Fortunes*, p. 75, for this quote and the following interchange.

66. This quote and the remaining in this section from McCracken are in Memorandum from the Chairman of the Council of Economic Advisers to President Nixon, June 2, 1971, reprinted in Bruce Duncombe, ed., *Foreign Relations of the United States, 1969–1976, vol. 3, Foreign Economic Policy: International Monetary Policy, 1969–1972* (Washington, DC: U.S. Government Printing Office, 2001), p. 438.

67. This quote and the remaining in this section from Connally are in Memorandum from Secretary of the Treasury Connally to President Nixon, June 8, 1971, reprinted in Duncombe, ed., *Foreign Relations of the United States,* vol. 3, pp. 440–41.

68. Memorandum from Jon Huntsman of the White House Staff to Secretary of the Treasury Connally, June 8, 1971, reprinted in ibid., pp. 442–43.

69. Dated July 27, 1971, Papers of Paul Volcker, Federal Reserve Bank of New York Archives, Box 0108477. The term *New Economic Policy* appeared in Nixon's speech announcing the program on August 15, 1971. See Transcript of the President's Address, *New York Times*, August 16, 1971, p. 14.

70. See the entry for August 2, 1971, in Haldeman, *The Haldeman Diaries*, pp. 335–36.

71. See Nixon Tape 562b (at 1 hour, 2 minutes) at www.nixontapes.org/chron2.htm.

72. See Nixon Tape 563b (at the 17-minute mark) at www.nixontapes.org/chron2.htm.

73. PIPAV.

74. See "Speculative Attacks Grow on U.S. Currency Abroad," *New York Times*, August 13, 1971, p. 35. Charles A. Coombs, who worked at the Federal Reserve Bank of New York during this period and was in charge of U.S. Treasury and Federal Reserve operations in the gold and foreign exchange markets, writes, "To protect the gold stock, the Federal Reserve . . . was forced to draw another $2.2 billion on swap lines." See Charles A. Coombs, *The Arena of International Finance* (New York: John Wiley, 1976), pp. vii and 217.

75. See Nixon Tape 273a (at the 48-minute mark, at 1 hour, 17 minutes, and at 1 hour, 34 minutes) at www.nixontapes.org/chron2.htm for these three quotes.

76. See Nixon Tape 273b at various points for the following discussion (see the following minute marks: 19, 26, 28, 32, 33, 36, 37, 38, and 43) at www.nixontapes.org/chron2.htm.

77. The decision to meet at Camp David on August 13 occurred as described here and had nothing to do with the British demand for $3 billion in gold. Two author/participants in these events (Haldeman, *The Haldeman Diaries*, p. 340; and Safire, *Before the Fall*, p. 512) mistakenly attribute the decision to the demand for gold by the United Kingdom. The British demand is never mentioned on the Nixon tape recordings of August 12, because it did not happen until the morning of August 13. Volcker recalls a telephone call received by Charles Coombs (see biographical information in note 74) conveying the demand by the United Kingdom on the morning of August 13. Volcker had invited Coombs, who wanted to make a plea to Connally against suspension, to the Treasury. The timing is also confirmed by a quotation in Safire (p. 514) from Connally at Camp David on the thirteenth: "The British came in today to ask us to cover $3 billion."

78. *New York Times*, August 16, 1971, p. 1.

5. Transformation

1. Nixon did not want to resort to the 1917 act, but according to the U.S. Senate Report 93-549, Emergency Powers Statutes (93rd Congress, 1st Sess.), the president needed the Trading with the Enemy Act to impose certain controls on imports. The key provision of the act, section 5(b), states, "During the time of war [or during any other period of national emergency declared by the President] the President may . . . investigate, regulate, direct and compel, nullify, void, prevent or prohibit, any acquisition, holding, withholding, use, transfer, withdrawal, transportation, importation or exportation of, or dealing in, or exercising any right, power, or privilege with respect to, or transactions involving, any property in which any foreign country or a national thereof has any interest by any person, or with respect to any property, subject to the jurisdiction of the United States." The wage-price freeze was imposed under the authority of the Economic Stabilization Act of 1970 (Public Law 91-379). The suspension of gold convertibility was authorized under the Gold Reserve Act of 1934.

2. See William Safire, *Before the Fall: An Inside View of the Pre-Watergate White House* (New York: Doubleday and Co., 1975), p. 518. Nixon was answering Peter G. Peterson, at the time serving as an assistant to the president for international economic affairs and executive director of the Council on International Economic Policy. Peterson had said that the State Department wanted to be at this meeting.

3. The following people signed the guest book: John Connally, Paul Mc-Cracken, Arthur Burns, Paul Volcker, Herbert Stein, Peter Peterson, H. R. Haldeman, John Ehrlichman, George Shultz, William Safire, Caspar Weinberger, Arnold Weber, Kenneth Dam, Michael Bradfield, and Larry Higby. Source: Bruce Duncombe, ed. *Foreign Relations of the United States, 1969–1976*, vol. 3, *Foreign Economic Policy; International Monetary Policy, 1969–1972* (Washington, DC: Government Printing Office, 2001), p. 466.

4. Based on an interview with Michael Bradfield.

5. The following conversation is based on Volcker's recollection, supplemented by H. R. Haldeman, *The Haldeman Diaries* (New York: G. P. Putnam's Sons, 1994), pp. 340–45, and Safire, *Before the Fall*, pp. 513–15.

6. Bryan actually ran three times as the Democratic nominee for president: 1896, 1900, and 1908.

7. See Safire, *Before the Fall*, p. 515.

8. In Tab B of Volcker's briefing book, in the section entitled "How Large an Exchange Rate Realignment Should the United States Seek," Volcker writes, "There are major uncertainties here . . . relevant studies in the U.S. Treasury and in the International Monetary Fund (IMF) produce rather different answers . . . The Treasury [estimates] slightly over $.5 billion improvement in the U.S. balance of payments position for each one percent exchange rate change . . . The IMF [estimates] a $.85 billion improvement . . . Therefore with the most optimistic assumption . . . the required exchange rate change would be an effective devaluation of 15 percent." Volcker (Paul Volcker and Toyoo Gyohten, *Changing Fortunes: The World's Money and the Threat to American Leadership* [New York: Times Books, 1992], p. 72) mentions a study he asked John Auten, a senior economist at Treasury, to undertake summarizing the academic literature on calculating exchange rate elasticity. That particular analysis has not been found, but numerous academic studies were submitted to the Volcker Group by prominent international economists at the time, including Richard N. Cooper, Paul Wonnacott, and Thomas Willett.

9. See Safire, *Before the Fall*, p. 520.

10. See the Transcript of the President's Address, *New York Times*, August 16, 1971, p. 14.

11. The Dow Jones Industrial Average rose by 3.7 percent, and the S&P 500 increased by 3.2 percent. The daily standard deviation of returns in the S&P 500 from January through July 1971 is 0.51 percent.

12. See "Abreast of the Market" column, *Wall Street Journal*, August 17, 1971, p. 33, and August 18, 1971, p. 29. GM and Ford did not trade on the sixteenth

because of an imbalance of buy orders. The increases reported in the text occurred on the seventeenth.

13. See "Abreast of the Market" column, *Wall Street Journal*, August 17, 1971, p. 33.

14. *Wall Street Journal*, August 17, 1971, p. 1.

15. The remaining text of the paragraph is based on ibid., p. 7.

16. See "Nixon: Flair for the Long Ball," *Wall Street Journal*, August 17, 1971, p. 14.

17. Ibid., p. 6.

18. Ibid.

19. Belgium, the Netherlands, and France (of course) converted $422 million into gold during the first week of May 1971 (*New York Times*, May 13, 1971, p. 65).

20. U.S. Treasury Department News, "Statement by Secretary Connally at the Opening of a News Conference and Transcript," August 16, 1971, Personal Papers of Paul Volcker.

21. *New York Times*, August 16, 1971, p. 1.

22. U.S. Treasury Department News, "Statement by Secretary Connally at the Opening of a News Conference and Transcript," August 16, 1971.

23. Ibid.

24. The details of the meeting are recorded in Memorandum of Conversation, August 16, 1971, reprinted in Duncombe, ed., *Foreign Relations of the United States, 1969–1976*, vol. 3, pp. 469–78. The news conference is reported in the *New York Times*, August 17, 1971, p. 19.

25. Ibid., pp. 469–78.

26. Ibid.

27. *New York Times*, August 18, 1971, p. 21.

28. See Memorandum of Conversation, August 16, 1971, reprinted in Duncombe, ed., *Foreign Relations of the United States, 1969–1976*, vol. 3, pp. 469–78.

29. On May 4, 1971, the dollar-mark exchange rate was 3.63 marks per dollar, and on August 13, 1971, the exchange rate was 3.388.

30. See chapter 4.

31. *Guardian*, August 29, 1971, p. 1.

32. See "Economic Poker Game," *New York Times*, September 15, 1971, p. 61.

33. *New York Times*, August 18, 1971, p. 21.

34. *New York Times*, November 29, 1971, p. 65 continued.

35. *Financial Times*, August 21, 1971.

36. *New York Times*, August 22, 1971, section 3, p. 1.

37. See Safire, *Before the Fall*, p. 515.

38. Ibid., p. 518.

39. Data for the afternoon gold fixing from August 17 through August 20 are $43.05; $43.15; $43.30; $43.30. On August 31 the fixing was $40.65.

40. *Newsweek*, January 27, 1997, p. 86.

41. The prices of precious metals often reflect their use as the monetary standard. For example, in analyzing the consequences of the demonetization of silver in 1873, Milton Friedman argues, "The most obvious, but by no means most important consequence of the U.S. return to gold rather than to a bimetallic standard was the sharp rise in the gold-silver price ratio." See "The Crime of 1973," in *Money Mischief: Episodes in Monetary History* (New York: Harcourt Brace and Company, 1992), p. 68.

42. The conversation is based on Telephone Logs of Paul Volcker, September 11, 1971, Federal Reserve Bank of New York Archives, Box 0108480.

43. A story with a similar theme is John Taintor Foote's *A Wedding Gift: A Fishing Story* (London: D. Appleton-Century Co., 1924). Volcker keeps a copy in his bookshelf at home.

44. *New York Times*, September 6, 1971, p. 24.

45. Between May 4, 1971, and August 13, 1971, the German mark appreciated from 3.63 marks per dollar to 3.38, an increase of 6.9 percent. By the end of November 1971 the mark had appreciated another 2.1 percent, to 3.31 marks per dollar. The Japanese kept the yen fixed at the official 360 per dollar until the end of August, when they allowed the yen to appreciate to 336 yen per dollar, just about matching the percentage increase in the mark. By the end of November the Japanese allowed the yen to appreciate to 327.25 yen per dollar, again almost matching the increase in the mark. The French franc remained fixed at 5.52 francs per dollar throughout this period. Unlike the Germans and the Japanese, the French could continue buying dollars to prevent their currency from appreciating without worrying so much about the inflationary consequences because the dollar inflows to France were much smaller. France also increased controls on capital inflows.

46. PIPAV.

47. See *Inside the Nixon Administration: The Secret Diary of Arthur Burns, 1969–1974*, edited by Robert H. Ferrell (Lawrence: University Press of Kansas, 2010), p. 65.

48. In 1971 the G-10 consisted of Britain, Canada, Japan, Sweden, the United States, and five of the six Common Market countries: Belgium, France, Italy, the Netherlands, and West Germany (*New York Times*, November 29, 1971, p. 65 continued).

49. *New York Times*, December 2, 1971, p. 73.

50. Letter from Burns to Nixon, October 14, 1971, reprinted in Duncombe, ed., *Foreign Relations of the United States, 1969–1976*, vol. 3, p. 516.

51. See the discussion of the meeting between Nixon, Connolly, and Burns of November 24, 1971, in ibid., pp. 565–66.

52. In August 1971 Switzerland and France held 65 and 55 percent, respectively, of their foreign exchange reserves in the form of gold. Japan held slightly less than 6 percent in gold (see the *Economist*, August 21, 1971, p. 54).

53. Volcker had written an outline of U.S. proposals prior to the G-10 meeting and had distributed it to the participants. It says that the United States would eliminate the 10 percent surcharge in exchange for an average 11 percent depreciation of the dollar against the major currencies. The document assumes continuation of suspension of convertibility and assumes no change in the dollar price of gold. A draft of the document is in the Personal Papers of Paul Volcker, and a version that John Connally sent to the White House appears in Duncombe, ed., *Foreign Relations of the United States, 1969–1976*, vol. 3, pp. 580–81.

54. The following quotes are from Volcker and Gyohten, *Changing Fortunes*, p. 86.

55. See Hubert Zimmerman, *Money and Security, 1950–1971* (Cambridge: Cambridge University Press, 2002), p. 226. The Blessing letter also helps explain why the suspension of convertibility had a relatively benign impact. Convertibility had been circumscribed in practice by the Blessing letter and by Japan's willingness to hold dollars rather than gold as reserves.

56. This and the following quotes are from Volcker and Gyohten, *Changing Fortunes*, p. 86.

57. The agenda for Pompidou's meeting with Nixon appeared in the *New York Times*, November 24, 1971, p. 5, and November 25, 1971, p. 1.

58. See Volcker and Gyohten, *Changing Fortunes*, p. 87.

59. *New York Times*, December 14, 1971, p. 1.

60. See "A Framework for Monetary and Trade Settlement," in Duncombe, ed., *Foreign Relations of the United States, 1969–1976*, vol. 3, pp. 597–99.

61. Under the new system, exchange rates could vary 2¼ percent on either side of parity compared with the 1 percent margins permitted under Bretton Woods.

62. See point 5 in "A Framework for Monetary and Trade Settlement," in Duncombe, ed., *Foreign Relations of the United States, 1969–1976*, vol. 3, p. 598.

63. *New York Times*, December 15, 1971, p. 91.

64. The exchange rates are the new central values of the dollar compared with the par values prior to the May 1971 crisis. See Duncombe, ed., *Foreign Relations of the United States, 1969–1976*, vol. 3, p. 601.

65. Recall that fixed exchange rates under Bretton Woods were not quite fixed (just as fat-free muffins are not quite fat-free). Central bankers could allow the

exchange rate to fluctuate 1 percent on either side of "parity." For example, the Bank of Japan could permit the yen, with a "par value" of 360 yen per dollar, to fluctuate between 363.3 and 356.4 before intervening in the marketplace. After the Smithsonian realignment the yen had a central value of 308 yen per dollar and could vary between 314.93 and 301.07.

66. *New York Times*, December 19, 1971, p. 1.

67. Volcker and Gyohten, *Changing Fortunes*, p. 90.

68. According to Volcker (ibid., p. 89), "The trade weighted depreciation of the dollar amounted to a little under 8 percent . . . Without Canada . . . the figure was 12 percent . . . Either way it was well short of what we felt we needed to restore solid equilibrium in our external payments."

6. Compromise

1. Letter from Pompidou to Nixon, dated February 4, 1972, Papers of Paul Volcker, Federal Reserve Bank of New York Archives, Box 108473, with response of Nixon to Pompidou, dated February 10, 1972, marked "PAV draft" in pencil.

2. The *New York Times*, February 3, 1972, p. 1, reports that gold touched fifty dollars an ounce during trading hours on February 2, 1972.

3. This quote and the remaining quotes are from the letter from Pompidou to Nixon dated February 4, 1972, Papers of Paul Volcker, Federal Reserve Bank of New York Archives, Box 108473.

4. On December 20, the day after the Smithsonian news conference, the overnight federal funds rate was 3.75 percent, the three-month Treasury bill rate was 4.12 percent, and the dollar bought 3.258 marks. On February 2, 1972, the funds rate had declined to 3.13 percent, the bill rate had dropped to 3.4 percent, and the dollar bought only 3.185 marks.

5. Quotes in this paragraph and in the two that follow are from Burton Abrams, "How Richard Nixon Pressured Arthur Burns: Evidence from the Nixon Tapes," *Journal of Economic Perspectives* 20, no. 4 (Fall 2006): 180–84.

6. The quotes are from Abrams (see ibid.). Shultz may have been referring to unconfirmed reports that Nixon had threatened to double the size of the Federal Reserve Board as a way to gain more control. See William Safire, *Before the Fall: An Inside View of the Pre-Watergate White House* (New York: Doubleday and Co., 1975), p. 492.

7. See February 4, 1972, Letter from Pompidou to Nixon, Papers of Paul Volcker, Federal Reserve Bank of New York Archives, Box 108473.

8. See Memorandum of Conversation, August 16, 1971, reprinted in Bruce Duncombe, ed., *Foreign Relations of the United States, 1969–1976*, vol. 3, *Foreign Economic Policy, 1969–1972; International Monetary Policy, 1969–1972*, p. 472.

9. *New York Times*, May 13, 1972, p. 43.

10. See Paul Volcker and Toyoo Gyohten, *Changing Fortunes: The World's Money and the Threat to American Leadership* (New York: Times Books, 1992), p. 84.

11. PIPAV.

12. *New York Times*, May 13, 1972, pp. 1, 43.

13. See *New York Times*, May 17, 1972, p. 63.

14. *Washington Post*, May 13, 1972, p. A1 continued.

15. *Washington Post*, May 17, 1972, p. A1.

16. *New York Times*, May 17, 1972, p. 47.

17. Connally writes in his autobiography, *In History's Shadow: An American Odyssey* (New York: Hyperion, 1993), p. 233, that he resigned because of interference by White House staffer John Ehrlichman in tax policy without clearing it with Connally.

18. PIPAV.

19. *Guardian*, June 13, 1972, p. 12.

20. *New York Times*, May 17, 1972, p. 46.

21. *Washington Post*, May 17, 1972, p. A1 continued.

22. *Washington Post*, May 18, 1972, p. A23.

23. The close on May 16 in the afternoon fixing in London (approximately 10:00 A.M. New York time) was $54.60. The opening in the morning fixing in London on May 17 (approximately 5:30 A.M. New York time) was $57.50. The announcement was made during the day on May 16, 1972, and the increase of 5 percent is statistically significant. The standard deviation of returns during the first four months of 1972 was .62 percent per day.

24. See *Wall Street Journal*, May 18, 1972, p. 5. The *Journal* reports that a contributing factor to the price jump was an announcement by South Africa that it would curtail gold sales.

25. *New York Times*, June 23, 1972, p. 47.

26. Ibid.

27. *New York Times*, June 24, 1972, p. 1.

28. PIPAV.

29. The remaining quotes in this paragraph are from a transcript of the June 23, 1972, Nixon Tapes, available at www.nixonlibrary.gov/forresearchers/find/tapes/watergate/wspf/741-002.pdf. Also available in *Time*, August 19, 1974.

30. The so-called smoking howitzer tape that forced Nixon's resignation recorded the conversation with Haldeman on the morning of June 23, 1972, the same day of the British devaluation. No wonder so few people remember the devaluation.

31. See George Willis, August 7, 1972, "The White Plan for an International Stabilization Fund: A Chronology," Personal Papers of Paul Volcker. According to the *Washington Post*, July 26, 1992, p. B5, Willis took a leave from Treasury in 1942 and served in the navy during the war, so he probably did not work on the design of Bretton Woods.

32. Memorandum from Willis to Volcker, Personal Papers of Paul Volcker, January 11, 1972.

33. The conversation is based on Volcker's recollection.

34. Ibid.

35. PIPAV.

36. See the interview with Shultz in SFGate.com, July 9, 2006.

37. The details that follow are from a series of memos from George Willis to Paul Volcker entitled "Main Principles of Plan X," August 1, 1972. See Plan X Folder, Personal Papers of Paul Volcker.

38. See Robert Solomon, *The International Monetary System, 1945–1981* (New York: Harper & Row, 1982), pp. 242–43.

39. *New York Times*, September 27, 1972, p. 70.

40. Ibid.

41. Shultz met with Friedman on September 21, 1972, and had left a telephone message for Volcker to join them (Telephone Logs of Paul Volcker, September 21, 1972, Federal Reserve Bank of New York Archives, Box 0108480). There is no record that a meeting ever took place.

42. Speculation against the dollar began on January 23, 1973, when the Swiss National Bank announced that it would allow the Swiss franc to float. The *New York Times* (January 24, 1973, p. 51) reported, "The dollar was 'hit' in the belief that other 'strong' currencies such as the West German mark would follow the franc's lead."

43. Cable from Brandt to Nixon via U.S. embassy in Washington, February 9, 1973, provisional translation, Hans Noebel, Chargé d'Affaires, Nixon Papers, Letters from German Embassy, National Archives II, College Park, MD.

44. Ibid. Germany had born the entire burden of keeping dollar-mark within the bands mandated by the Smithsonian Agreement. See the *Washington Post*, February 11, 1973, p. A1 continued, "In an effort to prevent the mark from rising . . . the West German central bank bought $6 billion with about 20 billion marks."

45. Message from Nixon to Brandt, February 10, 1973, via the State Department, Nixon Papers, Letters from German Embassy, National Archives II, College Park, MD.

46. On January 31, 1973, only days before Nixon's correspondence on the foreign exchange crisis, the front page of the *New York Times* featured an article on the guilty verdict against G. Gordon Liddy and James W. McCord in the Watergate burglary trial and one outlining American proposals for international monetary reform.

47. Message from Nixon to Tanaka, February 3, 1973, via John Ehrlichman, Nixon Papers, National Archives II, College Park, MD.

48. The following quotes are from the Memorandum of Conversation, February 8, 1973 (prepared by Sam Cross), Personal Papers of Paul Volcker.

49. Telephone Memorandum, February 10, 1973 (9:15 A.M.), from Ingersoll to Volcker through Jack Bennett, Volcker's deputy at Treasury, Personal Papers of Paul Volcker.

50. *New York Times*, February 12, 1973, p. 40.

51. Ibid.

52. The following quotes are from "Informal Notes on a Meeting in the Finance Ministry," February 10, 1973, Edward Hermberg, Financial Attaché, Personal Papers of Paul Volcker.

53. *New York Times*, February 13, 1973, p. 45.

54. *New York Times*, February 13, 1973, p. 1; *Washington Post*, February 13, 1973, p. 1; and the *Times* (London), February 14, 1973, p. 1.

55. See *New York Times*, February 14, 1973, p. 55. Also see Transcript, Press Briefing with Paul Volcker, February 13, 1973, p. 3, Papers of Paul Volcker, Federal Reserve Bank of New York Archives, Box 0108476.

56. Data on the yen are from the *New York Times*, February 14, 1973, p. 1 continued. Data on the German mark are from Datastream.

57. Tanaka is quoted in the *New York Times*, February 15, 1973, p. 89, and Schmidt is quoted in the *Washington Post*, February 14, 1973, p. A17.

58. *New York Times*, February 12, 1973, p. 40.

59. *New York Times*, February 17, 1973, p. 41.

60. Ibid.

61. *New York Times*, February 18, 1973, p. 209.

62. *New York Times*, March 4, 1973, p. 1.

63. According to the *New York Times* (March 6, 1973, p. 1), "When the major European governments announced that the international currency markets would be closed this simply meant that the government broker—who sets the official daily fixing of currency values—would not be in business."

64. The *Washington Post*, March 10, 1973, p. A1, reports that Canada, Indo-

nesia (representing the "poorer nations"), Japan, Sweden, and Switzerland were also invited.

65. See Volcker and Gyohten, *Changing Fortunes*, p. 112.

66. This conversation is based on the recollection of Paul Volcker.

67. From the testimony of Arthur Burns, *To Amend the Par Value Modification Act of 1972: Hearings Before the Subcommittee on International Finance of the Committee on Banking and Currency*, House of Representatives, 93rd Congress, 1st Sess., March 6, 1973, p. 119.

68. Volcker and Gyohten, *Changing Fortunes*, p. 113.

69. See *New York Times*, March 13, 1973, p. 49, for the floating arrangements, and *New York Times*, March 17, 1973, pp. 1 and 41, for the final communiqué.

70. See Volcker and Gyohten, *Changing Fortunes*, p. 113.

71. Ibid. The *New York Times*, March 17, 1973, p. 1, quotes Burns as saying, "whatever happens to the discount rate is decided in Washington, not in Europe."

72. PIPAV.

73. See *New York Times*, April 3, 1974, for Simon's political struggles.

74. Letter from Rumsfeld to Volcker, April 9, 1974, Papers of Paul Volcker, Federal Reserve Bank of New York Archives, Box 108473.

75. The ministers and central bank governors of the ten countries in the Group of Ten, sometimes called the G-10, met in Paris on March 16, 1973, under the chairmanship of Valéry Giscard d'Estaing (see www.ena.lu). Giscard d'Estaing was elected president of France on May 19, 1974.

76. This conversation was reported on the day after Volcker's resignation. See the *Washington Post*, April 9, 1974, p. D11.

77. *International Herald Tribune*, February 14, 1973.

78. Transcript, press conference, February 13, 1973, Personal Papers of Paul Volcker.

7. Prelude

1. For more details, see Lawrence Ritter, William Silber, and Gregory Udell, *Principles of Money, Banking and Financial Markets*, 12th ed. (Boston: Addison-Wesley, 2009).

2. PIPAV.

3. Burns would say later (see page 132) that he knew Volcker would not be a "rubber stamp," but he also disparaged Volcker in his diary (see the previous chapter).

4. PIPAV.

5. Details on the battle between Sproul and Martin appear in Robert P. Bremner, *Chairman of the Fed: William McChesney Martin Jr. and the Creation of the Modern American Financial System* (New Haven, CT: Yale University Press, 2004), pp. 99–102.

6. *New York Times*, May 12, 1970, p. 57.

7. See William Greider, *Secrets of the Temple: How the Federal Reserve Runs the Country* (New York: Simon & Schuster, 1987), p. 341.

8. *New York Times*, May 22, 1972, p. 53.

9. Burns questioned the travel budget in February 1970, ostensibly justifying a shift in international responsibilities from the New York bank to the board. See Allan Meltzer, *A History of the Federal Reserve System*, vol. 2, book 1 (Chicago: University of Chicago Press, 2009), p. 585n.

10. Letter from Russell Reynolds, chairman of Russell Reynolds and Associates, November 23, 1973, Personal Papers of Paul Volcker.

11. See *New York Times*, January 5, 1973, p. 23, and *New York Times*, January 9, 1975. Hunter disclosed that his annual salary was $150,000 but he signed a "pay package" worth $3.75 million over five years, which works out to $750,000 per year.

12. PIPAV.

13. *New York Times*, April 9, 1974, p. 55.

14. This information comes from Paul Volcker.

15. Volcker waited until June 1974 before leaving the Treasury, because he wanted to attend a Committee of Twenty meeting to promote a statement supporting "surveillance of the floating rate system . . . that takes international as well as national interests into account." The Committee of Twenty was set up by the International Monetary Fund in 1972 to discuss monetary reform. See *Washington Post*, June 14, 1974, p. A1.

16. This conversation is based on the recollection of Paul Volcker.

17. The chairman of the Board of Governors receives the same salary as a member of the president's cabinet, but bank presidents are paid at the discretion of each bank's board of directors, with the approval of the Board of Governors.

18. The 81 percent figure reflected the survey taken in October 1974, as reported in the *New York Times*, August 3, 1975, p. 36. See *New York Times*, July 14, 1974, p. 1, for the 15 percent number.

19. This quote and the remaining quotes in this paragraph are from the *New York Times*, July 14, 1974, p. 1 continued.

20. The Consumer Price Index rose by 12.1 percent from December 1973 through December 1974.

21. Venezuela increased the price of a barrel of crude oil to $14.08 on

December 28, 1973. According to the *New York Times* (December 29, 1973, p. 31), "The new posted price is 400 percent larger than the price last January 1."

22. Between 1955 and 1964 the Consumer Price Index increased at an annual compounded rate of 1.65 percent, and between 1965 and 1974 it increased at a 5.09 annual rate. These data are from Lawrence H. Officer and Samuel H. Williamson, available at www.measuringworth.com/inflation.

23. See "The Great Inflation: Lessons for Monetary Policy," monthly bulletin, European Central Bank, May 2010. Also see the forthcoming volume edited by Michael Bordo and Athanasios Orphanides, *The Great Inflation* (Chicago: University of Chicago Press), and especially the article in that volume by Andrew Levin and John B. Taylor, "Falling Behind the Curve: A Positive Analysis of Stop-Start Monetary Policies and the Great Inflation."

24. Narrow money supply (defined as currency plus demand deposits) grew at a 2.4 percent annual growth rate in the early period (December 1955 through December 1965) compared with an annual growth rate of 5.4 percent in the second period (December 1965 through December 1975). These are the annual geometric growth rates in the M1 data series labeled M1SL, available at research.stlouisfed.org/aggreg/.

25. *New York Times*, March 5, 1965, p. 45. Also see chapter 2 for an extensive discussion. Robert Barro suggested that the break with the past was signaled by the removal of silver from most American coins in 1964. See Barro, "United States Inflation and the Choice of Monetary Standard," in Robert Hall, *Inflation: Causes and Effects* (Chicago: University of Chicago Press, 1982), p. 104. Barro is correct with respect to circulating coins, but the removal of the gold cover seems more directly related to the Federal Reserve's discretionary control over the money supply.

26. See *New York Times*, June 19, 1974, p. 61, "House Unit Passes Gold Amendment," for the earliest indication that the purchase of gold would be legalized. Presidential Executive Order 11825 became effective on December 31, 1974. It invoked provisions of Public Law 93-373 to revoke earlier Executive Orders banning gold holding.

27. See *New York Times*, September 23, 1974, p. 55.

28. Ibid.

29. The morning fixing in London on December 30, 1974, was $197.50 compared with the final closing price on December 31, 1973, of $112.25.

30. *New York Times*, May 2, 1975, p. 45.

31. Ibid.

32. *New York Times*, April 5, 1974, p. 45.

33. Transcript, Federal Open Market Committee, January 17, 1977, Tape 7, p. 1, Papers of Arthur Burns, University of Michigan Library, Ann Arbor, MI.

34. Arthur Burns, "The Anguish of Central Banking," the 1979 Per Jacobsson Lecture, Belgrade, Yugoslavia, September 30, 1979, p. 15.

35. The inflation rate was 6.48 percent per year from December 1969 through December 1977 based on data from Lawrence H. Officer and Samuel H. Williamson, available at www.measuringworth.com/inflation/. Burns's tenure as Fed chairman is discussed in many articles and books, including William Poole, "Panel Discussion II: Safeguarding Good Policy Practice," in *Reflections on Monetary Policy 25 Years After October 1979*, *Federal Reserve Bank of St. Louis* 87, no. 2 (March/April 2005), part 2; Robert Hetzel, *The Monetary Policy of the Federal Reserve: A History* (New York: Cambridge University Press, 2008); and Meltzer, *A History of the Federal Reserve System*, vol. 2, book 2.

36. See Michael J. Haupert, "The Economic History of Major League Baseball," at eh.net/encyclopedia/article/haupert.mlb.

37. Burns, "The Anguish of Central Banking," p. 16.

38. Ibid.

39. The conversation is based on the recollection of Paul Volcker.

40. Memorandum of Discussion, Federal Open Market Committee, November 18, 1975, p. 39, Board of Governors of the Federal Reserve System, Washington, DC.

41. Transcript, Federal Open Market Committee, July 20, 1976, Tape 10, pp. 5 and 13, Papers of Arthur Burns, University of Michigan Library, Ann Arbor, MI.

42. *Washington Post*, August 14, 1975, p. A17.

43. PIPAV.

44. The Consumer Price Index rose 12.1 from December 1973 through December 1974 and rose 5.0 percent from December 1975 through December 1976.

45. The morning fixing in London on August 31, 1976, was $103.05.

46. *New York Times*, August 29, 1976, p. 105.

47. The price of gold reflects both supply and demand, of course, so that part of the drop in price reflected anticipated sales of gold from U.S. stockpiles and from the International Monetary Fund (see *New York Times*, September 3, 1976, p. D5). However, gold sales by the monetary authorities are only a small fraction of the stock of gold in the world—gold is indestructible, as in Charles de Gaulle's poetry. When speculators want gold as an inflation hedge, there is never enough to go around.

48. *New York Times*, September 2, 1976, p. 55.

49. For a discussion of the economic issues in the campaign, see the editorial in the *New York Times*, October 26, 1976, p. 38.

50. Inflation in 1969 was 5.9 percent.

51. Unemployment averaged 7.7 percent in 1976 and was 8.5 percent in 1975.

52. This quote and the remaining quotes in this paragraph are from the *New York Times*, June 5, 1978, p. 1.

53. According to Andrew Levin and John Taylor, inflationary expectations "reached a peak of about $4\frac{1}{2}$ percent in 1970 and then remained in the range of $3\frac{1}{2}$ to $4\frac{1}{2}$ percent over the next several years." See "Falling Behind the Curve: A Positive Analysis of the Stop-Start Monetary Policies and the Great Inflation," a manuscript prepared for the September 2008 NBER Conference on the Great Inflation, p. 6. Available at www.hber.org/public_html/confer/2008/gif08/gif08/levin.pdf.

54. Memorandum of Discussion, Federal Open Market Committee, August 19, 1975, p. 61–62, Board of Governors of the Federal Reserve System, Washington, DC.

55. See Robert E. Lucas Jr., "Expectations and the Neutrality of Money," *Journal of Economic Theory* 4, no. 2 (April 1972); and Robert E. Lucas Jr., "Econometric Policy Evaluation: A Critique," Carnegie-Rochester Conference Series, 1976.

56. See Thomas Sargent and Neil Wallace, "Rational Expectations, the Optimal Monetary Instrument, and the Optimal Money Supply Rule," *Journal of Political Economy* 83, no. 2 (April 1975); and Thomas Sargent and Neil Wallace, "Rational Expectations and the Theory of Economic Policy," *Journal of Monetary Economics* 2, no. 2 (April 1976).

57. See "Reconciling our Short- and Long-Run Goals in Economic Policy," a speech delivered to the Boston Economic Club, December 15, 1976, Personal Papers of Paul Volcker, pp. 11–12.

58. *New York Times*, December 17, 1978, p. F1.

59. The London morning fixing was $243.65 on October 31, 1978.

60. *New York Times*, December 17, 1978, p. F1.

61. Ibid.

62. Ibid.

63. Transcript, Federal Open Market Committee, February 28, 1978, p. 24. Volcker was referring to the possibility of accelerating inflation and the need to slow the economy to engineer a "soft landing" (to avoid a recession).

64. *New York Times*, December 20, 1977, p. 69.

65. *New York Times*, January 1, 1978, p. F1.

66. *New York Times*, December 29, 1977, p. 60.

67. *New York Times*, January 1, 1978, p. F1 continued.

68. PIPAV.

69. The following quotes are from the Transcript, Federal Open Market Committee, August 15, 1978, pp. 1–2.

70. See *Washington Post*, July 30, 1978, p. G1.

71. On August 8, 1978, the dollar bought only 1.98 marks, a new low, and on August 14 it declined to 1.95 marks, another new low.

72. Transcript, Federal Open Market Committee, August 15, 1978, p. 21.

73. PIPAV.

74. Transcript, Federal Open Market Committee, October 17, 1978, p. 40.

75. The conversation is based on Volcker's recollection.

76. Willes first dissented at the telephone conference of May 5, 1978, and at every regular meeting through October 17, 1978 (see FOMC transcripts). He credits Thomas Sargent and Robert Lucas with teaching him the importance of rational expectations and central bank credibility. See Interview with Mark H. Willes, www.minneapolisfed.org/about/role/history/willes .cfm.

77. Transcript, Federal Open Market Committee, July 18, 1978, p. 40.

78. The seasonally adjusted monthly rates of inflation in July, August, and September were .8, .6, and .9, which translate into an annual average of 9.2 percent.

79. This quote and those that follow are from the Transcript, Federal Open Market Committee, October 17, 1978, p. 40.

80. The exchange rate was 2.25 marks per dollar on October 31, 1977.

81. *Wall Street Journal*, October 31, 1978, p. 2.

82. Ibid.

83. *Washington Post*, November 1, 1978, p. A26.

84. *Wall Street Journal*, November 6, 1978, p. 1.

85. See *Wall Street Journal*, November 2, 1978, p. 1, and Robert Solomon, *The International Monetary System, 1945–1981* (New York: Harper & Row, 1982), pp. 349–50. Among the key components of the program were: (1) An increase in the discount rate from 8½ to 9½ percent; (2) the United States would issue $10 billion in foreign currency denominated bonds; and (3) the U.S. would draw $3 billion in foreign currency reserves from the International Monetary Fund for use in the dollar-support operation.

86. *New York Times*, November 13, 1978, p. D3.

87. PIPAV.

88. The dollar closed at 1.86 marks on November 1, which is 6 percent above the close of 1.754 on October 31. The standard deviation of overnight returns during the first ten months of 1978 is .686 percent.

89. The close on November 30 was 1.9281, which is 9.9 percent above the 1.754 close on October 31.

90. *Wall Street Journal*, November 2, 1978, p. 4.

91. Ibid.

92. The first three months of 1979 had monthly rates of inflation equal to 0.9,

1.0, and 1.0 percent, which translates (by adding them up and multiplying by four) into an annual rate of 11.6 percent.

93. Transcript, Federal Open Market Committee, March 20, 1979, p. 10.

94. PIPAV. Volcker adds an excuse for 1949: "I needed a job for six months, until I went to Harvard, and that's what I told them. They were very nice and polite when they said they did not hire temporary workers."

95. Transcript, Federal Open Market Committee, March 20, 1979, p. 21.

96. See public law 95-523, October 27, 1978, available at www.eric.ed.gov/PDFS/ED164974.pdf.

97. Public law 95-523 declares (section 102 [2g]) that "trade deficits are a major national problem requiring a strong export policy" but does not discuss exchange rates. The act is nicknamed after its sponsors, Senator Hubert Humphrey and Representative Augustus Hawkins. Prior to the Humphrey-Hawkins Act, the goals of the central bank were codified in the Federal Reserve Reform Act of 1977 as "maximum employment, stable prices, and moderate long-term interest rates." See David E. Lindsey, *A Modern History of FOMC Communication: 1975–2002*, Washington, DC: Board of Governors of the Federal Reserve System, July 24, 2003, p. 27.

98. Transcript, Federal Open Market Committee, March 20, 1979, p. 21.

99. "The Political Economy of the Dollar," the Fred Hirsch Memorial Lecture, Warwick University, Coventry, England, November 9, 1978, published simultaneously in the *Federal Reserve Bank of New York Quarterly Review* 3, no. 4 (Winter 1978–79), and in the January 1979 issue of the *Banker* (London). See *New York Times*, November 10, 1978, p. D2, and the *Times* (London), November 10, 1978, p. 27.

100. "Political Economy of the Dollar," *Quarterly Review*, pp. 10 and 12.

101. Transcript, Federal Open Market Committee, March 20, 1979, p. 21.

102. Frank Morris was not a voting member of the FOMC at this meeting, but he participated in the discussion, as was always the case with nonvoting presidents. His argument did not produce the easing that he wanted, just a policy of "maintaining the weekly average federal funds rate at about the current level" in the FOMC Directive (see Record of Policy Actions of the FOMC for the March 20 meeting, released on April 20, 1979, p. 11). The record also reports that "Messrs. [Paul] Volcker, [Philip] Coldwell, [Monroe] Kimbrel, and [Henry] Wallich dissented from this action because they favored a somewhat more restrictive policy posture, in view of strong inflationary forces."

103. *New York Times*, April 21, 1979, p. 29.

104. The annual rate of inflation averaged 12.8 percent during April, May, and June 1979, compared with an average of 11.6 during the first three months of 1979, and 8.4 during the last three months of 1978.

105. *New York Times*, February 1, 1979, p. A14.

106. This account comes from the *New York Times*, June 23, 1979, p. 19.

107. Ibid.

108. *New York Times*, June 10, 1979, p. 1.

109. This account comes from the *New York Times*, March 26, 1979, p. A14.

110. This quote and the remaining quotes in this paragraph are from the transcript of the talk as printed in the *New York Times*, July 16, 1979, p. A10.

111. See *Washington Post*, July 20, 1979, p. E1.

112. See *New York Times*, April 21, 1979, p. 29.

113. *New York Times*, July 20, 1979, p. A1 continued.

114. *Washington Post*, July 21, 1979, p. B1.

115. The afternoon fixing in London (10:00 A.M. New York time) on June 17 was $296.30. The morning fixing on July 18 was $303.85, a jump of 2.55 percent. The overnight standard deviation of gold returns during the first six months of 1979 was 1.28 percent.

116. *New York Times*, July 19, 1979, p. A1 continued.

117. This quote and the remaining ones in this paragraph are from the *New York Times*, July 21, 1979, p. 25.

118. *Washington Post*, July 24, 1979, p. A5, and *New York Times*, July 24, 1979, p. A1.

119. PIPAV.

120. The following conversation is based on my discussions with Ritter while we coauthored the textbook *Principles of Money Banking and Financial Markets*, and on discussions with Volcker and Kavesh.

8. Challenge

1. Personal Letters from 1979, Papers of Paul Volcker, Federal Reserve Bank of New York Archives, Box 95714.

2. PIPAV.

3. Personal Letters from 1979, Papers of Paul Volcker, Federal Reserve Bank of New York Archives, Box 95714.

4. Letter dated September 12, 1979, Federal Reserve Bank of New York Archives, Box 95714.

5. See interview with Shultz at www.turmoilandtriumph.org/shultz/economics_tradition.php.

6. Milton Friedman, "The Optimum Quantity of Money," in Friedman, *The Optimum Quantity of Money and Other Essays* (Chicago: Aldine, 1969), pp. 1–50.

7. See Milton Friedman, *Money Mischief: Episodes in Monetary History* (New York: Harcourt Brace and Company, 1994), p. 49.

8. Milton Friedman, "The Fed: At It Again," *Newsweek*, February 19, 1979, p. 65.

9. Interview with Milton Friedman, Academy of Achievement, Stanford, CA, July 31, 1991, p. 6, available at www.achievement.org.

10. *New York Times*, July 29, 1979, p. F1 continued.

11. Milton Friedman, "Burns on the Outside," *Newsweek*, January 9, 1978, p. 52.

12. Milton Friedman and Anna J. Schwartz, *A Monetary History of the United States, 1867–1960* (Princeton, NJ: Princeton University Press, 1963), p. 692. They are quoting and agreeing with Carl Snyder, who worked at the New York Fed.

13. Volcker's dissent on March 20, 1979, was discussed in detail in the previous chapter. He dissented in the following meeting on April 17, 1979, as well. See Transcript, Federal Open Market Committee, April 17, 1979.

14. *New York Times*, July 29, 1979, p. F1.

15. *Washington Post*, July 2, 1978, p. A6.

16. *Wall Street Journal*, July 10, 1978, p. 15.

17. *New York Times*, July 3, 1978, p. 32.

18. *New York Times*, July 30, 1979, p. D1.

19. The notes are in the Personal Papers of Paul Volcker and are reproduced in the section entitled "Personal Records and Correspondence."

20. This conversation is based on the recollection of Paul Volcker.

21. Dr. Michael Lockshin is the director of the Barbara Volcker Center for Women and Rheumatic Disease at the Hospital for Special Surgery in Manhattan. The center was endowed by a gift from Barbara and Paul Volcker.

22. Handwritten letter from Dillon to Volcker dated July 27, 1979, Personal Letters from 1979, Papers of Paul Volcker, Federal Reserve Bank of New York Archives, Box 95714.

23. PIPAV.

24. See www.federalreserve.gov/generalinfo/virtualtour/architecture.cfm.

25. The boardroom is fifty-six feet long and thirty-two feet wide. A regulation basketball court is ninety-four feet long and fifty feet wide, making half-court forty-seven feet by fifty feet. Thus the boardroom is longer and somewhat narrower than a half-court basketball court, but the high ceiling would make it eminently serviceable for a good game.

26. Transcript, Federal Open Market Committee Meeting, August 14, 1979, p. 1.

27. Ibid., p. 20.

28. Ibid., p. 21.

29. See the discussion in the last chapter of Volcker's speech to the Boston Economic Club in December 1976.

30. Transcript, Federal Open Market Committee Meeting, August 14, 1979, p. 21.

31. Ibid., p. 22–23.

32. Transcript, Federal Open Market Committee Meeting, September 18, 1979, p. 35.

33. Ibid., p. 44.

34. Ibid., p. 35.

35. *New York Times*, September 19, 1979, p. 1.

36. The Board of Governors approved a half-point increase in the discount rate to 10½ percent on August 16, 1979. See Minutes, Board of Governors, August 16, 1979.

37. PIPAV.

38. *New York Times*, September 19, 1979, p. 1.

39. *New York Times*, September 20, 1979, p. 1, continued on D9.

40. PIPAV.

41. *New York Times*, September 19, 1979, p. 1.

42. Ibid.

43. The intraday high on the Commodity Exchange on September 18 was 376.25 (*New York Times*, September 19, 1979, p. 1). The London afternoon gold fixing was 375.75 on September 18, compared with 351.75 on September 17, an increase of 6.8 percent. The standard deviation of daily returns on gold in the London fixing equaled 1.36 percent during the first eight months of 1979.

44. PIPAV.

45. *Washington Post*, September 19, 1979, p. A1.

46. Solomon's comments on gold are from the *New York Times*, September 23, 1979, p. E1. The Carter quote is from William Neikirk, *Volcker: Portrait of the Money Man* (New York: Congdon and Weed, 1987), p. 2.

47. Letter dated September 12, 1979, from Volcker to Kaufman, Personal Letters from 1979, Papers of Paul Volcker, Federal Reserve Bank of New York Archives, Box 95714.

48. Transcript, Federal Open Market Committee Meeting, September 18, 1979, pp. 13–14.

49. The untitled, unsigned draft, dated September 27, 1979, is from the Personal Papers of Paul Volcker. Interviews with Axilrod and Sternlight confirm that they began drafting their memorandum to Volcker within days of the September 18 discount rate announcement. Their final memorandum to the FOMC is dated October 4, 1979, Personal Papers of Paul Volcker.

50. This discussion relies on Edward Jay Epstein, *The Rise and Fall of Diamonds* (New York: Simon & Schuster, 1982), pp. 57–59.

51. See Transcript, Federal Open Market Committee, March 29, 1976, tape 5, pp. 16–17, Papers of Arthur Burns, University of Michigan Library, Ann Arbor, MI.

52. "The Role of Monetary Targets in an Age of Inflation," *Journal of Monetary Economics* 4, no. 2 (April 1978): 330.

53. Ibid., 332.

54. PIPAV.

55. William Greider, *Secrets of the Temple: How the Federal Reserve Runs the Country* (New York: Simon & Schuster, 1987), p. 105.

56. Transcript, Federal Open Market Committee Meeting, October 6, 1979, p. 19.

9. The Plan

1. Transcript, Federal Open Market Committee Conference Call, October 5, 1979, p. 5.

2. The remaining quotes in the telephone conference are from ibid., p. 3.

3. The following conversation is based on an interview with Charles Schultze.

4. The dollar had fluctuated between 1.81 and 1.83 marks during the two months since Volcker was appointed chairman. On September 18, the day of the split vote on the discount rate, the dollar closed at 1.8115 marks. The 1.74 figure is 4 percent below 1.8115.

5. *New York Times*, September 24, 1979, p. A1 continued.

6. The quotes in this paragraph are from the *New York Times*, September 30, 1979, p. 13, and anticipated in the *New York Times*, September 28, 1979, p. A1 continued.

7. Interview with Charles Schultze.

8. PIPAV. See Joseph Treaster, *Paul Volcker: The Making of a Financial Legend* (New York: John Wiley, 2004), p. 151, for a slightly different version of this quote: "Schmidt was at his irascible worst—or best."

9. *New York Times*, September 30, 1979, p. 13.

10. The lecture is published by the Per Jacobsson Foundation, International Monetary Fund, Washington, DC.

11. Ibid., p. 4.

12. Arthur Burns, "The Anguish of Central Banking," the 1979 Per Jacobsson Lecture, Belgrade, Yugoslavia, September 30, 1979, p. 7.

13. Ibid., p. 9.

14. Ibid., p. 13.

15. Milton Friedman, "Burns on the Outside," *Newsweek*, January 9, 1978, p. 52.

16. Burns, "The Anguish of Central Banking," p. 16.

17. The following quotes are from William Safire, *Before the Fall: An Inside View of the Pre-Watergate White House* (New York: Doubleday and Co., 1975), p. 515.

18. *New York Times*, October 1, 1979, p. D1.

19. *Wall Street Journal*, October 1, 1979, p. 6.

20. The London close on Friday, September 28, was 397.25, and the close on Monday, October 1, 1979, was $414.75, a close-to-close change of 4.4 percent. The daily standard deviation of returns on gold equaled 1.5 percent from January 1, 1979, through September 28, 1979.

21. See *New York Times*, October 3, 1979, p. D1. A nice description of the mechanics of the gold fixing appears in "Gold Fixing: London Tradition," *New York Times*, February 12, 1979.

22. *New York Times*, October 3, 1979, p. D1.

23. *Wall Street Journal*, October 3, 1979, p. 1.

24. *New York Times*, October 3, 1979, p. D1.

25. Ibid.

26. PIPAV.

27. I toured the Special Library in the summer of 2009 and discovered the following six nameplates attached to the table: Adolph Miller, Charles Hamlin, Paul Warburg, W. P. G. Harding, Daniel Crissinger, and the Comptroller of the Currency. Those nameplates belong to the original members of the first Federal Reserve Board appointed by Woodrow Wilson, except for Crissinger, who was appointed in 1923 by President Harding. The comptroller is ex officio (belonging to the Office of Comptroller), hence does not bear the name of John Skelton Williams, the first comptroller to sit on the Federal Reserve Board. My tour guide (Joseph Pavel) did not know why Crissinger's nameplate had replaced that of Frederic Delano, the sixth member of the first board. I provide an explanation of the missing seventh nameplate in the next paragraph.

28. The Board of Governors of the Federal Reserve System (at www.federal reserve.gov/bios/boardmembership.htm) lists Charles Hamlin as the first chairman of the Federal Reserve Board. Hamlin was, in fact, designated as governor by Woodrow Wilson. The first chairman of the Federal Reserve Board was William McAdoo, the secretary of the treasury at the time the Fed was created. See William L. Silber, *When Washington Shut Down Wall Street:*

The Great Financial Crisis of 1914 and the Origins of America's Monetary Supremacy (Princeton, NJ: Princeton University Press, 2007), p. 18.

29. Frederick Schultz, appointed vice-chairman of the board by Jimmy Carter, blamed "errors in judgment and structural flaws" for the Fed's poor performance during the Great Depression. The first structural problem mentioned is "The Treasury secretary sat on the Federal Reserve Board, so decisions were politicized." See Frederick Schultz, "The Changing Role of the Federal Reserve," in *Reflections on Monetary Policy 25 Years After October 1979, Federal Reserve Bank of St. Louis* 87, no. 2, part 2 (March/April 2005): 343.

30. See the discussion of the Minutes of the Board of Governors meeting on October 4, in David Lindsey, Athanasios Orphanides, and Robert Rasche, "The Reform of October 1979: How It Happened and Why," in *Reflections on Monetary Policy 25 Years After October 1979, Federal Reserve Bank of St. Louis* 87, no. 2, part 2 (March/April 2005): 199.

31. The following quote is from the Transcript, Federal Open Market Committee Meeting, October 6, 1979, p. 13. The Minutes of the Board of Governors meeting on October 4 (see the previous note) simply summarizes what was said without direct attribution. However, Partee's quote from October 6 is precisely the sentiment summarized in the Minutes of the October 4 meeting of the Board of Governors. Also note that Partee interrupts Volcker on October 6 (Transcript, Federal Open Market Committee Meeting, October 6, 1979, p. 12) to say "Lead went up 20 percent."

32. Transcript, Federal Open Market Committee Meeting, October 6, 1979, p. 4.

33. Ibid., pp. 7, 8.

34. Ibid., p. 8, 9.

35. Ibid., p. 9.

36. Ibid., p. 10.

37. Ibid., p. 24.

38. Ibid., p. 14.

39. Ibid.

40. Ibid.

41. Ibid.

42. Ibid., p. 19.

43. Ibid.

44. Ibid., pp. 19–20.

45. Ibid., p. 20.

46. See Joseph Coyne, "Reflections on the FOMC Meeting of October 6, 1979," in *Reflections on Monetary Policy 25 Years After October 1979, Federal Reserve Bank of St. Louis*, 313.

47. See page 1 of the transcript of the press conference with Paul Volcker, October 6, 1979, located at fraser.stlouisfed.org/historicaldocs/787.

48. See *Washington Post*, October 7, 1979, p. A1.

49. The questions and answers at the press conference are from the transcript of the press conference with Paul Volcker, October 6, 1979, located at fraser.stlouisfed.org/historicaldocs/787/, pp. 4, 7, 8.

50. See William Greider, *Secrets of the Temple: How the Federal Reserve Runs the Country* (New York: Simon & Schuster, 1987), p. 123. Greider wrote for *Rolling Stone* at the time he authored this book and had been a reporter for the *Washington Post* before that (see williamgreider.com/about).

51. This quote and the following interchange between Proxmire and Volcker are from *The Nomination of Paul A. Volcker to Be Chairman, Board of Governors of the Federal Reserve System: Hearings Before the Committee on Banking, Housing, and Urban Affairs*, U.S. Senate, 96th Congress, 1st Sess., July 30, 1979, U.S. Government Printing Office, Washington, DC, pp. 4–5.

52. *New York Times*, December 16, 2005, p. B13.

53. Transcript, Federal Open Market Committee Meeting, August 14, 1979, p. 21.

54. PIPAV. Volcker was referring both to Sargent (who won the Nobel Prize in Economics in 2011) and to Neil Wallace. Both men were at the University of Minnesota and were advisers to the Federal Reserve Bank of Minneapolis. Their work on the impotence of monetary policy includes Thomas Sargent and Neil Wallace, "Rational Expectations, the Optimal Monetary Instrument, and the Optimal Money Supply Rule," *Journal of Political Economy* 83, no. 2 (April 1975); and Thomas Sargent and Neil Wallace, "Rational Expectations and the Theory of Economic Policy," *Journal of Monetary Economics* 2, no. 2 (April 1976).

55. See the reference in chapter 7 to "Reconciling Our Short- and Long-run Goals in Economic Policy," a speech delivered to the Boston Economic Club, December 15, 1976, Personal Papers of Paul Volcker, pp. 11–12.

10. Sticking to It

1. *New York Times*, October 14, 1979, p. E18.

2. *New York Times*, October 21, 1979, p. D1.

3. *New York Times*, December 2, 1979, p. SM15. Meltzer's three-volume history, entitled *A History of the Federal Reserve System*, is published by the University of Chicago Press. Volume 1, published in 2003, covers the period

1913–1951; volume 2, book 1, published in 2009, covers 1951–1969; and volume 2, book 2, also published in 2009, covers 1970–1986.

4. PIPAV.

5. The exchange rate of 1.794 marks per dollar is reported "in Frankfurt" in the *New York Times* (October 9, 1979, p. A1) and the *Washington Post* (October 9, 1979, p. F1). The daily standard deviation of returns on dollar-mark equaled 0.38 percent, and the daily standard deviation of returns on gold equaled 2.0 percent from August 1, 1979, through September 30, the two months since Volcker's appointment. Thus the 2.0 percent increase in dollar mark is statistically significant, while the 3.3 percent decline in gold is not.

6. *New York Times*, October 9, 1979, p. A1 continued.

7. *Washington Post*, October 9, 1979, p. F1 continued.

8. Ibid., p. F1.

9. *Washington Post*, October 17, 1979, p. A23.

10. *New York Times*, October 11, 1979, p. D1.

11. The standard deviation of daily interest rate changes in the ten-year bond rate equaled .41 percent during the first nine months of 1979 and .45 percent from August 1, 1979, through September 30, the two months since Volcker's appointment. On October 9, 1979, the ten-year rate increased by 3.44 percent. (The numbers in this note are percentage change, not percentage points.)

12. For July 1975 the ten-year bond rate averaged 8.06 percent and the federal funds rate averaged 6.09 percent. For July 1974 the ten-year rate averaged 7.8 percent and the federal funds rate averaged 12.95 percent.

13. The rate on November 19, 1979, was 10.8 percent and it was 10.78 percent on November 20, 1979.

14. Transcript, Federal Open Market Committee Meeting, November 20, 1979, p. 29.

15. The transcript includes "Mark" in the omitted section in the previous quotation.

16. Transcript, Federal Open Market Committee Meeting, November 20, 1979, p. 30.

17. Ibid., p. 23.

18. Arthur Burns, "The Anguish of Central Banking," the 1979 Per Jacobsson Lecture, Belgrade, Yugoslavia, September 30, 1979, p. 16.

19. See Transcript, Federal Open Market Committee Meeting, November 20, 1979, p. 24, for the remaining quotes in this section .

20. William Greider, *Secrets of the Temple: How the Federal Reserve Runs the Country* (New York: Simon & Schuster, 1987), p. 105.

21. The $850 afternoon London gold fixing on January 21, 1980, was the highest recorded price until the $858.85 afternoon fixing on January 3, 2008.

The price rose during January 2008 and ended at $923.00 on January 31, 2008.

22. See *New York Times*, January 19, 1980, p. 29, for gold responding to the Russian invasion of Afghanistan, and *New York Times*, December 6, 1979, p. D12, for gold responding to rumors of the murder of American hostages in Iran. The annual rate of inflation during the last three months of 1979 was 13.2, 13.2, and 14.4 for October, November, and December, respectively.

23. The afternoon gold fixing on November 19, 1979, was $389.85.

24. The quotes and reports in this paragraph are from the *New York Times*, January 12, 1980, p. 27.

25. The quotes and reports in this paragraph are from the *New York Times*, January 27, 1980, p. WC1.

26. On April 1, 1980, the afternoon fixing in London was $509.50. On April 30 it was $518.00.

27. *Washington Post*, November 4, 1979, p. M1.

28. *New York Times*, March 8, 1980, p. 29.

29. Okun is quoted in the *New York Times*, March 7, 1980, p. D2. He died on March 23, 1980, two weeks after his prediction, so he did not live to see his forecast validated.

30. The prime rate was 17.75 percent on March 7, when Okun made his statement. It rose to 20 percent on April 2. The all-time high of 21.5 percent occurred in December 1980.

31. Reports of the Cincotta protest appeared in the *Chicago Tribune*, April 15, 1980, p. C1, and April 17, 1980, p. B2, and in the *New York Times*, April 15, 1980, p. D7.

32. *Chicago Tribune*, April 15, 1980, p. C1.

33. See Joseph Coyne, "Reflections on the FOMC Meeting of October 6, 1979," in *Reflections on Monetary Policy 25 Years After October 1979*, Federal Reserve Bank of St. Louis 87, no. 2, part 2 (March/April 2005): 314.

34. *Chicago Tribune*, April 17, 1980, p. B2.

35. The annual rates of inflation in the first four months of 1980 were 16.8, 15.6, 16.8, and 12.0 percent, for an average of 15.2 percent.

36. See the transcript of Carter's message in the *New York Times*, March 15, 1980, p. 34.

37. See Paul Volcker and Toyoo Gyohten, *Changing Fortunes: The World's Money and the Threat to American Leadership* (New York: Times Books, 1992), p. 171.

38. *New York Times*, October 10, 1979, p. D5.

39. *New York Times*, October 13, 1979, p. 31.

40. *New York Times*, October 10, 1979, p. D5.

41. From *Implementation of the Credit Control Act Pursuant to Executive Order 12201: Hearings before the Senate Committee on Banking, Housing, and Urban Affairs*, 96th Congress, 2nd Sess., March 14, 1980, U.S. Government Printing Office, Washington, DC, March 18, 1980, p. 17.

42. See *New York Times*, March 19, 1980, p. D4; and ibid.

43. See Stacey L. Schreft, "Credit Controls: 1980," *Federal Reserve Bank of Richmond Economic Review* 76, no. 6 (November/December 1990): 25–43.

44. See *New York Times*, March 30, 1980, p. F1.

45. Ibid.

46. See Monetary Aggregates and Money Market Conditions, prepared for the May 16, 1980, FOMC meeting, pp. 1–5. The so-called blue book (named for the color of the cover) begins with "The record decline in demand deposits in April led to a contraction in all of the targeted monetary aggregates last month . . . The underlying weakness in money supply over the past several weeks most likely reflects not only the lagged effect of previous high interest rates, but also net repayment of bank debt at a time of sizable reduction in economic activity."

47. The federal funds rate was 11.57 percent on May 6, compared with 19.78 percent on April 7.

48. Transcript, Federal Open Market Committee Meeting, May 6, 1980, p. 4.

49. Ibid., p. 5.

50. The Federal Open Market Committee's Directive since October 6, 1979, established a reserve growth path consistent with its money-supply target combined with a wide band on the federal funds rate, usually four percentage points. Whenever the funds rate slipped towards its lower or upper band there would be consultation (as with the May 6, 1980, conference call) among the committee members about whether to widen the bands. Also see David E. Lindsey, *A Modern History of FOMC Communication*, Washington, DC: Board of Governors of the Federal Reserve System, June 24, 2003, p. 45.

51. Transcript, Federal Open Market Committee Meeting, May 6, 1980, p. 5.

52. See Transcript, Federal Open Market Committee Meeting, October 6, 1979, p. 43, for the following exchange among Volcker, Wallich, and Teeters:

> VOLCKER: Let me say again that if we adopt this technique, I don't think we can be at all sure where the fed funds rate will go in the very short run.
>
> WALLICH: It doesn't matter all that much.
>
> VOLCKER: And it doesn't matter all that much.
>
> WALLICH: It would disavow us.
>
> VOLCKER: No.

TEETERS: It matters to you, Henry, if it goes down.

WALLICH: Yes.

TEETERS: It doesn't matter to me if it goes down.

53. Transcript, Federal Open Market Committee Meeting, May 6, 1980, p. 5.

54. Transcript, Federal Open Market Committee Meeting, October 6, 1979, p. 20.

55. Transcript, Federal Open Market Committee Meeting, May 6, 1980, p. 5.

56. The federal funds rate averaged 19.38 percent during the first week of April 1980 and averaged 9.44 percent during the first week of July.

57. *New York Times*, July 21, 1980, p. D4.

58. The afternoon gold fixing on April 1, 1980, was $509.50. The dollar-mark exchange rate on April 1 was 1.9615 and on July 1 it was 1.7615.

59. See *New York Times*, May 31, 1980, p. 23. I wrote this op-ed article, which is entitled "Rates of Interest," and sent it to Volcker before it was accepted for publication. He sent the following note to me, dated May 27, 1980 (before the article was published): "Dear Bill: Thanks for sending me the piece you submitted to the Times. The analysis is right on the mark and the message needs to be fully understood. Sincerely, Paul."

60. For a comparison of the monetary growth rates (M1, M2, and M3) for the first half of 1980 with 1979, see *The Federal Reserve's Second Monetary Policy Report for 1980: Hearings Before the Senate Committee on Banking, Housing and Urban Affairs*, 96th Congress, 2nd Sess., July 21, 22, 1980, U.S. Government Printing Office, Washington, DC, 1980, pp. 150–52.

61. *New York Times*, July 21, 1980, p. D4.

62. See Thomas Sargent, "The Ends of Four Big Inflations," in Thomas Sargent, *Rational Expectations and Inflation* (New York: Harper & Row, 1986). The first draft of "The Ends of Four Big Inflations" was completed in August 1980, and the first reference to it appeared in Preston Miller, "Deficit Policies, Deficit Fallacies," *Federal Reserve Bank of Minneapolis Quarterly Review* 4, no. 3 (Summer 1980). Miller was an assistant vice president in the Federal Reserve Bank of Minneapolis.

63. Sargent, "The Ends of Four Big Inflations," pp. 97 and 100.

64. The quote is from Thomas Sargent, "Stopping Moderate Inflations: The Methods of Poincare and Thatcher," in Thomas Sargent, *Rational Expectations and Inflation*, 2nd ed. (New York: HarperCollins, 1993), p. 122, including note 3. Sargent made this point in connection with a discussion of Margaret Thatcher's policies to control inflation in Britain. He said (pp. 121–22), "Mrs. Thatcher came to power against the background of over 20 years of stop-go or reversible government policy actions. Her economic policy actions are

vigorously opposed both by members of the Labor Party and by a strong new party, the Social Democrats . . . In addition, throughout her administration, speculation has waxed and waned about whether Mrs. Thatcher herself would be driven to implement a U-turn in macroeconomic policy actions, and whether her stringent monetary policy actions would be reversed by the Conservative Party itself, by choosing a new party leader . . . For all of these reasons, it is difficult to interpret Thatcher's policy actions in terms of the kind of once-and-for-all, widely believed, uncontroversial, and irreversible regime change that rational expectations equilibrium theories assert can cure inflation at little or no cost in terms of real output."

65. PIPAV. Volcker also recognized the limitations of the Thatcher experiment. "If you want to know about the difficulties of monetarism, look [at the English experience]. They have a government with a five-year lease on life, totally dedicated to the proposition of monetary restraint as the way to kill inflation and totally prepared, [at least] verbally, to take the budgetary measures that they thought appropriate to accompany that . . . [But] they are battling . . . to establish their credibility . . . I wish Mrs. Thatcher well, but I don't think she has all that much of a constituency in the United Kingdom now." (See Transcript, Federal Open Market Committee Meeting, December 18–19, 1980, pp. 61–62.)

11. New Territory

1. *New York Times*, October 3, 1980, pp. A1 and A19.
2. *New York Times*, October 4, 1979, p. 1.
3. Ibid.
4. *Washington Post*, October 4, 1980, p. C1.
5. Transcript, Federal Open Market Committee Meeting, October 21, 1980, p. 54.
6. The discount rate was last increased during an election year on August 24, 1956, a month earlier than in 1980. The increase was from 2.75 percent to 3.00 percent (see research.stlouisfed.org/fred2/data/).
7. See Minutes of the Board of Governors of the Federal Reserve System, September 25, 1980, p. 3.
8. *New York Times*, September 27, 1980, p. 29.
9. *New York Times*, October 5, 1980, p. E4. According to Abrams, "How Richard Nixon Pressured Arthur Burns: Evidence from the Nixon Tapes," *Journal of Economic Perspective* 20, no. 4 (2006): 186, "Most empirical studies

of the behavior of the Federal Reserve prior to presidential elections have not uncovered evidence of a political monetary cycle, which has supported the view that the Fed is independent. However . . . without invoking political pressure, the surge of expansionary monetary policy leading up to the 1972 election seems hard to explain."

10. *Wall Street Journal*, October 6, 1980, p. 34.

11. PIPAV.

12. Ibid.

13. *Wall Street Journal*, June 3, 1980, p. 6.

14. *New York Times*, October 31, 1980, p. D2.

15. See Record of Policy Actions of the Federal Open Market Committee Meeting held on October 6, 1979, pp. 4–5. "Most [FOMC] members strongly supported a shift in the conduct of open market operations to an approach placing emphasis on supplying the volume of bank reserves estimated to be consistent with the desired rates of growth in monetary aggregates, while permitting much greater fluctuations in the federal funds rate than heretofore. A few members, while urging strong action to restrain monetary growth, expressed some preference for continuing to direct daily open market operations toward maintenance of levels of the federal funds rate . . . Committee members recognized that for a number of reasons the relationship between growth of various reserve measures and growth of the monetary aggregates was not precise; thus the shift in emphasis to controlling reserves improved prospects for achievement of the Committee's objectives for monetary growth over the next few months but did not assure it."

16. For example, the Federal Open Market Committee's Directive on September 16, 1980, p. 10, reads: "In the short run, the Committee seeks expansion of reserve aggregates consistent with growth of [alternative measures of the money supply] M-1A, M-1B, and M-2, over the August to December period at annual rates of about 4 percent, $6\frac{1}{2}$ percent, and $8\frac{1}{2}$ percent respectively, provided that in the period before the next regular meeting the weekly average federal funds rate remains within a range of 8 to 14 percent. If it appears during the period before the next meeting that the constraint on the federal funds rate is inconsistent with the objective for the expansion of reserves, the Manager for Domestic Operations is promptly to notify the Chairman, who will then decide whether the situation calls for supplementary instructions from the Committee."

17. See Marvin Goodfriend and Robert G. King, "The Incredible Volcker Disinflation," *Journal of Monetary Economics* 52, no. 5 (July 2005), esp. pp. 1007–12, for an excellent description of Volcker's mixed strategy of controlling reserves and interest rates over different time horizons.

18. *New York Times*, December 31, 1980, p. D2.

19. *Wall Street Journal*, June 3, 1980, p. 6.

20. The following interchange among Lawrence Roos, Paul Volcker, and Lyle Gramley on the predictability and relevance of money growth comes from the Transcript of the FOMC Meeting of September 16, 1980, pp. 8–9.

21. See Minutes of the Board of Governors of the Federal Reserve System, September 25, 1980, p. 3. The FOMC had voted no change in policy in the meeting of September 16, 1980. The immediate cause for the change in the discount rate on September 25 was that "the federal funds rate, which averaged 10.85 percent in the latest statement week, now was around 11.25 percent; and weekly average borrowings from the Federal Reserve had risen to $1.6 billion." (See Minutes of the Board of Governors of the Federal Reserve System, September 25, 1980, p. 3.)

22. See Record of Policy Actions of the Federal Open Market Committee Meeting held on October 21, 1980, p. 8. Four dissents, led by Larry Roos and Henry Wallich, urged even more restraint (see p. 13).

23. On September 24, 1980, the federal funds rate was 10.92 percent, and on November 3, 1980, it was 14.06 percent.

24. The quotes in this paragraph are from Jimmy Carter, *White House Diary* (New York: Farrar, Straus and Giroux, 2010), pp. 347–48.

25. Volcker's Daily Planner for 1980 lists a 5:30 P.M. meeting on November 19 with Burns.

26. The meeting Burns attended is reported in the *Los Angeles Times*, November 14, 1980, p. B10.

27. The following conversation is based on Paul Volcker's recollection and the document cited in the next note.

28. The exact quote Burns refers to is as follows: "The Federal Reserve is an independent agency. However, independence should not mean lack of accountability for what it does. In practice, independence has not meant that the Federal Reserve is immune to Presidential and Congressional influence. The problem is to assure accountability while preserving independence." It appears on page 11 of "Economic Strategy for the Reagan Administration: A Report to President-Elect Ronald Reagan from His Coordinating Committee on Economic Policy," dated November 16, 1980 (Murray Weidenbaum Papers, University Archives, Department of Special Collections, Washington, University Libraries, Box 8). It is signed by George Shultz (chairman), Arthur Burns, Milton Friedman, Alan Greenspan, Michael Halbouty, Jack Kemp, James Lynn, Paul McCracken, William Simon, Charls Walker, Murray Weidenbaum, Caspar Weinberger, and Walter Wriston.

29. PIPAV.

30. See *New York Times*, June 8, 1980, p. F1 continued. A reporter describes Friedman's view as "the monetary authorities don't even have to look at the money supply itself . . . all they have to do is keep adding reserves at a steady rate." A luncheon companion said to Friedman, "In other words, you would not need the Fed, only a computer." Friedman replied, "Indeed."

31. The *New York Times*, December 5, 1980, p. D2, reported, "Mr. Wriston has made Citibank famous as a center of monetarist thought and policy advice."

32. Milton Friedman and Robert Roosa, *The Balance of Payments: Free Versus Fixed Exchange Rates* (Washington, DC: American Enterprise Institute, 1967).

33. PIPAV.

34. A letter from Reagan to Gordon Luce (CEO of a California savings bank) dated July 23, 1981, reads as follows: "Dear Gordon. Thanks very much for your letter and for the observations about the Federal Reserve . . . I've passed your essay on to our economic types to see if they have an answer to whether the Federal Reserve is really necessary." See *Reagan: A Life in Letters*, ed. Kiron Skinner, Annelise Anderson, and Martin Anderson (New York: Free Press, 2003), pp. 298-99.

35. This and the next quote are from the Transcript, Federal Open Market Committee Meeting, November 18, 1980, pp. 51-52.

36. The 13 percent discount rate established on December 5, 1980, matched the 13 percent rate established on February 15, 1980. The federal funds rate first broke through 20 percent on December 11, 1980. (The highest level before that was 19.96 percent on April 3, 1980.) The federal funds rate remained above 20 percent between December 16 and December 19, 1980. It hit an all-time high of 22 percent on the last day of the year.

37. Transcript, Federal Open Market Committee Meeting, December 18-19, 1980, p. 49.

38. Ibid., p. 53.

39. Allan Meltzer, *A History of the Federal Reserve*, vol. 2, book 2 (Chicago: University of Chicago Press, 2009), p. 1073, treats Partee's statement as simply recognizing that inflation is now an explicit Federal Reserve target. Given that Partee's point follows Gramley's proposal for a weak economy, I think Partee is complaining that this policy requires a judgment on the trade-off against a weak economy. Volcker confirms this interpretation despite his quote from the transcript in the next paragraph.

40. The following quotes are from the Transcript, Federal Open Market Committee Meeting, December 18-19, 1980, pp. 61-63.

41. Moral hazard is the concept that insurance against loss changes the insured's behavior to make that loss more likely. Economist Kenneth Arrow was one of the first to use moral hazard in the economics literature. See "Uncer-

tainty and the Welfare Economics of Medical Care," *American Economic Review* 43, no. 5 (December 1963): 941–73.

42. William Shakespeare, *Timon of Athens*, Act 3, Scene 5.

43. Transcript, *Issues and Answers*, ABC, August 30, 1981, p. 15.

44. See Paul Volcker, "We Can Survive Prosperity," Remarks at the Joint Meeting of the American Economic Association—American Finance Association, San Francisco, CA, December 28, 1983, p. 5.

45. Inflation during the last three months of 1980 was 12.0, 13.2, and 10.8 percent per annum.

46. *Chicago Tribune*, December 15, 1980, p. C2.

47. Ibid.

48. *Washington Post*, November 30, 1980, p. H1 continued.

49. See Martin Anderson, *Revolution: The Reagan Legacy* (Stanford, CA: Hoover Institution Press, 1988), pp. 250–53, for his recollection of this incident. It differs from Volcker's. Anderson writes that Volcker did not want to come to the Oval Office to meet the president, while Volcker recalls that Anderson did not offer that option.

50. PIPAV.

51. The year-over-year inflation rate in December 1980 was 12.4 percent, compared with 13.3 percent for December 1979.

52. The ten-year Treasury bond rate was 11.75 percent on September 24, 1980, compared with 12.43 on December 31, 1980.

53. The following conversation is based on three sources: Anderson, *Revolution*, pp. 250–51; the *New York Times*, January 24, 1981, p. 1; and the recollection of Paul Volcker. I deferred to Volcker's version on crucial details. (He insists he was sitting on the president's left, not on the right, as Anderson claims.)

54. *New York Times*, December 14, 1980, p. E5. Donald Regan's complete quote is "Well, the Federal Reserve is tightening money. That's the price we have to pay for the inflation that this country finds itself in. It's the only game in town—it's the only way that inflation can be stopped at the current moment. When this administration takes over we'll have a new economic policy with which we'll deal with inflation in several ways at once rather than just one way."

12. The Only Game in Town

1. *New York Times*, January 20, 1982, p. A1 continued.

2. The Kemp-Roth tax bill, more formally known as the Economic Recovery Tax Act of 1981, was signed by the president on August 13, 1981.

3. Civilian Unemployment Rate, U.S. Department of Labor: Bureau of Labor Statistics, for January 1982 versus January 1981 (source: research.stlouisfed .org/fred2/).

4. The annual rate of inflation from December 1980 through December 1981 was 8.9 percent, compared with 12.4 percent for December 1979 through December 1980.

5. *The Reagan Diaries*, ed. Douglas Brinkley, vol. 1 (New York: HarperCollins, 2009), p. 65.

6. *New York Times*, July 26, 1981, p. F18. Schmidt was referring to Germany. Edward Hyman, an economist with the brokerage firm C. J. Lawrence, commented, "Believe it or not, real interest rates in the United States have been this high or higher before." He cites 1920, 1921, and 1930.

7. On January 20, 1981, the ten-year government bond rate stood at 12.5 percent. On January 19, 1982, the ten-year bond rate was 14.8 percent.

8. The monthly payment on a 12 percent twenty-year mortgage of $100,000 is $1,100. If the rate were 14 percent, the monthly payment would rise to $1,243. The difference of $143 times 12 equals $1,716.

9. See Transcript, *New York Times*, January 20, 1982, p. A20.

10. *The Conduct of Monetary Policy, Pursuant to the Full Employment and Balanced Growth Act of 1978: Hearings Before the House Committee on Banking, Finance and Urban Affairs*, P.L. 95-523, 97th Congress, 1st Sess., July 14, 21–23, 1981, pp. 211 and 212.

11. Gonzalez threatened impeachment in July 1981 (see ibid.) but did not act until January 1983. See *Congressional Record*, 98th Congress, 1st Sess., January 6, 1983, p. 143.

12. *New York Times*, September 2, 1981, p. D2.

13. Monthly inflation for October, November, and December of 1981 measured 0.3, 0.4, and 0.3 percent, which translates into an annual average of 4 percent, while in the last three months of 1980 it measured 1.0, 1.1, and 0.9 percent, for an annual average of 12 percent.

14. In 1982 the survey measured expected inflation for one year forward, so the numbers do not match the long-term horizon that is relevant for the ten-year bond rate. The one-year-forward expected inflation in the fourth quarter of 1981 measured 7.52 percent compared with 9.37 percent in 1980. Expectations for all future time horizons should move in the same direction, although by smaller amounts. For example, a simple linear regression from 1992 through 2008 of quarterly changes in the ten-year inflation forecast versus changes in the one-year inflation forecast produces a statistically significant regression coefficient of .16. The Survey of Professional Forecasters began in 1968 and was conducted by the American Statistical Association and the

National Bureau of Economic Research. The Federal Reserve Bank of Philadelphia took over the survey in 1990.

15. The structural deficit is the deficit that would prevail at full employment. Benjamin Friedman, "Learning from the Reagan Deficits," *American Economic Review* 82, no. 2 (May 1992): 299–304, shows in Table 1 that the structural deficit measured 2.3 percent of GNP between 1981 and 1985 compared with 1.3 percent of GNP between 1971 and 1980. The 1984 Economic Report of the President, Washington, DC, p. 36, reports that the structural deficit jumped from $48 billion to $101 billion in fiscal year 1983 (which began in October 1982, a year after the tax cut was enacted). The Congressional Budget Office's publication *Budget and Economic Outlook: Fiscal Years 2011–2021* (available at www.cbo.gov/doc.cfm?index=12039) shows in Table E-13 that approximately two thirds of the increase in the deficit (without automatic stabilizers) came from reduced revenues between 1981 and 1985. I would like to thank Rudolph Penner for a discussion of these calculations.

16. *Administration's Fiscal Year 1983 Budget Proposal: Hearings Before the Senate Committee on Finance, United States Senate*, 97th Congress, 2nd Sess. February 23, 1982, Government Printing Office, Washington, DC, 1982, p. 10.

17. See *Second Concurrent Resolution on the Budget—Fiscal Year 1982: Hearings Before the Senate Committee on the Budget, United States Senate*, 97th Congress, 1st Sess., September 16, 1981, Government Printing Office, Washington, DC, 1981, p. 137.

18. *Administration's Fiscal Year 1983 Budget Proposal: Hearings Before the Senate Committee on Finance, United States Senate*, 97th Congress, 2nd Sess., February 23, 1982, Government Printing Office, Washington, DC, 1982, p. 180.

19. See Marvin Goodfriend and Robert G. King, "The Incredible Volcker Disinflation," *Journal of Monetary Economics* 52, no. 5 (July 2005), esp. pp. 1012–13, for evidence of no greater stability in money supply growth during the Volcker period compared with earlier.

20. See the previous chapter describing how the Fed raised interest rates starting in September 1980 and tightened further after the election to rein in excess growth in the money supply. The combination of erratic money supply growth and compensatory adjustments in real interest rates characterized Volcker's chairmanship of the Fed. See Goodfriend and King, "The Incredible Volcker Disinflation." Goodfriend and King conclude (p. 1012), "During the [Volcker] disinflation, then, our sense is that the Volcker-led FOMC undertook a delicate balancing act. It sought to manage short-term interest rates and to respect monetary targets."

21. See the previous chapter.

22. See *New York Times*, January 30, 1981, p. D2.

23. The quote is from Milton Friedman, *Newsweek*, September 21, 1981, p. 39.

24. See the quote in chapter 9 from Milton Friedman, "Burns on the Outside," *Newsweek*, January 9, 1978, p. 52: "We have been having inflation . . . because . . . John Q. Public has been demanding inflation [by] . . . asking Congress to provide us with ever more goodies—yet not raise our taxes."

25. Milton Friedman, *Money Mischief: Episodes in Monetary History* (New York: Harcourt Brace, 1994), p. 207.

26. All quotes are from the *Second Concurrent Resolution on the Budget Fiscal Year 1982. Hearings Before the Senate Committee on the Budget*, 97th Congress, 1st Sess., September 16, 1981, Government Printing Office, Washington, DC, 1981, p. 73.

27. See Rudolph Penner, ed., *The Great Fiscal Experiment* (Washington, DC: Urban Institute Press, 1991), p. 5; and Rudolph Penner and Alan Abramson, *Broken Purse Strings: Congressional Budgeting, 1974 to 1988* (Washington, DC: Urban Institute Press, 1988), esp. chapter 5.

28. The following quotes are from *Extension of the Temporary Limit on Public Debt: Hearings Before the Senate Subcommittee on Taxation and Debt Management Generally of the Committee on Finance*, 96th Congress, 2nd Sess., April 2, 1980, Government Printing Office, Washington, DC, 1980, pp. 12–13.

29. This is known as the Ricardian equivalence argument, after David Ricardo (1772–1823), the English political economist. Ricardo mentions this possible response by savers but rejects it as unlikely. Robert Barro resurrected the argument and sums up the discussion in Robert Barro, "The Ricardian Approach to Budget Deficits," *Journal of Economic Perspectives* 3, no. 2 (Spring 1989): 37–54.

30. A summary of the most recent empirical evidence on the impact of deficits on interest rates appears in Thomas Laubach, "New Evidence on the Interest Rate Effects of Budget Deficits and Debt," *Journal of the European Economic Association* 7, no. 4 (June 2009): 858–85. As discussed in the remainder of this paragraph, all empirical estimates suffer from a variety of errors in variables problems, which bias the estimated coefficients downward. Special thanks to Kenneth Garbade and Thomas Sargent for extensive discussions on this topic.

31. Penner actually quotes Henry Aaron (a budget expert at the Brookings Institution, not the baseball player) in Rudolph Penner, *Errors in Budget Forecasting* (Washington, DC: Urban Institute Press, 2001), p. 1.

32. The paper by James Barth et al. and the comment by Frank de Leeuw in Penner, ed., *The Great Fiscal Experiment*, esp. p. 149, report that econometric

models that "attempt to measure expected future deficits rather than actual current deficits" are more likely to show positive impacts of the deficit on interest rates. The phrase "each circumstance is unique" translates into an econometric problem where "initial conditions" matter a lot in estimation. For a similar problem with measuring the impact of fiscal policy, see Jonathan Parker, "On Measuring the Effects of Fiscal Policy in Recessions," *Journal of Economic Literature* 49, no. 3 (September 2011): 703–18.

33. *New York Times*, September 11, 1981, p. D6.

34. *New York Times*, January 10, 1982, p. NES10.

35. William Greider, "The Education of David Stockman," *Atlantic Monthly*, December 1981, pp. 16–17.

36. Goodfriend and King, "The Incredible Volcker Disinflation," pp. 1001–2, describe the increase in long-term rates between January and October 1981 as "the second inflation scare." They point to anti-inflationary statements at various FOMC meetings to support their point. But the fact that members of the FOMC worried about reducing inflationary expectations during this period, which they did, does not imply that increased inflationary expectations were responsible for the increase in long-term rates. Another possible source of the increase in the risk premium on real long-term rates in January 1982 compared with a year earlier is an increase in the volatility of short-term rates in the immediately preceding year. In fact, the reverse occurred. The daily standard deviation of percent change in the three-month Treasury bill rate during 1981 was 2.16 percent, compared with 2.49 percent during 1980.

37. See *Administration's Fiscal Year 1983 Budget Proposal: Hearings Before the Senate Committee on Finance*, 97th Congress, 2nd Sess., February 23, 1982, Government Printing Office, Washington, DC, 1982, pp. 181–2. Meltzer ignores the "uncertainty over the deficit" explanation for high real interest rates in his *A History of the Federal Reserve*, vol. 2, book 2 (Chicago: University of Chicago Press, 2009), p. 1103. Instead, he blames the high rate of interest on the uncertainty that inflation will remain low after the economy rebounds from recession. That explanation is inconsistent with the decline in the price of gold from 1981 to 1982. Meltzer also cites foreign purchases of U.S. bonds and the failure of the deficit after 2001 to raise interest rates as evidence that the deficit did not raise interest rates in 1982. Circumstances were quite different in those two periods, however. Foreign purchases could certainly have financed the deficit without raising U.S. rates, but that would have been unlikely if foreigners had not been confident in the Federal Reserve's stance against inflation.

38. Thomas Sargent describes the same confrontation as "a game of chicken." See his "Interpreting the Reagan Deficits," in Thomas Sargent, *Rational*

Expectations and Inflation, 2nd ed. (New York: HarperCollins, 1993), pp. 211–26.

39. *New York Times*, January 10, 1982, p. NES10.

40. *New York Times*, August 28, 1981, p. D2.

41. See *New York Times*, January 28, 1982, p. D6, and January 30, 1982, p. 29.

42. See Record of Policy Actions of the Federal Open Market Committee, February 1–2, 1982, p. 3. "M1 [checking accounts plus currency] grew at an annual rate of 11½ percent in December and accelerated in January to a rate estimated to be above twenty percent."

43. Ibid.

44. Transcript, Federal Open Market Committee Meeting, February 1–2, 1982, p. 41.

45. Ibid., p. 46.

46. Ibid., p. 90.

47. Ibid., pp. 90–91.

48. See Record of Policy Actions of the Federal Open Market Committee, February 1–2, 1982, p. 14.

49. See "Kennedy Urges End to Federal Reserve Autonomy," *New York Times*, April 7, 1982, p. A24.

50. Transcript, Federal Open Market Committee Meeting, February 1–2, 1982, p. 104.

51. Interview with Murray Weidenbaum.

52. Based on Volcker's Daily Planner for 1982 and an official White House photograph of Reagan and Volcker on February 15, 1982.

53. Douglas Brinkley, ed., *The Reagan Diaries*, vol. 1, *January 1981–October 1985* (New York: HarperCollins, 2009), p. 110.

54. *New York Times*, February 19, 1982, p. A20.

55. The following conversation is based on an interview with Murray Weidenbaum.

56. See "Reagan's 'First Friend,'" *New York Times*, March 21, 1982, p. SM26.

57. *Washington Post*, March 30, 1982, p. A1.

58. Ibid., p. A1 continued.

59. Ibid.

60. *New York Times*, August 15, 1982, p. E4.

61. *New York Times*, October 24, 1982, p. 25 continued.

62. *New York Times*, August 15, 1982, p. E4.

63. *Washington Post*, August 7, 1982, p. A1.

64. Ibid.

65. See *Washington Post*, August 20, 1982, p. A1. The vote was 226–207 in the House and 52–47 in the Senate.

13. The End of the Beginning

1. The letter is from the Personal Papers of Paul Volcker.

2. The annual rate of inflation for the year ending August 1982 was 6 percent compared with 12.6 percent for the year ending November 1980.

3. The story is from an interview with Jerry Corrigan.

4. *Time*, March 8, 1982, and *People*, May 10, 1982.

5. Transcript, Federal Open Market Committee Meeting, May 18, 1982, p. 41.

6. *Washington Post*, August 7, 1982, p. A1, reported a 9.8 percent unemployment rate for July, "the highest in 41 years, since late 1941." The total number of unemployed equaled 10.8 million for July 1982, according to the Bureau of Labor Statistics.

7. The unemployment rate reached a peak of 10.8 percent in November and December 1982, corresponding to twelve million unemployed workers.

8. Housing starts averaged 936,000 units from January through June 1982, compared with 2,020,000 units in 1978. See *Economic Report of the President*, February 1983, Washington, DC, Government Printing Office, p. 216.

9. See Joseph Treaster, *Paul Volcker: The Making of a Financial Legend* (New York: John Wiley, 2004), p. 5.

10. *Washington Post*, April 7, 1982, p. D7 continued.

11. The quotes in this paragraph and the next are from "Paying More for Money," the cover story in *Time*, March 8, 1982.

12. PIPAV. Also see Andrew Tobias, "A Talk with Paul Volcker," *New York Times*, September 19, 1982, p. 271.

13. The New York Mercantile Exchange had not yet launched its crude oil futures contract, but the International Monetary Fund published an average monthly price index of Brent, Dubai, and West Texas crude oil beginning 1980. The index reached a monthly peak of 73.71 in January 1981 and declined to 60.15 in August 1982 (source: www.imf.org/external/np/res/commod/index.asp).

14. *Wall Street Journal*, January 5, 1982, p. 34.

15. Transcript, Federal Open Market Committee Meeting, October 5, 1982, p. 19.

16. See Milton Friedman and Anna J. Schwartz, *A Monetary History of the United States, 1867–1960* (Princeton, NJ: Princeton University Press, 1963), p. 434, "Federal insurance of bank deposits was the most important structural change in the banking system to result from the 1933 panic, and . . . the structural change most conducive to monetary stability since state bank notes were taxed out of existence immediately after the Civil War." They also note (p. 437) that "The reduction in [bank] failures is not of

NOTES TO PAGES 220–222

course attributable to any correspondingly drastic improvement in the quality of bank officials or in the effectiveness of the supervisory authorities."

17. Insurance was set at $2,500 per account in the original legislation and was raised in a series of steps to $100,000 in 1980. See Lawrence Ritter and William Silber, *Principles of Money, Banking, and Financial Markets* (New York: Basic Books, 1983), 4th ed., p. 106.

18. See chapter 17 for more on the financial crisis that began in August 2007.

19. PIPAV.

20. The document "U.S. Bank Claims on Mexico (end-1981: adjusted for guarantees)," Personal Papers of Paul Volcker, appears without a date but has a cover sheet that says, "Please Transmit Promptly to the Office of Chairman Volcker for Ms. Sandy Wolfe." It is combined with a telegram dated August 18, 1982, from the Mexican minister of finance, Jesús Silva Herzog, to Edwin Truman at the Federal Reserve Board. Data on bank size is from *History of the Eighties: Lessons for the Future*, Federal Deposit Insurance Corporation, Washington, DC, 1997, p. 237.

21. See *Washington Post*, August 4, 1982, p. D7 continued. In *History of the Eighties: Lessons for the Future*, p. 237, Table 7.1 lists Continental as the eighth-largest in assets as of the end of 1981.

22. See chapter 6 in Irvine Sprague, *Bailout: An Insider's Account of Bank Failures and Rescues* (New York: Basic Books, 1986), for a discussion of Penn Square.

23. The devaluation began on February 17, 1982, when Mexico allowed the peso to float versus the dollar. It traded at 27 pesos per dollar before February 17 and traded at 45 pesos per dollar on August 6, 1982. See *Washington Post*, August 7, 1982, p. D8.

24. See Joseph Kraft, *The Mexican Rescue* (New York: Group of Thirty, 1984), p. 8.

25. Paul Volcker and Toyoo Gyohten, *Changing Fortunes: The World's Money and the Threat to American Leadership* (New York: Times Books, 1992), p. 199.

26. See Kraft, *The Mexican Rescue*, p. 4.

27. The following discussion is based on ibid., pp. 9–14; Volcker and Gyohten, *Changing Fortunes*, pp. 200–207; and the recollection of Paul Volcker.

28. The telephone numbers appear in the document "U.S. Bank Claims on Mexico (end-1981: adjusted for guarantees)," Personal Papers of Paul Volcker.

29. See Ron Chernow, *The House of Morgan: An American Banking Dynasty and the Rise of Modern Finance* (New York: Atlantic Monthly Press, 1990), p. 127.

30. At the FOMC meeting on August 24, 1982 (Transcript, Federal Open Market Committee Meeting, August 24, 1982, p. 1), Volcker says, "Mr. Solomon

made a little introductory statement . . . indicating that there was some expectation of some private new money as part of this [negotiation]." According to the *New York Times* (August 21, 1982, p. 32): "The Mexican government and United States officials put heavy pressure on commercial banks . . . to agree to a program under which the banks would postpone repayments of $10 billion in Mexican debt . . . Despite denials by the Federal Reserve that it had anything to do with the meeting and that it had merely provided the group with a room, Anthony Solomon, president of the Federal Reserve Bank of New York, made an opening statement to the participants . . . that the Federal Reserve fully supported the plan that was presented by Mr. Silva Herzog."

31. Transcript, Federal Open Market Committee Meeting, August 24, 1982, p. 18.

32. *International Financial Markets and Related Problems: Hearings Before the House Committee on Banking, Finance and Urban Affairs*, 98th Congress, February 2, 1983, p. 76, Table V.

33. The federal funds rate was 14.73 percent on July 1, 1982, versus 9.03 percent on August 24, 1982. The ten-year rate was 14.4 percent on July 1, 1982, and 12.35 percent on August 24, 1982.

34. Transcript, Federal Open Market Committee Meeting, August 24, 1982, p. 23.

35. Transcript, Federal Open Market Committee Meeting, October 5, 1982, p. 38.

36. Transcript, Federal Open Market Committee Meeting, August 24, 1982, p. 30.

37. Transcript, Federal Open Market Committee Meeting, October 5, 1982, p. 19.

38. See Milton Friedman and Anna Schwartz, *A Monetary History of the United States, 1867–1960* (Princeton, NJ: Princeton University Press, 1963), pp. 313–14.

39. Transcript, Federal Open Market Committee Meeting, October 5, 1982, p. 20.

40. Ibid., p. 70.

41. The transcript for the October 5, 1982 meeting (esp. pp. 10–11 and pp. 34–42) cites technical problems associated with the All-Savers certificate program, making the narrow money supply figures suspect. But this was only a temporary phenomenon. See Allan Meltzer, *A History of the Federal Reserve*, vol. 2, book 2 (Chicago: University of Chicago Press, 2009), pp. 1104–31, for further discussion.

42. Transcript, Federal Open Market Committee Meeting, October 5, 1982, pp. 53.

43. See Marvin Goodfriend and Robert G. King, "The Incredible Volcker Disinflation," *Journal of Monetary Economics* 52, no. 5 (2005): 1003.

44. Ibid., p. 985, claims that the Volcker disinflation did not gain credibility until much later. Goodfriend and King argue that "the behavior of intermediate and long term interest rates is evidence that the [Volcker] disinflation" was not credible. They cite the rise in the ten-year rate from 13 percent to 14 percent from the beginning of 1981 to 1982 as evidence. I argued in the previous chapter that this increase in rates was a consequence of the increase in the budget deficit and the uncertainty over the magnitude of the increased deficit.

45. See Transcript of the Press Conference at the Business Council Meeting, Hot Springs, Virginia, October 9, 1982. He had told the FOMC at the October 5 meeting that he would indicate the change in policy before the release of the minutes six weeks later to avoid concern in the markets about movements in the money supply. See Transcript, Federal Open Market Committee Meeting, October 5, 1982, p. 53.

46. *New York Times*, October 13, 1982, p. A30, and October 14, 1979, p. E18.

47. *New York Times*, October 13, 1982, p. A30.

48. *New York Times*, October 12, 1982, p. D1 continued.

49. *International Debt: Hearings Before the Senate Subcommittee on International Finance and Monetary Policy of the Committee on Banking, Housing and Urban Affairs*, 98th Congress, 1st Sess., February 14, 1983.

50. See Board of Governors of the Federal Reserve System, *Federal Reserve System: Purposes and Functions*, Washington, DC, 9th ed., 2005, chapter 5, for the supervisory responsibilities of the Federal Reserve and other agencies.

51. *International Debt: Hearings Before the Senate Subcommittee on International Finance and Monetary Policy of the Committee on Banking, Housing and Urban Affairs*, 98th Congress, 1st Sess., February 17, 1983, p. 258.

52. Ibid., p. 237.

53. Ibid., p. 239.

54. For this and the remaining quotes immediately following, see *International Debt: Hearings Before the Senate Subcommittee on International Finance and Monetary Policy of the Committee on Banking, Housing and Urban Affairs*, 98th Congress, 1st Sess., February 14, 1983, p. 247.

55. *New York Times*, July 6, 1978, p. D1.

56. PIPAV.

57. See Board of Governors of the Federal Reserve System, *Federal Reserve System: Purposes and Functions*, Washington, DC, 5th ed., 1963.

58. *New York Times*, December 10, 1985, p. B6. This comment by Martin came after the failure of Continental Illinois (discussed in the next chapter) and was not a response to Mexico per se.

59. PIPAV.

60. *Washington Post*, January 28, 1983, p. C9.

61. See Volcker's Daily Planner, 1983.

62. This conversation is based on the recollection of Paul Volcker.

63. Volcker had received an honorary degree the previous June at Princeton. The valedictorian at the graduation ceremony applied Churchill's words to mark the end of their tutorial on life. See *New York Times*, June 9, 1982, p. B2.

64. The monthly inflation rates announced in January 1983 through May 1983 were 0.2, 0.1, 0.1, 0.7, and 0.4. Annualizing those numbers (add them up and divide by 5 and then multiply by 12) produces an inflation rate of 3.6 per annum.

65. On May 4, 1983, the federal funds rate was 8.64 percent and the ten-year bond rate was 10.12 percent, compared with October 5, 1982, the day of the FOMC meeting, when the funds rate was 10.27 percent and the ten-year bond rate was 11.69 percent.

66. In July 1975 the federal funds rate had declined to a monthly average of 6 percent compared with an average of 13 percent a year earlier, while over that same period, the ten-year government bond rate rose from an average of 7.8 percent to over 8.0 percent (see chapter 10).

67. See Transcript, Federal Open Market Committee Meeting, October 5, 1982, p. 38.

68. *New York Times*, November 22, 1980, p. 9.

69. On May 31, 1983, the dollar bought 2.52 German marks compared with 1.97 marks on December 31, 1982.

70. See Benjamin Friedman, "Learning from the Reagan Deficits," *American Economic Review* 82, no. 2 (May 1992): 299–304, for a discussion of the unprecedented size of the Reagan deficits as a percentage of GNP compared with the post–World War II experience until then, and the transformation of the United States from a net exporter of capital to a net importer.

71. *Washington Post*, May 12, 1983, p. A23.

72. On May 31, 1983, the dollar bought 7.54 French francs compared with 4.55 French francs on December 31, 1980.

73. *Washington Post*, May 12, 1983, p. A23.

74. See Martin Anderson, *Revolution: The Reagan Legacy* (Stanford, CA: Hoover Institution Press, 1990), p. 239.

75. *Washington Post*, April 19, 1983, p. A1.

76. See William Safire "To Pay Paul," *New York Times*, May 16, 1983, p. A19.

77. Friedman's remark is quoted in Harry Anderson and Rich Thomas, "Voting for Volcker to Stay," *Newsweek*, June 20, 1983, p. 53.

78. In describing the incident, William Safire wrote, "The Friedman savaging continued . . . Paul Volcker did not feel the need to respond." See *New York Times*, May 16, 1983, p. A19.

79. *Washington Post*, April 21, 1983, p. D11.

80. The discussion and conversation that follow are from the Transcript, Federal Open Market Committee Meeting, May 24, 1983. See p. 31 for "snugging up" and 59–60 for the rest.

81. The following conversation is based on the recollection of Paul Volcker.

82. The quote is as written in the June 6 entry to Reagan's diary, with the exception that the question mark in the diary appears before the word *Do*. See Douglas Brinkley, ed., *The Reagan Diaries*, vol. 1 (New York: HarperCollins, 2009), p. 233.

83. *Washington Post*, June 9, 1983, p. A1 continued.

84. See *New York Times*, June 19, 1983, p. 26. Also see "Reagan's 'First Friend,'" *New York Times*, March 21, 1982, p. SM26.

85. See "Final Choice of Volcker Is Attributed to His Experience and Solid Support," *New York Times*, June 19, 1983, p. 26.

86. See entry for June 7, continued on page 234, Brinkley, ed., *The Reagan Diaries*, vol. 1.

87. See Greenspan's note, dated July 28, 1983, Personal Papers of Paul Volcker.

88. *Washington Post*, June 19, 1983, p. A1 continued.

89. Reagan made the following entry for June 18 in his diary: "About 11am I phoned Paul Volcker in N.Y. & asked him to accept re-appointment as Chmn. of the Fed." See Brinkley, ed., *The Reagan Diaries*, vol. 1, p. 238.

90. *Washington Post*, June 19, 1983, p. A1 continued.

14. Follow-Through

1. *The Re-nomination of Paul Volcker: Hearings Before the Senate Committee on Banking, Housing and Urban Affairs*, U.S. Senate, 98th Congress, 1st Sess., July 14, 1983, pp. 1–2.

2. Ibid., pp. 3–4.

3. *New York Times*, July 22, 1983, p. D11.

4. *The Re-nomination of Paul Volcker: Hearings Before the Senate Committee on Banking, Housing and Urban Affairs*, U.S. Senate, 98th Congress, 1st Sess., July 14, 1983, p. 10.

5. Personal Papers of Paul Volcker.

6. Ibid.

7. *New York Times*, July 28, 1983, p. D20.

8. Ibid.

9. The unemployment rate was 10.8 percent in November 1982 and 7.8 percent in February 1984.

10. *The Federal Reserve's First Monetary Policy Report for 1984: Hearings Before the Senate Committee on Banking, Housing and Urban Affairs*, 98th Congress, 2nd Sess., February 8, 1984, pp. 12–13. Volcker's remarks also cited the balance-of-payments deficit.

11. See Annual Report of the Council of Economic Advisers, February 1984, Washington, DC, p. 37.

12. *New York Times*, March 18, 1984, p. SM34.

13. See chapter 12 for a discussion of the difficulty of testing the general proposition that deficits increase real interest rates. That discussion provides evidence from the 1981 tax cut of a positive impact of the deficit, and uncertainty over the deficit, on interest rates, but that evidence certainly does not resolve the issue more generally. The evidence presented here will also show that the persistence of the structural deficit under President Reagan during 1984 pushed up real interest rates as the economy recovered. For a contemporaneous dismissal of the relationship between deficits and interest rates, see Shadow Open Market Committee, Policy Statement and Position Papers, March 11–12, 1984 (available at shadowfed.org/archives/1984/september-30 -1984-washington-d-c), which begins by saying (p. 5), "There is no careful study showing a direct connection between actual or expected budget deficits and market interest rates." That statement is correct because "initial conditions" in the economy matter a lot in whether the deficit raises real rates, which is a good reason for looking at each particular historical episode as a separate case study.

14. See Economic Report of the President, transmitted to the Congress, February 2, 1984, Washington, DC, 1984, pp. 4 and 6.

15. *The Federal Reserve's First Monetary Policy Report for 1984: Hearings Before the Senate Committee on Banking, Housing and Urban Affairs*, 98th Congress, 2nd Sess., February 8, 1984, pp. 106 and 107.

16. Ibid., p. 107.

17. Heinz's position on the 1981 tax cut is discussed in David Stockman, *The Triumph of Politics* (New York: Harper & Row, 1986), pp. 252–53.

18. Transcript, Federal Open Market Committee Meeting, August 14, 1979, p. 22.

19. See Ellen Meade and David Stasavage, "Two Effects of Transparency on the Quality of Deliberation," mimeo., September 2005: "In 1993 the FOMC began releasing verbatim transcripts of its meetings, albeit with a five year delay. Before 1993 the FOMC did not release transcripts, but as was subsequently revealed, all pre-1993 meetings had been taped, and contrary to the expectations of participants, these earlier records had been preserved. After 1993 the verbatim records of these earlier meetings were also released to the public."

20. See "Contingency Planning: Options for the International Monetary Problem," March 14, 1971, Papers of Paul Volcker, Federal Reserve Bank of New York Archives, Box 0108477, p. 59, and the discussion in chapter 4.

21. Volcker weighed 240 pounds at this time and has caught Atlantic salmon weighing 35 pounds. Even the biggest fish stories do not report Atlantic salmon exceeding 100 pounds. Volcker claims he once caught a 120-pound tarpon.

22. This quote and those that follow are from *The Federal Reserve's First Monetary Policy Report for 1984: Hearings Before the Senate Committee on Banking, Housing and Urban Affairs*, 98th Congress, 2nd Sess., February 8, 1984, p. 108.

23. The discount rate was last increased on May 5, 1981, from 13 to 14 percent. It was then reduced in nine steps to 8.5 percent. It remained at that level from December 14, 1982, until April 9, 1984, when it was increased from 8.5 to 9.0 percent.

24. On February 1, 1984, the ten-year rate equaled 11.64 percent. On May 30, 1984, it reached 13.99 percent.

25. The long-term rate might increase a little because long-term rates reflect the current and expected future short-term rates, but that need not occur if inflationary expectations are reduced in the process.

26. See "Coming Out of the Recession: The Economy in 1984," an address before the Wharton Entrepreneurial Center, April 30, 1984, p. 2, available at fraser.stlouisfed.org/historicaldocs/831/download/29536/Volcker_19840430.pdf. Also see Allan Meltzer, *A History of the Federal Reserve*, vol. 2, book 2 (Chicago: University of Chicago Press, 2009), p. 1165.

27. The Shadow Open Market Committee was founded in 1973 by Karl Brunner of the University of Rochester and Allan Meltzer of Carnegie Mellon University. For this quote, see Shadow Open Market Committee, Policy Statement and Position Papers, March 11–12, 1984, p. 6, available at shadowfed.org/archives/1984/.

28. Meltzer's quote refers to August 1984. See Meltzer, *A History of the Federal Reserve*, p. 1167.

29. Transcript, Federal Open Market Committee Meeting, March 27, 1984, p. 85.

30. Ibid., p. 52. Wallich repeated his concern at the May 22, 1984, meeting of the FOMC (p. 5).

31. Goodfriend wrote, "The Fed tightened in an effort to resist the ongoing

inflation scare, raising the funds rate to an 11.6 percent peak in August of 1984." See Marvin Goodfriend, "Interest Rate Policy and the Inflation Scare Problem: 1979–1992," *Federal Reserve Bank of Richmond Economic Quarterly* 79, no. 1 (Winter 1993): 14.

32. The afternoon London gold fixing was $277.50 on the last day of June 1979 and ended the year at $524.00.

33. See chapter 10.

34. The monthly averages are of the daily afternoon London gold fixing. The price at the beginning of the period and the end of the period show almost no change: The London afternoon fixing on February 1, 1984, was $378, and on May 31 it was $384.

35. See the discussion of 1981 in chapter 12.

36. Steinhardt Partners was one of the most successful hedge funds ever, earning a gross annual return of 30 percent during its first twenty-one years of existence, compared with an annual return of 8.9 percent in the S&P 500 index over the same period. See the chapter on Michael Steinhardt in Jack Schwager, *Market Wizards: Interviews with Top Traders* (New York: New York Institute of Finance, 1989), esp. pp. 207–209, for a discussion of his speculation in Treasury bonds. Also see Dan Dorfman, "Superstar Betting $400 Million on Falling Interest Rates," *Chicago Tribune*, May 24, 1984, p. A1.

37. Dorfman, "Superstar Betting $400 Million."

38. Ibid. attributes this view to Steinhardt, but it is not a direct quote from him.

39. See Prepared Statement by Paul Volcker in *The Federal Reserve's First Monetary Policy Report for 1984: Hearings Before the Senate Committee on Banking, Housing and Urban Affairs*, 98th Congress, 2nd Sess., February 8, 1984, p. 18.

40. Ibid., p. 108.

41. See "How the Panic Followed the Sun in Debacle at Chicago Bank," *Chicago Tribune*, May 27, 1984, p. 1.

42. Continental is mentioned as the seventh-largest bank in 1984 in *History of the Eighties: Lessons for the Future* (Washington, DC: Federal Deposit Insurance Corporation, 1997), p. 236. Table 7.1 on the following page shows Continental as the eighth-largest in total assets at the end of 1981.

43. See *Managing the Crisis: The FDIC and RTC Experience, 1980–1994* (Washington, DC: Federal Deposit Insurance Corporation, August 1998), p. 548.

44. Wallace's quote is from the *Chicago Tribune*, May 20, 1984, p. W1. Continental's balance sheet showed that only 16 percent of its funding came from core deposits of local customers. See George Hanc, *History of the Eighties: Lessons for the Future* (Washington, DC: Federal Deposit Insurance Corporation, 1997), p. 255, Table 7A.1.

45. See Table 7A.1, ibid., p. 255, for foreign office deposits. The *Chicago Tribune*, May 27, 1984, p. 1, gives the $8 billion that was renewed each day.

46. See *Chicago Tribune*, May 20, 1984, p. W1.

47. The $3.6 billion is reported in the *Chicago Tribune*, May 27, 1984, p. 1. Volcker told the Federal Reserve Board on Monday, May 14, 1984, that "Continental Illinois had been borrowing 3–5 billion daily at the discount window." (See Federal Reserve Board Minutes, May 14, 1984, p. 8.)

48. Borrowing by all 5,800 banks averaged $955 million during the previous eighteen months. The data on borrowing at the discount window is the average of monthly figures available at research.stlouisfed.org/fred2/series/BORROW.

49. See *Chicago Tribune*, May 27, 1984, p. 1.

50. Transcript, Federal Open Market Committee Meeting, May 22, 1984, p. 41.

51. The principle of Too Big to Fail in the United States, usually associated with large bank failures, antedates Continental Illinois. See Benton Gup in *Too Big to Fail: Policies and Practices in Government Bailouts* (Westport, CT: Praeger Publishers, 2004), who makes the case that Too Big to Fail applies to a wide range of firms and industries, from Chrysler and Lockheed Aircraft in the early 1970s to New York City in 1975. I argue in *When Washington Shut Down Wall Street* (Princeton, NJ: Princeton University Press, 2007), pp. 123–26, that the Too Big to Fail doctrine goes back much further, to 1914, when Treasury Secretary William McAdoo subsidized banks to help prevent New York City from declaring bankruptcy. (Yes, New York was in trouble even back then.)

52. The Office of the Comptroller of the Currency (OCC) was created as a bureau within the U.S. Treasury by the National Currency Act of February 25, 1863. The comptroller is a presidential appointee subject to Senate confirmation. The act was designed to implement a uniform national currency based on federally chartered banks to replace the multiple currencies issued by individual state-chartered banks. To accomplish that goal, the OCC was charged with the responsibility of monitoring the safety and soundness of national banks and to conduct periodic on-site examinations.

53. The FDIC was established by the Banking Act of 1933, signed by President Franklin Roosevelt on June 16, 1933. The legislation is also known by the more popular title, the Glass-Steagall Act, after its cosponsors Senator Carter Glass and Representative Henry Steagall. Among other things, the act established the FDIC as an independent federal agency governed by a five-person board, each appointed by the president of the United States and confirmed by the Senate. The FDIC's insurance fund is financed by premiums charged to insured banks, but the agency is ultimately backed by the "full faith and credit" of the U.S. Treasury as a backstop to its accumulated capital.

54. Details of the meeting vary according to the source. The clearest description is in the *Chicago Tribune*, May 27, 1984, p. 1 continued. Also see William Isaac with Philip Meyer, *Senseless Panic: How Washington Failed America* (New York: John Wiley, 2010), pp. 67–68; and Irvine Sprague, *Bailout: An Insider's Account of Bank Failures and Rescues* (New York: Basic Books, 1986), pp. 154–55.

55. Isaac, with Meyer, *Senseless Panic*, p. 67.

56. PIPAV.

57. See *Statement of C. T. Conover, Comptroller of the Currency, Before the House Subcommittee on Financial Institutions, Supervision, Regulation, and Insurance*, 98th Congress, 2nd Sess., September 18, 19, and October 4, 1984, p. 205. Also see the interchange between Conover and Representative Wylie on pp. 291–92. Finally, see *Continental Illinois National Bank: Report of an Inquiry into Its Federal Supervision and Assistance: Hearings Before the House Committee on Banking, Finance and Urban Affairs*, 99th Congress, 1st Sess., July 1985, p. 164.

58. The FDIC's investment represented almost 15 percent of its $15 billion insurance fund (see *Wall Street Journal*, May 23, 1984, p. 1 continued).

59. The impetus for this meeting came from Treasury Secretary Donald Regan. Volcker had suggested that Connor and Isaac discuss the rescue plans with Regan. The treasury secretary suggested that they would have a greater chance of success with private bankers participating. See Sprague, *Bailout*, p. 156.

60. At last count (June 2011), Volcker has received sixty-one honorary degrees from universities in the United States and abroad. Alphabetically, they begin with Adelphi and Amherst and end with Yeshiva and York (Toronto). He likes them all but is especially proud of the honors he received from his alma maters, Princeton and Harvard. (Yale conferred one as well, just to keep up.) The University of London conferred an honorary degree and considers him an alumnus even though he never finished his doctoral dissertation during his stay there. His family connections with Rensselaer, where his father went, and with Fairleigh Dickinson in Teaneck, where he grew up, make them special as well.

61. PIPAV.

62. The description of this meeting is based on a number of sources, including the recollection of Paul Volcker; Isaac, with Meyer, *Senseless Panic*; and Sprague, *Bailout*. I have noted in the text specific quotes attributed to each source.

63. As reported in the *New York Times*, May 21, 1984, p. D6, by one of the participants.

64. See Isaac, with Meyer, *Senseless Panic*, p. 69.

65. PIPAV. Also see Isaac, with Meyer, *Senseless Panic*, p. 69.

66. See Isaac, with Meyer, *Senseless Panic*, p. 69.

67. PIPAV. Isaac confirms Volcker's opposition to the 100 percent guarantee: "Volcker was negative," Isaac, with Meyer, *Senseless Panic*, p. 69.

68. PIPAV. Isaac complained more formally in testimony before the Senate Banking Committee, "The Federal Reserve does not take any risk . . . The only agency that is at risk in the banking system, the true lender of last resort, is the FDIC." See Hearings Before the Committee on Banking, Housing and Urban Affairs, U.S. Senate, 99th Congress, 1st Sess., Deposit Insurance Reform and Related Supervisory Issues, July 23, 1985, p. 27. Also see Sprague, *Bailout*, p. 162, for the relationship between the 100 percent guarantee and the $2 billion capital infusion. "After infusing $2 billion in the bank, we could make the guarantee because then it would be more cost effective to do an assisted merger or bailout than a payoff."

69. PIPAV.

70. This is the third paragraph of the press release on May 17, 1984, distributed jointly by the Office of the Comptroller, the FDIC, and the Federal Reserve Board. See Sprague, *Bailout*, p. 276, for the entire document.

71. See *New York Times*, July 26, 1984, p. D1, for a detailed account of Treasury's objections. William Isaac argues that debt covenants of the holding company precluded the FDIC's investing directly in the bank itself (other than as a loan) and that the creditors were protected by the assets of the holding company upon liquidation. See Isaac, with Meyer, *Senseless Panic*, pp. 74–75.

72. PIPAV.

73. *Wall Street Journal*, May 18, 1984, p. 3.

74. Transcript, Federal Open Market Committee Meeting, May 22, 1984, p. 32.

75. See Federal Reserve Press Release, July 20, 1984, pp. 1–13. The committee members discussed this omission at the meeting (see Transcript, May 22, 1984, pp. 38–39) and claimed that the professional Fed watchers could read between the lines and detect the subtle changes in the directive (which is what they are paid to do).

76. Volcker summarized the discussion at the meeting on May 22, 1984 (transcript, pp. 27–28): "My bottom line is that we've run out of room for the time being for any tightening . . . [but] I don't have any sense here that we should be easing."

77. The increase in the Consumer Price Index measured 3.4 percent from August 1, 1984, through August 1, 1985, compared with 12.9 percent from August 1, 1979, through August 1, 1980.

78. Unemployment stood at 7.1 percent in August 1985. The last time it was that low (or lower) was April 1980, when it was 6.9 percent.

79. The average price of the afternoon London gold fixing was $414 during November 1982, compared with an average of $317 during the month of July 1985. Gold was high in November 1982 because of the Mexican crisis. Using June 1982 as a benchmark, when the price of gold averaged $315, shows virtually no change. On August 6, 1985, the price closed at $319.80.

80. Robert L. Hetzel, *The Monetary Policy of the Federal Reserve: A History* (New York: Cambridge University Press, 2008), p. 178, writes, "The year 1985 should have been a time of satisfaction for the FOMC. It had brought down trend inflation to 4%. With dramatic increases in the funds rate [in] 1984, it had confronted and subdued the inflationary expectations created by a strong economic recovery." The Annual Report of the Council of Economic Advisers, February 1986, Washington, DC, p. 37, said: "The current expansion that began in November 1982 marks an important departure from the pattern of persistently rising inflation rates . . . What is particularly unusual compared with the average postwar expansion is that the inflation rate has continued to decelerate during the third year of this expansion."

81. *The Re-nomination of Paul Volcker: Hearings Before the Senate Committee on Banking, Housing and Urban Affairs*, 98th Congress, 1st Sess., July 14, 1983, p. 18.

82. See chapter 13 and Reagan's diary entry for June 7, 1983, in Douglas Brinkley, ed., *The Reagan Diaries*, vol. 1 (New York: HarperCollins, 2009), p. 234.

83. The ten-year rate was 10.65 percent on August 6, 1985, compared with an average of 13.42 percent during the entire month of May 1984, and 13.99 percent on May 30, 1984. It was 8.91 on August 6, 1979.

84. The ten-year rate was 8.91 percent on August 6, 1979, and was 10.65 percent on August 6, 1985. The monthly payment at 8.91 percent equals $893 versus $1,008 at 10.65 percent, for a difference of $115 per month or $1,380 per year.

85. For August 1985 the overnight federal funds rate averaged 7.92 percent, the year-over-year inflation in the Consumer Price Index measured 3.4 percent, and the Survey of Professional Forecasters reported (for the third quarter) a one-year expected inflation of 4.21 percent. For August 1979 the numbers are 10.94 percent for federal funds, CPI inflation of 11.8 percent, and an expected inflation of 8.03 percent. Although the expected inflation forecasts are for one year ahead the ten-year expected rate moves in the same direction, although by a smaller amount.

86. The 5 percent deficit number comes from an estimated deficit of $202 billion for 1986 and a GNP of $3,992 billion for 1985. See Annual Report of the Council of Economic Advisers, February 1986, Washington, DC, pp. 252 and 339.

87. See "Plan to End Deficit in 1991 Gaining Wide Support," *New York Times*, October 4, 1985, p. A32.

88. See William Niskanen, *Reaganomics: An Insider's Account of the Policies and the People* (New York: Oxford University Press, 1988), p. 66.

89. *Washington Post*, December 12, 1985, p. A1.

90. On October 1, 1985, the day before the bill was introduced, the yield on the ten-year bond was 10.29 percent, and on December 11, 1985, it was 9.2 percent.

91. The ten-year bond rate traded at 7.99 percent and 7.93 percent on the first two trading days of March 1986 (before the cut in the discount rate on March 7). On March 22, 1978, the ten-year traded at 7.98 percent, which was the last time it was below 8 percent.

92. PIPAV.

93. In October 1985 the federal funds rate averaged 8.01 percent and the London afternoon gold fixing averaged $325.84, compared with February 1986, when the overnight rate averaged 7.87 percent and gold averaged $338.89. William Greider, *Secrets of the Temple: How the Federal Reserve Runs the Country* (New York: Simon & Schuster, 1987), p. 696, argues that falling oil prices "from $26 a barrel to $12 in a few short weeks at the end of 1985" cheered investors because of the favorable outlook for inflation. The facts are that crude oil futures prices (the "front month") declined from $29.75 on December 2, 1985 (the first trading day of the month), to $26.30 on December 31, 1985. Moreover, if the outlook for inflation had improved, the price of gold should have declined during this period.

94. *New York Times*, December 24, 1985, p. D1.

95. *New York Times*, January 20, 1986, p. D5.

96. See "The Budget Noose Remains," *New York Times*, February 8, 1985, p. 26: "In throwing out a key provision of the Gramm-Rudman-Hollings law, a Federal court addressed only procedure, not substance. The rest of the law remains in place and so does the first task for the President and Congress: to find a mutually acceptable way to reduce the deficit . . . The law calls on the Comptroller General, head of the General Accounting Office, to determine whether the deficit reduction goals are met. But the Comptroller General's office is subject to Congressional authority. That's the vulnerability found by a three-judge district court in Washington yesterday, ruling in a case brought by members of Congress. Giving him such responsibility intrudes improperly into executive branch terrain, the court held."

97. *New York Times*, February 8, 1986, p. 9.

98. Ibid.

99. See *Wall Street Journal*, March 3, 1986, p. 1.

100. Rudolph Penner and Alan Abramson, *Broken Purse Strings: Congressional Budgeting, 1974 to 1988* (Washington, DC: Urban Institute Press, 1988), p. 70.

101. Thomas Sargent describes the battle between the monetary and fiscal authorities more generally as follows: "While the authorities are playing this game of chicken, we would observe large . . . government deficits, low rates of monetization of government debt . . . and maybe also high real rates of interest on government debt." See Thomas Sargent, *Rational Expectations and Inflation*, 2nd ed. (New York: HarperCollins, 1993), p. 221.

102. *Washington Post*, December 12, 1985, p. A1 continued.

103. *Wall Street Journal*, January 21, 1986, p. 64.

104. Ibid.

105. PIPAV and *Wall Street Journal*, January 21, 1986, p. 64.

15. The Resignations

1. The following conversation is based on the recollection of Paul Volcker.

2. See *Washington Post*, January 9, 1985, p. A1, for the announcement of the job switch.

3. On August 6, 1979, the day before Volcker took office, the mark closed at 1.8295 marks per dollar and the yen closed at 217.15 yen per dollar. On September 20, 1985, the last trading day before the Plaza Agreement, the mark was at 2.8475, a 56 percent increase in the value of the dollar, and the yen was at 241, an increase in the dollar of 11 percent.

4. PIPAV.

5. Transcript, Federal Open Market Committee Meeting, October 1, 1985, p. 25.

6. On September 20, 1985, the Friday before the Plaza Agreement, the yen closed at 241 yen per dollar and the mark closed at 2.8475 marks per dollar. On February 3, 1986, the yen closed at 191.6 yen per dollar, a 20 percent decline in the value of the dollar, and the mark closed at 2.4 marks per dollar, a 15.7 percent drop in the value of the dollar. According to Volcker, the expected depreciation at the Plaza meeting was about 10–12 percent. See Paul Volcker and Toyoo Gyohten, *Changing Fortunes: The World's Money and the Threat to American Leadership* (New York: Times Books, 1992), p. 254.

7. The FOMC consists of the seven-member board plus a rotating group of five presidents of the regional Federal Reserve banks, with the exception of the president of the New York Fed, who is a permanent member of the FOMC.

8. See *New York Times*, October 11, 1985, p. D1.

9. The phrase "Gang of Four" as applied to the Reagan appointees to the Federal Reserve Board appears in a headline in the *Washington Post*, January 30, 1986, p. A25.

10. See *New York Times*, October 11, 1985, p. D1.

11. See Minutes of the Board of Governors of Federal Reserve System, January 27, 1986, p. 5: "At several previous meetings, most recently on January 21, 1986, the Board had considered but taken no action on requests by some Reserve Banks to lower the discount rate." The last discount rate change was on May 20, 1985, a decline from 8.0 percent to 7.5.

12. This quote and the remaining quotes in this conversation are based on the recollection of Paul Volcker and on the reports in the *New York Times*, March 24, 1986, p. A1, and the *Washington Post*, March 17, 1986, p. A11. The Minutes of the Board of Governors of Federal Reserve System, February 24, 1986, pp. 2–3, gives a general description.

13. *Washington Post*, March 19, 1986, p. A1.

14. PIPAV.

15. *Washington Post*, February 20, 1986, p. A15.

16. Ibid.

17. The following conversation is based on the recollection of Paul Volcker.

18. PIPAV.

19. See Minutes of the Board of Governors of Federal Reserve System, February 24, 1986, p. 6, for a description of the afternoon meeting. The face-saving on all sides is reflected in the following quote: "In view of the improved prospects for coordinated actions, a consensus was recorded to reconsider the decision reached earlier today to reduce the discount rate."

20. *Washington Post*, March 8, 1986, p. A1.

21. Ibid.

22. Ibid.

23. *Washington Post*, March 17, 1986, p. A11.

24. *Washington Post*, March 22, 1986, p. A1.

25. Ibid.

26. See the twelfth annual survey of "Who Runs America," *U.S. News & World Report*, May 20, 1985, p. 54.

27. PIPAV. Also see Bob Woodward, *Maestro: Greenspan's Fed and the American Boom* (New York: Simon & Schuster, 2000), p. 19.

28. *Washington Post*, March 27, 1986, p. A1.

29. Letter dated August 6, 1979, Personal Letters from 1979, Papers of Paul Volcker, Federal Reserve Bank of New York Archives, Box 95714.

30. Response to Carlock, dated August 16, 1979, Personal Letters from 1979, Papers of Paul Volcker, Federal Reserve Bank of New York Archives, Box 95714.

31. Letter dated June 19, 1983, Personal Papers of Paul Volcker.

32. *Newsweek*, February 24, 1986, p. 46.

33. Ibid.

34. PIPAV.

35. *New York Times*, March 31, 1987, p. B6.

36. PIPAV.

37. *Washington Post*, February 28, 1987, p. A21.

38. *Washington Post*, March 14, 1987, p. A21.

39. See "Bank Curb Eased in Volcker Defeat," *New York Times*, May 1, 1987, p. D1.

40. See Minutes of the Federal Reserve Board, "Citicorp; J.P. Morgan & Co.; Bankers Trust New York Corporation, all of New York, New York— Applications to underwrite and deal in certain securities," April 29, 1987.

41. *New York Times*, May 1, 1987, p. D1.

42. Ibid.

43. *Wall Street Journal*, May 4, 1987, p. 66.

44. The following dialogue is based on the recollection of Paul Volcker and on the *Wall Street Journal*, June 3, 1987, p. 20, and the *Washington Post*, June 3, 1987, p. A1 continued. Reagan's diary entry (see the next note) confirms Volcker's recollection that he chose not to be reappointed. Bob Woodward in *Maestro*, p. 23, claims that Volcker asked Baker, "If I were [interested] would the President reappoint me?" Woodward also claims that Volcker then suggested (without quotes), let me think about it. The public record fails to confirm Woodward's version.

45. See the entry for May 27, 1987, in Douglas Brinkley, ed., *The Reagan Diaries*, vol. 2 (New York: HarperCollins, 2009), p. 728.

46. Paul Laxalt, Reagan's best friend in the U.S. Senate, as quoted in the *Washington Post*, March 30, 1982, p. A1.

47. See Woodward, *Maestro*, p. 21.

48. Ibid., p. 19.

49. The sale of arms to Iran in violation of a U.S. embargo was exposed in November 1986. President Reagan appointed a commission chaired by Senator John Tower to investigate. The Tower Commission called the president to testify and later exonerated him from direct knowledge but criticized him for not properly monitoring his subordinates.

50. *Wall Street Journal*, June 3, 1987, p. 20.

51. See *New York Times*, June 2, 1987, p. D1, for this precise quote and the article in the *Wall Street Journal*, June 1, 1987, p. 3, entitled, "Fed's Volcker Is Likely to Be Reappointed If He Wants, White House Aide Indicates."

52. *New York Times*, June 3, 1987, p. D26.

53. *Washington Post*, June 3, 1987, p. A1.

54. Ibid. Also see Ecclesiastes 3:1 "For everything there is an appointed time."

55. Ibid.

56. *Wall Street Journal*, June 3, 1987, p. 20.

57. The closing prices on June 2, 1987, versus June 1, 1987, reflect the market's assessment of the news during the day. The value of the dollar fell from 1.834 marks to 1.804 marks, a decline of 1.6 percent, which is statistically significant compared with a daily average standard deviation of returns equal to 0.74 percent. Gold rose from $443 to $455, an increase of 2.7 percent, which is significant when compared with a daily standard deviation of returns equal to 1.25 percent. The daily standard deviations are measured from January through May of 1987.

58. See "Markets Decline After Volcker Steps Down," *Washington Post*, June 3, 1987, p. G1 continued.

59. Letter dated June 4, 1987, Personal Papers of Paul Volcker.

60. See "Hill Reaction to Greenspan Is Varied," *Washington Post*, June 3, 1987, p. G1 continued.

61. *Wall Street Journal*, June 3, 1987, p. 20.

62. *Washington Post*, June 3, 1987, p. G1 continued.

63. *Wall Street Journal*, June 3, 1987, p. 20.

64. The increase in the ten-year bond rate from 8.45 percent to 8.72 percent is a jump of 3.2 percent and is statistically significant compared with a daily average standard deviation of yield changes (measured from January through May of 1987) of 0.97 percent.

16. An Equestrian Statue

1. Seven black binders containing each letter and response in a separate cellophane wrapping are available in the Personal Papers of Paul Volcker.

2. The letter is dated June 6, 1987, Personal Papers of Paul Volcker.

3. The letter is dated June 10, 1987, Personal Papers of Paul Volcker.

4. The letter is dated June 2, 1987, Personal Papers of Paul Volcker.

5. The letter is dated August 1, 1987, Personal Papers of Paul Volcker.

6. The letter is dated June 5, 1987, Personal Papers of Paul Volcker.

7. The letter is dated June 3, 1987, Personal Papers of Paul Volcker.

8. *Wall Street Journal*, June 3, 1987, p. 1 continued.

9. "The Triumph of Central Banking?" 1990 Per Jacobsson Lecture, Washington, DC, September 23, 1990.

10. Both talks were given at the joint meeting of the World Bank and International Monetary Fund.

11. "The Triumph of Central Banking?" 1990 Per Jacobsson Lecture, Washington, DC, September 23, 1990, p. 3.

12. Morse said after Volcker spoke, "The great deflation of the 1930s . . . was not very well handled, and . . . the politicians and the commentators were able to put much of the blame onto the central banks . . . Now, if in the 1980s there was a successful disinflation . . . and if at the same time the reputation of central banks were enhanced . . . then no one takes more credit for that than Paul Volcker." See "The Triumph of Central Banking?," p. 18.

13. Ibid., p. 14.

14. Ibid.

15. PIPAV.

16. Interview with Milton Friedman, October 1, 2000, at www.pbs.org/wgbh/commandingheights/shared/minitext/int_miltonfriedman.html.

17. Paul Volcker and Toyoo Gyohten, *Changing Fortunes: The World's Money and the Threat to American Leadership* (New York: Times Books, 1992), p. 175.

18. *Newsweek*, February 24, 1986, p. 46.

19. Alan Blinder, "Panel Discussion I: What Have We Learned Since October 1979?" in *Reflections on Monetary Policy 25 Years After October 1979*, *Federal Reserve Bank of St. Louis* 87, no. 2, part 2 (March/April 2005): 283.

20. Blinder cites Otto Eckstein, a leading Keynesian econometrician (Otto Eckstein, *Core Inflation* [Englewood Cliffs, NJ: Prentice-Hall, 1981]), as an example of someone predicting an especially poor trade-off—which Blinder implies was not representative of the mainstream. But Arthur Okun, in "Efficient Disinflationary Policies," *American Economic Review* 68, no. 2 (May 1978), surveyed the existing econometric evidence that provides a range of estimates at that time. According to Marvin Goodfriend and Robert King in "The Incredible Volcker Disinflation," *Journal of Monetary Economics* 52, no. 5 (July 2005): 982–83, Okun's article implies that Volcker's "6 percentage point

reduction in inflation . . . would have led to a modern Great Contraction," which it did not. None of this is meant to imply that the increase in unemployment was trivial. It was not. It implies only that Volcker's disinflation was less costly than professional economists expected.

21. Volcker defined stable prices as "a situation in which expectations of generally rising (or falling) prices over a considerable period are not a pervasive influence on economic and financial behavior." (See Paul Volcker, "We Can Survive Prosperity," remarks at the Joint Meeting of the American Economic Association—American Finance Association, San Francisco, CA, December 28, 1983, p. 5.) That definition was later echoed by Alan Greenspan: "Price stability is that state in which expected changes in the general price level do not effectively alter business or household decisions" (see Transcript, Federal Open Market Committee Meeting, July 3, 1996, p. 51).

22. See Goodfriend and King, "The Incredible Volcker Disinflation," esp. pp. 1008–12.

23. See Milton Friedman, "How to Give Monetarism a Bad Name," in *Essays Prepared for the Joint Economic Committee*, Congress of the United States, June 27, 1985, Washington, DC, pp. 51–61; and see Allan Meltzer in *Administration's Fiscal Year 1983 Budget Proposal: Hearings Before the Senate Committee on Finance*, 97th Congress, 2nd Sess., February 23, 1982, Government Printing Office, Washington, DC, 1982, p. 180.

24. *New York Times*, December 31, 1983, p. 29.

25. *Newsweek*, February 24, 1986, p. 46.

26. For evidence on the response of monetary policy to inflation during the Volcker-Greenspan period compared with earlier, see Richard Clarida, Jordi Gali, and Mark Gertler, "Monetary Policy Rules and Macroeconomic Stability: Evidence and Some Theory," *Quarterly Journal of Economics* 115, no. 1 (February 2000): 147–80. They summarize (p. 148): "During the Volcker-Greenspan era the Federal Reserve adopted a proactive stance toward controlling inflation: it systematically raised real as well as nominal short term interest rates in response to higher expected inflation."

27. See chairman's remarks in *Reflections on Monetary Policy 25 Years After October 1979*, Federal Reserve Bank of St. Louis 87, no. 2, part 2 (March/April 2005): 138.

28. The letter is dated August 28, 1984, Personal Papers of Paul Volcker.

29. See chapter 12.

30. Alan Greenspan, *The Age of Turbulence* (New York: Penguin, 2007), p. 35.

31. Politics prevented, in Burns's words, "the Federal Reserve . . . [from] frustrating the will of Congress to which it was responsible—a Congress that

was intent on providing additional services to the electorate." See Arthur Burns, "The Anguish of Central Banking," 1979 Per Jacobsson Lecture, Belgrade, Yugoslavia, September 30, 1979, p. 16.

32. *New York Times*, August 28, 1981, p. D2.

33. *The Federal Reserve's First Monetary Policy Report for 1984: Hearings Before the Senate Committee on Banking, Housing and Urban Affairs*, 98th Congress, 2nd Sess., February 8, 1984, p. 108.

34. See *New York Times*, August 12, 1983, p. D2.

35. *The Nomination of Alan Greenspan: Hearings Before the Senate Committee on Banking, Housing and Urban Affairs*, 100th Congress, 1st Sess., July 21, 1987, pp. 25 and 27.

36. Rudolph G. Penner and C. Eugene Steuerle ("Budget Rules," *National Tax Journal* 57, no. 3 [September 2004]: 549) describe the history of the budget control rules legislated in the Budget Enforcement Act of 1990 as follows: "When it became apparent that GRH [Gramm-Rudman-Hollings] was not working, President George H. W. Bush began difficult, bipartisan negotiations with the Democratically-controlled Congress. The result was a significant deficit reduction package . . . The rules embodied in the agreement, which were adapted and extended under President Clinton's 1993 budget agreement, worked extremely well through 1997." The 1998 surplus is described as a surprise on page 550 of the same article.

37. Bob Woodward, *Maestro: Greenspan's Fed and the American Boom* (New York: Simon & Schuster, 2000), p. 221.

38. A nice survey of the causes of the Great Moderation, and the starting date, is in Peter M. Summers, "What Caused the Great Moderation? Some Cross-Country Evidence," *Federal Reserve Bank of Kansas City Economic Review* (3rd quarter 2005): 5–32. Summers mentions three standard explanations (p. 11): "Better monetary policy, structural changes in inventory management, and good luck." Volcker's chairmanship of the Federal Reserve Board begins the regime of better monetary policy that continues through the Greenspan period (see Clarida, Gali, and Gertler, "Monetary Policy Rules and Macroeconomic Stability"). Ben Bernanke, in a talk entitled "The Great Moderation" before the Meetings of the Eastern Economic Association on February 20, 2004, suggests that the inventory improvement explanation may in fact be related to improved monetary policy (p. 15). "High and unstable inflation increases the variability of relative prices and real interest rates, for example, distorting decisions regarding consumption, capital investment, and inventory investment, among others."

17. In Retrospect

1. The crisis is sometimes called the subprime mortgage crisis because the mortgage securities that were the source of the initial problem were below the top credit ratings. The label "World Financial Crisis" appears in *The Squam Lake Report* (Princeton, NJ: Princeton University Press, 2010), a brief book coauthored by fifteen financial economists offering detailed recommendations to guide financial reform. For a discussion of the development of the crisis, see Stephen Cecchetti, "Symposium: Early Phases of the Credit Crunch," *Journal of Economic Perspectives* 23 (Winter 2009): 51–75. An exhaustive description of the origins of the crisis is in *The Financial Crisis Inquiry Report*, submitted by the Financial Crisis Inquiry Commission Pursuant to Public Law 111-21, January 2011, available at U.S. Government Printing Office, Washington, DC 20402.

2. See "Radical Shift for Goldman and Morgan," *New York Times*, September 22, 2008, p. A1.

3. The demise of Lehman is told in Andrew Ross Sorkin, *Too Big to Fail: The Inside Story of How Wall Street and Washington Fought to Save the Financial System from Crisis—and Themselves* (New York: Viking, 2009). See William D. Cohan, *House of Cards: A Tale of Hubris and Wretched Excess on Wall Street* (New York: Doubleday, 2009), for the Bear Stearns story.

4. PIPAV.

5. See Paul Volcker, "Commercial Banks Must Match Profitability with Discipline," *Financier*, August 1990, Personal Papers of Paul Volcker.

6. The quote is from *Financial Services Competitiveness Act of 1995, Glass-Steagall Reform, and Related Issues: Hearings Before the House Committee on Banking and Financial Services*, 104th Congress, 1st Sess., March 29, April 5, 6, 1995, Washington, DC: Government Printing Office, p. 89. A related observation is made by Hyman Minsky, *Can "It" Happen Again? Essays on Instability and Finance* (Armonk, NY: M. E. Sharpe, 1982), p. 101: "Stability—or tranquility—in a world with a cyclical past and capitalist financial institutions is destabilizing."

7. The legislation in 1999 was the Gramm-Leach-Bliley Act, passed on November 12, 1999, which repealed the provisions of the Banking Act of 1933, commonly called the Glass-Steagall Act. The earlier Fed permissiveness refers to the 1987 decision discussed in chapter 15 dealing with bank underwriting. Volcker dissented from that ruling (see Minutes of the Federal Reserve Board, "Citicorp; J.P. Morgan & Co.; Bankers Trust New York Corporation, all of

New York, New York—Applications to underwrite and deal in certain securities," April 29, 1987).

8. See "Symposium: Early Phases of the Credit Crunch."

9. See *The Financial Services Competitiveness Act of 1995, Glass-Steagall Reform, and Related Issues: Hearings Before the House Committee on Banking and Financial Services*, 104th Congress, 1st Sess., March 29, April 5, 6, Washington, DC: Government Printing Office, p. 88. Volcker began his remarks with a reference to Goldman Sachs because the previous day Congressman Toby Roth raised the hypothetical issue of bailing out Goldman Sachs (see *Hearings*, p. 44).

10. For more details on James D. Wolfensohn and Company, see Joseph Treaster, *Paul Volcker: The Making of a Financial Legend* (New York: John Wiley, 2004), pp. 194–98.

11. *New York Times*, May 23, 1996, p. D1.

12. Letter to Paul Volcker from Deborah Sale, vice president, Hospital for Special Surgery, dated March 4, 1997, Personal Papers of Paul Volcker.

13. PIPAV.

14. September 25, 1996, p. A20.

15. See *The Disposition of Assets Deposited in Swiss Banks by Missing Nazi Victims: Hearings Before the House Committee on Banking and Financial Services*, 104th Congress, 2nd Sess., Washington, DC, December 11, 1996, p. 49.

16. See "Under Fire, Andersen Puts Trust in Volcker," *New York Times*, February 4, 2002, p. A18.

17. See Volcker's testimony on the UN investigation before Congress in *Corruption in the United Nations Oil-for-Food Program: Reaching a Consensus on United Nations Reform: Hearings Before the Senate Committee on Homeland Security and Government Affairs*, 109th Congress, 1st Sess., Washington, DC, October 31, 2005, pp. 11–26.

18. PIPAV.

19. Statement by Paul Volcker in Support of Barack Obama, Personal Papers of Paul Volcker, excerpted in *Wall Street Journal*, Washington Wire, Eastern edition, February 1, 2008.

20. *Wall Street Journal*, October 21, 2008, p. A1.

21. Ibid.

22. From an interview with Austan Goolsbee.

23. See *Wall Street Journal*, November 8, 2008, p. A4, for the three contenders for the job as treasury secretary: former Clinton treasury secretary Lawrence Summers, Federal Reserve Bank of New York president Timothy Geithner, and Volcker.

24. This story is from Austan Goolsbee. Buffett was born on August 30, 1930, which makes him three years younger than Volcker.

25. The conversation is based on Volcker's recollection.

26. For a discussion of the transition team, see *Washington Post*, November 6, 2008, p. A1, and November 14, 2008, p. A6; and *New York Times*, November 24, 2008, p. A1.

27. See *New York* magazine, May 31, 2010, p. 25.

28. *New York Times*, November 27, 2008, p. A29.

29. *New York Times*, December 6, 1992, p. A1 continued. This quote also refers to the investment banker Felix G. Rohatyn, head of the Municipal Assistance Corporation in New York.

30. *Wall Street Journal*, November 26, 2008, p. A4.

31. *Washington Post*, November 27, 2008, p. A1.

32. The Dodd-Frank Wall Street Reform and Consumer Protection Act, signed by President Obama on July 21, 2010, is named after Senate Banking Committee chairman Christopher Dodd and House Banking Committee chairman Barney Frank. The Volcker Rule prohibitions against bank proprietary trading activities and certain relationships with hedge funds are contained in Section 619 of the act.

33. *Prohibiting Certain High Risk Investment Activities by Banks and Bank Holding Companies: Hearing Before the Senate Committee on Banking, Housing and Urban Affairs*, 111th Congress, 2nd Sess., Washington, DC, February 2, 2010, p. 3.

34. Ibid., pp. 3–4.

35. Volcker's key PERAB memo to Obama is contained in a cover letter dated June 2, 2009, supported by a statement on systemic risk dated June 3, 2009 (Personal Papers of Paul Volcker). The following excerpt on bank regulation forms the basis of what became the Volcker Rule: "Bank holding companies that engage in non-bank financial services, such as hedge funds, private equity funds, proprietary trading, and certain aspects of derivatives trading and other 'transaction-oriented' services, subject their firms to complex risks and, to the extent they also serve customers in a fiduciary capacity, raise potentially unreconcilable [*sic*] conflicts of interest. Recent events have revealed that these threats, and the implications for the maintenance of management control, are very real and can have severe systemic consequences. As a result, banks should be discouraged from, and in some cases completely prohibited from, engaging in some risk-prone transaction-oriented capital market activities. It will not be necessary to return to Glass-Steagall, which prohibited some 'relationship-oriented' services, such as underwriting corporate securities for business customers. However, some revision of Gramm-Leach-

Bliley will be required to reinforce protections against banking/commerce combinations and hedge fund or private equity fund sponsorships. The control of banks by individual hedge funds, private equity funds, or commercial firms should be prohibited."

36. See *Prohibiting Certain High Risk Investment Activities by Banks and Bank Holding Companies*, p. 49.

37. See Paul Volcker op-ed, "How to Reform Our Financial System," *New York Times*, January 31, 2010, p. WK1.

38. PIPAV.

39. See U.S. Treasury, "Financial Regulatory Reform: A New Foundation—Rebuilding Financial Supervision and Regulation," June 19, 2009, available at web.archive.org/web/20100623205517/http://www.financialstability.gov/docs/regs/FinalReport_web.pdf.

40. Leverage enhances profits when prices rise but can lead to bankruptcy when prices decline. For example, suppose a family with $100,000 in savings pays that amount for a home a few miles outside of Cleveland or Dallas. A drop of $20,000 in the price of the house means a 20 percent loss on the $100,000 investment, but they still have a net worth of $80,000 and can enjoy the benefits of living close to downtown. A family with only $10,000 to begin with could also buy the same house but would have to borrow the remaining $90,000 to complete the purchase. After this *leveraged* transaction, the identical $20,000 price decline would turn the family's net worth from plus $10,000 to minus $10,000—the house is worth only $80,000, but they still owe $90,000. The price decline might even force the family to vacate the premises. Leverage can cause bankruptcy when asset prices decline.

41. *Prohibiting Certain High Risk Investment Activities by Banks and Bank Holding Companies*, p. 22.

42. Ibid., p. 21.

43. Ibid., p. 22.

44. See Markus Brunnermeier, "Deciphering the Liquidity and Credit Crunch of 2007–2008," *Journal of Economic Perspectives* 23, no. 1 (Winter 2009): 80–81. "In hindsight, it is clear that one distorting force leading to the popularity of structured investment vehicles was regulatory and ratings arbitrage. The Basel I Accord (an international agreement that sets guidelines for bank regulation) required that banks hold capital of at least 8 percent of the loans on their balance sheets; this capital requirement (called a 'capital charge') was much lower for contractual credit lines."

45. See "Citigroup Says It Will Absorb SIV Assets," MarketWatch, December 13, 2007, available at www.marketwatch.com/story/citi-plans-to-absorb-49-billion-in-siv-assets-onto-balance-sheet.

46. This quote and the following quotes by Senator Johanns and Volcker come from *Prohibiting Certain High Risk Investment Activities by Banks and Bank Holding Companies*, pp. 26–28.

47. For a detailed argument against the power of the Volcker Rule to prevent a crisis, and for arguments in favor of more capital, see Lawrence J. White, "The Gramm-Leach-Bliley Act of 1999: A Bridge Too Far? Or Not Far Enough?" *Suffolk University Law Review* 43 (2009–2010): 937–56.

48. Sorkin, *Too Big to Fail*, tells the Lehman story well.

49. See "Dollar Hits Two-Year Low vs. Yen; Subprime-Battered Investors Pull Back from 'Carry Trade,'" *Wall Street Journal*, November 13, 2007, p. C2. Also see "Yen Gets Lift from Turmoil in the Market; Strength Amid Distress Reveals Investor Caution as Carry Trades Unwind," *Wall Street Journal*, January 24, 2008, p. C1.

50. *Prohibiting Certain High Risk Investment Activities by Banks and Bank Holding Companies*, p. 36.

51. Shelby had asked "what constitutes excessive growth" at the largest financial firms? And Volcker gave the pornography answer. See ibid., p. 14.

52. This quote and the remaining quotes in the chapter are from ibid., p. 37.

18. The Rule

1. *Guardian*, London, February 3, 2010, p. 22.

2. The article is entitled "On the Nature of Trading: Do Speculators Leave Footprints?" *Journal of Portfolio Management* 29, no. 4 (July 2003): 64–70. It was written in connection with my work as an expert witness in a legal dispute over a corporate takeover. The court case was *Consolidated Edison, Inc. v. Northeast Utilities*. I was retained by Shearman & Sterling on behalf of Consolidated Edison to provide deposition testimony and an expert report analyzing the nature of customer-based trading versus speculation. I applied that analysis to the behavior of the Northeast Utilities energy trading subsidiary in connection with Con Edison's bid to terminate its takeover of Northeast.

3. I traded on the New York Futures Exchange, the COMEX, and the New York Mercantile Exchange as a scalper, or market maker, and wrote a paper describing that activity entitled "Marketmaker Behavior in an Auction Market: An Analysis of Scalpers in Futures Markets," *Journal of Finance* 39, no. 4 (September 1984): 937–54. I traded for a hedge fund called Odyssey Partners, run by Jack Nash and Leon Levy, from 1988 through 1996.

4. The letter, entitled "Congress Should Implement the Volcker Rule for

Banks," was signed by W. Michael Blumenthal, Nicholas Brady, Paul O'Neill, George Shultz, and John Snow, and appeared in Letters to the Editor, *Wall Street Journal*, February 22, 2010, p. A18.

5. Brady (1988–1993), O'Neill (2001–2002), Shultz (1972–1974), and Snow (2003–2006) served in Republican administrations; Blumenthal (1977–1979) served in a Democratic administration.

6. Milton Friedman was born on July 31, 1912, and died on November 16, 2006.

7. See Bloomberg news report "Ex–Treasury Secretary Brady Running with 'Volcker,'" at www.nj.com/business/index.ssf/2010/08/ex-treasury_secretary_brady_ru.html.

8. Letter dated May 19, 2010, Personal Papers of Paul Volcker.

9. *New York Times*, July 11, 2010, p. BU1.

10. See John Cassidy, "The Volcker Rule," *New Yorker*, July 26, 2010, p. 25.

11. A copy of the 849-page bill, Public Law 111-203–July 21, 2010, is available at the online Government Printing Office with the following specific address: www.gpo.gov/fdsys/pkg/PLAW-111publ203/pdf/PLAW-111publ203.pdf.

12. Public Law 111-203—July 21, 2010, 124 Stat. 1620.

13. Ibid., 124 Stat. 1621.

14. Ibid., 124 Stat. 1394. Section 111 of the Dodd-Frank Act established the Financial Stability Oversight Council (124 Stat 1392).

15. The council consists of ten voting members and five nonvoting members. The voting members are the secretary of the treasury; the chairman of the Board of Governors of the Federal Reserve System; the comptroller of the currency; the director of the Bureau of Consumer Financial Protection; the chairman of the Securities and Exchange Commission; the chairman of the Federal Deposit Insurance Corporation; the chairman of the Commodity Futures Trading Commission; the director of the Federal Housing Finance Agency; the chairman of the National Credit Union Administration Board; and an independent member with insurance expertise who is appointed by the president and confirmed by the Senate for a six-year term. The nonvoting members, who serve in an advisory capacity, are the director of the Office of Financial Research; the director of the Federal Insurance Office; a state insurance commissioner designated by the state insurance commissioners; a state banking supervisor designated by the state banking supervisors; and a state securities commissioner (or officer performing like functions) designated by the state securities commissioners.

16. See FSOC 2011 Annual Report, available at www.treasury.gov/initiatives/fsoc/Pages/annual-report.aspx, esp. p. 127.

17. See Cassidy, "The Volcker Rule," for a detailed account of the negotiations.

18. See "Banks Dodge a Bullet as Congress Dilutes Rules," Bloomberg, June 25, 2010.

19. See WSJ.com, February 3, 2010, 9:16 P.M.

20. Volcker's letter is addressed to Timothy Geithner as chairman of the FSOC, and is dated October 29, 2010. His footnote reads, "I understand that NYU Professor William Silber, who has served as expert witness in cases requiring identification of, and distinctions between, 'proprietary' and 'market-making' activity, is providing FSOC with relevant analysis." My letter to committee chairman Timothy Geithner, dated November 2, 2010, included the following: "The methodology outlined in my paper can be applied to the ban on proprietary trading contained in Section 619 of the Dodd-Frank Act but it should not be viewed as a substitute for a comprehensive approach to implementing the Volcker Rule. In conversations with some of the staff at Treasury I have suggested that you instruct regulators to adapt the practical skills of managers in financial firms whose job it is to distinguish between speculation and market making. For example, during the years I spent as a trader on a number of futures exchanges I was impressed by the ability of my clearing firm to monitor each of their traders' risk exposure and to impose different capital requirements depending on whether the trader was a market maker or a speculator. The manager at the clearing firm looked at the sequence of a trader's transactions, the rate of inventory turnover, end-of-day positions, and then supplemented those numerical facts with surprise visits to the trading floor to see what a suspected 'closet speculator' was actually doing. I think that regulators monitoring the implementation of the Volcker Rule ban on speculation should arm themselves with a variety of methodologies, including the analysis outlined in 'Do Speculators Leave Footprints?' They should establish the same type of multi-dimensional approach that the IRS uses to identify tax evasion, including face-to-face audits where that is indicated."

21. See "Wall St. Faces Specter of Lost Trading Units," *New York Times*, August 6, 2010, p. B1.

22. See "Morgan Stanley Team to Exit in Fallout from Volcker Rule," *Wall Street Journal*, January 11, 2011, p. C1.

23. See "Wall St. Faces Specter of Lost Trading Units," *New York Times*, August 6, 2010, p. B1.

24. See "With Big Banks Forced to Exit, Look for Speculators to Step In," *Wall Street Journal*, September 7, 2010, p. C10.

25. See Michael Lewis, "Wall Street Proprietary Trading Under Cover," Bloomberg Opinion, October 27, 2010, 4:48 P.M.

26. Study & Recommendations on Prohibitions on Proprietary Trading & Certain Relationships with Hedge Funds & Private Equity Funds, Financial

Stability Oversight Council, January 2011, p. 4, at www.treasury.gov/initiatives/ Documents/Volcker%20sec%20%20619%20study%20final%201%2018%2011 %20rg.pdf.

27. For a complete list of the metrics see ibid., pp. 39–43.

28. Ibid., p. 44.

29. *Prohibiting Certain High Risk Investment Activities by Banks and Bank Holding Companies*, p. 37.

30. See page 2 of Volcker's letter addressed to Timothy Geithner as chairman of the FSOC, dated October 29, 2010.

31. Study & Recommendations on Prohibitions on Proprietary Trading & Certain Relationships with Hedge Funds & Private Equity Funds, p. 3.

32. Ibid., pp. 35–36.

33. See "Volcker Rule May Work Even If Vague," *New York Times*, January 21, 2011, p. B1.

34. "Volcker Rule Should Require Sign-off by Bank CEOs, Panel Says," Bloomberg, January 19, 2011, available at www.bloomberg.com/news/2011-01-19/volcker -rule-should-require-bank-ceos-to-certify-compliance-panel-says.html.

35. Ibid.

36. See "Volcker Rule May Work Even If Vague," p. B1.

37. Paul Volcker, Mais Lecture, Cass Business School, London, July 14, 2011.

19. Trust

1. The *Wall Street Journal* ran an op-ed piece by Lewis Lehrman on August 15, 2011, the fortieth anniversary of the suspension of dollar convertibility, entitled "The Nixon Shock Heard 'Round the World." The facts are mostly right, with one big exception. Lehrman writes (*Wall Street Journal*, August 15, 2011, p. A13), "At least one Camp David participant, Paul Volcker, regretted what transpired that weekend." The suspension of convertibility was, in fact, Volcker's idea (see chapter 3), and he does not think it was a mistake.

2. See chapter 2 on the gold cover. The requirement that the Federal Reserve hold gold certificates against bank reserves was removed in 1965, and the requirement against Federal Reserve notes was eliminated in 1968.

3. This inscription appears on the face of every Federal Reserve note. Check your pocket.

4. See Friedman's testimony in "Gold Cover," Hearings Before the Committee on Banking and Currency, U.S. Senate, 90th Congress, 2nd Sess., February 1, 1968, p. 152.

5. Irving Fisher was a professor of economics at Yale University from 1898

until 1935. His most important books include *The Rate of Interest* (Macmillan, 1907), *The Purchasing Power of Money* (Macmillan, 1911), and *The Making of Index Numbers* (Houghton Mifflin, 1922). In *Money Mischief* (New York: Harcourt Brace, 1994), p. 37, Milton Friedman calls Fisher "the greatest economist the United States has ever produced."

6. The quotes in this paragraph are from Friedman, *Money Mischief*, pp. 252 and 254.

7. For a general discussion on the origins of the Great Inflation, see Allan Meltzer, "Origins of the Great Inflation," and Christina Romer, "Commentary," in *Reflections on Monetary Policy 25 Years After October 1979, Federal Reserve Bank of St. Louis* 87, no. 2, part 2 (March/April 2005).

8. See chapter 14 for the discussion of the passage of the Gramm-Rudman-Hollings amendment to balance the budget.

9. Federal Reserve press release available at www.federalreserve.gov/news events/press/monetary/20110809a.htm.

10. PIPAV.

11. Paul Volcker, "A Little Inflation Can Be a Dangerous Thing," *New York Times*, September 19, 2011, p. A27.

12. According to Federal Reserve chairman Ben Bernanke, "Even after economic conditions have returned to normal, the nation faces a sizable structural budget gap. Both the Congressional Budget Office and the Committee for a Responsible Federal Budget project that the budget deficit will be almost 5 percent of GDP in fiscal year 2015, assuming that current budget policies are extended and the economy is then close to full employment." See "Fiscal Sustainability," Remarks by Ben S. Bernanke, Annual Conference of the Committee for a Responsible Federal Budget, Washington, DC, June 14, 2011, p. 1, available at www.federalreserve.gov/newsevents/speech/2011speech.htm.

13. Paul Volcker, "A Little Inflation Can Be a Dangerous Thing," *New York Times*, September 19, 2011, p. A27.

14. See WSJ.com, October 19, 2011, 10:27 A.M.

15. See "Fiscal Sustainability," Remarks by Ben S. Bernanke, Annual Conference of the Committee for a Responsible Federal Budget, Washington, DC, June 14, 2011, available at www.federalreserve.gov/newsevents/speech/2011speech.htm.

Selected Bibliography

Books, Articles, Reports

Abrams, Burton. 2006. "How Richard Nixon Pressured Arthur Burns: Evidence from the Nixon Tapes." *Journal of Economic Perspectives* 20, no. 4 (Fall): 177–88.

Anderson, Harry, and Rich Thomas. 1983. "Voting for Volcker to Stay." *Newsweek*, June 20, p. 53.

Anderson, Martin. 1990. *Revolution: The Reagan Legacy*. Stanford, CA: Hoover Institution Press, Stanford University.

Arrow, Kenneth. 1963. "Uncertainly and the Welfare Economics of Medical Care." *American Economic Review* 43, no. 5 (December): 941–73.

Barro, Robert. 1982. "United States Inflation and the Choice of Monetary Standard." In Robert Hall, ed. *Inflation: Causes and Effects*. Chicago: University of Chicago Press, pp. 99–110.

———. 1989. "The Ricardian Approach to Budget Deficits." *Journal of Economic Perspectives* 3, no. 2 (Spring): 37–54.

Bell, Geoffrey. 1973. *The Euro-Dollar Market and the International Financial System*. New York: John Wiley.

Bernanke, Ben S. 2004. "The Great Moderation." Remarks at the Meetings of the Eastern Economic Association, February 20, 2004. Available at fraser .stlouisfed.org/historicaldocs/1191/download/64784/bernanke_20040220 .pdf.

———. 2010. "Paul Volcker," *Time*, April 29, 2010. Available at www.time.com/ time/specials/packages/article/0,28804,1984685_1984745_1984803,00 .html.

———. 2011. "Fiscal Sustainability." Remarks at the Annual Conference of the Committee for a Responsible Federal Budget. Washington, DC,

June 14, 2011. Available at www.federalreserve.gov/newsevents/speech/2011speech.htm.

Bernstein, Peter L. 2000. *The Power of Gold: The History of an Obsession.* New York: John Wiley.

Blinder, Alan. 2005. "Panel Discussion I: What Have We Learned Since October 1979?" *Reflections on Monetary Policy 25 Years After October 1979, Federal Reserve Bank of St. Louis* 87, no. 2, part 2 (March/April).

Board of Governors of the Federal Reserve System. 1963. *Federal Reserve System: Purposes and Functions.* 5th ed. Washington, DC: Board of Governors of the Federal Reserve System.

———. 2005. *Federal Reserve System: Purposes and Functions.* 9th ed. Washington, DC: Board of Governors of the Federal Reserve System.

———. Various dates. *Minutes.* Washington, DC: Board of Governors of the Federal Reserve System.

———. Various dates. *Press Releases.* Washington, DC: Board of Governors of the Federal Reserve System.

Bordo, Michael D., and Athanasios Orphanides (eds.) (forthcoming). *The Great Inflation.* Chicago: University of Chicago Press.

Boughton, James. 1998. "Harry Dexter White and the International Monetary Fund." *Finance and Development* 35, no. 3 (September).

Bremner, Robert P. 2004. *Chairman of the Fed: William McChesney Martin Jr. and the Creation of the Modern American Financial System.* New Haven, CT: Yale University Press.

Brunnermeier, Markus. 2009. "Deciphering the Liquidity and Credit Crunch of 2007–2008." *Journal of Economic Perspectives* 23, no. 1 (Winter): 77–100.

Burns, Arthur F. 1979. *The Anguish of Central Banking.* Belgrade, Yugoslavia: The 1979 Per Jacobsson Lecture. Available at www.perjacobsson.org/lectures/1979.pdf.

———. 2010. *Inside the Nixon Administration: The Secret Diary of Arthur Burns, 1969–1974.* Robert H. Ferrell, ed. Lawrence: University Press of Kansas.

Carter, Jimmy. 2010. *White House Diary.* New York: Farrar, Straus and Giroux.

Cassidy, John. 2010. "The Volcker Rule." *New Yorker* 86, no. 21, July 26.

Chernow, Ron. 1990. *The House of Morgan: An American Banking Dynasty and the Rise of Modern Finance.* New York: Atlantic Monthly Press.

Clarida, Richard, Jordi Gali, and Mark Gertler. 2000. "Monetary Policy Rules and Macroeconomic Stability: Evidence and Some Theory." *Quarterly Journal of Economics* 115, no. 1 (February): 147–180.

Cohan, William D. 2009. *House of Cards: A Tale of Hubris and Wretched Excess on Wall Street*. New York: Doubleday.

Connally, John B. 1993. *In History's Shadow: An American Odyssey*. New York: Hyperion.

Coombs, Charles A. 1976. *The Arena of International Finance*. New York: John Wiley.

Council of Economic Advisers. Various dates. *Annual Report*. Washington, DC.

———. Various dates. *Economic Report of the President*. Washington, DC.

Coyne, Joseph H. 2005. "Reflections on the FOMC Meeting of October 6, 1979." *Reflections on Monetary Policy 25 Years After October 1979, Federal Reserve Bank of St. Louis* 87, no. 2, part 2 (March/April): 313–16.

Dornbusch, Rudiger, and Jeffrey Frankel. 1989. "The Flexible Exchange Rate System: Experience and Alternatives." National Bureau of Economic Research Working Paper No. 2464. Available at www.nber.org/papers/w2464.pdf.

Duncombe, Bruce, ed. 2002. *Foreign Relations of the United States, 1969–1976*, vol. 3, *Foreign Economic Policy 1969–1972; International Monetary Policy, 1969–1972*. Washington, DC: U.S. Government Printing Office.

Eckstein, Otto. 1981. *Core Inflation*. Englewood Cliffs, NJ: Prentice-Hall.

Epstein, Edward Jay. 1982. *The Rise and Fall of Diamonds: The Shattering of a Brilliant Illusion*. New York: Simon & Schuster.

Federal Deposit Insurance Corporation. 1998. *Managing the Crisis: The FDIC and RTC Experience, 1980–1994*. Washington, DC.

Federal Open Market Committee. Various dates. *Memorandum of Discussion*. Washington, DC: Board of Governors of the Federal Reserve System.

———. Various dates. *Record of Policy Actions*. Washington, DC: Board of Governors of the Federal Reserve System.

———. Various dates. *Transcripts*. Papers of Arthur Burns. University of Michigan Library, Ann Arbor, MI.

———. Various dates. *Transcripts*. Washington, DC: Board of Governors of the Federal Reserve System.

Feldstein, Martin S. 1994. "American Economic Policy in the 1980s: A Personal View." In Martin Feldstein, ed. *American Economic Policy in the 1980s*. Chicago: University of Chicago Press.

Financial Stability Oversight Council. 2011. *Annual Report*. Available at www.treasury.gov/initiatives/fsoc/Pages/annual-report.aspx.

———. 2011. "Study & Recommendations on Prohibitions on Proprietary Trading & Certain Relationships with Hedge Funds & Private Equity

Funds." Available at www.treasury.gov/initiatives/Documents/Volcker%20sec%20%20619%20study%20final%201%2018%2011%20rg.pdf.

Fisher, Irving. 1907. *The Rate of Interest* New York: Macmillan.

———. 1911. *The Purchasing Power of Money.* New York: Macmillan.

———. 1922. *The Making of Index Numbers.* Boston: Houghton Mifflin.

Fleming, J. M. 1962. "Domestic Financial Policies Under Fixed and Under Floating Exchange Rates." *IMF Staff Papers* 9, no. 3, (November): 369–80.

Foote, John Taintor. 1924. *A Wedding Gift; A Fishing Story.* London: D. Appleton-Century Co.

French, Kenneth R., et al. 2010. *The Squam Lake Report: Fixing the Financial System.* Princeton, NJ: Princeton University Press.

Friedman, Benjamin. 1992. "Learning from the Reagan Deficits." *American Economic Review* 82, no. 2 (May): 299–304.

Friedman, Milton. 1968. "The Role of Monetary Policy." *American Economic Review* 58, no. 1 (March): 1–17.

———. 1969. "The Optimum Quantity of Money." In *The Optimum Quantity of Money and Other Essays.* Chicago: Aldine.

———. 1978. "Burns on the Outside." *Newsweek*, January 9, p. 52.

———. 1985. "How to Give Monetarism a Bad Name." In *Essays Prepared for the Joint Economic Committee*, June 27, 1985. Washington, DC.

———. 1994, 1992. *Money Mischief: Episodes in Monetary History.* New York: Harcourt Brace.

———. 2000. "Interview," October 1. Available at www.pbs.org/wgbh/commandingheights/shared/minitext/int_miltonfriedman.html.

Friedman, Milton, and Robert V. Roosa. 1967. *The Balance of Payments: Free Versus Fixed Exchange Rates.* Washington, DC: American Enterprise Institute for Public Policy Research.

Friedman, Milton, and Anna J. Schwartz. 1963. *A Monetary History of the United States, 1867–1960.* Princeton, NJ: Princeton University Press.

Goodfriend, Marvin. 1993. "Interest Rate Policy and the Inflation Scare Problem: 1979–1992." *Federal Reserve Bank of Richmond Economic Quarterly* 79, no. 1 (Winter): 1–24.

Goodfriend, Marvin, and Robert G. King. 2005. "The Incredible Volcker Disinflation." *Journal of Monetary Economics* 52, no. 5 (July): 981–1015.

Graham, Frank D., and Charles R. Whittlesey. 1934. "Fluctuating Exchange Rates, Foreign Trade, the Price Level." *American Economic Review* 24, no. 3 (September): 410–16.

Greenspan, Alan. 2005. "Chairman's Remarks." *Reflections on Monetary Policy 25 Years After October 1979, Federal Reserve Bank of St. Louis* 87, no. 2, part 2 (March/April).

———. 2007. *The Age of Turbulence: Adventures in a New World.* New York: Penguin Books.

Greider, William. 1981. "The Education of David Stockman." *Atlantic Monthly*, December.

———. 1987. *Secrets of the Temple: How the Federal Reserve Runs the Country.* New York: Simon & Schuster.

Gup, Benton E. 2004. *Too Big to Fail: Policies and Practices in Government Bailouts.* Westport, CT: Praeger Publishers.

Haldeman, H. R. 1994. *The Haldeman Diaries.* New York: G. P. Putnam's Sons.

Hanc, George. 1997. *History of the Eighties: Lessons for the Future.* Washington, DC: Federal Deposit Insurance Corporation.

Hansen, Lars Peter, and Thomas J. Sargent. 1991. *Rational Expectations Econometrics.* Boulder, CO: Westview Press.

Harper, Christine. 2010. "Banks 'Dodged a Bullet' as U.S. Congress Dilutes Trading Rules," June 25. Available at www.bloomberg.com/news/2010 -06-25/banks-dodged-a-bullet-as-congress-dilutes-u-s-trading-rules-in -overhaul.html.

Haupert, Michael J. 2007. "The Economic History of Major League Baseball." Available at eh.net/encyclopedia/article/haupert.mlb.

Hayek, Friedrich A. 1944, 1994. *The Road to Serfdom.* Chicago: University of Chicago Press.

Herren, Robert S. 1991. "Paul A. Volcker." In Bernard Katz, ed. *Biographical Dictionary of the Board of Governors of the Federal Reserve.* New York: Greenwood Press.

Hetzel, Robert L. 2008. *The Monetary Policy of the Federal Reserve: A History.* New York: Cambridge University Press.

Hume, David. 1752, repr. 1963. *Essays: Moral, Political, and Literary.* London: Oxford University Press.

International Monetary Fund. Various dates. *Annual Report.* Washington, DC.

Isaac, William, with Philip C. Meyer. 2010. *Senseless Panic: How Washington Failed America.* New York: John Wiley.

Katz, Ian. 2011. "Volcker Rule Should Require Sign-off by Bank CEOs, Panel Says," January 19. Available at www.bloomberg.com/news/2011-01-19/ volcker-rule-should-require-bank-ceos-to-certify-compliance-panel -says.html.

Kindleberger, Charles. 1934. "Competitive Currency Depreciation Between Denmark and New Zealand." *Harvard Business Review* 12, no. 4 (July).

Kraft, Joseph. 1984. *The Mexican Rescue.* New York: Group of Thirty.

Laubach, Thomas. 2009. "New Evidence on the Interest Rate Effects of Budget Deficits and Debt." *Journal of the European Economic Association* 7, no. 4 (June): 858–85.

Levin, Andrew, and John Taylor. 2008. "Falling Behind the Curve: A Positive Analysis of the Stop-Start Monetary Policies and the Great Inflation." Manuscript prepared for the September 2008 NBER Conference on the Great Inflation. Available at www.nber.org/public_html/confer/2008/gif08/levin.pdf.

Lewis, Michael. 2010. "Proprietary Trading Goes Under Cover," October 27. Available at www.bloomberg.com/news/2010-10-27/wall-street-proprie tary-trading-under-cover-commentary-by-michael-lewis.html.

Lindsey, David, Athanasios Orphanides, and Robert Rasche. 2005. "The Reform of October 1979: How It Happened and Why." *Reflections on Monetary Policy 25 Years After October 1979, Federal Reserve Bank of St. Louis* 87, no. 2, part 2 (March/April): 187–236.

Lindsey, David E. 2003. *A Modern History of FOMC Communication: 1975–2002*. Washington, DC: Board of Governors of the Federal Reserve System. Available at fraser.stlouisfed.org/docs/publications/books/20030624_lindsey_modhistfomc.pdf.

Lucas, Robert E. Jr. 1972. "Expectations and the Neutrality of Money." *Journal of Economic Theory* 4, no. 2 (April): 103–24.

———. 1976. "Econometric Policy Evaluation: A Critique." *Carnegie-Rochester Conference Series*, pp. 19–46.

Lutz, Friedrich A. 1954. "The Case for Flexible Exchange Rates." *Banca Nazionale del Lavoro Quarterly Review* 7 (December): 175–85.

Mehrling, Perry. 2001. "An Interview with Paul A. Volcker." *Macroeconomic Dynamics* 5, no. 3 (June): 434–60.

Meltzer, Allan H. 2003. *A History of the Federal Reserve*, vol. 1, *1913–1951*. Chicago: University of Chicago Press.

———. 2005. "Origins of the Great Inflation." *Reflections on Monetary Policy 25 Years After October 1979, Federal Reserve Bank of St. Louis* 87, no. 2, part 2 (March/April): 145–76.

———. 2009. *A History of the Federal Reserve*, vol. 2, book 1, *1951–1969*. Chicago: University of Chicago Press.

———. 2009. *A History of the Federal Reserve*, vol. 2, book 2, *1970–1986*. Chicago: University of Chicago Press.

Meyer, Lawrence H. 2004. *A Term at the Fed: An Insider's View*. New York: HarperBusiness.

Miller, Preston. 1980. "Deficit Policies, Deficit Fallacies." *Federal Reserve Bank of Minneapolis Quarterly Review* 4, no. 3 (Summer).

Morgenstern, Oskar. 1937. *The Limits of Economics*. London: William Hodge and Company.

———. 1963. *On the Accuracy of Economic Observations*. Princeton, NJ: Princeton University Press.

Mundell, Robert A. 1963. "Capital Mobility and Stabilization Policy Under Fixed and Flexible Exchange Rates." *The Canadian Journal of Economics and Political Science* 29 (November): 475–85.

Naftali, Timothy J., ed. 2001. *John F. Kennedy: The Great Crises*. Vol. 1. New York: W. W. Norton and Company.

Neikirk, William. 1987. *Volcker: Portrait of the Money Man*. New York: Congdon and Weed.

Neumann, John von, and Oskar Morgenstern. 1944. *Theory of Games and Economic Behavior*. Princeton, NJ: Princeton University Press.

New York Times. Various dates.

Newsweek. Various dates.

Niskanen, William. 1988. *Reaganomics: An Insider's Account of the Policies and the People*. New York: Oxford University Press.

Nixon, Richard. Various dates. Nixon Papers. National Archives II, College Park, MD.

Nixon Tapes. Various dates. Available at www.nixontapes.org/chron2.html.

Obstfeld, Maurice, Jay C. Shambaugh, and Alan M. Taylor. 2005. "The Trilemma in History: Tradeoffs Among Exchange Rates, Monetary Policies, and Capital Mobility." *Review of Economics and Statistics* 87, no. 3 (August): 423–38.

Officer, Lawrence H., and Samuel H. Williamson. Annual Inflation Rates in the United States, 1775–2009, and United Kingdom, 1265–2009. Available at www.measuringworth.com/inflation/.

Okun, Arthur M. 1978. "Efficient Disinflationary Policies." *American Economic Review* 68, no. 2 (May).

Onaran, Yalman. 2009 "Volcker Gets Less Than He Wants in Curbing Excesses." June 25. Available at www.bloomberg.com/apps/news?pid=newsarchive&sid=a_S7ikIYpN8g.

Penner, Rudolph. 2001. *Errors in Budget Forecasting*. Washington, DC: Urban Institute. Available at www.urban.org/url.cfm?ID=310086.

———. ed. (1991). *The Great Fiscal Experiment*. Washington, DC: Urban Institute Press.

Penner, Rudolph G., and Alan J. Abramson. 1988. *Broken Purse Strings: Congressional Budgeting, 1974 to 1988*. Washington, DC: Urban Institute.

Penner, Rudolph G., and C. Eugene Steuerle. 2004. "Budget Rules." *National Tax Journal* 57, no. 3 (September): 547–57.

Pollak, Amy. 2010. "Homes for Under $100,000." Available at Kiplinger.com, November 8.

Poole, William. 2005. "Panel Discussion II: Safeguarding Good Policy Practice." *Reflections on Monetary Policy 25 Years After October 1979, Federal Reserve Bank of St. Louis* 87, no. 2, part 2 (March/April).

Reagan, Ronald. 2003. *Reagan: A Life in Letters.* Annelise Graebner Anderson, Kiron K. Skinner, and Martin Anderson, eds. New York: Free Press.

———. 2007. *The Reagan Diaries.* Douglas Brinkley, ed. New York: Harper-Collins.

Ritter, Lawrence S. 1966. *The Glory of Their Times: The Story of the Early Days of Baseball Told by the Men Who Played It.* New York: Macmillan.

Ritter, Lawrence S., and William L. Silber. 1970, 1984. *Money.* New York: Basic Books.

———. 1974. *Principles of Money, Banking, and Financial Markets.* New York: Basic Books.

Ritter, Lawrence S., William L. Silber, and Gregory Udell. 2009. *Principles of Money, Banking and Financial Markets*, 12th ed. New York: Addison-Wesley.

Rodda, Richard. "Oral History of Teaneck." Teaneck Public Library. Available at www.teaneck.org/virtualvillage/oralhistory/index.html.

Romer, Christina D. 2005. "Commentary." *Reflections on Monetary Policy 25 Years After October 1979, Federal Reserve Bank of St. Louis* 87, no. 2, part 2 (March/April): 177–86.

Roosa, Robert V. 1956. *Federal Reserve Operations in the Money and Government Securities Markets.* New York: Federal Reserve Bank of New York.

———. 1965. *Monetary Reform for the World Economy.* New York: Harper & Row.

———. 1967. *The Dollar and World Liquidity.* New York: Random House.

Safire, William. 1975. *Before the Fall: An Inside View of the Pre-Watergate White House.* New York: Doubleday.

Samuelson, Paul A., and Robert M. Solow. 1960. "Analytical Aspects of Anti-Inflation Policy." *American Economic Review* 50, no. 2 (May).

Samuelson, Robert J. 2008. *The Great Inflation and Its Aftermath: The Past and Future of American Affluence.* New York: Random House.

Sargent, Thomas J. 1986. "The Ends of Four Big Inflations." In Thomas J. Sargent, ed. *Rational Expectations and Inflation.* New York: Harper & Row.

———. 1993. "Interpreting the Reagan Deficits." In Thomas J. Sargent, ed. *Rational Expectations and Inflation,* 2nd ed. New York: HarperCollins.

———. 1993. "Stopping Moderate Inflations: The Methods of Poincare and Thatcher." In Thomas J. Sargent, ed. *Rational Expectations and Inflation*, 2nd ed. New York: HarperCollins.

———., ed. 1993, 1986. *Rational Expectations and Inflation*. New York: HarperCollins.

Sargent, Thomas J., and Neil Wallace. 1975. "Rational Expectations, the Optimal Monetary Instrument, and the Optimal Money Supply Rule." *Journal of Political Economy*, 83, no. 2 (April).

———. 1976. "Rational Expectations and the Theory of Economic Policy." *Journal of Monetary Economics* 2, no. 2 (April).

Schlesinger, Arthur M. 1965. *A Thousand Days: John F. Kennedy in the White House*. Boston: Houghton Mifflin Company.

Schreft, Stacey L. 1990. "Credit Controls: 1980." *Federal Reserve Bank of Richmond Economic Review* 76, no. 6 (November/December).

Schultz, Frederick H. 2005. "The Changing Role of the Federal Reserve." *Reflections on Monetary Policy 25 Years After October 1979, Federal Reserve Bank of St. Louis* 87, no. 2, part 2 (March/April): 343–48.

Shadow Open Market Committee. 1984. "Policy Statement and Position Papers, March 11–12, 1984." Available at shadowfed.org/archives/1984/.

Shultz, George, et al. 1980. "Economic Strategy for the Reagan Administration, A Report to President-elect Ronald Reagan from His Coordinating Committee on Economic Policy," November 16. Murray Weidenbaum Papers. University Archives, Department of Special Collections, Washington, University Libraries.

Silber, William L. 1984. "Marketmaker Behavior in an Auction Market: An Analysis of Scalpers in Futures Markets." *Journal of Finance* 39, no. 4 (September): 937–54.

———. 2003. "On the Nature of Trading: Do Speculators Leave Footprints?" *Journal of Portfolio Management* 29, no. 4 (July): 64–70.

———. 2007. *When Washington Shut Down Wall Street: The Great Financial Crisis of 1914 and the Origins of America's Monetary Supremacy*. Princeton, NJ: Princeton University Press.

———. 2009. "Why Did FDR's Bank Holiday Succeed?" *Federal Reserve Bank of New York Economic Policy Review* 15, no. 1 (July): 19–30.

Solomon, Robert. 1982. *The International Monetary System, 1945–1981*. New York: Harper & Row.

Sorensen, Theodore. C. 1965. *Kennedy*. New York: Harper & Row.

Sorkin, Andrew Ross. 2009. *Too Big to Fail: The Inside Story of How Wall Street and Washington Fought to Save the Financial System from Crisis—and Themselves*. New York: Viking.

Sparks, Jared. 1834. *The Writings of George Washington: Being His Correspondence, Addresses, Messages, and Other Papers, Official and Private.* Vol. IV. Boston: Russell, Odiorne and Metcalf, and Hilliard, Gray, and Co.

Sprague, Irvine H. 1986. *Bailout: An Insider's Account of Bank Failures and Rescues.* New York: Basic Books.

Sproul, Allan. 1980. *Selected Papers of Allan Sproul.* Lawrence Ritter, ed. New York: Federal Reserve Bank of New York.

Stein, Herbert. 1984. *Presidential Economics: The Making of Economic Policy from Roosevelt to Reagan and Beyond.* New York: Simon & Schuster.

Stern, Gary H. 2009. "Paul A. Volcker: In Conversation with Gary H. Stern." *The Region* (Federal Reserve Bank of Minneapolis) 23, no. 3 (September).

Stern, Gary H., and Ron J. Feldman. 2004. *Too Big to Fail: The Hazards of Bank Bailouts.* Washington, DC: Brookings Institution Press.

Stockman, David A. 1986. *The Triumph of Politics: How the Reagan Revolution Failed.* New York: Harper & Row.

Summers, Peter M. 2005. "What Caused the Great Moderation? Some Cross-Country Evidence." *Federal Reserve Bank of Kansas City Economic Review*, 3rd quarter, pp. 5–32.

"Symposium: Early Phases of the Credit Crunch." 2009. *Journal of Economic Perspectives* 23, no. 1 (Winter): 3–119.

"The Great Inflation: Lessons for Monetary Policy." 2010. *European Central Bank Monthly Bulletin*, no. 5 (May): 99–110.

Time. Various dates.

Treaster, Joseph B. 2004. *Paul Volcker: The Making of a Financial Legend.* New York: John Wiley.

U.S. Census Bureau. 1975. *Historical Statistics of the United States.* Washington, DC: Government Printing Office.

U.S. Congress. Various dates. *The Congressional Record.* Washington, DC: Government Printing Office.

U.S. News & World Report. Various dates.

U.S. Senate. 1973. "Emergency Powers Statutes (U.S. Senate Report 93-549)," 93rd Congress, 1st Sess. Washington, DC: Government Printing Office.

Volcker, Paul A. 1949. *The Problems of Federal Reserve Policy Since World War II.* Thesis submitted to the Department of Economics, Princeton University, Mimeograph (January 7).

———. 1978. *The Rediscovery of the Business Cycle.* New York: Free Press.

———. 1978. "The Role of Monetary Targets in an Age of Inflation." *Journal of Monetary Economics* 4, no. 2 (April).

———. 1978/1979. "The Political Economy of the Dollar." The Fred Hirsch

Lecture, Warwick University, Coventry, England, November 9, 1978. *Federal Reserve Bank of New York Quarterly Review* 3, no. 4 (Winter).

———. 1983. "We Can Survive Prosperity." Remarks at the Joint Meeting of the American Economic Association, American Finance Association, San Francisco, CA, December 28. Available at fraser.stlouisfed.org/docs/historical/volcker/Volcker_19831228.pdf.

———. 1984. "Coming Out of the Recession: The Economy in 1984." Address before the Wharton Entrepreneurial Center, April 30, 1984. Available at fraser.stlouisfed.org/historicaldocs/831/download/29536/Volcker _19840430.pdf.

———. 1990. "Commercial Banks Must Match Profitability with Discipline." *Financier* 14, no. 8 (August): 55–60.

———. 1990. *The Triumph of Central Banking?* Washington, DC. The 1990 Per Jacobsson Lecture. Available at www.perjacobsson.org/lectures/1990 .pdf.

———. 2002. "Monetary Policy Transmission: Past and Future Challenges." *Federal Reserve Bank of New York Economic Policy Review* 8, no. 1 (May): 7–11.

———. 2010. "How to Reform Our Financial System," *New York Times*, January 31, 2010. Available at www.nytimes.com/2010/01/31/opinion/31volcker .html?pagewanted=all.

———. 2011. "A Little Inflation Can Be a Dangerous Thing." *New York Times*, September 19, 2011. Available at www.nytimes.com/2011/09/19/opinion/ a-little-inflation-can-be-a-dangerous-thing.html.

———. Various dates. Personal Papers of Paul Volcker.

———. Various dates. Papers of Paul Volcker. Federal Reserve Bank of New York Archive.

———. Various dates. Undersecretary for Monetary Affairs, National Archives II, College Park, MD.

Volcker, Paul A., and Toyoo Gyohten. 1992. *Changing Fortunes: The World's Money and the Threat to American Leadership*. New York: Times Books.

Wall Street Journal. Various dates.

Wallace, Neil. 1979. "Why Markets in Foreign Exchange Are Different from Other Markets." *Federal Reserve Bank of Minneapolis Quarterly Review* 14, no. 1 (January): 12–18.

Washington Post. Various dates.

Wennerlind, Carl. 2005. "David Hume's Monetary Theory Revisited: Was He Really a Quantity Theorist and Inflationist?" *Journal of Political Economy* 113, no. 1 (February): 223–37.

Wessel, David. 2009. *In Fed We Trust: Ben Bernanke's War on the Great Panic.* New York: Crown Business.

White, Lawrence J. 2009–2010. "The Gramm-Leach-Bliley Act of 1999: A Bridge Too Far/Or Not Far Enough?" *Suffolk University Law Review* 43: 937–56.

Woodward, Bob. 2000. *Maestro: Greenspan's Fed and the American Boom.* New York: Simon & Schuster.

Zimmermann, Hubert. 2002. *Money and Security: Troops, Monetary Policy and West Germany's Relations with the United States and Britain, 1950–1971.* Cambridge, UK: Cambridge University Press.

Congressional Hearings

Administration's Fiscal Year 1983 Budget Proposal: Hearings Before the Senate Committee on Finance. 97th Congress, 2nd Sess. February 23, 1982. Washington, DC: Government Printing Office.

Conduct of Monetary Policy, Pursuant to the Full Employment and Balanced Growth Act of 1978: Hearings Before the Committee on Banking, Finance and Urban Affairs. P.L. 95-523, 97th Congress, 1st Sess. July 14, 21–23, 1981. Washington, DC: Government Printing Office.

Continental Illinois National Bank: Report of an Inquiry into Its Federal Supervision and Assistance: Hearings Before the House Committee on Banking, Finance and Urban Affairs. 99th Congress, 1st Sess. July 1985. Washington, DC: Government Printing Office.

Corruption in the United Nations Oil-for-Food Program: Reaching a Consensus on United Nations Reform: Hearings Before the Senate Committee on Homeland Security and Government Affairs. 109th Congress, 1st Sess. October 31, 2005. Washington, DC: Government Printing Office.

Deposit Insurance Reform and Related Supervisory Issues, Part 1: Hearings Before the Senate Committee on Banking, Housing and Urban Affairs. 99th Congress, 1st Sess. July 23, 25, and 31, 1985. Washington, DC: Government Printing Office.

The Disposition of Assets Deposited in Swiss Banks by Missing Nazi Victims: Hearings Before the House Committee on Banking and Financial Services. 104th Congress, 2nd Sess. December 11, 1996. Washington, DC: Government Printing Office.

Experts' Perspectives on Systemic Risk and Resolution Issues: Hearings Before the House Committee on Financial Services. 111th Congress, 1st Sess. September 24, 2009. Washington, DC: Government Printing Office.

Extension of the Temporary Limit on Public Debt: Hearings Before the Senate Subcommittee on Taxation and Debt Management Generally. 96th Congress, 2nd Sess. April 2, 1980. Washington, DC: Government Printing Office.

Federal Reserve's First Monetary Policy Report for 1984: Hearings Before the Senate Committee on Banking, Housing and Urban Affairs. 98th Congress, 2nd Sess. February 8–9, 1984. Washington, DC: Government Printing Office.

The Federal Reserve's Second Monetary Policy Report for 1980: Hearings Before the Senate Committee on Banking, Housing and Urban Affairs. 96th Congress, 2nd Sess. July 21–22, 1980. Washington, DC: Government Printing Office.

The Financial Services Competitiveness Act of 1995, Glass-Steagall Reform, and Related Issues: Hearings Before the House Committee on Banking and Financial Services. 104th Congress, 1st Sess. March 29, April 5 and 6, 1995. Washington, DC: Government Printing Office.

Gold Cover: Hearings Before the Senate Committee on Banking and Currency. 90th Congress, 2nd Sess. January 30–February 1, 1968. Washington, DC: Government Printing Office.

Implementation of the Credit Control Act Pursuant to Executive Order 12201, March 14, 1980: Hearings Before the Senate Committee on Banking, Housing and Urban Affairs. 96th Congress, 2nd Sess. March 18, 1980. Washington, DC: Government Printing Office.

Inquiry into Continental Illinois Corp. and Continental Illinois National Bank House: Hearings Before the Subcommittee on Financial Institutions, Supervision, Regulation, and Insurance. 98th Congress, 2nd Sess. September 18–19 and October 4, 1984. Washington, DC: Government Printing Office.

International Debt: Hearings Before the Senate Subcommittee on International Finance and Monetary Policy. 98th Congress, 1st Sess. February 14, 15, and 17, 1983. Washington, DC: Government Printing Office.

International Financial Markets and Related Problems: Hearings Before the Committee on Banking, Finance and Urban Affairs. 98th Congress, 1st sess. February 2, 8, and 9, 1983. Washington, DC: Government Printing Office.

The Nomination of Alan Greenspan: Hearings Before the Senate Committee on Banking, Housing and Urban Affairs. 100th Congress, 1st Sess. July 21, 1987. Washington, DC: Government Printing Office.

The Nomination of Paul A. Volcker to Be Chairman, Board of Governors of the Federal Reserve System: Hearings Before the Senate Committee on Banking,

Housing and Urban Affairs. 96th Congress, 1st Sess. July 30, 1976. Washington, DC: Government Printing Office.

Prohibiting Certain High-Risk Investment Activities by Banks and Bank Holding Companies: Hearings Before the Senate Committee on Banking, Housing and Urban Affairs. 111th Congress, 2nd Sess. February 2, 2010. Washington, DC: Government Printing Office.

Reduction in Reserve Ratio for Federal Reserve Notes and Deposits: Hearing Before the Senate Committee on Banking and Currency. 79th Congress, 1st Sess. February 20 and 28 and March 7, 1945. Washington, DC: Government Printing Office.

The Re-nomination of Paul A. Volcker: Hearings Before the Senate Committee on Banking, Housing and Urban Affairs. 98th Congress, 1st Sess. July 14, 1983. Washington, DC: Government Printing Office.

Repealing Certain Legislation Relating to Reserves Against Deposits in Federal Reserve Banks: Hearings Before the House Committee on Banking and Currency. 89th Congress, 1st Sess. February 1, 1965. Washington, DC: Government Printing Office.

Second Concurrent Resolution on the Budget Fiscal Year 1982: Hearings Before the Senate Committee on the Budget. 97th Congress, 2nd Sess. September 15 and 16, 1981. Washington, DC: Government Printing Office.

To Amend the Par Value Modification Act of 1972: Hearings Before the Subcommittee on International Finance of the Committee on Banking and Currency. 93rd Congress, 1st Sess. March 6, 1973. Washington, DC: Government Printing Office.

Index

A Note on the Author

William L. Silber is one of America's most respected experts on finance and banking. He is currently Marcus Nadler Professor of Finance and Economics and director of the Glucksman Institute for Research in Securities Markets, at the Stern School of Business, New York University. He has written numerous books and articles on economics and financial history, most recently *When Washington Shut Down Wall Street: The Great Financial Crisis of 1914 and the Origins of America's Monetary Supremacy.*